First World War
and Army of Occupation
War Diary
France, Belgium and Germany

16 DIVISION
49 Infantry Brigade
Princess Victoria's (Royal Irish Fusiliers)
7th Battalion, 8th Battalion, 7/8th Battalion and 11 Battalion
1 February 1916 - 27 February 1918

WO95/1978

The Naval & Military Press Ltd
www.nmarchive.com
Published in association with The National Archives

Published by

The Naval & Military Press Ltd

Unit 10 Ridgewood Industrial Park,

Uckfield, East Sussex,

TN22 5QE England

Tel: +44 (0) 1825 749494

www.naval-military-press.com

www.nmarchive.com

This diary has been reprinted in facsimile from the original. Any imperfections are inevitably reproduced and the quality may fall short of modern type and cartographic standards.

Contents

Document type	Place/Title	Date From	Date To
Heading	WO95/1978/1		
Heading	7th Bn. Roy. Ir. Fus. 49 Bde 16th Div. France (Feb 1916-Feb. 1918) December Feb 1918 amalgamated 8 Bn. Oct 1916 Oct 7/8 Bn		
War Diary	Bordon	01/02/1916	17/02/1916
War Diary	Southampton	18/02/1916	20/02/1916
War Diary	Horace	21/02/1916	22/02/1916
War Diary	Nedonchelle	23/02/1916	26/02/1916
War Diary	Busnettes	27/02/1916	01/03/1916
War Diary	Sailly La Bourse And Vermelles	02/03/1916	02/03/1916
War Diary	Vermelles	03/03/1916	19/03/1916
War Diary	Sailly Labourse	20/03/1916	21/03/1916
War Diary	Raimbert	22/03/1916	27/03/1916
War Diary	Mazingarbe	28/03/1916	31/03/1916
War Diary	Puits 14 Bis Sector	01/04/1916	09/04/1916
War Diary	Philosophe	10/04/1916	12/04/1916
War Diary	Noeux Les Mines	13/04/1916	20/04/1916
War Diary	Hulloch Section	21/04/1916	06/05/1916
War Diary	Mazingarbe	07/05/1916	17/05/1916
War Diary	Loos Section	18/05/1916	21/05/1916
War Diary	Philosophe East	22/05/1916	25/05/1916
War Diary	Loos Section	26/05/1916	09/06/1916
War Diary	Puits 14 Bis Sector	10/06/1916	13/06/1916
War Diary	W.H.S.	14/06/1916	20/06/1916
War Diary	Philosophe W	21/06/1916	24/06/1916
War Diary	Puits 14 Bis Section	25/06/1916	30/06/1916
Miscellaneous	Special Order. by Lieut. Col. F.T.T. Moore, Commanding 7th Battn Royal Irish Fusiliers.	27/06/1916	27/06/1916
Heading	War Diary 7th (S) Battalion Royal Irish Fus. 1st July to 31st. July 1916 Volume 6		
War Diary	Noeux Les Mines	01/07/1916	03/07/1916
War Diary	Loos Right Sub-Section	04/07/1916	16/07/1916
War Diary	Loos	16/07/1916	16/07/1916
War Diary	Philosophe E	17/07/1916	18/07/1916
War Diary	Mazingarbe	19/07/1916	20/07/1916
War Diary	Hulluch Sector	21/07/1916	30/07/1916
War Diary	Tenth Avenue	31/07/1916	31/07/1916
Heading	War Diary. 7th Royal Irish Fusiliers. Month Of August, 1916 Volume 7		
War Diary	Tenth Avenue	01/08/1916	03/08/1916
War Diary	14 Bis	04/08/1916	06/08/1916
War Diary	Puits 14 Bis.	07/08/1916	07/08/1916
War Diary	Mazingarbe	08/08/1916	12/08/1916
War Diary	14 Bis.	13/08/1916	16/08/1916
War Diary	Tenth Avenue	17/08/1916	20/08/1916
War Diary	Puits 14 Bis.	20/08/1916	25/08/1916
War Diary	Marles Bis Mines	26/08/1916	28/08/1916
War Diary	Vaux Sur Somme	29/08/1916	31/08/1916
Heading	War Diary 7th Royal Irish Fusiliers For Month Of September, 1916 Volume 8		

War Diary	Happy Valley	01/09/1916	02/09/1916
War Diary	Citadel	03/09/1916	03/09/1916
War Diary	Chimpanzee Trench	04/09/1916	04/09/1916
War Diary	Falfamont Farm	05/09/1916	05/09/1916
War Diary	Angle Wood	06/09/1916	06/09/1916
War Diary	Guillemont	07/09/1916	07/09/1916
War Diary	Bernafay Wood	08/09/1916	08/09/1916
War Diary	Quarry Guillemont	09/09/1916	09/09/1916
War Diary	Billon Farm	10/09/1916	10/09/1916
War Diary	Sailly Le Sec	11/09/1916	19/09/1916
War Diary	Fontaine	18/09/1916	20/09/1916
War Diary	Locre	21/09/1916	22/09/1916
War Diary	Kemmel	23/09/1916	26/09/1916
War Diary	Kemmel Chateau	27/09/1916	30/09/1916
Operation(al) Order(s)	49th. Infantry Brigade Order No. 53-4/9/16	04/09/1916	04/09/1916
Operation(al) Order(s)	15th. Infantry Brigade Order No. 59	05/09/1916	05/09/1916
Miscellaneous	15th Infy. Bde.	05/09/1916	05/09/1916
Miscellaneous	A Form Messages And Signals.		
Operation(al) Order(s)	49th Infantry Brigade Order No. 54-7/9/16	07/09/1916	07/09/1916
Operation(al) Order(s)	49th Infantry Brigade Order No. 55-8/9/16	08/09/1916	08/09/1916
Miscellaneous	49th. Inf. Bde. No. B.O. 55/2-8/9/16	08/02/1916	08/02/1916
Miscellaneous	C Form (Duplicate).Messages And Signals.		
Miscellaneous	C Form (Original). Messages And Signals.		
Operation(al) Order(s)	49th. Infantry Brigade Order No. 56-9/9/16	09/09/1916	09/09/1916
Miscellaneous	7th R. Irish Fusiliers. 49th Inf. Bde.		
Miscellaneous	C Form (Original). Messages And Signals.		
Map			
Miscellaneous	Special Order of The Day. By Brigadier-General P. Leveson-Gower Commanding 49th. Infantry Brigade 16th. Division, Wednesday, 13th. September 1916	03/09/1916	03/09/1916
Map	Ginchy & Guillemont		
War Diary	Kemmel	01/10/1916	03/10/1916
War Diary	Locre	04/10/1916	09/10/1916
War Diary	Kemmel	10/10/1916	13/10/1916
War Diary	Locre	14/10/1916	15/10/1916
Operation(al) Order(s)	95th Infy. Bde Operation Order No. 162	05/09/1916	05/09/1916
Heading	WO95/1978/2		
Heading	8 Bn. Roy. In Fus. 49th Bde 16th Div (Feb. 1916-1918) Disbanded Feb. 1918 France Commanding March 7 Bn Oct. 1916 Then 7/8 Bn. 1916 Feb-1916 Oct.		
War Diary	Bordon	01/02/1916	18/02/1916
War Diary	S. Hampton	19/02/1916	19/02/1916
War Diary	Havre	20/02/1916	21/02/1916
War Diary	Berghette	22/02/1916	22/02/1916
War Diary	Bellery	23/02/1916	26/02/1916
War Diary	Gonnehem	27/02/1916	04/03/1916
War Diary	Petit Sains	05/03/1916	18/03/1916
War Diary	Maroc	19/03/1916	22/03/1916
War Diary	Petit Sains	23/03/1916	23/03/1916
War Diary	Noeux-Les Mines	24/03/1916	31/03/1916
War Diary	Loos	01/04/1916	03/04/1916
War Diary	Philosophe	04/04/1916	06/04/1916
War Diary	Northern Up.	07/04/1916	08/04/1916
War Diary	Tenth Avenue	09/04/1916	09/04/1916
War Diary	Loos	10/04/1916	12/04/1916
War Diary	Mazingarbe.	13/04/1916	20/04/1916

War Diary	10th Avenue	21/04/1916	24/04/1916
War Diary	9th Avenue	25/04/1916	28/04/1916
War Diary	Philosophe West	29/04/1916	30/04/1916
Diagram etc	Sketch Map Of Hulluch Craters 18.4.16		
Diagram etc			
Miscellaneous	Maintaining Communications.	30/04/1916	30/04/1916
Miscellaneous	Head Quarters 49th Infy. Bde.	11/07/1916	11/07/1916
Miscellaneous	Further Information Obtained regarding raid Carried and on 11.7.16	11/07/1916	11/07/1916
Miscellaneous			
War Diary	Philosophe West	01/05/1916	02/05/1916
War Diary	9th Avenue	03/05/1916	06/05/1916
War Diary	Noeux-Les-Mines	07/05/1916	16/05/1916
War Diary	Philosophe East	17/05/1916	20/05/1916
War Diary	Loos	21/05/1916	24/05/1916
War Diary	Village Line	25/05/1916	27/05/1916
War Diary	E. Way.	28/05/1916	28/05/1916
War Diary	Loos	29/05/1916	31/05/1916
Miscellaneous	The A.G. 3rd Echelon		
War Diary	Loos	01/06/1916	01/06/1916
War Diary	Mazingarbe	02/06/1916	09/06/1916
War Diary	Reserve Trench	10/06/1916	13/06/1916
War Diary	10th Avenue	14/06/1916	19/06/1916
War Diary	Reserve Trench	20/06/1916	24/06/1916
War Diary	Philosophe West	25/06/1916	25/06/1916
War Diary	Noeux-Les-Mines	26/06/1916	30/06/1916
Heading	War Diary 8th (S) Battalion Royal Irish Fus. 1st. July to 31st. July 1916 Volume No. 6		
War Diary	Noeux Les Mines	01/07/1916	02/07/1916
War Diary	Philosophe East	03/07/1916	06/07/1916
War Diary	Loos	07/07/1916	11/07/1916
War Diary	Philosophe East	12/07/1916	15/07/1916
War Diary	Loos	16/07/1916	19/07/1916
War Diary	Mazingarbe	20/07/1916	20/07/1916
War Diary	Fosse Way.	21/07/1916	24/07/1916
War Diary	Mazingarbe	25/07/1916	30/07/1916
War Diary	Reserve Trench 14 Bis.	31/07/1916	31/07/1916
Miscellaneous	Scheme For Battalion Raid W 289	02/07/1916	02/07/1916
Heading	War Diary. 8th Royal Irish Fusiliers Month Of August 1916 Volume 7		
War Diary	Reserve Trench 14 Bis	01/08/1916	03/08/1916
War Diary	10th Avenue	04/08/1916	07/08/1916
War Diary	Reserve Trench	08/08/1916	11/08/1916
War Diary	Mazingarbe	12/08/1916	15/08/1916
War Diary	Reserve Trench 14 Bis	16/08/1916	19/08/1916
War Diary	10th Avenue	20/08/1916	24/08/1916
War Diary	Houchin	25/08/1916	26/08/1916
War Diary	Lapugnoy	27/08/1916	28/08/1916
War Diary	Sailly-Le-Sec	29/08/1916	30/08/1916
War Diary	Happy Valley near Bray	31/08/1916	31/08/1916
Heading	War Diary 8th Royal Irish Fusiliers For Month Of September, 1916 Volume 8		
War Diary	Happy Valley near Bray.	01/09/1916	03/09/1916
War Diary	Casement Trench	04/09/1916	04/09/1916
War Diary	Chimpanzee Trench	05/09/1916	05/09/1916
War Diary	Leuze Wood	05/09/1916	06/09/1916

War Diary	Arrow Head Copse	07/09/1916	09/09/1916
War Diary	Near Guillemont	10/09/1916	10/09/1916
War Diary	Billon Farm	11/09/1916	11/09/1916
War Diary	Sailly-Le-Sec	12/09/1916	18/09/1916
War Diary	Hallencourt (near Abbeville)	19/09/1916	21/09/1916
War Diary	Bailleul	22/09/1916	22/09/1916
War Diary	Westoutre	23/09/1916	23/09/1916
War Diary	Kemmel	24/09/1916	27/09/1916
War Diary	Fort Victoria	28/09/1916	30/09/1916
Miscellaneous	Special Order of The Day. By Brigadier-General P. Leveson-Gower. Commanding 49th. Infantry Brigade, 16th. Division.	13/09/1916	13/09/1916
Diagram etc			
Miscellaneous	8th R. Irish Fus. W. 412 H.Qrs. 49th Inf. Bde.	10/09/1916	10/09/1916
Operation(al) Order(s)	Operation Order No. 32 by Lt. Col. S.T. Watson Comdg 8 R. Irish Fusiliers.	08/09/1916	08/09/1916
War Diary	Fort Victoria Near Kemmel	01/10/1916	03/10/1916
War Diary	Kemmel Shelters	04/10/1916	09/10/1916
War Diary	Fort Victoria Near Kemmel	10/10/1916	14/10/1916
War Diary	Locre	15/10/1916	16/10/1916
War Diary	Kemmel Shelters	17/10/1916	19/10/1916
War Diary	Kemmel Chateau	20/10/1916	25/10/1916
War Diary	Kemmel Shelters	26/10/1916	31/10/1916
Heading	WO95/1978/3		
Heading	16th Division 49 Bde 7/8th Bn Roy H. Fus. Nov 1916-Feb 1918 Disbanded Feb 1916		
Heading	War Diary For Month Of November 1916. Volume 2. 7/8th R. Irish Fusiliers.		
War Diary	Kemmel Shelters	01/11/1916	01/11/1916
War Diary	Kemmel Chateau	02/11/1916	05/11/1916
War Diary	Kemmel Shelters	07/11/1916	12/11/1916
War Diary	Kemmel Chateau	13/11/1916	19/11/1916
War Diary	Kemmel Shelters	20/11/1916	24/11/1916
War Diary	Kemmel Chateau	25/11/1916	29/11/1916
War Diary	Kemmel Shelters	30/11/1916	30/11/1916
Heading	War Diary For Month Of December, 1916. Volume 31 7/8th R. Irish Fusiliers.		
War Diary	Kemmel Shelters	01/12/1916	04/12/1916
War Diary	La Polka	06/12/1916	11/12/1916
War Diary	Kemmel Shelters	12/12/1916	17/12/1916
War Diary	La Polka	18/12/1916	23/12/1916
War Diary	Locre	24/12/1916	30/12/1916
War Diary	La Polka	31/12/1916	31/12/1916
Miscellaneous		18/12/1916	18/12/1916
Map	Secret		
Operation(al) Order(s)	49th Infantry Brigade Order No. 81-20-12-16	20/12/1916	20/12/1916
Miscellaneous	49th Infy Bde No. B.O. 81/2-22-12-16	22/12/1916	22/12/1916
Miscellaneous	49th Infy Bde No. B.O. 81/1 P 21-12-16	21/12/1916	21/12/1916
Heading	War Diary for month of January, 1917. Volume 4. 7/8th Btn Rl Irish Fusiliers.		
War Diary	La Polka	01/01/1917	05/01/1917
War Diary	Locre	06/01/1917	10/01/1917
War Diary	La Polka	11/01/1917	17/01/1917
War Diary	Mount Kemmel	18/01/1917	22/01/1917
War Diary	La Polka	23/01/1917	29/01/1917
War Diary	Curragh Camp	30/01/1917	31/01/1917

Heading	War Diary For Month Of February, 1917. Volume 5. Unit:- 7/8th Irish Fusiliers.		
Map	Secret		
Miscellaneous	Orders For Raid By Lieut. Col. K.C. Weldon D.S.O. Commanding 7/8th. Royal Irish Fusiliers.		
War Diary	Curragh Camp	01/02/1917	06/02/1917
War Diary	La Polka	06/02/1917	09/02/1917
War Diary	Newport Dugouts	10/02/1917	14/02/1917
War Diary	Wakefield Camp	15/02/1917	22/02/1917
War Diary	Newport Dugouts	23/02/1917	26/02/1917
War Diary	Doctors House	27/02/1917	28/02/1917
Heading	War Diary For Month of March, 1917. Volume 6 Unit 7/8th Bde R Irish Fusiliers.		
War Diary	Doctors House	01/03/1917	02/03/1917
War Diary	Kemmel D Locre	03/03/1917	18/03/1917
War Diary	Rossignol	19/03/1917	22/03/1917
War Diary	Harley House	23/03/1917	31/03/1917
Heading	War Diary For Month Of April, 1917. Volume 7 Unit 7/8th R Irish Fusiliers.		
War Diary	Doncaster	01/04/1917	07/04/1917
War Diary	Kemmel	08/04/1917	12/04/1917
War Diary	Kemmel Shelters	13/04/1917	15/04/1917
War Diary	Tournehem	16/04/1917	27/04/1917
War Diary	Wizernes	28/04/1917	28/04/1917
War Diary	Hazebrouck	29/04/1917	29/04/1917
War Diary	Locre	30/04/1917	30/04/1917
Operation(al) Order(s)	Operation Orders No. 41 by Lieut. Colonel K.C. Weldon D.S.O. Commanding Royal Irish Fusiliers.	13/04/1917	13/04/1917
Operation(al) Order(s)	Operation Orders No. 39. By Lieut. Colonel K.C. Weldon D.S.O. Commanding 7/8th Royal Irish Fusiliers	07/04/1917	07/04/1917
Operation(al) Order(s)	Operation Orders No. 40. by Lieut. Colonel K.C. Weldon D.S.O. Commanding Royal Irish Fusiliers.	12/04/1919	12/04/1919
Operation(al) Order(s)	Operation Orders No. 41. by Lieut. Colonel K.C. Weldon D.S.O. Commanding Royal Irish Fusiliers.	14/04/1917	14/04/1917
Operation(al) Order(s)	Operation Orders No. 44. by Lieut. Colonel K.C. Weldon D.S.O. Commanding Royal Irish Fusiliers	27/04/1917	27/04/1917
Operation(al) Order(s)	Operation Orders No. 43. by Lieut Colonel K.C. Weldon D.S.O. Commanding Royal Irish Fusiliers	25/04/1917	25/04/1917
Operation(al) Order(s)	Operation Orders No. 46. By Lieut. Colonel K.C. Weldon D.S.O.		
Diagram etc			
Miscellaneous	Sheet 2		
Heading	War Diary Volume 8 For Month Of May, 1917. Unit 7/8th Royal Irish Fusiliers.		
War Diary	Ridge Wood (N.5 a. 5)	01/05/1917	04/05/1917
War Diary	Brasserie (N.6. c. 1.9)	05/05/1917	06/05/1917
War Diary	Brasserie	07/05/1917	09/05/1917
War Diary	Butterfly Farm	10/05/1917	13/05/1917
War Diary	York House N.16 c. 9.3	14/05/1917	15/05/1917
War Diary	York House N.16 c. 9.3	14/05/1917	17/05/1917
War Diary	York Hse	18/05/1917	18/05/1917
War Diary	Doncaster Huts	19/05/1917	31/05/1917
Heading	War Diary For Month Of June, 1917. Volumes 9 Unit 7/8th Battn R. Irish. Fusiliers.		
War Diary	Doncaster Huts	01/06/1917	05/06/1917
War Diary	S.P. 13	06/06/1917	06/06/1917

War Diary	Locre	07/06/1917	07/06/1917
War Diary	York. Rd	08/06/1917	08/06/1917
War Diary	Locre	09/06/1917	12/06/1917
War Diary	Moolenacker	13/06/1917	16/06/1917
War Diary	Clare Camp	17/06/1917	17/06/1917
War Diary	Moolenacker	18/06/1917	19/06/1917
War Diary	Near Steenvoorde	20/06/1917	21/06/1917
War Diary	Broxelles Area	22/06/1917	29/06/1917
War Diary	Cormettes	30/06/1917	30/06/1917
Miscellaneous	7/8th. (S) Battalion Royal Irish Fusiliers Order No. I.	04/06/1917	04/06/1917
Operation(al) Order(s)	Operation Order No. 2 June 1917	02/06/1917	02/06/1917
Operation(al) Order(s)	Continuation of Operation Order No. 1. Issued on /6/17. Sheet 8. Dated 4th./June 1917	00/09/1917	00/09/1917
Operation(al) Order(s)	D.K. Operation Order No. 9. Reference Wytschaete Sheet 28. S.W. 2. Edition 5. A.	06/06/1917	06/06/1917
Operation(al) Order(s)	49th Infantry Brigade Order No. 150	06/06/1917	06/06/1917
Map	Second Army Barrage Map June 1917		
Diagram etc			
Miscellaneous	Conversion Table Minutes Hours		
Map			
Map	Secret G/16/1 Copy No. 1		
Miscellaneous			
Map	Map A		
Operation(al) Order(s)	49th Infantry Brigade Order No. 131	09/06/1917	09/06/1917
Operation(al) Order(s)	7/6th Battalion Royal Fusiliers Order No. 3	12/06/1917	12/06/1917
Miscellaneous	Special Order	09/06/1917	09/06/1917
Miscellaneous	Special Order	06/06/1917	06/06/1917
Miscellaneous	Confidential Not To Be Issued To Commanders Of Lower Rank Than Battalion Battery To And Field Company Commanders And Not To Be Taken Into Front Line Trenches	04/06/1917	04/06/1917
Map	IX Corps Topo. Sec.; 9. C. T. S.3		
Miscellaneous	Confidential Not To Be Issued To Commanders Of Lower Rank Than Battalion Battery And Field Company Commanders An Not To Be Taken Into Front Line Trenches	08/06/1917	08/06/1917
Map	IX Corps Tops Sec. 9.C.T.S.4		
Miscellaneous	IX Corps No. G.221/218		
Operation(al) Order(s)	7/8th. Royal Irish Fusiliers Order No. 4	16/06/1917	16/06/1917
Miscellaneous	Issued Through Signals at 9.0. P.M. 16th June 1917	16/06/1917	16/06/1917
Operation(al) Order(s)	7/8th. (S) Battalion Royal Irish Fusiliers Order No. 6	19/06/1917	19/06/1917
Operation(al) Order(s)	7/8th. (S) Battalion Royal Irish Fusiliers Order No. 7	21/06/1917	21/06/1917
Operation(al) Order(s)	7/8th. (S) Battalion Royal Irish Fusiliers Order No. 8	29/06/1917	29/06/1917
Heading	War Diary For Month Of July, 1917. Volume 10 Unit 7/8th Irish Royal Fusiliers.		
War Diary	Cormettes	01/07/1917	07/07/1917
War Diary	Robrouck	08/07/1917	08/07/1917
War Diary	Winnezeele	09/07/1917	26/07/1917
War Diary	Watau Area No 2	27/07/1917	29/07/1917
War Diary	Branhoek No. 1 Area	30/07/1917	31/07/1917
Miscellaneous	The attached Instructions are issued to you today, they are not complete and will added to from time to time.	28/07/1917	28/07/1917
Diagram etc			
Miscellaneous	Sheet. 2		
Operation(al) Order(s)	7/8th. (S) Battalion Royal Irish Fusiliers Order No. 16	29/07/1917	29/07/1917
Operation(al) Order(s)	7/8th. (S) Battalion Royal Irish Fusiliers Order No. 15	25/07/1917	25/07/1917

Diagram etc	Steenvoorde N Training Area		
Diagram etc	Steenvoorde Training Area		
Miscellaneous	Allotment Of Training And Sports Field.	20/07/1917	20/07/1917
Miscellaneous	To Be Read In Conjuction With O.O. No. 9 Dated 5/6/17	05/06/1917	05/06/1917
Operation(al) Order(s)	7/8th. Royal Irish Fusiliers Battalion Order No. 10	07/07/1917	07/07/1917
Operation(al) Order(s)	7/8th. (S) Battalion Royal Irish Fusiliers Order No. 11 July 8th. 1917	08/07/1917	08/07/1917
Operation(al) Order(s)	July 11th. 1917 7/8th (S) Battalion Royal Irish Fusiliers Order No. 18	11/07/1917	11/07/1917
Miscellaneous	O.C. "A" Coy.	27/07/1917	27/07/1917
Miscellaneous	Instruction For The Offensive No. 3. Reference Maps Attached "A" & "B" 28. N.W. 28. N.E.	28/07/1917	28/07/1917
Miscellaneous	Appendix "A" To Be Read In Conjunction With Para 7	28/07/1917	28/07/1917
Miscellaneous	XIXth Corps.		
Miscellaneous	Instruction For The Offensive.	29/07/1917	29/07/1917
Miscellaneous	Appendix "B" To Be Read In Conjuction With Map "C"	29/07/1917	29/07/1917
Miscellaneous	Instruction For The Offensive	30/07/1917	30/07/1917
Operation(al) Order(s)	7/8th. S. Bn. R. Irish Fusiliers, Order No. 14	13/07/1917	13/07/1917
Miscellaneous	Issued For Training Purposes Only. July 5th 1917	05/07/1917	05/07/1917
Miscellaneous	Programme or Training For "C" and "D" Companies for Period 19th. July to 25th. July 1917	25/07/1917	25/07/1917
Miscellaneous	Issued through Signals at 3.0 p.m.		
Heading	War Diary Of 7/8th R. Irish Fus for August 1917		
Heading	War Diary. For Month Of August, 1917. Volume Unit 7/8th Royal Irish Fusiliers		
War Diary	Query Camp G.6 A.7.4	01/08/1917	02/08/1917
War Diary	Ecole	03/08/1917	05/08/1917
War Diary	Vlamertinghe	05/08/1917	07/08/1917
War Diary	Verlorenhoek	08/08/1917	10/08/1917
War Diary	Square Farm	11/08/1917	11/08/1917
War Diary	H.16.a.9.4	12/08/1917	16/08/1917
War Diary	Cambridge Rd	17/08/1917	17/08/1917
War Diary	H.17.a.1.8	18/08/1917	19/08/1917
War Diary	K.17 b	20/08/1917	20/08/1917
War Diary	Eecke	21/08/1917	21/08/1917
War Diary	Eecke	22/08/1917	22/08/1917
War Diary	Achiet le Petit	23/08/1917	28/08/1917
War Diary	Hamlincourt	29/08/1917	31/08/1917
Map	Creeping Barrage Map		
Map			
Miscellaneous	Headquarters 15th Division.	06/08/1917	06/08/1917
Miscellaneous	Of The Work Which Has Once	09/08/1917	09/08/1917
Miscellaneous	To The O.C. 7/8 Royal Irish Fus	10/08/1917	10/08/1917
Miscellaneous	Herewith Copy. No. 12 or Operation Order No. 4 They are not Complete and Will Probably have to be amended as Information in received on Several Points	14/08/1917	14/08/1917
Operation(al) Order(s)	August 14th. 1917 Operation Order No. 4. By Lieut. Colonel. K.C. Weldon D.S.O. Comdg Royal Irish Fusiliers Provisional Orders for the Attack.	14/08/1917	14/08/1917
Miscellaneous	Reference Operation Orders No. 4 Issued To Day Please Note The Rolling Amendment.		
Miscellaneous	7/8th. (S) Battalion The Royal Irish Fusiliers Order. No. 18. Aug.7/7	07/08/1917	07/08/1917

Heading	War Diary. For Month Of September, 1917. Volume Unit:- 7/8th Btn Royal Irish		
War Diary	Armagh Camp S23.c.5.0	01/09/1917	02/09/1917
War Diary	Left Support Fontaines Sector	03/09/1917	09/09/1917
War Diary	Front Line L. Sub Sector Fontaines Sector	10/09/1917	16/09/1917
War Diary	Armagh Camp	17/09/1917	27/09/1917
War Diary	Left Support	28/09/1917	30/09/1917
Heading	War Diary for Month of October, 1917. Unit 7/8th Royal Irish Fuslrs. Volume Number 13		
War Diary	Left Sub Section Fontaine	01/10/1917	10/10/1917
War Diary	Armagh Camp	11/10/1917	21/10/1917
War Diary	Left Sub Section Fontaine	22/10/1917	27/10/1917
War Diary	Left Support Croisilles	28/10/1917	31/10/1917
Miscellaneous			
Operation(al) Order(s)	7/8th. (S) Battalion The Royal Irish Fusiliers Order No. 30	25/10/1917	25/10/1917
Operation(al) Order(s)	October 27th. 1917 7/8th. (S) Battalion The Royal Irish Fusiliers Order No. 31	27/10/1917	27/10/1917
Operation(al) Order(s)	October 27th. 1917 7/8th. (S) Battalion The Royal Fusiliers Order No.	27/10/1917	27/10/1917
Miscellaneous	October 26th. 1917. 7/8th. Royal Irish Fusiliers. Order No. 29	26/10/1917	26/10/1917
Miscellaneous	7/8th. R. Irish Fusiliers. Action In The Event Of An Enemy Withdrawal	17/10/1917	17/10/1917
Operation(al) Order(s)	October 3rd.1917 7/8th. (S) Battalion The Royal Irish Fusiliers Order No. 27	03/10/1917	03/10/1917
Operation(al) Order(s)	October 9th. 1917. 7/8th.S. Bn. R. Irish Fusiliers, Order No. 28	09/10/1917	09/10/1917
Operation(al) Order(s)	October 31st 1917. 7/8th. (S) Battalion The Royal Irish Fusiliers Order No. 32	31/10/1917	31/10/1917
Heading	War Diary For Month Of November, 1917. Volume:-14 Unit:- 7/8th R. Irish Fusiliers		
War Diary	Armagh Camp	01/11/1917	18/11/1917
War Diary	Right Sub Section Fontaine Leg Croisilles	19/11/1917	21/11/1917
War Diary	T.23.c.4.9	22/11/1917	22/11/1917
War Diary	Armagh Camp	23/11/1917	25/11/1917
War Diary	Left Sub Section Fontaine Lez Croisilles	26/11/1917	26/11/1917
War Diary	Left Sub Section	26/11/1917	28/11/1917
War Diary	Left Section Fontaine	29/11/1917	30/11/1917
Map	To Accompany 10th Div. Order No. 167 D/24-10-17		
Map	18 Pdr. Barrage S.O.S. Line S.O.S Divisional Boundary		
Map	16/49/2-16/49/3 Reference		
Miscellaneous	November 6th. 1917 7/8th. (S) Battalion The Royal Irish Fusiliers Warning Order.	06/11/1917	06/11/1917
Miscellaneous	November 6th. 1917 7/8th (S) Battalion The Royal Irish Fusiliers Order No. 34	06/11/1917	06/11/1917
Operation(al) Order(s)	11th November 1917 7/8th. (S) Battalion The Royal Irish Fusiliers Order No. 35	11/11/1917	11/11/1917
Operation(al) Order(s)	November 17th 1917 7/8th (S) Battalion The Royal Irish Fusiliers Order No. 33	17/11/1917	17/11/1917
Operation(al) Order(s)	November 16th.1917. 7/8th. (S) Battalion The Royal Irish Fusiliers Order No. 36	16/11/1917	16/11/1917
Operation(al) Order(s)	November 21st. 1917 7/8th. (S) Battalion The Royal Irish Fusiliers Order No 36	21/11/1917	21/11/1917
Operation(al) Order(s)	22nd. November 1917 7/8th. (S) Battalion The Royal Irish Fusiliers A Order No. 37	22/11/1917	22/11/1917

Operation(al) Order(s)	49th Inf. Bde. Order No. 188	04/11/1917	04/11/1917
Miscellaneous	Battalion Orders, No. 39, By Lieut. Colonel K.C. Weldon, D.S.O., Comdg. 7/8th. R. Irish Fusiliers.	29/11/1917	29/11/1917
Heading	War Diary For Month Of December, 1917. Volume:-15. Unit:-7/8th Ro. Irish Fusiliers		
War Diary	Armagh Camp Hamlincourt	01/12/1917	01/12/1917
War Diary	Achiet-Le-Petit	02/12/1917	03/12/1917
War Diary	Barastre	04/12/1917	04/12/1917
War Diary	Tincourt	05/12/1917	05/12/1917
War Diary	St. Emelie	06/12/1917	15/12/1917
War Diary	Epehy	16/12/1917	18/12/1917
War Diary	Hamel	19/12/1917	22/12/1917
War Diary	St. Emelie	23/12/1917	28/12/1917
War Diary	Lempire	29/12/1917	31/12/1917
Operation(al) Order(s)	December 2nd.1917 7/8th (S) Battalion The Royal Irish Fusiliers Order No. 40	02/12/1917	02/12/1917
Miscellaneous	December 12th. 1917 7/8th. (S) Battalion The Royal Irish Fusiliers Order No.	12/12/1917	12/12/1917
Operation(al) Order(s)	December 16th.1917 7/8th (S) Battalion The Royal Irish Fusiliers Order No. 43	16/12/1917	16/12/1917
Miscellaneous	December 17th.1917 7/8th. (S) Battalion The Royal Irish Fusiliers Order to be Read in Conjunction With Order No. 43 Dated 16.12.17	17/12/1917	17/12/1917
Operation(al) Order(s)	December 28th.1917 Bn. Royal Irish Fusiliers Order No. 45	28/12/1917	28/12/1917
Operation(al) Order(s)	December 31st. 1917 7/8th (S) Battalion The Royal Irish Fusiliers Order No. 46	31/12/1917	31/12/1917
Operation(al) Order(s)	19th Inf. Bde. Order No. 188	03/12/1917	03/12/1917
Operation(al) Order(s)	March Table To Accompany 19th Inf. Bde. Order No. 188		
Operation(al) Order(s)	19th Inf. Bde. Order No. 189	04/12/1917	04/12/1917
Operation(al) Order(s)	March Table To Accompany Brigade Order No. 189		
Operation(al) Order(s)	19th Inf. Bde. Order No. 190	03/12/1917	03/12/1917
Operation(al) Order(s)	Table To Accompany 19th Inf. Bde. Order No. 190		
Operation(al) Order(s)	49th Infantry Brigade Order No. 191	06/12/1917	06/12/1917
Operation(al) Order(s)	49th. Inf. Bde. Order No. 192	07/12/1917	07/12/1917
Operation(al) Order(s)	49th Inf. Bde. Order No. 193	08/12/1917	08/12/1917
Operation(al) Order(s)	19th Inf. Bde. Order No. 198	15/12/1917	15/12/1917
Miscellaneous	49th Infantry Brigade. Administrative Instruction No. 29	16/12/1917	16/12/1917
Miscellaneous	49th Infantry Brigade. Administrative Instructions No. 30	16/12/1917	16/12/1917
Operation(al) Order(s)	19th Inf. Bde. Order No. 199	16/12/1917	16/12/1917
Operation(al) Order(s)	Move Table To Accompany 49th Inf. Order No. 199		
Operation(al) Order(s)	49th Inf. Bde. Order No. 200	20/12/1917	20/12/1917
Operation(al) Order(s)	Relief Table To Accompany Inf. Bde. Order No. 200		
Operation(al) Order(s)	19th Inf. Bde. Order No. 201	25/12/1917	25/12/1917
Miscellaneous	Special Order.	17/12/1917	17/12/1917
Heading	War Diary, For Month Of January, 1918. Volume:-16 Units:-7/8th R. Irish Fusiliers		
War Diary	Left Sub Sec Right Sect. H.2. Lempire	01/01/1918	03/01/1918
War Diary	Right Left Sub Section Right	04/01/1918	04/01/1918
War Diary	Hamel	05/01/1918	10/01/1918
War Diary	Left Support Lempire	11/01/1918	17/01/1918
War Diary	Left Sub Section Epeny	17/01/1918	20/01/1918
War Diary	Epeny	22/01/1918	22/01/1918
War Diary	St. Emelie	23/01/1918	31/01/1918

Operation(al) Order(s)	January 3rd.1918 7/8th. (S) Battalion The Royal Irish Fusiliers Order No. 47	03/01/1918	03/01/1918
Operation(al) Order(s)	January 9th. 1916 7/8th. (S) Battalion The Royal Irish Fusiliers Order No. 46	09/01/1918	09/01/1918
Operation(al) Order(s)	January 18th.1916 7/8th. (S) Battalion The Royal Irish Fusiliers Order No. 40	18/01/1918	18/01/1918
Operation(al) Order(s)	January 21st.1918.7/8th. (S) Battalion The Royal Irish Fusiliers Order No. 50	21/01/1918	21/01/1918
Operation(al) Order(s)	January 27th.1918 7/8th. (S) Battalion The Royal Irish Fusiliers Order No. 51	27/01/1918	27/01/1918
Heading	War Diary. For Month Of February, 1918. Volume:- 17 Unit:-7/8th Ro. Irish Fusils.		
War Diary	Left Sub Section Epeny	01/02/1918	03/02/1918
War Diary	Villers Faucon	04/02/1918	07/02/1918
War Diary	Hamel	08/02/1918	11/02/1918
Operation(al) Order(s)	7/8th (S) Battalion The Royal Irish Fusiliers Order No. 52	02/02/1918	02/02/1918
Operation(al) Order(s)	February 6th. 1918 7/8th. (S) Battalion the Royal Irish Fusiliers Order No. 33	06/02/1918	06/02/1918
Operation(al) Order(s)	February 8th.1918 7/8th. (S) Battalion the Royal Irish Fusiliers Order No. 54	08/02/1918	08/02/1918
Heading	WO95/1978/4		
Heading	11th. Bn Roy In. Fus 7th 48 Bde. 16th Div France (formed June1918) France July1918. absorbed by 5th Bn. Aug 1918 1918 July-1918 Aug Absorbed Coy. 5 Bn		
War Diary	Courset	01/08/1918	22/08/1918
War Diary	Barlin	23/02/1918	27/02/1918
Miscellaneous	7 RDF Vol 2 June D.A.G. 3rd Echelon G.A.Q.	23/09/1918	23/09/1918
Miscellaneous	11 R. Ir. Fus.	07/06/1918	07/06/1918
Miscellaneous	Headquarters, Division.	03/09/1918	03/09/1918

7th Bn. Roy. Ir. Fus.

49 Bde 16th DIV.

France. (Feb 1916 - Feb. 1918)

Disbanded Feb 1918

Amalgamated with 8th Bn. Oct 1916. then 7/8th Bn

Feb - Sep 1916

1916 FEB — 1916 ~~SEP~~ OCT

AMALGAMATED WITH 8 BN

7th Bn
8th Bn
7/8th Bn

See 7/8 BN

Instructions regarding War Diaries and Intelligence Summaries are contained in F. S. Regs., Part II. and the Staff Manual respectively. Title pages will be prepared in manuscript.

WAR DIARY
or
INTELLIGENCE SUMMARY.
(Erase heading not required.)

Army Form C. 2118.

Place	Date	Hour	Summary of Events and Information	Remarks and references to Appendices
Bordon	1/2/16		Orders to mobilize	[illegible]
	5/2/16		Mobilization complete	[illegible]
"	17/2/16		Battalion entrained in three train loads – on arrival at Southampton received instructions that the Battalion would proceed to the Rest Camp for the night. The 1st Line Transport however was embarked & proceeded.	[illegible]
Southampton	18/2/16 & 19/2/16		Received instructions for 600 men to leave camp at 3 pm and 300 men to leave camp at 3·30 pm to proceed to the Docks. The first party embarked on S/S "La Marguerite" & proceeded to sea at 6 pm but owing to heavy weather the ship had to put back and anchored in Southampton Water. After re-coaling the ship again proceeded and arrived at Havre at 1 am 20/2/16 – disembarkation being commenced at 7·30 am. The Second Party embarked on S/S Connaught & arrived at Havre at 8 am 19/2/16. The Battalion went into Rest Camp at Havre.	[illegible]
Havre	21/2/16		Orders received for 3 officers + 125 O.Rs to leave Rest Camp at 2 pm & the Battalion (less 3 officers + 125 O.Rs) to leave Rest Camp at 4·30 pm to entrain at Points 3 & 6 respectively.	
	22/2/16	5 pm 10 "	The Battalion detrained at LILLERS and marched to NÉDONCHELLE where the Battalion went into billets. There having been a fall of snow followed by frost it was impossible to bring the 1st Line transport along. It was therefore parked at [illegible] 1 mile outside LILLERS. (FRANCE Sheet 36A, U 10c)	[illegible]

2353 Wt. W2544/1454 700,000 5/15 D. D. & L. A.D.S.S./Forms/C. 2118.

7th R Irish Fus

Army Form C. 2118.

Instructions regarding War Diaries and Intelligence Summaries are contained in F. S. Regs., Part II. and the Staff Manual respectively. Title pages will be prepared in manuscript.

WAR DIARY

or

~~INTELLIGENCE SUMMARY.~~

(Erase heading not required.)

Place	Date	Hour	Summary of Events and Information	Remarks and references to Appendices
NEDONCHELLE	23/2/16		Continued frost + snow showers. Transport still parked.	
"	24/2/16		" " " " Transport brought in by numbers finally arriving complete at 7-10 pm	
"	25/2/16		Further fall of snow + continued frost. Inspected by G.O.C. 16th Division	
"	26/2/16		Marched out of billets at NEDONCHELLE to billets at BUSNETTES. Road difficult at first but thaw setting in about midday it became easy travelling + the battalion arrived at billets complete at 4.55 pm.	
BUSNETTES	27/2/16		Inspection of equipment, kits etc. and general interior economy.	
BUSNETTES	28/2/16	10-4 am	Orders received that the Brigade will move forward to the trenches on 1st March. This battalion to be attached to the 12th Division till 16th March.	

F Moore Lt Col Comdg 7th R. I. Fus

2353 Wt. W2544/1454 700,000 5/15 D. D. & L. A.D.S.S./Forms/C. 2118.

Instructions regarding War Diaries and Intelligence Summaries are contained in F. S. Regs., Part II. and the Staff Manual respectively. Title pages will be prepared in manuscript.

WAR DIARY or ~~INTELLIGENCE SUMMARY.~~

(Erase heading not required.)

7th Royal Irish Fusiliers

Army Form C. 2118.

1

Place	Date	Hour	Summary of Events and Information	Remarks and references to Appendices
BUSNETTES	1/3/16	9-15 am	Battalion marched from Billets at BUSNETTES to Billets in SAILLY LABOURSE (Sheet 36B L.3 B 3 5) via CHOCQUES, BETHUNE, and BEUVRY arriving at 2.20 pm. Being attached to the 12th Division for training the Commanding Officer called at Headquarters & had an interview with the Divisional Commander and being informed that the Battalion would be attached to the 35th Brigade proceeded to the Brigadier General's dug out. It was decided that the training should commence with individual attachment, progressing by Platoon attachment, Company attachment, to Battalion training. Orders were then received that A & B Coy would on the 2/3/16 march from SAILLY LABOURSE so as to arrive at VERMELLES (Sheet 36c G 8 C 6.8) at 10 am and for 'C' & 'D' Coys to march out so as to arrive at VERMELLES at 2 pm.	LBD
SAILLY LABOURSE and VERMELLES	2/3/16	8-30 am	A & B Coys marched out of SAILLY LABOURSE to VERMELLES where they were met by guides from the 7th Suffolk Regt (to which unit these Coys. are attached for training) and conducted into the trenches	This Battn being attached only all Official reports as to operations were forwarded by the 7th Suffolk & 5th Berkshires to their own Brigade. the 35th
		12-30	C & D Coys marched out and on arrival at VERMELLES were put into Billets	
VERMELLES	3/3/16		'A' & 'B' Coys came out of the trenches with the 7th Suffolk Regt and C & D Coys (attached to 5th R. BERKSHIRE Rgt) went into the trenches in relief	
"	4/3/16		A & B Coys in Billets. C & D Coys in trenches	
	5/3/16		A & B Coys in Billets. C & D Coys came out of the trenches and were also Billeted in VERMELLES.	
"	6/3/16	2/pm	A & B Coys attached to 5th R BERKSHIRE Rgt proceeded into the trenches for Platoon attachment. 'C' Coy marched to Billets at LABOURSE and	LBD

2353 Wt. W2544/1454 700,000 5/15 D. D. & L. A.D.S.S./Forms/C. 2118.

Instructions regarding War Diaries and Intelligence Summaries are contained in F. S. Regs., Part II. and the Staff Manual respectively. Title pages will be prepared in manuscript.

WAR DIARY

or

~~INTELLIGENCE SUMMARY.~~

(Erase heading not required.)

7th Royal Irish Fusiliers

Army Form C. 2118. 2

Place	Date	Hour	Summary of Events and Information	Remarks and references to Appendices
			D Coy marched to billets at SAILLY LABOURSE	WBD
VERMELLES	7/3/16		D Coy received instructions direct from H.Q. 12th Division to leave their billets & march to others at LABOURSE (Sheet 36B. L 2. a.7.5)	WBD
"	8/3/16		NIL.	
"	9/3/16	2 pm	A & B Coys came out of trenches with 5th R. BERKSHIRE REGT. and marched to billets at LABOURSE. C & D Coys. marched from their billets and went into the trenches with 7th SUFFOLK REGT.	WBD
"	12/3/16		C & D Coys came out of trenches & A & B Coys went in	WBD
"	14/3/16		A & B Coys came out of trenches & C & D Coys went in attached to 9th Battn Royal Fusiliers (36th Inf. Brigade)	
"	17/3/16		C & D Coys came out of trenches & marched to billets at LABOURSE. A & B Coys attached to 5th R Sussex Regt. went into trenches	WBD
"	19/3/16		Battalion Headquarters moved from VERMELLES to SAILLY LABOURSE	WBD
SAILLY LABOURSE	20/3/16		A & B Coys came out of trenches & marched to LABOURSE where they went into billets. Training finished on this day.	WBD
"	21/3/16	9.45 am	Battalion marched from LABOURSE to RAIMBERT (Sheet 36B. C 15 & 16) arriving at 4.5 pm	
RAIMBERT	22-26 3.16		Training & reorganising the battalion	
"	24 3.16		Orders received that on the relief of the 15th Division by the 16th Division this Battn would move to MAZINGARBE (Sheet 36 B. L 23).	49th Inf Bde order No 7 attached to original.
"	27 3.16	7.50 am	Battalion less Transport marched to LAPUGOY (Sheet 36 B D 21 d.) where it entrained. Detrained at NOEUX les Mines (Sheet 36 B. K.18.) and marched to Billets at MAZINGARBE, arriving at 12.50 pm. The 1st Line Transport Brigaded and moving by march route arrived at	WBD

2353 Wt. W2544/1454 700,000 5/15 D. D. & L. A.D.S.S./Forms/C. 2118.

WAR DIARY

~~or~~

~~INTELLIGENCE SUMMARY.~~

(Erase heading not required.)

7th Royal Irish Fusiliers.

Army Form C. 2118.

Instructions regarding War Diaries and Intelligence Summaries are contained in F. S. Regs., Part II. and the Staff Manual respectively. Title pages will be prepared in manuscript.

Place	Date	Hour	Summary of Events and Information	Remarks and references to Appendices
	27/3/16 (Cont'd)		3.40 pm less half a Field Kitchen, the axle of which broke en route. The Transport after removing required stores proceeded to its permanent lines at NOEUX.	WDF
MAZINGARBE	28/3/16		At MAZINGARBE	
	29/3/16			
	30/3/16			
	31/3/16	3/pm	Battalion less 'D' Coy moved up into Support in PUITS BIS 14. trenches 'D' Coy in Reserve with Reserve Battalion at PHILOSOPHE	WDF

F Moore . Lieut. Col.
Comdg. 7th. (S) Bn. Rl. Irish Fus.

7th Royal Irish Fusiliers

Instructions regarding War Diaries and Intelligence Summaries are contained in F. S. Regs., Part II. and the Staff Manual respectively. Title pages will be prepared in manuscript.

WAR DIARY

~~or~~

~~INTELLIGENCE SUMMARY.~~

(Erase heading not required.)

XVI

Army Form C. 2118.

7/R Ir Fus
Vol 3

Place	Date	Hour	Summary of Events and Information	Remarks and references to Appendices
PUIS 14 BIS Sector	1/4/16 2/4/16		Battalion less D Coy. in Brigade Support Line Trenches. D Coy in Brigade Reserve at PHILOSOPHE	
	3/4/16		Battalion moved up to Right Sub-Sector + took over the line from 8th Royal IRISH FUSILIERS.	
	4/4/16		Normal conditions with the usual amount of rifle grenades, trench mortars etc. exchanged.	
	5/4/16		Quiet day. A small mine was blown by the enemy opposite the front of the Battalion on our right. Our men stood to and there was a lively exchange of rifle fire, rifle grenades and artillery fire which last until 1 am. on the 6/4/16.	
	6/4/16		Enemy somewhat aggressive with rifle grenades but was quickly silenced by our sending back 3 to his 1. We were warned that a camouflet would be blown on our right at 8 pm but this failed to explode.	
	7/4/16		Normal conditions. The camouflet mentioned above was blown at 9 pm. + there was a lively exchange of fire for 2 hours afterwards.	
	8/4/16		Normal conditions	
	9/4/16		Normal conditions. At 8 pm. the first platoon of the 8th ROYAL IRISH FUSILIERS arrived in relief of this Battalion. The relief was finally completed at 11 pm without anything untoward happening to interfere with the operation, and	

2353 Wt. W2544/1454 700,000 5/15 D. D. & L. A.D.S.S./Forms/C. 2118.

7TH (S) BATTN ROYAL IRISH FUSILIERS.

Army Form C. 2118.

II

WAR DIARY

or

~~INTELLIGENCE SUMMARY.~~

(Erase heading not required.)

Instructions regarding War Diaries and Intelligence Summaries are contained in F. S. Regs., Part II. and the Staff Manual respectively. Title pages will be prepared in manuscript.

Place	Date	Hour	Summary of Events and Information	Remarks and references to Appendices
			The Battalion then marched to Billets at PHILOSOPHE EAST into Brigade Reserve	
PHILOSOPHE	10/4/16 – 11/4/16		Nothing of moment occurred. Large working & carrying parties were sent out each night in accordance with Brigade requirements.	
	12/4/16		The Battalion was relieved by the 8th ROYAL DUBLIN FUSILIERS in the afternoon and on completion marched to billets at NOEUX les MINES (Sheet 36B. K. 18.) in DIVISIONAL Reserve.	
NOEUX les MINES	13/4/16 to 19/4/16		In billets in DIVISIONAL Reserve.	
"	20/4/16		marched from billets + took over Left Sub Sector of HULLOCH SECTION from 7th LEINSTER REGT.	
HULLOCH SECTION	21/4/16		Normal conditions with exchange of Rifle Grenades & trench mortars	
	22/4/16		– – – – –	
	23/4/16		– – – –	
	24/4/16		Relieved by 8th Royal IRISH FUSILIERS and this Battalion moved back into BRIGADE Support.	
	25/4/16		Battalion practiced Gas alarm in the morning by Companies and in the afternoon by battalion.	
	26/4/16		RESERVE TRENCH heavily shelled by enemy with 5.9's. They made a direct hit on the dug out the officers of B Coy were in. Major M.W. LITTON + 2nd/Lieut. R.D	

7TH (S) BATTN ROYAL IRISH FUSILIERS.

III

Army Form C. 2118.

Instructions regarding War Diaries and Intelligence Summaries are contained in F. S. Regs., Part II. and the Staff Manual respectively. Title pages will be prepared in manuscript.

WAR DIARY

~~or~~

~~INTELLIGENCE SUMMARY~~.

(Erase heading not required.)

Place	Date	Hour	Summary of Events and Information	Remarks and references to Appendices
			GREER being seriously wounded and Capt. T. F. O'DONNELL slightly wounded	
HULLOCH SECTION	27/4/16	3.45 am	The enemy discharged clouds of gas which was followed by a raid on the RIGHT SUB SECTION. 'C' Coy. of this battalion was moved up into RESERVE TRENCH and put under the orders of O.C. 7th R. INNISKILLING FUSILIERS. Trenches were very heavily shelled while the gas was on and Capt H. W. C. WELDON, O.C. 'B' Coy. was Killed in RESERVE TRENCH	
	28/4/16		Battalion moved up into Left Sub Sector in relief of 8th Royal IRISH FUSILIERS.	
	29/4/16	3.50 am	Enemy discharged gas but after about 20 minutes the gas appeared to be blown back across their lines. Numbers of the enemy left their trenches + ran towards their rear. They were caught by our artillery barrage + suffered casualties. Our casualties from gas were heavy and Lieut. C. J. FULTON died from its effects. Operations ceased about 11 am + the rest of the day was quiet. D Coy was moved up into the line + distributed between 'C' Coy + 'B' Coy. a Coy. of 16th DIVISIONAL CYCLISTS being sent up to occupy portion of RESERVE TRENCH in place of 'D' Coy.	
	30.4.16		about 1 am the enemy attempted to occupy SMITHS CRATER but was driven out by our bombers. The day passed quietly with only small exchange of rifle grenades etc.	

F. Moore. Lieut. Col.
Comdg. 7th. (S) Bn. Rl. Irish Fus.

2353 Wt. W2544/1454 700,000 5/15 D. D. & L. A.D.S.S./Forms/C. 2118.

7th Royal Irish Fusiliers

WAR DIARY

or

~~INTELLIGENCE SUMMARY.~~

(16)

7 R Ir Fus

Army Form C. 2118.

Vol 4

Instructions regarding War Diaries and Intelligence Summaries are contained in F. S. Regs., Part II. and the Staff Manual respectively. Title pages will be prepared in manuscript.

(*Erase heading not required.*)

Place	Date	Hour	Summary of Events and Information	Remarks and references to Appendices
HULLOCH SECTION	1/5/16		Quiet day. but 'Gas alert' being notified. There were two false alarms during the night.	
	2/5/16		The 8th R. IRISH FUSILIERS relieved this battalion + LEFT SUB SECTOR and we moved back into BRIGADE RESERVE in billets at PHILOSOPHE WEST.	
	3/5/16		working + carrying parties furnished but nothing of importance occurred	
	4/5/16		- - - - - -	
	5/5/16		- - - - - -	
	6/5/16		Battalion was relieved by 8th R DUBLIN FUSILIERS on the BRIGADE going back into DIVISIONAL RESERVE – the Battalion being billetted in MAZINGARBE.	
MAZINGARBE	7/5/16		Nothing of importance	
	8/5/16		- -	
	9/5/16		Brigadier General P. LEVESON-GOWER inspected & addressed the battalion	
	10/5/16		Nothing of importance. men being practiced in bombing + wiring.	
	11/5/16		orders received at 6 30 pm to 'stand to' owing to a strafe on the Division on our Left. The Battn. was not ordered out as things quietened down.	
	~~12/5/16~~			
	12/5/16 13/5/16 14/5/16 15/5/16 16/5/16		men being practiced in bombing, wiring etc. working parties furnished at night.	M. 99 19

2353 Wt. W2544/1454 700,000 5/15 D. D. & L. A.D.S.S./Forms/C. 2118.

7th Royal Irish Fusiliers

II

Army Form C. 2118.

Instructions regarding War Diaries and Intelligence Summaries are contained in F. S. Regs., Part II. and the Staff Manual respectively. Title pages will be prepared in manuscript.

WAR DIARY

~~or~~

~~INTELLIGENCE SUMMARY.~~

(*Erase heading not required.*)

Place	Date	Hour	Summary of Events and Information	Remarks and references to Appendices
MAZINGARBE	17/5/16		Battalion relieved 2nd K.R.R + 1st LOYAL NORTH LANCS REGT in LOOS Section Companies being disposed as follows from Right to Left:- D Coy from HAYMARKET inclusive to DEAD MANS SAP exclusive A Coy from DEAD MANS SAP inclusive to FIR STREET inclusive B Coy from FIR STREET exclusive to NORTH STREET exclusive C Coy in Support in cellars S. of ENCLOSURE The relief commenced at 9 P.M.	
LOOS SECTION	18/5/16 19/5/16 20/5/16		This tour in the front line trenches was carried out under normal conditions There was nothing of exceptional interest happened. There was the usual exchange of rifle grenades. trench mortars etc.	
	21/5/16		The 8th Royal Irish Fusiliers relieved this Battalion on this night. This Battalion then proceeded to Billets in PHILOSOPHE EAST into Brigade Reserve.	
PHILOSOPHE EAST	22/5/16 23/5/16 24/5/16		We furnished working parties each night under orders received from the Brigade Office	
	25/5/16		Relieved the 8th Royal Irish Fusiliers in Right Sub Section - LOOS SECTION - the relief commencing at 9.30 pm.	
LOOS SECTION	26/5/16		Warning was received that the enemy appeared to be concentrating opposite the 1st Corps front. 2 Coys. of the 8th Royal IRISH Fusiliers were placed under the orders of this Battalion in case of attack.	
	27/5/16		Day passed quietly but a sharp look out was kept.	

2353 Wt. W2544/1454 700,000 5/15 D. D. & L. A.D.S.S./Forms/C. 2118.

III

7th Royal Irish Fusiliers

WAR DIARY

or

~~INTELLIGENCE SUMMARY~~.

(*Erase heading not required.*)

Army Form C. 2118.

Instructions regarding War Diaries and Intelligence Summaries are contained in F. S. Regs., Part II. and the Staff Manual respectively. Title pages will be prepared in manuscript.

Place	Date	Hour	Summary of Events and Information	Remarks and references to Appendices
LOOS SECTION	28/5/16		Normal conditions. with customary exchange of rifle grenades etc.	
	29/5/16		Relieved by 8th Royal IRISH Fusiliers and we then went into Brigade Support, Battn. Headquarters & 'C' Coy. being in E. WAY. 'B' Coy & 'D' Coy in the ENCLOSURE, and 'A' Coy. in cellars near SCOTTS ALLEY.	
	30/5/16 31/5/16		The days passed very quietly. During the nights the Battalion was employed on working & carrying parties.	

[signature] Major
Comdg 7 Royal Irish Fusiliers

2353 Wt. W2544/1454 700,000 5/15 D. D. & L. A.D.S.S./Forms/C. 2118.

Instructions regarding War Diaries and Intelligence Summaries are contained in F. S. Regs., Part II. and the Staff Manual respectively. Title pages will be prepared in manuscript.

Army Form C. 2118.

XVI

WAR DIARY
or
~~INTELLIGENCE SUMMARY.~~
(Erase heading not required.)

7th (S) Battn. Royal Irish Fusiliers

Place	Date	Hour	Summary of Events and Information	Remarks and references to Appendices
LOOS SECTION	1/6/16		Battn. in Bde Support. Hdqrs and one Coy in E WAY TRENCH. 2 Coys in ENCLOSURE LOOS. 1 Coy in cellars near SCOTS ALLEY.	W.H.S.
	2/6/16		do. On night 2/3 Bde. was relieved by 48th Inf. Bde. This Battn. marched to billets in NOEUX-LES-MINES	W.H.S.
	3/6/16		Training in NOEUX-LES-MINES	W.H.S.
	4/6/16			W.H.S.
	5/6/16			W.H.S.
	6/6/16			W.H.S.
	7/6/16			W.H.S.
	8/6/16			W.H.S.
	9/6/16			W.H.S.
PUITS 14 BIS SECTOR	10/6/16		Bde. relieved 47th Inf. Bde. This Battn. relieved the 7th LEINSTER REGT in Bde Support in TENTH AVENUE.	W.H.S.
	11/6/16		Work carried out in TENTH AVENUE, NORTHERN SAP REDOUBT and 65 METRE PT. REDOUBT.	W.H.S.
	12/6/16		no operations to report.	W.H.S.
	13/6/16			W.H.S.
~~PUITS~~ W.H.S.	14/6/16		On night 14/15 June Battn. relieved 8 Royal Irish Fusiliers in Right Sub-Section PUITS 14 BIS	
	~~15~~ 14/6/16		about 3 AM enemy shelled H.25.b.4.6. with "Whizzbangs" from direction WINGLES. Trench mortar shells and rifle grenades were also sent over at same time. Our artillery and STOKES guns retaliated and silenced the enemy about 3.40 AM	W.H.S.

2353 Wt. W2544/1454 700,000 5/15 D. D. & L. A.D.S.S./Forms/C. 2118.

M4

Instructions regarding War Diaries and Intelligence Summaries are contained in F. S. Regs., Part II. and the Staff Manual respectively. Title pages will be prepared in manuscript.

WAR DIARY
or
~~INTELLIGENCE SUMMARY~~.
(Erase heading not required.)

Army Form C. 2118.

7th (S) Battn. Royal Irish Fusiliers

Place	Date	Hour	Summary of Events and Information	Remarks and references to Appendices
~~14.6.16~~ (~~cont~~)	~~14.6.16~~ (cont)		2 patrols went out at H.31.6 and H.31.8. No enemy patrols or wiring parties were discovered.	W.H.S
	15.6.16		Nothing of importance to report.	W.H.S.
	16.6.16		About 3.10 AM our artillery shelled the enemys lines opposite the left Battn and this Battn front between 3PM and 5PM. We sent over rifle grenades but the enemy did not retaliate. At 11.30PM a German patrol was seen opposite Boyau 52. It was dispersed by M.G fire.	W.H.S.
	17.6.16		About 6PM Enemy shelled our Front and Support lines with "Whizzbangs". Our artillery retaliated and firing ceased. At dawn an attempt was made by the enemy to raid our front line where the HULLOCK road enters our line near Boyau 60. Our M.G's opened fire and the enemy took cover in shell holes. We bombed them out and they retreated to their own lines.	W.H.S.
	18.6.16		7 patrols were sent out in the early hours. No hostile patrols were encountered. During the day enemys artillery registered on our trenches, especially CHALK PIT ALLEY above RESERVE TRENCH.	W.H.S.
	19.6.16		A patrol went out at H.31.7 and brought back information that the enemy was cutting the grass between front line and wire. During the afternoon our artillery fired 24 rounds into enemys front system and one of our T.M's registered 5 shots on enemys front line. There was no retaliation.	W.H.S.

2353 Wt. W2544/1454 700,000 5/15 D. D. & L. A.D.S.S./Forms/C. 2118.

Instructions regarding War Diaries and Intelligence Summaries are contained in F. S. Regs., Part II. and the Staff Manual respectively. Title pages will be prepared in manuscript.

WAR DIARY

or

~~INTELLIGENCE SUMMARY~~. 7th (S) Battn. Royal Irish Fusiliers.

(*Erase heading not required.*)

Army Form C. 2118.

Place	Date	Hour	Summary of Events and Information	Remarks and references to Appendices
	19.6.16 (cont.)		mining operations were detected about 30x to 40x from our line between Boyaux 53 and 54, 56 and 57, and about 49.	W.H.S.
	20.6.16.		Patrols reported everything quiet on our front. About 1 P.M enemy put 6 4.2's and 25 'Whizzbangs' into Firing and Support lines of RIGHT Coy. Between 3 P.M and 4 P.M we sent over an organized straffe of 50 rifle grenades into enemy's firing line. Not a shot was fired in retaliation.	W.H.S.
PHILOSOPHE W	21.6.16		On night 20/21 June Battn. was relieved by 8th Royal Irish Fusiliers and marched to PHILOSOPHE W as Battn. in Bde Reserve. Hdqrs and B·C 2 Coys in PHILOSOPHE W. A Coy in 65 METRE POINT and D Coy in TENTH AVENUE	W.H.S.
	22.6.16		In Brigade Reserve.	W.H.S.
	23.6.16			W.H.S.
	24.6.16			W.H.S.
PUITS 14 bis SECTION			On afternoon Battn. relieved 8 Royal Irish Fusiliers in Right - Sub-section PUITS 14 BIS Section. During the evening until 11 P.M our artillery and Stokes guns shelled enemy's wire and front system about H. 31 b 2.5. At 11.45 P.M the artillery commenced firing again.	
"	25.6.16		About 12.30 A.M enemy commenced a heavy bombardment of our front lines and communication trenches of left and centre Coys., especially around CHALK PIT. Ten minutes later artillery fire lifted unto our support lines	W.H.S.

2353 Wt. W2544/1454 700,000 5/15 D. D. & L. A.D.S.S./Forms/C. 2118.

Vol 5

Army Form C. 2118.

June

Instructions regarding War Diaries and Intelligence Summaries are contained in F. S. Regs., Part II. and the Staff Manual respectively. Title pages will be prepared in manuscript.

WAR DIARY
or
~~INTELLIGENCE SUMMARY.~~ 7 (S) Battn. Royal Irish Fusiliers
(Erase heading not required.)

Place	Date	Hour	Summary of Events and Information	Remarks and references to Appendices
	25.6.16 (cont)		and a German raiding party, estimated at about 60. came along both sides of the road which enters our line at H.25 d. 2.8½. They came through a gap in our wire and spread out on both sides. M.G. fire, rifle fire and bombs being directed on them. Only a few of the enemy managed to reach our parapet, but none of them succeeded in entering our trenches. After a very brisk action the enemy were put to flight, leaving 3 dead on our parapet. On examination these proved to belong to 2nd Battn. 5th Bavarian Reserve Regt, IV Division, II Bavarian Corps.	Special order of the day is attached and marked 1.
			From papers found in pocket of German it was learnt that each bomber was to carry rifle, bayonet fixed, 30 rounds ammunition in pockets, 3 bombs and a small dagger.	W.H.S.
	25.6.16		At 1.10 AM. the situation became quieter, and shelling intermittant.	
	26.6.16		Early morning passed very quietly. Our artillery continued their bombardment, which did not evoke much retaliation.	W.H.S.
			about 10.P.M Battn. was relieved by 1st. Battn. Royal MUNSTER FUSILIERS. 48th INF BDE. Battn. marched to NOEUX-LES-MINES, accomodated in huts.	
	27.6.16		BDE in Divisional Reserve. Training carried out	W.H.S.
	28.6.16			W.H.S.
	29.6.16			W.H.S.
	30.6.16			W.H.S.

J More Lieut-Col
Commdg. 7 Royal Irish Fusiliers.

2353 Wt. W2544/1454 700,000 5/15 D. D. & L. A.D.S.S./Forms/C. 2118.

I

SPECIAL ORDER.
by
Lieut.Col.F.T.T.Moore,
Commanding 7th Battn Royal Irish Fusiliers.

-- June 27th 1916.

The following message has been received from MAJOR-GENERAL W.B.HICKIE.C.B.Commanding 16th(IRISH)Division, is to be communicated to all ranks :-

Divisional Headquarters.

25th June 1916..

Please accept my hearty congratulations and convey them to Officers and men concerned.

(Signed) W.B.HICKIE.Major - General.
Commanding 16th(IRISH) Division.

(Signed) W.D.Thompson.Captain & Adjutant.
7th Bn Royal Irish Fusiliers........

W A R   D I A R Y

7th (S) Battalion
Royal Irish Fus.

1st. July to 31st.July 1916.

VOLUME No. ~~7~~ 6

16
7. R. I. Fus
July
Vol 6

M5

7th S. Battn Royal Irish Fusiliers

Instructions regarding War Diaries and Intelligence Summaries are contained in F. S. Regs., Part II. and the Staff Manual respectively. Title pages will be prepared in manuscript.

WAR DIARY or ~~INTELLIGENCE SUMMARY.~~

(Erase heading not required.)

JULY 1916

Army Form C. 2118.

Place	Date	Hour	Summary of Events and Information	Remarks and references to Appendices
NOEUX LES MINES	1 7 16		49 Inf Bde in Divisional Reserve	W.H.S.
	2 7 16		Battn. quartered in huts.	W.H.S.
	3 7 16		Training	W.H.S.
			49 Inf Bde relieved 47 Inf Bde in LOOS SECTOR. This Battn. relieved the 7th Leinsters in Right sub-section on afternoon. During the night 3/4 our MG's traversed the enemys wire.	
LOOS Right sub-section	4 7 16		The night passed quietly. Between 11 and 12 PM the enemy sent over a large number of rifle grenades and aerial torpedoes. Between 4 and 5 PM enemy shelled ENCLOSURE with 4.2's. Between 5.30 and 6.30 PM enemy shelled firing line between Boyaux 31 and 32 causing considerable damage. Our artillery retaliated with good results. This shelling was in retaliation to our 60 pounder trench mortar which was cutting enemys wire S. of HARRISONS CRATER. At 7 PM we blew a camouflet successfully opposite Boyau 32. During the night 4/5 we sent out 2 patrols. Enemy were throwing wire out on end of poles.	W.H.S.
	5 (6) 16		At 5 AM 3 Germans were seen on left lip of HARRISONS CRATER wearing dark grey spiked helmets. At 5.10 PM enemy blew a camouflet under our no 5 shaft which runs out from SUNKEN ROAD. No surface damage. Casualties 5 killed 1 gassed. A slight bombardment followed from TM's	W.H.S.
	6 (6) 16		Our MG's traversed enemys wire. During the night 5/6 from 11.30 PM to 1.30 AM enemy subjected our trenches to a heavy bombardment with artillery	W.H.S.

2353 Wt. W2544/1454 700,000 5/15 D. D. & L. A.D.S.S./Forms/C. 2118.

7th (S) Battn. Royal Irish Fusiliers

Instructions regarding War Diaries and Intelligence Summaries are contained in F. S. Regs., Part II. and the Staff Manual respectively. Title pages will be prepared in manuscript.

WAR DIARY
or
~~INTELLIGENCE SUMMARY.~~
(Erase heading not required.)

July 1916.

Army Form C. 2118.

Place	Date	Hour	Summary of Events and Information	Remarks and references to Appendices
LOOS Right sub-section	6.7.16		T.M's rifle grenades. This was owing to us sending gas over from the	
			PUITS 14 bis SECTOR. We retaliated eventually silencing enemy about 1.30AM	
			Between 6AM and 9AM enemy sent over a few whizz-bangs.	
			With the exception of an Exchange of rifle grenades.	W.H.S.
			At 3AM enemy bombarded our line at M.6.5 with T.M's. Our Stokes guns	
	7.7.16		fired on M.6.a.10 5½. 3-5PM. our artillery shelled intermittently behind	
			HARRISONS CRATER. On night 7/8 our M.G's were active during the night.	
			Two patrols went out at M.6.c.1.6 and M.5.d.2.6 to examine gaps which	W.H.S.
			were shelled by our artillery and T.M's. These gaps were only partially open	
	8.7.16		Battn was relieved by the 8 Royal Irish Fusiliers about 11 P.M. on 7th inst.	
			Battn moved into Brigade Support. Battn Hdqrs in DUKE STREET	
			B Coy in PIP STREET and A Coy in DUKE STREET both attached to 7th Royal	
			INNISKILLING FUSILIERS who were holding left sub-section. C and D Coys. in	
			ENCLOSURE under 8th ROYAL IRISH FUSILIERS who were holding Right sub-section.	W.H.S.
	9.7.16		Coys on fatigues under battalions mentioned above.	W.H.S.
			Battn Hdqrs moved to PHILOSOPHE E	
	10.7.16		Same as 9th inst.	W.H.S.
			Relieved 8 Royal Irish Fusiliers in Right sub-section. 4 Coys. in front line.	
	11.7.16		2 Coys of 8 Royal Irish Fusiliers in ENCLOSURE as reserve attached to this	
			Battn. The night passed quietly	W.H.S.

2353 Wt. W2544/1454 700,000 5/15 D. D. & L. A.D.S.S./Forms/C. 2118.

7th 15th Battn. Royal Irish Fusiliers

Instructions regarding War Diaries and Intelligence Summaries are contained in F. S. Regs., Part II. and the Staff Manual respectively. Title pages will be prepared in manuscript.

WAR DIARY
or
~~INTELLIGENCE SUMMARY.~~
(Erase heading not required.)

July 1916

Army Form C. 2118.

Place	Date	Hour	Summary of Events and Information	Remarks and references to Appendices
LOOS Right Sub section	12.7.16		Our trench mortars effectively shelled enemys front line near the CRASSIER. At 3 p.m we bombarded the enemys front support and communication trenches with artillery T.M's and rifle grenades. At about 5 p.m enemy retaliated on QUARRY, HAY HILL, and ENCLOSURE. At 10 P.M we carried out a similar bombardment to the 3 P.M Straffe. Throughout the night our M.G's were very active	W.H.S.
	13.7.16		About 9.30 AM enemy sent over 'Whizzbangs' and T.M's from Boyau 31 to HARTS CRATER doing some damage. We retaliated with Stokes Gun and whizzbangs. 5 copies of latest news from SOMME with map showing how far the allies had advanced, were attached to rifle grenades and sent into German lines.	W.H.S.
			During the night 13/14 enemy traversed our parapets with M.G's.	
	14.7.16		The day passed very quietly. On night 14/15 our M.G's fired on German wiring party claiming 2 hits.	W.H.S.
	15.7.16		A large number of T.M's were sent into our lines. Our artillery continued to fire on enemy communications at intervals.	
	16.7.16		Night 15/16 passed quietly until 11 P.M when enemy shelled our lines heavily with schrapnel. This was retaliation for a large mine the Battalion on our left blew at 11 P.M under SEAFORTH CRATER and a small raid carried out by them. Our artillery retaliated strongly.	W.H.S.

2353 Wt. W2544/1454 700,000 5/15 D. D. & L. A.D.S.S./Forms/C. 2118.

7th (S) Battn Royal Irish Fusiliers

WAR DIARY
or
~~INTELLIGENCE SUMMARY~~.
(Erase heading not required.)

Army Form C. 2118.

Instructions regarding War Diaries and Intelligence Summaries are contained in F. S. Regs., Part II. and the Staff Manual respectively. Title pages will be prepared in manuscript.

July 1916

Place	Date	Hour	Summary of Events and Information	Remarks and references to Appendices
LOOS.	16.7.16		The situation becoming normal about 12.30 AM. The day passed quietly. At 5 p.m we blew a small mine to the left of HARTS CRATER blowing in enemy's passages. No artillery operations followed.	W.H.S.
			About 6 P.M Battn was relieved by 8 (S) Battn Royal Irish Fusiliers, and moved into Bd. Reserve in PHILOSOPHE E.	W.H.S.
PHILOSOPHE E	17.7.16 / 18.7.16		Working parties and fatigues	W.H.S.
MAZINGARBE	19.7.16		Bde was relieved by 48 Infantry Bde and moved into Divisional Reserve. This Battn in NORTHERN HUTS ~~NOEUX LES~~ (W.H.S.) MAZINGARBE	W.H.S.
	20.7.16		Cleansing up and changing clothes etc	W.H.S.
HULLUCH Sector	21.7.16		49 Inf. Bde relieved 45th Inf Bde in ~~Right~~ ~~Sub-section~~ HULLUCH SECTOR. This Battn relieved 13 Royal Scots in Right sub-section during the day. Right Flank VENDIN ALLEY left flank BOYAU 75. The afternoon and evening passed very quietly. At night enemy was busy sniping. Shots seemed mostly to come from fixed rifle rests.	W.H.S.

2353 Wt. W2544/1454 700,000 5/15 D. D. & L. A.D.S.S./Forms/C. 2118.

7(S) Battn Royal Irish Fusiliers

Instructions regarding War Diaries and Intelligence Summaries are contained in F. S. Regs., Part II. and the Staff Manual respectively. Title pages will be prepared in manuscript.

WAR DIARY
or
~~INTELLIGENCE SUMMARY.~~
(Erase heading not required.)

July 1916.

Army Form C. 2118.

Place	Date	Hour	Summary of Events and Information	Remarks and references to Appendices
HULLUCH SECTOR	22.7.16		Our Stokes guns were active. There was little or no retaliation to our Stokes guns and rifle grenades. At 10 PM a patrol went out opposite Boyau 73. Nothing to report except enemy working hard on front line trenches opposite this point.	W.H.S.
	23.7.16		About 10 AM hostile aeroplane dropped 2 smoke bombs near ESSEX LANE about 100 x E. of NINTH AVENUE. Nothing followed this.	W.H.S.
			About 11 30 PM small enemy's patrol observed near LONG SAP. Bombs were thrown and patrol dispersed. Day quiet.	W.H.S.
	24.7.16		About 1 PM enemy shelled RESERVE TRENCH with about 20 5.9s. We retaliated silencing enemy. 48 Inf Bde relieved 49 Inf Bde in HULLOCH SECTOR. On relief 49 Inf Bde moved into Divisional Reserve. This Battn on being relieved by 7 ROYAL IRISH RIFLES proceeded about 2 PM to NORTHERN HUTS MAZINGARBE.	W.H.S.
	25.7.16		Cleaning up. Kit inspections etc.	W.H.S.
	26.7.16		Squad drill. Training specialists etc.	W.H.S.
	27.7.16		Working parties. Physical training etc.	W.H.S.
	28.7.16		Training in MAZINGARBE	W.H.S.
	29.7.16		″	W.H.S.
	30.7.16		″	W.H.S.
	~~31.7.16~~			

2353 Wt. W2544/1454 700,000 5/15 D. D. & L. A.D.S.S./Forms/C. 2118.

7 (S) Battn. Royal Irish

Instructions regarding War Diaries and Intelligence Summaries are contained in F. S. Regs., Part II. and the Staff Manual respectively. Title pages will be prepared in manuscript.

WAR DIARY

or

~~INTELLIGENCE SUMMARY.~~

(Erase heading not required.)

July 1916

Army Form C. 2118.

Place	Date	Hour	Summary of Events and Information	Remarks and references to Appendices
TENTH AVENUE	31-7-16		49 Inf Bde relieved 47 Inf Bde in 14 BIS SECTOR This Battn relieved 6 Battn. ROYAL IRISH REGIMENT in Brigade Support in TENTH AVENUE. One Company (B) in GUN TRENCH. Weather very hot. In evening carrying rations for 2 Battalions in firing line.	[illegible]

J Moore. Lieut. Colonel

Commanding 7 (S) Battn Royal Irish Fusiliers,

1/8/16

2353 Wt. W2544/1454 700,000 5/15 D. D. & L. A.D.S.S./Forms/C. 2118.

Vol 7

49/16

W A R D I A R Y.

7th Royal Irish Fusiliers

MONTH OF AUGUST, 1916.

VOLUME:- 7

9 W

7th (S) Battn Royal Irish Fusiliers.

Instructions regarding War Diaries and Intelligence Summaries are contained in F. S. Regs., Part II. and the Staff Manual respectively. Title pages will be prepared in manuscript.

WAR DIARY
or
~~INTELLIGENCE SUMMARY~~.
(Erase heading not required.)

August 1916

Army Form C. 2118.

Place	Date	Hour	Summary of Events and Information	Remarks and references to Appendices
TENTH AVENUE	1/8/16		Battalion in Bde Support PUITS 14 BIS SECTOR. Repairing trenches etc. Supplying working parties.	W.H.S.
"	2/8/16		do.	W.H.S.
"	3/8/16		do.	W.H.S.
14 BIS	4/8/16		Battalion relieved 8th ROYAL IRISH FUSILIERS in RIGHT SUB-SECTION, PUITS 14 BIS SECTOR on afternoon of 8th. Enemys T.M.s were active firing from opposite Boyaux 62 and 56 at about 8 PM and 10 PM respectively we retaliated effectively with W bizzybangs and Stokes Guns. Enemys snipers active throughout the night.	W.H.S.
14 BIS.	5/8/16		Our medium T.M's fired on enemys wire at H 31 b 1.5. breaking it in several places and on SUPPORT trench in retaliation to enemy T.M's. Enemys T.M. were active during the night. During the night the enemy kept up a slow fire with rifle grenades. We replied with Stokes guns.	W.H.S.
"	6/8/16		Our Lewis Gunners were active and surprised a working party at 1 AM. About 3 PM. our T.M's and Stokes engaged enemy who retaliated	

T.2134. Wt. W708—776. 500000. 4/15. Sir J. C. & S.

7 (S) Battn. Royal Irish Fusiliers

Instructions regarding War Diaries and Intelligence Summaries are contained in F. S. Regs., Part II. and the Staff Manual respectively. Title pages will be prepared in manuscript.

WAR DIARY
or
~~INTELLIGENCE SUMMARY.~~
(Erase heading not required.)

August 1916

Army Form C. 2118.

Place	Date	Hour	Summary of Events and Information	Remarks and references to Appendices
			in kind feebly. About 11 PM a patrol left our lines at Boyau 54 and proceeded towards PUITS 14 BIS. returning about 12.30 AM. They reported all quiet in enemys lines.	W.H.S.
Puits 14 BIS.	7/8/16		At 2 AM our Stokes Guns bombarded enemys lines for ½ hour without drawing any retaliation. Our Lewis Guns were active. An enemys M.G. was located. We carried out a very successful dummy raid on enemys trenches in vicinity of H 31 b 1.7. A Bangalore torpedo was put in position close to the enemys wire at H 31 b ½.7. At 12.15 AM Artillery Lewis Guns Vickers Guns, Stokes and TM's opened fire on enemys front line trenches between PUITS 14 BIS and communication trench immediately S. of BOIS RASÉ. The torpedo was fired successfully and at the end of 2 minutes the bombardment lifted. After 5 minutes the bombardment was switched back to original objective. Enemy retaliation was half-hearted and erratic. Our shooting appeared accurate and as the enemy had been heard working and talking in his front line;	

T2134. Wt. W708–776. 500000. 4/15. Sir J. C. & S.

7(S) Battn. Royal Irish Fusiliers

Instructions regarding War Diaries and Intelligence Summaries are contained in F. S. Regs., Part II. and the Staff Manual respectively. Title pages will be prepared in manuscript.

WAR DIARY

or

~~INTELLIGENCE SUMMARY.~~

(Erase heading not required.)

Army Form C. 2118.

August 1916

Place	Date	Hour	Summary of Events and Information	Remarks and references to Appendices
			the results must have been satisfactory. Our stokes dealt with enemys retaliation	W.H.S.
MAZINGARBE	8/8/16		Morning passed quietly. Battalion on being relieved on afternoon by 8 ROYAL IRISH FUSILIERS moved into Brigade Reserve, NORTHERN HUTS, MAZINGARBE.	W.H.S.
do.	9/8/16		Re-equipping, physical drill etc.	W.H.S.
do.	10/8/16			
do.	11/8/16			
	12/8/16		Relieved the 8 Battalion Royal Irish Fusiliers in the right subsection ~~Bet~~ PUITS 14 bis. SECTOR. relief complete 9.0 P.M. Weather warm. Our Stokes Guns replied during the night to aerial torpedoes and T.M's. On every occasion we silenced the enemy.	W.H.S.
14 BIS.	13/8/16		Our Lewis Guns dispersed a wiring party working from opposite Boyau 61 northwards. Our Medium T.M and Stokes Guns fired at enemys wire etc. The enemy replied with 4.2's but did not reply to 12 rounds fired from our Field Guns. At 9.30 P.M the enemy	

T.2134. Wt. W708–776. 500000. 4/15. Sir J. C. & S.

7th (S) Battn. Royal Irish Fusiliers

Instructions regarding War Diaries and Intelligence Summaries are contained in F. S. Regs., Part II. and the Staff Manual respectively. Title pages will be prepared in manuscript.

WAR DIARY
or
~~INTELLIGENCE SUMMARY~~.
(Erase heading not required.)

August 1916

Army Form C. 2118.

Place	Date	Hour	Summary of Events and Information	Remarks and references to Appendices
			bombarded our left Coy's front and support lines with whizzbangs, T.M's and rifle grenades, doing a little damage to Support line between Boyaux 63 and 64. Our retaliation effectively silenced him.	W.H.S.
14 Bis.	14/8/16		The day passed quietly. During the Day 49 Inf Bde No. S.O. 676 received being orders for discharge of gas from Boyau 61 to Boyau 79 at 11.15 P.M on night 14/15 August. This Battn was to carry out a raid on German Trenches opposite Boyau 63. to ascertain damage done by our gas and to obtain identifications, inflict damage etc. Owing to weather conditions these operations had to be postponed. A patrol of 1 officer and 1. O.R. went out opposite Boyau 62 and stayed out from 11.45 PM to 12.30 A.M. Owing to brightness of moon, little information could be obtained.	W.H.S.
do.	15/8/16		At 6.30 P.M. our medium T.M. cut wire around sap at H.25 b.5.5½. This was in preparation for our raid; as Operations as laid down in 49 I.B S.O. 676 were to be carried out, but again had to be postponed owing to the weather.	W.H.S.

T2134. Wt. W708—776. 500000. 4/15. Sir J. C. & S.

7(S) Battn. Royal Irish Fusiliers

Instructions regarding War Diaries and Intelligence Summaries are contained in F. S. Regs., Part II. and the Staff Manual respectively. Title pages will be prepared in manuscript.

WAR DIARY

or

~~INTELLIGENCE SUMMARY~~.

(Erase heading not required.)

August 1916.

Army Form C. 2118.

Place	Date	Hour	Summary of Events and Information	Remarks and references to Appendices
14 Bis	16/8/16		Our Lewis Guns traversed enemy's wire during night 15/16. Our Field Guns shelled enemy front and support lines about 2.30 A.M.; this did not provoke any retaliation. Operations as laid down in 49 Inf Bde S.O. 676 were to take place at same time etc on night 16/17 but were again put off. This Battn was relieved by the 8th Royal Irish Fusiliers and moved into Bde. Support relieving the 8th Royal Inniskilling Fusiliers. C Coy occupied GUN TRENCH D.B.A TENTH AVENUE from POSEN ALLEY to RAILWAY ALLEY reading from (R. to L) Weather warm and showery. One casualty.	W.H.S.
TENTH AVENUE	17/8/16		Situation quiet. Our 9.2s shelled a suspected gun emplacement opposite Posen 50 with good results. Operations as for 14/15 inst were to have taken place on night 17/18 but were postponed.	W.H.S.
	18/8/16		Day passed quietly. Our artillery appeared to be very active. Discharge of Gas along Divisional Front, etc. had to be postponed, weather being unsuitable. LIEUT.-COL F. T. T. MOORE visited the operations in the SOMME area this day.	W.H.S.

T2134. Wt. W708–776. 500000. 4/15. Sir J. C. & S.

7 (S) Battn. Royal Irish Fusiliers.

Instructions regarding War Diaries and Intelligence Summaries are contained in F. S. Regs., Part II. and the Staff Manual respectively. Title pages will be prepared in manuscript.

WAR DIARY
or
~~INTELLIGENCE SUMMARY~~.
(*Erase heading not required.*)

Army Form C. 2118.

August 1916.

Place	Date	Hour	Summary of Events and Information	Remarks and references to Appendices
TENTH AVENUE	19/8/16		The day passed quietly. Discharge of gas was again postponed weather being unfavourable.	W.H.S.
	20/8/16		The morning passed quietly. In the afternoon this Battalion relieved 8' Battn. ROYAL IRISH FUS. in the LEFT SUB-SECTION PUITS 14 BIS SECTION. 3 Coys front and support lines, one Coy in RESERVE. Operations as laid down in S.O. 676 were carried out. At 10.30 PM gas was discharged from Boyau 61 to Boyau 79. At 10.35 PM the enemy sent up rockets which burst into a red and green light. At 10.36 PM. hostile retaliation commenced, consisting chiefly of TM's but a small amount of artillery was sent over. This retaliation was aimed chiefly at our front and support lines. Rifle, machine gun fire and aerial torpedoes were sent over from the right of the gas cloud into our lines. The MG's firing down No Mans Land and traversing our parapets. The gas was turned off about 10.50 PM. From 11PM to midnight our 18 pounders retaliated for the TM fire, eventually silencing the enemy about mid-night. About 12.15 AM. an officers' patrol left our line between Boyau 62 and 63	

T2134. Wt. W708-776. 500000. 4/15. Sir J. C. & S.

7 (S) Battn. Royal Irish Fusiliers

Instructions regarding War Diaries and Intelligence Summaries are contained in F. S. Regs., Part II. and the Staff Manual respectively. Title pages will be prepared in manuscript.

WAR DIARY
or
~~INTELLIGENCE SUMMARY~~.
(Erase heading not required.)

August 1916

Army Form C. 2118.

Place	Date	Hour	Summary of Events and Information	Remarks and references to Appendices
POITS 14 BIS.	20/8/16		and made for the sap directly opposite where gaps had been cut in the wire. These gaps had been filled up and our sap patrols were unable to gain entrance to the hostile trenches. After 1 AM the night passed quietly. Casualties 1 O.R. SHOCK SHELL. 3 O.R. wounded. No 13462 C.S.M. WALLS H. was awarded the MILITARY CROSS for service on 1/2. 5. 16.	W.H.S.
do.	21/8/16		There was increased T.M. and rifle grenade activity. Enemy's T.M. replied with especial vigour between Boyaux 55 & 61 from 2.30 PM to 4 PM and again at 9.45 PM. An aerial torpedo battery was located firing from sap at H25d. 4/2. 4¾. At 10.30 PM an officers patrol heard enemy working hard in sap at H.25 b. 3.7 and in front line. Casualties O.R. 1 died of wounds 1 wounded.	W.H.S.
	22/8/16		The day passed quietly. Our stokes guns were active on enemy front and support lines. During the night our Lewis guns traversed enemy's parapets and fired at gaps in wire. About 4 PM over 20 minenwerfer and heavy TM's fired into FORREST TRENCH doing considerable damage. An officers patrol went out	

T2134. Wt. W708—776. 500000. 4/15. Sir J. C. & S.

Instructions regarding War Diaries and Intelligence Summaries are contained in F. S. Regs., Part II. and the Staff Manual respectively. Title pages will be prepared in manuscript.

WAR DIARY
or
INTELLIGENCE SUMMARY.
(Erase heading not required.)

Army Form C. 2118.

Place	Date	Hour	Summary of Events and Information	Remarks and references to Appendices
Pruits 14 BIS. (continued).	22.8.16		opposite Boyau 56 and found enemy very busy in his front line. Casualties LIEUT E.P. HARPUR wounded. O.R 1 killed and 1 died of wounds.	W.H.S.
do	23.8.16		Our artillery fired intermittently on enemys front and support lines from 12 mid-night to 2AM. At 4 p.m our artillery, 2" TM's and stokes guns bombarded enemy front, support and communication trenches between H 25d. 8.9 and H 25 b 5¾. 4. Fire lasted from 4PM to 4.7 pm and was intense. This provoked practically no retaliation. On the night	W.H.S.
do.	24.8.16		23/24 our Lewis Guns were very active. Casualties on 23rd. 3 O.R. wounded During the afternoon the Enemy sent over a few whizzbangs and aerial torpedoes in answer to our Stokes guns and 2" TM's. At 11.40 P.M our artillery commenced a heavy bombardment of the enemys lines along the divisional front. A certain number of Batteries were switched off their normal zones for the purpose of assisting the Divisional and Corps artillery in this bombardment. The bombardment lasted until about 1A.M. Enemy retaliation was feeble chiefly consisting of Minenwerfer and T.M., their retaliation ceased as soon as the bombardment	

T2134. Wt. W708—776. 500000. 4/15. Sir J. C. & S.

7th (S) Battn. Royal Irish Fusiliers

Instructions regarding War Diaries and Intelligence Summaries are contained in F. S. Regs., Part II. and the Staff Manual respectively. Title pages will be prepared in manuscript.

WAR DIARY
or
~~INTELLIGENCE SUMMARY.~~
(Erase heading not required.)

August 1916.

Army Form C. 2118.

Place	Date	Hour	Summary of Events and Information	Remarks and references to Appendices
			was finished. Our casualties amounted to 1 killed 1 wounded.	W.H.S
Puits 14 Bis	25.8.16.		The morning passed quietly. The Bde was relieved by the 112th Bde on the afternoon of the 25th inst. This Battn. was relieved by the 6th Battn BEDFORDS. and on relief marched to NOEUX-les-MINES being billeted in the town.	W.H.S.
MARLES-les-MINES.	26.8.16		At 3 P.M the Battn with full transport commenced to march to MARLES-les-MINES via X Roads J. 17 b. railway crossing in J. 4 C. On arrival the Battn. was billeted in the village.	W.H.S
do	27.8.16		The day was taken up with Divine Service, Baths etc.	W.H.S.
do	28.8.16		The Battn. proceeded on a short route march via LOZINGHEM, AUCHEL returning after a 2½ hour march.	W.H.S.
VAUX en SOMME	29.8.16		The Battalion marched to FOUQUERUIL from MARLES les Mines and entrained with full transport, for journey to the SOMME area on being transferred to the IV Army XIV. Corps. The journey commenced at midday and lasted until 7 P.M. when the Battn. detrained at LONGUEAU. Detrainment being completed the Battn marched to billets in	

T.2134. Wt. W708—776. 500000. 4/15. Sir J. C. & S.

7th (S) Battn. Royal Irish Fusiliers

Instructions regarding War Diaries and Intelligence Summaries are contained in F. S. Regs., Part II. and the Staff Manual respectively. Title pages will be prepared in manuscript.

WAR DIARY
or
INTELLIGENCE SUMMARY.
(*Erase heading not required.*)

August 1916.

Army Form C. 2118.

Place	Date	Hour	Summary of Events and Information	Remarks and references to Appendices
VAUX sur SOMME			VAUX sur SOMME.	W.H.S.
	30-8-16.		The day was spent in billets awaiting orders to move further up.	
	31-8-16		At 7AM the Battn. marched off from VAUX sur SOMME to HAPPY VALLEY where the 16 Div. became Corps Reserve. The Battn. was under canvas in the valley.	W.H.S.

F. Moore. Lieut.-Col
Commdg 7th (S) Battn. Royal Irish Fusiliers.

3/9/16

T.2134. Wt. W708—776. 500000. 4/15. Sir J. C. & S.

WAR DIARY

7th Royal Irish Fusiliers

FOR MONTH OF SEPTEMBER, 1916.

VOLUME 8

Vol 8

47

49/16

7th (S) Battn. Royal Irish Fusiliers

WAR DIARY
or
~~INTELLIGENCE SUMMARY.~~
(Erase heading not required.)

September 1916

Army Form C. 2118.

Instructions regarding War Diaries and Intelligence Summaries are contained in F. S. Regs., Part II. and the Staff Manual respectively. Title pages will be prepared in manuscript.

Place	Date	Hour	Summary of Events and Information	Remarks and references to Appendices
HAPPY VALLEY	1.9.16		The Battn. was bivouaced in the Valley. Orders were received that the Battn. was under 3 hours notice to proceed to the line. The day was spent organising and drill.	W.H.S.
do.	2.9.16		The Battn bathed by Coys. in the SOMME. The remaining Companies were training at extended order drill and the machine gunners and signallers at specialist training	W.H.S.
CITADEL do	3.9.16		At 9 A.M. the Battn marched to the CITADEL where the Brigade bivouaced partly in huts partly under canvas. The Bde. came under 3 hours notice. The day was spent with inspections and settling down. About 7 P.M an order was received from Bde Hdqrs to be prepared to move at once. At 7.41 P.M. an order was received for the Battn to move to BILLON FARM at 8 P.M. Transport less G.S. wagons to move under Bde Transport Officers orders QM Stores to remain at CITADEL. The Battn. marched across country and reported to G.O.C 49 Inf Bde at BILLON FARM, where orders were received to march to DUBLIN TRENCH near BRIQUETERIE where we came under 5th Div. and were in Div. Res. The Battn. remained in DUBLIN TRENCH until 3 PM on	
CHIMPANZEE TRENCH	4.9.16		4.9.16 when orders were received to occupy slits near CHIMPANZE TRENCH as the Battn. was under orders of 15 Inf Bde, as the XIV Corps were continuing offensive operations in conjunction with the French. (49 Inf Bde Oper. Order marked 1. attached) About 7.30 PM. B and C. Coys were ordered forward to occupy a trench behind ANGLE WOOD. The Coys remained in these positions during the night. During the afternoon while in the slits the Battn was subjected to	W.H.S.

7th (S) Battn Royal Irish Fusiliers

Instructions regarding War Diaries and Intelligence Summaries are contained in F. S. Regs., Part II. and the Staff Manual respectively. Title pages will be prepared in manuscript.

WAR DIARY
or
INTELLIGENCE SUMMARY.
(*Erase heading not required.*)

September 1916

Army Form C. 2118.

Place	Date	Hour	Summary of Events and Information	Remarks and references to Appendices
4.9.6 (continued)			Considerable artillery fire, causing the following casualties, 2nd Lt F. C. BERNARD wounded, O.R 1 Killed 4 wounded. The weather was very inclement.	
FALFAMONT. FARM.	5.9.16		In accordance with 15th Infy Brigade Oper. Orders 59 & 60 attached & marked 2 & 3 respectively, A & B Companies moved up with head quarters to ANGLE WOOD. On arrival there 50 men were sent out at once to dig in strong points some 300 yds in front of FALFAMONT FARM. At dusk B. C & D Companies were to go out & connect up these strong posts with a trench & A Compy to garrison FALFAMONT FARM. Patrols to connect up with 95th Infy Brigade on Left & the French on right. At 3.15 pm verbal orders were received to take the German trench which runs from middle of S.E side of LEUZE. Wood to a point S. W of COMBLES, This trench was reported to be very lightly held if held at all, as the Artillery Barage was to lift at 4 pm This gave very little time for preparation & no time for reconnaissance— At 4 pm B compy advanced in two lines followed by C Company in similar formation They advanced about 500 yards in excellent formation and met comparatively little resistance until they found themselves opposed by very thick barbed wire quite uncut, they gallantly attempted to break through this but were met by a withering fire from machine guns, they at once proceeded to dig in where they were— During this time Battn H. Q and the reserve companies were subjected to very heavy artillery fire. At 7 pm having reported the situation the following order was	JM

2353 Wt. W2544/1454 700,000 5/15 D. D. & L. A.D.S.S./Forms/C. 2118.

7th (S) Battn Royal Irish Fusiliers

Instructions regarding War Diaries and Intelligence Summaries are contained in F. S. Regs., Part II. and the Staff Manual respectively. Title pages will be prepared in manuscript.

WAR DIARY
or
~~INTELLIGENCE SUMMARY.~~
(*Erase heading not required.*)

Army Form C. 2118.

September 1916

Place	Date	Hour	Summary of Events and Information	Remarks and references to Appendices
~~Fal~~ FALFAMONT FARM. (continued)	5/9/16		Received from G.O.C 15th Infy Brigade "LEUZE WOOD in our hands, French report COMBLES deserted, capture trench at all costs" – D & A Companies were then pushed up, but despite repeated gallant attempts were unable to break through the wire ~~and~~ owing to heavy machine gun fire and also artillery fire – The report about LEUZE, WOOD & COMBLES proved to be false and the Battn was heavily enfiladed from both flanks – When dark the companies fell back about 300 yds and commenced digging in about 400 yds NE of FALFAMONT FARM.	
			Portion of order stating that trench must be taken at all costs & expressing Brigadiers pleasure at progress made is attached & marked 4.	4
ANGLE WOOD	6.9.16		At ~~8~~ dawn what remained of the Battn on relief by the SOUTH KENSINGTON REGT moved back to ANGLE WOOD. – Great gallantry & devotion was shown by all ranks in this advance – The following casualties occurred – Died of wounds LIEUT. E.P HARPUR 2nd LIEUT L.M. DAVENPORT. Wounded LIEUT F.H LEDGERWOOD, 2nd Lt T. GERATY, 2nd Lt H.S. LEE. 2nd Lt E.A EVANSON. 2nd Lt J. TURNER, 2nd Lt W.M. MOORE, 2nd Lt W.D BRADLEY. Wounded at duty Capt C.F. BRADY. R.A.M.C	
			Total other ranks, killed wounded & missing 236.	
			at about 8 pm the Battn was suddenly relieved by the 2nd London Regt, with orders to rejoin the 49th Infy Brigade at GUILLEMONT and take over from 7th & 8th	

2353 Wt. W2544/1454 700,000 5/15 D. D. & L. A.D.S.S./Forms/C. 2118.

7/8 Bn Royal Irish Fusiliers

Army Form C. 2118.

WAR DIARY
or
INTELLIGENCE SUMMARY.
(Erase heading not required.)

September 1916

Instructions regarding War Diaries and Intelligence Summaries are contained in F. S. Regs., Part II. and the Staff Manual respectively. Title pages will be prepared in manuscript.

Place	Date	Hour	Summary of Events and Information	Remarks and references to Appendices
ANGLE WOOD. (Continued)	6 9/16		Rl Inniskilling Fusiliers	
			The Battn continued consolidating the defences of GUILLEMONT – during the evening the Battn was heavily shelled – 49 Ify Bg. Op order No 54 attached & marked 5.	Fm
GUILLEMONT	7 9/16		The Battn was relieved at dawn by 11th HANTS and moved to BERNAFAY WOOD, where 49th Infy Brigade became Divisional Reserve (49th I. B. op order No 55 attached marked 6) –	Fm
BERNAFAY WOOD.	8. 9/16		In evening the 49th Infy Brigade moved forward, the Battn moving into the QUARRIES & STATION of GUILLEMONT –	Fm
QUARRY GUILLEMONT	9 9/16		orders were issued for the 48th Infy Brigade to attack ~~Guillem~~ GINCHY at 4.45 P.M. at 2.45 p.m orders were received for this Battn to take part in the attack on GINCHY owing to one battn of 48th Infy Brigade being very week, the battn had only barely time to move from the QUARRIES to the left flank of the 7th Rl Irish Rifles with whom they were to attack the first objective – at 4.45, This Battn and the Irish Rifles attacked in 4 waves going as if they were on parade and in 12 minutes gained their objective. Part of the Battn went forward with the R. DUBLIN. FUS to the final objective. The position was consolidated and orders received that the Battn was to be relieved at 10 PM by the WELSH GUARDS. Part of the Battn was relieved at this hour, but the remainder was only relieved at 10 AM. on 10/9/16 (vide no 10) message of congratulations from G.O.C. 48 Inf. Bde attached & marked No 11	Fm WHS.

2353 Wt. W2544/1454 700,000 5/15 D. D. & L. A.D.S.S./Forms/C. 2118.

7 (S) Battn Royal Irish Fusiliers

Instructions regarding War Diaries and Intelligence Summaries are contained in F. S. Regs., Part II. and the Staff Manual respectively. Title pages will be prepared in manuscript.

WAR DIARY
or
~~INTELLIGENCE SUMMARY.~~

(*Erase heading not required.*)

Sept 1916

Army Form C. 2118.

Place	Date	Hour	Summary of Events and Information	Remarks and references to Appendices
	9.9.16		Sketch showing objectives (no 12 attached) Our casualties were as follows:- Killed 2LIEUT G M PICKETT aaa Died of wounds 2LIEUT J. O DWYER aaa wounded CAPT G ROBINSON, CAPT. WV EDWARDS, CAPT DC LISTON, 2LIEUT J.L. CHALMERS (wounded at duty), 2LIEUT J.J. MICHIE, 2LIEUT F.K. WALKINGTON, 2LIEUT J.B LANE, 2LIEUT P.H WRAY, 2LIEUT F.M. EAGAR, 2LIEUT A.C YOUNG, aaa missing LIEUT C.P.M. IRWIN. Other ranks killed wounded and missing total 130. All ranks were congratulated by G.O.C 49 Inf Bde on their magnificent achievement and the courage coolness and daring shewn.	W.H.S.
BILLON FARM	10.9.16		On relief the Battalion moved to Bde Transport lines near BILLON FARM. The total strength of the Battn amounted to 14 officers and O.R.	W.H.S.
SAILLY le SEC	11.9.16		The Bde moved to SAILLY le SEC and were accomodated in billets.	W.H.S.
do	12.9.16		Organising, resting and re-equipping	
do	13.9.16		do	W.H.S.
	14.9.16		Lewis Gunners and signallers training in their specialist duties. Remainder of Battn. Squad drill, company drill extended order, etc.	W.H.S.
.	15.9.16		The G.O.C 49 Inf Bde inspected the Battn with full transport, and congratulated the Battn on its gallantry and great achievements near FALFAMONT FARM and at GINCHY.	W.H.S.
.	16.9.16		Squad drill etc. Specialists training by themselves.	W.H.S.
"	17.9.16		Orders were received for the 16' Div. to concentrate by evening of 18' inst. in Area 5.	

2353 Wt. W2544/1454 700,000 5/15 D. D. & L. A.D.S.S./Forms/C. 2118.

7 (S) Battn. ROYAL IRISH FUSILIERS

Instructions regarding War Diaries and Intelligence Summaries are contained in F. S. Regs., Part II. and the Staff Manual respectively. Title pages will be prepared in manuscript.

WAR DIARY
or
~~INTELLIGENCE SUMMARY.~~
(Erase heading not required.)

September 1916

Army Form C. 2118.

Place	Date	Hour	Summary of Events and Information	Remarks and references to Appendices
	19.9.16 (cont)		which lies in the neighbourhood of HALLENCOURT 20 miles W.N.W of AMIENS. The transport left SAILLY-le-SEC under Bde Transport Officer at 1.45 P.M. for FONTAINE	W.H.S.
FONTAINE	18.9.16		The Battn marched to LA NEUVILLE. At LA NEUVILLE the Battn entered buses, which brought it to FONTAINE, where billets were provided.	W.H.S.
	19.9.16		cleaning up etc	W.H.S.
	20.9.16		do.	W.H.S.
LOCRE	21.9.16		During the afternoon the Battn and Transport marched to PONT REMY and entrained for transfer to II Army.	W.H.S.
"	22.9.16		About 5.30 AM the Battalion detrained at BAILLEUL and marched to LOCRE where it was accomodated in huts.	W.H.S.
KEMMEL	23.9.16		In the afternoon the Battn marched to KEMMEL SHELTERS where it relieved part of the 72nd CANADIAN BATTN. thus becoming the Reserve Battn to the 49th INF BDE in the Right Section of the Divisional Line.	W.H.S.
"	24.9.16		Training etc. Special attention being paid to specialists	W.H.S.
"	25.9.16		do	W.H.S.
"	26.9.16		do. ~~The 49~~	W.H.S.
KEMMEL CHATEAU	27.9.16		The 16 Div. front was was readjusted as follows 47 Inf Bde on left 48 Inf Bde in ~~Right~~ Centre, 49 Inf Bde on Right. Front of 49 Inf Bde N.29 d 9.4 to N24 a 2.3 This Battn relieved 8 R. INNIS FUS. and 7 R. INNIS. FUS. in left subsection on afternoon 27 inst. A + D Coys in front line C Coy and 1 platoon B Coy in YONCE Redoubt. 2 platoons B Coy in S.P.10 and remaining platoon in FORT REGINA.	

2353 Wt. W2544/1454 700,000 5/15 D. D. & L. A.D.S.S./Forms/C. 2118.

7(S) Battn Royal Irish Fusiliers

Instructions regarding War Diaries and Intelligence Summaries are contained in F. S. Regs., Part II. and the Staff Manual respectively. Title pages will be prepared in manuscript.

WAR DIARY
or
~~INTELLIGENCE SUMMARY.~~
(Erase heading not required.)

September 1916.

Army Form C. 2118.

Place	Date	Hour	Summary of Events and Information	Remarks and references to Appendices
KEMMEL CHATEAU	27.9.16 (cont.)		The evening passed very quietly. 5 patrol went out and reported enemys wire to be very thick. Our own wire is weak. Enemy was very quiet.	W.H.S.
"	28.9.16		The day passed very quietly. Our T.M's and Stokes Gun were active, provoking very little retaliation.	W.H.S.
"	29.9.16		Our patrols were busy on night 28/29 patrolling enemys wire. Very little sound was heard in enemys lines. Only 2 Very lights were put up by the enemy during the night opposite this front. About 3.30 PM our medium TM and Stokes Guns were very active. Enemy retaliated with T.M, Aerial torpedo and rifle grenades doing considerable damage.	W.H.S.
"	30.9.16		Our lewis guns were active during the early hours of the morning. The day passed quietly	W.H.S.

T. F. O'Donnell Capt
Commdg 7(S) Battn. Royal Irish Fusiliers.

T2134. Wt. W708–776. 500000. 4/15. Sir J. C. & S.

SECRET.

Copy No.....3.....

49th. Infantry Brigade Order No. 53 - 4/9/16.

==*==*==*==*==*==*==*==

Reference Trench Map 1/10,000.

1. The XIV Corps attack yesterday met with considerable success. Over 500 prisoners have been taken; the French to the South have taken over 2000 prisoners.

2. Our line runs along the WEDGE WOOD - GINCHY ROAD from WEDGE WOOD to T.20.a.1.5.

3. The attack will be renewed to-day.

4. At 3.10 p.m. the 5th. Division will attack the line B.2.d.4.8 - WEDGEWOOD and the trench from T.26.c.4.5 to T.26.a.8.5½.

The French Corps will simultaneously attack the trench from OAKHANGER WOOD to B.2.d.4.8.

The 7th. Division will simultaneously clear up the situation in GINCHY.

5. Subsequently, the exact hour being notified later, the 5th. and 20th. Divisions will capture the line LEUZE WOOD - T.20.a.6.5.

The dividing line between Divisions will be the W. corner of LEUZE WOOD (T.26.b.8.8½).

6. The 47th. and 48th. Inf. Bdes. at the disposal of the 20th. Division and the two Battalions of the 49th. Inf. Bde. at the disposal of the 5th. Division, are available for this operation.

7. The 49th. Inf. Bde. (less the two Battalions at the disposal of the 5th. Division) will be at one hour's notice. The remainder of the 16th. Division will be at 3 hours notice.

8. The attack will be preceded by a bombardment commencing at 7 a.m.

9. All the transport, surplus Officers, N.C.Os. &c., of the 7th. & 8th. R. Irish Fus. now out of the trenches, and the surplus officers, N.C.Os., spare machine gunners and transport less cookers, Water Carts, Mess Carts and Maltese Carts of the 7th. & 8th. Inniskilling Fus. will return to the Citadel to-day and will form a permanent base there.

The M.G. Coy. will also form a permanent base at the Citadel.

10. Acknowledge.

W. W. Willen.
Captain,
Brigade Major, 49th. Infantry Brigade.

Issued through Signals :

Copy No. 1 to 7th. R. Innis. Fus.
.. 2 .. 8th. R. Innis. Fus.
.. 3 .. 7th. R. Irish Fus.
.. 4 .. 8th. R. Irish Fus.
.. 5 .. 49th. M.G. Company.
.. 6 .. 49th. T.M. Battery.
.. 7 .. Bearer Div. 113th. Field Ambce.
.. 8 .. 157th. Field Coy. R.E.
.. 9 .. 16th. Division.
.. 10 .. 144 Coy. A.S.C.
.. 11 .. Bde. Supply Officer.
.. 12 .. Bde. Transport Officer.
.. 13 .. Bde. Signals.
.. 14 - 15 War Diary.
.. 16 .. File.

2

SECRET.

15th Infantry Brigade Operation Order No. 59.

5th September, 1916.

O.C., 1st BEDFORDSHIRE Regiment.

As the situation in FALFEMONT FARM is not yet clear the Division order that the Farm shall be taken from the direction of WEDGE WOOD.

The 1st CHESHIRE Regiment are in possession of the Line from B.2.a.7/5, thence NORTH through T.23.c.7/1 to T.26.c.8/5, thence to Valley Trench.

The 1st NORFOLK Regiment are hung up just SOUTH of FALFEMONT FARM. It is more than probable that they have established themselves at S.W. Corner of FARM as our Troops have been observed there. This matter, however, must not be left to doubt and you will, therefore, with the remainder of your Regiment, and the two Companies of the 1st ROYAL WEST KENT Regiment, assault the FARM with the bayonet and establish yourself in it. You can call on one Company of the 7th ROYAL IRISH FUSILIERS, now in NEW TRENCH, SOUTH of ANGLE WOOD, to support you if you consider that the Troops at your disposal are not sufficient.

This attack must take place at once by night and be carried through with the utmost vigour.

You will endeavour to establish yourself in QUARRY in T.26.c. 2/1.

ACKNOWLEDGE, please.

[signature] Captain,

5/9/1916. Brigade Major, 15th Infantry Brigade.

Issued at 12-30 a.m.

Copies to :-
B.G.C.
5th Division.
13th Infy. Bde.
95th Infy. Bde.
1st Norfolks.
1st Cheshires.
16th R.Warwicks.
15th M.G.Coy.
15th T.M.Battery.
7th R.Irish Fus.
1st R.W.Kents.

S E C R E T .

15th Infy. Bde.

O.C., 7th R. IRISH FUSILIERS.

We have now taken FALFEMONT FARM and are bombing down trenches to Point 48. The French have been asked to make good their first objective and join us at Point 48.

Our Line now runs as follows :-

We are entrenched 30 yards from German line from Point 48 to S.E. Corner of FALFEMONT FARM.

We hold FALFEMONT FARM, thence NORTH along Road in T.23.c., to about T.23.a.8/5. Our flank is turned back and runs in a Northwesterly direction to Valley Trench about T.23.c.5/3. We also hold from T.23.c.8/7 to T.23.a.8/1.

You will relieve Troops of this Brigade as follows :-

For the purposes of relief the line as now held by us has been divided into two areas - Area 'A' and Area 'B'.

Area 'A' is from the right of Western end of FALFEMONT FARM.

Area 'B', thence to left of our line.

Please relieve as many as possible in Area 'A' and Area 'B' by daylight.

Tropps relieved in Area 'A' by you will come back and occupy the Support Trenches to old Main Fire Trench and right part of New Trench SOUTH of ANGLE WOOD. Those relieved by you in Area 'B' in left part of New Trench SOUTH of ANGLE WOOD.

Eventually these troops will be sorted out and a sufficient local reserve will be behind you which will be in New Trench SOUTH of ANGLE WOOD.

Those of the 15th Infantry Brigade and R. W. KENT Regiment, not forming the local reserve, will withdraw to Brigade Reserve in Slit Trenches EAST of CHIMPANZEE Trench.

If the QUARRY in T.23.d 1/1 is not occupied by us you will immediately occupy it.

The Battalion H.Q. of Area 'A' is in B.2.c.4/5.
The Battalion H.Q. of Area 'B' is in WEDGE WOOD, B.2.a.9/8.

Area 'A' will be relieved first, Area 'B' second.

The O.C., 1st BEDFORDSHIRE Regiment has been instructed to send a representative to meet you at the Battalion H.Q. in Area 'A'.

ACKNOWLEDGE, please.

Captain

5/9/1916. Brigade Major, 15th Infantry Brigade.

Copies to :- B.G.C., 5th Division, 13th Infy. Bde. 95th Infy. Bde.
1st Norfolks. 1st Bedfords. 1st Cheshires.
16th R. Warwicks. 15th M.G.Coy. 15th T.M.Battery.
1st R. West Kents

"A" Form. Army Form C. 2121.

MESSAGES AND SIGNALS. No. of Message............

Prefix........... Code.............m. Office of Origin and Service Instructions.	Words	Charge	This message is on a/c of: ....Service. (Signature of "Franking Officer.")	Recd. at..........m. Date.......... From.......... By..........
	Sent At..........m. To.......... By..........		4	

TO O.C. Redan

* Sender's Number	Day of Month	In reply to Number	AAA
R.T. 17	5		

The B.G.C. is very pleased at the progress you have made and as presumably you are digging in on this line I am ordering up two Coys of South Kensingtons to FALFEMONT FARM two Coys will go to ANGLE WOOD also Batt by [illegible] aaa You must at all costs get your first objective aaa This must be done and I suggest cutting wire and penetrating the line in driblets then bombing up and down as probably the trench is lightly held, aaa having done this you will send forward patrols right into the town and ascertain if the town is held. The French are of the opinion it is not held and are also patrolling it.

From
Place
Time

The above may be forwarded as now corrected. (Z)

.... Censor. Signature of Addressor or person authorised to telegraph in his name.

* This line should be erased if not required.

(A1) O. Ltd., London— W.14042/M.44. 150,000 Pads. 12/15. Form C.2121.

5

SECRET. Copy No....3...

49th. Infantry Brigade Order No. 54 - 7 /9/ 16.

==*==*==*==*==*==*==*==

1. 49th. Infantry Brigade will be relieved to-night. The 168th. Infantry Brigade will take over the line N. corner of LEUZE WOOD to T.20.d.1.5. on the GUILLEMONT -COMBLES Road, including trench running from West corner of LEUZE WOOD to T.20.d.1.3. and the GINCHY WEDGE WOOD Line from our present right to Cross Roads T.20.c.2.4.
The 4th. London Regt. will be on right and 12th. London Regt. on left. Details of relief to be arranged between C.Os. concerned.

2. The 47th. Infantry Brigade will take over the line from T.20.d.2.5 to GINCHY WEDGE WOOD Road exclusive with the 6th. R. Irish Regt. The 8th. Inniskilling Fus. will have necessary guides at Cross-Roads T.20.c.2.5. at 10 p.m. to guide the 6th. R. Irish Regt.

3. The 7th. R. Irish Fus. will be relieved in the Defences of GUILLEMONT by the 11th. Hants. Regt.

4. The 8th. R. Irish Fus. will be relieved by the 7th. Leinster Regt. Guides will be sent to Bde. H.Q. as soon as possible.

5. O.C. 49th. M.G. Companywill arrange the relief of his guns with O.C. 168th. M.G. Coy. and 47th. M.G. Coy.

6. The 49th. T.M. Batty. is not being relieved but will withdraw their personnel and guns at dusk.

7. No troops will be withdrawn from the line until relieved by corresponding troops of the incoming Brigades.

8. All spare ammunition, bombs, tools, &c., must be handed over.

9. As much work as possible must be done on line from N. corner of LEUZE WOOD to T.20.c.5.6. before relief.

10. On relief 49th. Brigade will move into Divisional Reserve in BERNAFAY WOOD, where Guides will meet Battalions.

11. On relief Bde. H.Q. will be at S.29.b. Central.

12. Acknowledge.

13. Completion of relief to be reported to present Bde. HQ

[signature] Captain,
Brigade Major, 49th. Infantry Brigade.

Issued through Signals at

Copy No. 1 to 7th. R. Innis. Fus.
.. 2 .. 8th. R. Innis. Fus.
.. 3 .. 7th. R. Irish Fus.
.. 4 .. 8th. R. Irish Fus.
.. 5 .. 49th. T.M. Battery.
.. 6 .. 49th. M.G. Company.
.. 7 .. 168th. Brigade.
.. 8 .. 47th. Brigade.
.. 9 .. 48th. Brigade.
.. 10 .. 16th. Division.
.. 11 .. Bde. Transport Officer.
.. 12 .. Bde. Supply Officer.
.. 13 - 14 War Diary.
.. 15 .. File.

SECRET.   6   Copy No. 3 ......

49th. Infantry Brigade Order No. 55 - 8 /9/ 16.

Reference Map
GUILLEMONT Sheet 1/20000.

1. (a) The Fourth Army will renew the attack on September 9th. at an hour to be notified later.
(b) XIV Corps is to capture the German position from T.27.b.1.5½ - T.21.d.5½.2½ - Point 141.7 (1000 yards East of GINCHY) - the trench along the GINCHY-MORVAL Road to Trench junction T.14.c.5.4½ - T.14.a.4.2 and thence to junction of trenches at T.7.d.4.0.
(c) XV Corps will carry out a simultaneous operation on left of XIV Corps.

2. (a) The XIV Corps attack will be carried out by 56th. Division on the right and 16th. Division on left.
Dividing line between 56th. and 16th. Divisions will be the line from the GUILLEMONT-LEUZE WOOD Road at T.20.d.1.5 to Trench Junction at T.14.d.8½.4. (inclusive to 56th. Division).
(b) Dividing line between 16th. Division and 55th. Division (XV Corps) attack will be T.13.c.6½.1½. - T.13(Central) - Trench Junction T.7.d.4.0.
(c) The objectives allotted to 56th. Division are as follows :
First Objective T.27.b.1.5½. - T.21.d.5½.2½. - T.21.a.6.2½. - T.20.b.4½.3½.
Second Objective. T.21.a.6.2½. - T.15.c.1.4½ - T.14.d.8½.4.

3. The 16th. Division attack will be carried out by 47th. Inf. Bde. on right and 48th. Inf. Bde. on left. Dividing line between Brigades will be the GINCHY-WEDGEWOOD Road from present front line to T.20.a.1.6 (to 48th. Inf. Bde.) and thence the trench running to T.14.c.5.4½ (to 47th. Inf. Bde.)

4. The objectives allotted to Brigades are as follows :-

First Objective.

(a) 47th. Inf. Bde. - T.20.b.4½.3½ - point where trench crosses GINCHY-LEUZE WOOD Road at T.14.c.3½.1½.

Second Objective.

Trench Junction at T.14.d.8½.4 (exclusive) - point where trench crosses road at T.14.c.5.4½ (inclusive).

First Objective.

(b) 48th. Inf. Bde. - Point where trench crosses GINCHY-LEUZE WOOD Road at T.14.c.3½.1½. (exclusive) - road junction T.13.d.7.3½. - T.13. (Central).

Second Objective.

Point where trench crosses road at T.14.c.5.4½ (exclusive) -T.14.a.4.2. - Trench Junction T.7.d.4.0.

5. (a) At Zero time 47th. Inf. Bde. will advance with two Battalions in front line to their first objective and consolidate.
(b) At zero plus 40 minutes the remaining two Battalions will advance to their second objective and consolidate.
(c) 47th. Inf. Bde. are establishing strong points at T.20.a.8.9 and T.14.c. (Central).

6. (a) At Zero time 48th. Inf. Bde. will advance with two Battalions to their first objective and consolidate.
(b) At Zero plus 40 minutes the remaining two Battalions will advance to the second objective and consolidate.
(c) 48th. Inf. Bde. are arranging for parties to clear all cellars and dug-outs in GINCHY.
(d) 48th. Inf. Bde. are establishing strong points at T.14.a.4.2. at the northern corner of GINCHY and at T.7.d.4.0.

7. The 49th. Infantry Brigade will be in Divisional Reserve.

8. 7th. Inniskillings will relieve the garrison of GUILLEMONT (11th. HantsR.) on night 8th/9th. September. The H.Q. of 11th. Hants is at T.19.c.9.4.

The 8th. Inniskillings will occupy new trenches at N.E. corner of GUILLEMONT T.19.b.0.3. to T.19.d.10.7.

The 7th. R, Irish Fus. will occupy the old British Line from The Gridiron to T.20.b.8.9.

The 8th. R. Irish Fus. will remain in present position.

Bde. H.Q. is in BERNAFAY WOOD S.28.b. Central.

The 49th. M.G. Company will attach one Section to each Battalion. O.Cs. Sections will be under the orders of Battalion Commanders.

4 Sections will be held in Reserve at the South end of SHERWOOD Trench.

The 49th. Trench Mortar Battery will remain at Bde. H.Q. and will be utilized as carrying parties.

The above moves will be completed by 5 a.m. on 9th.

9. Dumps will be formed under Bde. arrangements at following places:-

Main Forward Dump near ARROW HEAD COPSE.
Forward Dumps on Road at T.19.b.0.2.
" " on Road at T.19.d.5.4.

Water, S.A.A., R.E. material, rockets, flares, &c., will be at these dumps.

The main Dump will be distinguished by 3 rifles tied horizontally on poles and at night by a miner's lamp.

10. A forward Brigade report centre will be at the Quarry at T.19.c.0.3. There will be a representative of the Brigade at this point

11. Battalions will carry two days rations and full water bottles, 220 rounds of S.A.A. and 2 bombs per man will be carried.

12. Observation on to the ORVAL-LESBOEUFS Line is a necessity. Infantry Brigade therefore, on reaching their objectives will at once push forward patrols and establish posts from which this information can be obtained.

13.(a) The attack will be preceded by a deliberate Heavy Artillery bombardment commencing at 7 a.m. and continuing until Zero time with an interval from 11.20 a.m. to 11.50 a.m. for photography.

During this bombardment certain trenches may have to be cleared from time to time.

14. Fifty per cent of the Field Artillery Guns covering the Division will be employed for stationary barrage and fifty per cent for creeping barrage.

The creeping barrage will in all cases advance at the rate of 50 yards per minute in front of the Infantry.

When the creeping barrage reaches the stationary barrage the stationary will lift on to the next barrage line.

At Zero, when the Infantry advance to their first objective, an intense Field Artillery barrage will open.

At Zero plus 40 minutes when the Infantry advance to their second objective, the barrage will again become intense.

15. No. 9 Squadron R.F.C. will have two contact aeroplanes in the air from zero to zero plus two hours, after that one contact aeroplane until dark and one from 5.30 a.m. to 8 a.m. on 10th. September.

Flares will be lit as follows :-

(a) On obtaining each objective.
(b) At 6.30 p.m. on September 9th.
(c) At 6 a.m. on September 10th.

16. Watches will be synchronized at 6 p.m. on September 8th. and at 9 a.m. on September 9th.

17. All prisoners are to be sent to the Advanced Prisoners of War Post on the MONTAUBAN-CARNOY Road at the Craters (A.8.a.8.4.) where they will be searched under arrangements to be made by A.P.M. 16th. Division.

Receipts will be given for prisoners and escorts will then return to their units.

18. Acknowledge.

[signature] Captain,

Brigade Major, 49th. Infantry Brigade.

Issued through Signals :

Copy No. 1 to 7th. R. Innis. Fus.
" 2 " 8th. R. Innis. Fus.
" 3 " 7th. R. Irish Fus.
" 4 " 8th. R. Irish Fus.
" 5 " 49th. M.G. Company.
" 6 " 49th. T.M. Battery.
" 7 " 47th. Infantry Brigade.
" 8 " 48th. Infantry Brigade.
" 9 " 16th. Division.
" 10 " Staff Captain.
" 11 " 11th. Hants Regt.
" 12 - 13 War Diary.
" 14 " File.

S E C R E T.

7th. R. Innis. Fus.
8th. R. Innis. Fus.
7th. R. Irish Fus.
8th. R. Irish Fus.
49th. M.G. Company.
49th. T.M. Battery.

49th. Inf. Bde. No. B.O. 55/2 - 8 /9/16.

The following information has been received subsequent to Bde. Order No. 55 being published :

1. Medical Arrangements.

(a) Left Brigade Advanced Bearer Post at BERNAFAY WOOD (S.23.c.1.1½.
Right Brigade Advanced Bearer Post at BRIQUETERIE (A.4.b.7.4.)

(b). Advanced Dressing Station at :-
CARNOY (A.13.d.3.8.)
Sapper Corner (L.25.b.).

(c) XIV Corps Walking Wounded Collecting Post at A.14.c.5.1.

(d) Main Dressing Station at DINE COPSE (J.24.b.).

2. Walking wounded proceed direct to Walking Wounded Collecting Post.

3. German Wounded, if walking, will be sent in charge of a slightly wounded British to Advanced Dressing Station at CARNOY, if stretcher cases will be evacuated to Bearer Posts.

4. During the Operations a Divisional Collecting Post will be established at T.19.c.0.0. All Medical Officers of Regiments should get in touch with this Post by 5 a.m. on 9th. inst. Any change of Regimental Aid should be notified to this Post immediately.

5. Besides Bearers at Advanced Bearer Posts at BERNAFAY WOOD and BRIQUETERIE a reserve of Bearers will be stationed at MONTAUBAN and CARNOY.

6. The 49th. Infantry Brigade in Reserve will be prepared to send such reinforcements as they may require to the 47th. and 48th. Infantry Brigades for the accomplishment of their tasks.
Two Battalions will normally be available to reinforce each Brigade.

7. Relieving troops will be at hand, a heavy barrage will be kept up in front of the ~~first~~ final objective, and arrangements have been made to relieve all Infantry Brigades as soon after dark as possible.

8. It must be impressed upon all ranks taking part in the attack that this is the last effort that they will be called upon to make and that the capture of GINCHY and the trenches to the East of the GINCHY-WEDGE WOOD Road is of paramount importance to the Divisions fighting on each flank and to the success of the Army in future operations.

9. The attack of the XV Corps on the left of the XIV Corps will be made at the second bound Zero plus 40 minutes.

10. On relief Battalions will hand over all spare ammunition, bom rations (except iron rations), Water, &c.
Battalions will bring out as many German Machine guns and rifles as possible as G.H.Q. require them.
The Hants Pioneers have established a dump of Bombs, and S.A.A. at T.19.c.3.2.

11. German prisoners captured by XV Corps state there are machine guns in position at T.19.b.6½.9., and T.13.d.2.7.

Captain,
Bde Major 49th Inf Bde

7

"C" Form (Duplicate).
MESSAGES AND SIGNALS.

Army Form C. 2123.
(In books of 50's in duplicate.)
No. of Message

48 BDE HQ 2/8 Res

Charges to Pay. £ s. d.

Office Stamp.

Service Instructions. Recite Priority

Handed in at RECITE Office 2/35 m. Received 2/56 m.

TO REDAN

Sender's Number	Day of Month	In reply to Number	AAA
BM 88	9	G 96	

REDAN will come under the orders of REACH for the attack aaa REDANS HQ is at Quarry TRAY C 1.24 aaa REDAN will get into touch with REACHS Signal station at Quarries T19 C 1.4 and get orders

FROM RECITE

PLACE & TIME 2-30pm

Wt. 452—M437 500,000 Pads. H W V 5/16 Forms C.2123.

5

"C" Form (Original).
MESSAGES AND SIGNALS.

Army Form C. 2123.
(In books of 50's in duplicate.)
No. of Message

Prefix ... Code ... Words ...	Received	Sent, or sent out	Office Stamp.
£ s. d. Charges to collect	From ... By ...	At ... m. To ... By ...	
Service Instructions.			

Handed in at ... Office ... m. Received ... m.

TO RAZOR 7th ROYAL IRISH FUS

*Sender's Number	Day of Month	In reply to Number	AAA
BHB 878	ninth		

Your Batt has been placed at my disposal aaa I wish you immediately to get in touch with OC RAZOR at T19b73 to whom I have [illegible] that you will support him in the attack on the first objective arranging to reach his line at ZERO hour aaa Should this operation be impossible I leave it to Colonel FRANCIS to decide whether he would prefer to amalgamate RASHER with his Batt and that you should replace RASHER and take the second objective AAA Colonel FRANCIS will explain all the details of the attack to you

FROM
PLACE & TIME

* This line should be erased if not required.

Wt. 492—M437 500,000 Pads. H W V 5 16 Forms C.2123.

"C" Form (Original).

Army Form C. 2123.
(In books of 50's in duplicate.)

MESSAGES AND SIGNALS. No. of Message

Prefix Code Words | Received From By | Sent, or sent out At m. To By | Office Stamp.

£ s. d.
Charges to collect

Service Instructions.

Handed in at Office m. Received m.

TO

*Sender's Number | Day of Month | In reply to Number | AAA

aaa addressed 7th IRISH FUSILIERS
repeated RAZOR AAA ack urgent

FROM
PLACE & TIME

REACH
2·50 pm

* This line should be erased if not required.

132—M437 500,000 Pads. H W V 5 16 Forms C.2123.

10

SECRET.

Copy No. 3....

49th. Infantry Brigade Order No. 56 - 9/9/16.

Reference Maps
ALBERT Combined Sheet.
LONGUEVAL Sheet 1/10,000.

1. The Guards Division is to relieve the 16th. Division in the Left Sector of the XIV Corps Front.

2. The 1st. Welsh Guards are relieving the 48th. Infantry Brigade on the night of the 9th/10th.

3. Details as to Units which are relieving the 49th. Infantry Brigade on the night of the 9th/10th. and the times will be notified later.

4. Under no circumstances will any troops be withdrawn until they are properly relieved and the Commanders of the relieving Units are satisfied as to the situation.

5. All maps, plans, &c., are to be handed over on relief to incoming Units.

6. Bde. H.Q. will ~~remain at present position for night 9th/10th.~~ on relief move to Bde Transport Lines

7. On the 10th. Sept. the 16th. Division will move to HAPPY VALLEY and MORLANCOURT. Troops at the Craters will not be required to move before 12 noon. Orders for this move will be issued later.

8. Battalions must ensure that all Lewis Guns handcarts are taken back.

9. On relief all Units of the 49th. Infantry Brigade will assemble at the Brigade Transport Lines F.29.b. Guides from the Transport will meet Battalions at Main Forward Dump near ARROW HEAD COPSE S.30.d.5.7.
Quartermasters have been informed and a hot meal will be provided.

W.B. Wills Captain,
Brigade Major, 49th. Infantry Brigade.

Issued through Signals :
Copy No. 1 to 7th. R. Innis. Fus.
.. 2 .. 8th. R. Innis. Fus.
.. 3 .. 7th. R. Irish Fus.
.. 4 .. 8th. R. Irish Fus.
.. 5 .. Qr.Masters 7th. R. Innis. Fus.
.. 6 .. .. 8th. R. Innis. Fus.
.. 7 .. .. 7th. R. Irish Fus.
.. 8 .. .. 8th. R. Irish Fus.
.. 9 .. 49th. M.G. Company.
.. 10 .. 49th. T.M. Battery.
.. 11 .. Staff Captain,.
.. 12 .. Bde. Signal Officer.
.. 13 .. Bde. Supply Officer.
.. 14 .. Bde. Transport Officer.
.. 15 .. 16th. Division.
.. 16 .. 47th. Infantry Brigade.
.. 17 .. 48th. Infantry Brigade.
.. 18 & 19 - War Diary.
.. 20 .. File.

7th R.Irish Fusiliers.

49th Inf. Bde.

Report on Operations resulting in capture of GINCHY on the 9th Sept. 1916.

On evening of 8th Sept. I moved my battn. up to West of GUILLEMONT where we entrenched and took up a position suitable to our role as Divisional Reserve.

At 3 p.m. on the 9th. Sept. I received orders by telephone to proceed at once to H.Q. of 7th R.Irish Regt. and put my Btn. at disposal of the officer commanding that Battalion to assist him in the attack on GINCHY. I at once gave orders for the Batt to stand to to be ready to move at a moments notice. I then proceeded to H.Q., 7th R.Irish Rifles. In consultation with O.C. of this battn. I decided to move my battalion up into some disused trench to West his assembly trenches. This was a somewhat difficult operation owing to these trenches being very exposed and also to the very short time at my disposal as the Battalion had to be in its new position and attack at 4.45 p.m., however, the last company were just in position at 4.45 p.m. when the whole Battalion got up and went over in 4 waves on the left of the 7th R.Irish Rifles, both Battalions going as if they were on parade and in about 12 minutes they had obtained their objective, owing however to the very short time to point out the objective and also to three of my Company commanders being knocked out, part of my Battalion went forward with the Dublin Fusiliers to the final objective, this eventually was rather fortunate as they were badly needed up there.

The position was consolidated and orders were received that we would be relieved at 10 p.m. part of my battalion were relieved and passed down in the early hours of the morning, but as at about 8 a.m. a part of my battalion and a mixture of Dublins. Munsters &c. had not been relieved I consulted with O.C. Welsh Guards who had relieved me and we came to the conclusion that I had better go and see the Brigadier of the 3rd. Guards Bde and show him exactly the situation. My adjutant & I were fortunate enough to get through a rather heavy barrage and on pointing out the situation they were at once relieved by some of the Grenadiers.

I would like to take this opportunity of mentioning Major. K.C. WELDON my second in command who did most excellent work in consolidating the position, also Capt. T.F.O'DONNELL who led over the first wave in a most gallant manner and gave great assistance in consolidating the position. In a case like this where everyone did well it is hard to pick individuals, but the above two officers sis excellently.

(Sd) F. MOORE Lt.Col.

Commanding 7th R.Irish Fusiliers.

"C" Form (Original).

Army Form C. 2123.
(In books of 50's in duplicate.)

MESSAGES AND SIGNALS.

No. of Message ....

Prefix .... Code .... Words ....

£ s. d.

Charges to collect

Service Instructions.

Received From .... By ....

Sent, or sent out At .... m. To .... By ....

Office Stamp. ARMY POST OFFICE YE 10.IX.16 FR ... SIGNALS

Handed in at Reach Office 12 30 m. Received .... m.

TO 7th Royal Irish

*Sender's Number	Day of Month	In reply to Number	AAA
BMB901	10		

The GOC 48th INF BDE wishes to thank all ranks of 7th Royal Irish Fusiliers for their gallant and successful effort in assisting in the capture of GINCHY aaa The courage and spirit displayed by all ranks was beyond all praise aaa He very much regrets the heavy casualties sustained amongst all ranks aaa Addsd 7th Royal Irish Fusiliers repd 49 BDE

FROM 48 INF BDE

PLACE & TIME 11 40 am

* This line should be erased if not required.

Wt. 432—M437 500,000 Pads. H W V 5 16 Forms C.2123.

12

FINAL OBJECTIVE
BOUNDARY BETWEEN CORPS
BOUNDARY BETWEEN DIVISIONS
BOUNDARY BETWEEN BRIGADES

Scale:- 1:10,000

Guillemont

Leuze Wood

SPECIAL ORDER OF THE DAY.

BY

BRIGADIER-GENERAL P. LEVESON - GOWER,
COMMANDING 49TH. INFANTRY BRIGADE, 16TH. DIVISION,

WEDNESDAY, 13TH. SEPTEMBER, 1916.

o-o-o-o-o-o-o-o-o-o-o-o-o-o-o-o-o-o-o-o-o-o-o-o-o-o-o-o-o-o-o-o-o-o-o-o-

The Brigadier wishes to express his admiration for the conduct and gallantry of all ranks of the 49th. Infantry Brigade during the recent operations, during which they have added greatly to the honour of their Regiments and Corps and also their Country. The discipline displayed and the bravery exhibited by all ranks was most marked.

The following has been received from 16th. Division :-

"General Wilson Commanding lV Corps wires Hearty congratulations "to 16 Div. from lV Corps. AAA

South African Brigade wires to 16 Division Hearty congratulations "on your success Ends".

(sd) L.B.Brierley, Captain,

Staff Captain, 49th. Inf. Brigade.

2ND EDITION
GINCHY & GUILLEMONT
ROTTEN ROW
CAMPBELL ST
KING ST
SOUTH ST.
ELSOM
BASIL ST
HANS CRESCENT
BRUNTON ST.
Ginchy
Waterlot Farm Cellar (40-60 men)
HIGH HOLBORN
FLEET ST
4 deep Dugouts
BROMPTON ROAD
HILL ST
AUDLEY ST
NORTH ST
MOUNT ST
Quarry
PARK LANE
NORFOLK
CHURCH SQ.
CRESCENT
SOUTH ST
DOWN ST
Cemetery
Guillemont
Screen
SCALE 1:5,000
Yards 100
1700 Yards
1 Mile
CORRECTED UP TO 3·8·16
Note: the fact that an obstacle is not represented on the map, does not mean necessarily that one does not exist
REFERENCE.
Any trench apparently organised for fire
Other trenches in good or fair order
Damaged or disused trenches
Wire entanglements
Gun positions
Observation posts
Dug outs
Supply dumps
Well defined tracks used by enemy
Buried pipe line or cable
Hedges
Hedge, wall or ditch, (not known which)
Buildings in ruins
(504)

[illegible] Battn Royal Irish Fusiliers

Instructions regarding War Diaries and Intelligence Summaries are contained in F. S. Regs., Part II. and the Staff Manual respectively. Title pages will be prepared in manuscript.

WAR DIARY
or
~~INTELLIGENCE SUMMARY.~~
(Erase heading not required.)

October 1916

Army Form C. 2118.

Place	Date	Hour	Summary of Events and Information	Remarks and references to Appendices
KEMMEL	1.10.16		Enemy very quiet. Spasmodic bursts of machine gun fire throughout the night. Our patrols met with no opposition.	T.F.O'D T.F.O'D
	2.10.16		Enemy again quiet. We dispersed several working parties and again our patrols met with no opposition	T.F.O'D T.F.O'D
	3.10.16		The battalion was relieved by the 8th R. Inniskilling Fusiliers and went into Divisional Reserve at LOCKE	T.F.O'D T.F.O'D
LOCKE	4th–8th		Training at LOCKE and improving the camp	T.F.O'D
	9.10.16		The battalion relieved the 8th R. Inniskilling Fusiliers in the trenches	T.F.O'D
KEMMEL	10.10.16		The enemy seemed to be annoyed because we persisted in dispersing his working-parties. He directed Machine gun fire and rifle grenades on certain portions of our trenches. Little damage was done and our retaliation was most effective.	T.F.O'D
	11.10.16		Our Machine Gun and Trench Mortars were active, and provoked little retaliation from the enemy, who were unusually quiet, possibly on account of a suspected relief	T.F.O'D.
	12.10.16		We dispersed some working parties, and the enemy sent a few small shells about our front line.	T.F.O'D
	13.10.16		Enemy slightly active with rifle grenades and Trench Mortars. Little damage was done, and our retaliation was effective.	T.F.O'D

T.2134. Wt. W708—776. 500000. 4/15. Sir J. C. & S.

7th (S) Battn. Royal Irish Fusiliers

Instructions regarding War Diaries and Intelligence Summaries are contained in F. S. Regs., Part II. and the Staff Manual respectively. Title pages will be prepared in manuscript.

WAR DIARY
or
~~INTELLIGENCE SUMMARY.~~
(Erase heading not required.)

October 1916

Army Form C. 2118.

Place	Date	Hour	Summary of Events and Information	Remarks and references to Appendices
LOCRE	14.10.16		The Battn. was relieved by the 8 (S) Battn R. INNIS. FUS. and proceeded to LOCRE thus becoming Divisional Reserve	W.H.S.
	15.10.16		The Battn. was amalgamated with the 8 (S) Battn. Royal IRISH FUSILIERS under the title 7/8 (S) Battn. ROYAL IRISH FUSILIERS under the Temporary Command of CAPT. T.F. O'DONNELL M.C. Notification was received on 5th inst that CAPT. T.F. O'DONNELL had been granted the Military Cross.	W.H.S.

W.H. Stitt. Capt. Adj
7/8 Battn. Royal Irish Fusiliers

Secret. 5th Sept 1916. A 1

95th Infy. Bde Operation Order

No 162

Reference 1/10,000 Trench map & Sketch.

1. The 15th Bde have taken the line point 48 – FALFEMONT – WEDGE WOOD and state there are no Germans between them and COMBLES. DEVONS have occupied the W edge of LEUZE WOOD and consolidated. 49th Bde hold from LEUZE WOOD to COMBLES ROAD.

2. The 5th Division will attack and capture the German line running through LEUZE WOOD and S. of it from T 21 C 4.7. to T28 C 0.3.

Boundaries of objective

95th Bde

Point where German line enters wood at T 21.C 4.7. to point where it leaves at T 27 a 70.75.

15th Bde. T 27 a 70.75 to T 28.c.0.3.

3. The attack will be carried out as under.

ASSAULTING DEVONS

SUPPORTING E. SURREYS

RESERVE. D.C.L.I. Stand fast.

GLOSTERS move to GINCHY – WEDGE WOOD road.

The 8th R. I. FUSILIERS will remain in present position.

A 2

4/ The bombardment on the objective will be at 4 p.m.

The assaulting waves will advance close up to the barrage through the wood ready to rush the German trenches as soon as the barrage lifts.

5/. Special parties will be detailed beforehand for the following.

(a). To bomb up the German trench northwards from T 21 C 4.7 and establish a block.

N.B. If the division on our ~~right~~ left attack this line ~~there~~ this will ~~be~~ not be ~~necessarily~~ necessary.

(b). To establish strongpoint at T 21 C 4.7.

(c). " " " " " T 21 c 52.32. where track crosses trench

(d). At T 27 a 70.75. where trench leaves wood.

6/. When DEVONS assault 2 Coys SURREYS will move up and occupy trenches at present held by DEVONS and two companies now in GINCHY road will move forward and occupy trenches at present held by their two forward Coys.

7. On arrival at objective it will be at once consolidated and patrols pushed forward to the N.E. + E. edge of wood to reconnoitre.

A3

[illegible] If necessary a chain of posts must be dug to connect our left with 16th Div. right.

8. If the above line is gained a fresh Brigade will be sent up tonight to take it over.

Should it be found impossible to gain the objective a line will be established as close as possible to it.

9. Flares will be lighted on reaching objectives and at 7 p.m.

10. Cornwalls & Glosters will provide carrying parties for Devons and Surreys as required and will assist with Stretcher bearers if necessary.

11. Four Vickers guns will be attached to E. SURREYS and will be sent up to objectives as soon as Devons are established.

12. Bde H.Q. will not move.

Acknowledge.

Signed D.A. McLeod Capt.
Bde Major.
95th Infy. Bde.

True Copy.

Stewart Lt. Col.
8 R. Irish Fus.

~~7~~ 8th Bn. Roy. Ir. Fus.

49th Bde 16th DIV (Feb. 1916 - Feb. 1918)

Disbanded Feb. 1918

France

Amalgamated with 7th Bn. Oct. 1916 then 7/8 Bn.

1916 FEB — 1916 OCT ~~1918~~

~~DISBANDED~~

See 7/8 BN

Army Form C. 2118.

Instructions regarding War Diaries and Intelligence Summaries are contained in F. S. Regs., Part II. and the Staff Manual respectively. Title pages will be prepared in manuscript.

2/6th

WAR DIARY
or
~~INTELLIGENCE SUMMARY~~.
(Erase heading not required.)

Place	Date	Hour	Summary of Events and Information	Remarks and references to Appendices
	1916			
BORDON	1-2-16		Order received to mobilize	T.S.A
"	2-2		Nil	T.S.A
"	3-2		Nil	T.S.A
"	4-2		Nil	T.S.A
"	5-2		Nil	T.S.A
"	6-2		Nil	T.S.A
"	7-2		Nil	T.S.A
"	8-2		Nil	T.S.A
"	9-2		Nil	T.S.A
"	10-2		Nil	T.S.A
"	11-2		Nil	T.S.A
"	12-2		Nil	T.S.A
"	13-2		Nil	T.S.A
"	14-2		Nil	T.S.A
"	15		Nil	T.S.A
"	16		Nil	T.S.A
"	17		Nil	T.S.A

2353 Wt. W2544/1454 700,000 5/15 D. D. & L. A.D.S.S./Forms/C. 2118.

Army Form C. 2118.

Instructions regarding War Diaries and Intelligence Summaries are contained in F. S. Regs., Part II. and the Staff Manual respectively. Title pages will be prepared in manuscript.

WAR DIARY
or
~~INTELLIGENCE SUMMARY.~~
(Erase heading not required.)

8th Bn R. IRISH FUSILIERS.

Place	Date	Hour	Summary of Events and Information	Remarks and references to Appendices
	1916			
BORDON	18-2		Entrained for SOUTHAMPTON	J.A.B.
S.HAMPTON	19-2	6 P.M	Embarked for HAVRE	J.A.B.
HAVRE	20-2	7 AM	Disembarked & marched to rest camp No 1	J.A.B.
HAVRE	21-2	6 p.m	Entrained for BERGHETTE	J.A.B.
BERGHETTE	22-2	6 p.m	Detrained at BERGHETTE & marched to Billets at BELLERY	J.A.B.
BELLERY	23-2	2.30 am	Arrived	J.A.B.
"	24		nil	J.A.B.
"	25		nil	J.A.B.
"	26	10 am	Marched to new billets at GOMMEHEM arriving at 2.45 p.m	J.A.B.
GONNEHEM	27th		Battalion remained in billets. Major S.T. WATSON 6th Bn The Queen's Regt arrived to take over command of the battalion pending the appointment of a C.O.	STW
"	28th		Drill and field operations practiced by the battalion.	STW
"	29th		Colonel J.S. ~~Brown~~ BROWN, Major T. CARSON (2nd in command) and Lt Col. M.A. TIGHE returned to England on leave.	STW

S.T. Watson Major.
Comg 8th R. Irish Fus.

2353 Wt. W2544/1454 700,000 5/15 D. D. & L. A.D.S.S./Forms/C. 2118.

1916

WAR DIARY
or
~~INTELLIGENCE SUMMARY~~.
(Erase heading not required.)

Army Form C. 2118.

Instructions regarding War Diaries and Intelligence Summaries are contained in F. S. Regs., Part II. and the Staff Manual respectively. Title pages will be prepared in manuscript.

8th Bn. R. Irish Fusiliers.

Place	Date	Hour	Summary of Events and Information	Remarks and references to Appendices
GONNEHEM	March 1st.		Battalion remained in rest billets.	Sgd.
"	2nd		" " " " . 31 men medically unfit left the Battalion to be posted to 16th Infantry Base Depot at HAVRE. MAJOR T.H. BOARDMAN 20th Royal Fusiliers joined the battalion and took over command of D Company.	Sgd. Sgd.
"	3rd		Orders received from Brigade that the battalion will be attached to 3rd Infantry Brigade from 5th inst until 22nd inst for instruction in trench warfare.	Sgd.
"	4th.		Battalion paraded at 9.30 am. to march to PETIT SAINS for attachment to 3rd Infy. Brigade. Arrived at 2.15 pm.	
PETIT SAINS	5th.		A Company (under command of Capt. GALVIN) paraded at 5.15 pm. to be attached to 1st Bn S. WALES BORDERERS. One platoon was attached to each company 1st S.W.B for instruction in trench warfare. B Company (under command of Capt. ALEXANDER) paraded at the same time for similar attachment to 1/6th THE WELCH REGIMENT. The regiments mentioned above were in reserve and support trenches respectively in LES BREBIS and MAROC.	Sgd.
"	6th.		A + B Companies, attached respectively to 1st S. WALES BORDERERS and 1/6th THE WELCH REGIMENT, moved up to the front trenches with those units. C + D companies remained rest billets and found working parties on communication trenches.	Sgd.
"	7th.		Companies were situated as on 6th inst. Captain E.W.P. UNIACKE 2nd KING EDWARDS HORSE joined as 2nd in command.	Sgd.
"	8th.		C Company (under command of Capt GREVILLE) paraded at 5.15 pm. to be attached to 1st Bn. GLOSTERSHIRE REGT. One platoon was attached to each company for instruction in trench warfare. D Company (under command of Major BOARDMAN) paraded at the same time for similar attachment to 2nd Bn R. MUNSTER FUSILIERS.	Sgd.

2353 Wt. W2544/1454 700,000 5/15 D. D. & L. A.D.S.S./Forms/C. 2118.

Army Form C. 2118. 2

WAR DIARY
or
~~INTELLIGENCE SUMMARY.~~
(*Erase heading not required.*)

Instructions regarding War Diaries and Intelligence Summaries are contained in F. S. Regs., Part II. and the Staff Manual respectively. Title pages will be prepared in manuscript.

8th Bn R. Irish Fusiliers.

Place	Date	Hour	Summary of Events and Information	Remarks and references to Appendices
PETIT SAINS	8th (continued)		A and B Companies returned to billets at about 11 pm.	S.W.
"	9th		Companies were situated as on 8th inst. C+D Companies moved up to the fire trenches.	S.W.
"	10th		Companies were situated as on 9th inst.	S.W.
"	11th		A+B Companies paraded at 5.15 pm. for attachment to 1st S.W. Borderers and 1/6th THE WELCH REGT. respectively. The companies were now rationed from these battalions. D Company returned to billets at about 8.45 pm. and C Company at about 11 pm.	S.W.
"	12th		Companies attached to 1st S.W. Borderers and 1/6th THE WELCH REGT. moved up to front line with those units and took over a Section of the fire trench as companies.	S.W.
"	13th		Companies were situated as on 12th inst.	S.W.
"	14th		C+D Companies paraded at 5.15 pm. to take over that portion of the front line held by A+B Companies. A+B Companies returned to billets at 11.30 pm and 1 am. on 15th.	S.W.
"	15th		Companies were situated as on 14th inst.	S.W.
"	16th		ditto.	S.W.
"	17th		C+D Companies were relieved in the front line trenches and returned to billets about 8.45 pm. The following telegram received from GENERAL SIR CHARLES MUNRO Commanding 1st Army. "Please convey to all ranks my best wishes on ST PATRICK'S DAY and my feeling of confidence that they will prove themselves to be the stern, hard fighters that	

2353 Wt. W2544/1454 700,000 5/15 D. D. & L. A.D.S.S./Forms/C. 2118.

Army Form C. 2118.

WAR DIARY
or
INTELLIGENCE SUMMARY.
(Erase heading not required.)

Instructions regarding War Diaries and Intelligence Summaries are contained in F. S. Regs., Part II. and the Staff Manual respectively. Title pages will be prepared in manuscript.

8th R Irish Fusiliers.

Place	Date	Hour	Summary of Events and Information	Remarks and references to Appendices
PETIT SAINS	17th (Continued)		Irishman have always shown themselves to be" Shamrock was received from Mr JOHN REDMOND M.P. and distributed to A+B Companies on parade. Shamrock was sent up to the trenches to be distributed to the companies in the trenches.	[signature]
"	18th		Remained in billets.	[signature]
MAROC	19th		The battalion took over a part of MAROC sub-section of the front line from 2nd Bn NORTHAMPTONS and were attached to 2nd Infantry Brigade. Relief started at 7.15 pm and was completed at 8.35 p.m. Companies were situated as follows. B Coy from trench 13 (M 9 b 9 9) to Sap D (M 9 b 8.4.) A Company Sap C (M 9 b 8 2.) to Sap B (M.9.d.8.6). D Company from Sap A (M 9 d 8.5.) to junction of CALONNE ALLEY with front line. C Coy, one platoon formed the crater party at (M 9 d 5 3, one formed the garrison of CALONNE KEEP and two platoons were in local reserve in building in S. MAROC. Battalion H.Q were situated at M 3 c 2 1.	[signature]
"	20th		Battalion situated as above. CAPTAIN N.G. ALEXANDER wounded	[signature]
"	21st		Battalion situated as on 19th.	[signature]
"	22nd		Battalion was relieved by 1st Bn NORTHAMPTONSHIRE REGT commencing at 6.30 pm. The relief was complete by 8.15 pm. and platoons marched back independently to PETIT SAINS where they occupied the same billets vacated on 19th inst. The casualties during the time the battalion was in the front line was 6 other ranks including one ~~others~~ accidental.	[signature]
PETIT SAINS	23rd		The battalion paraded at 3 pm. to march to NOEUX-LES-MINES to be billeted there. They were accomodated in huts. Attachment to 1st Division for instruction terminated.	[signature]

Instructions regarding War Diaries and Intelligence Summaries are contained in F. S. Regs., Part II. and the Staff Manual respectively. Title pages will be prepared in manuscript.

WAR DIARY
or
~~INTELLIGENCE SUMMARY~~.
(Erase heading not required.)

Army Form C. 2118.

4

8th Bn R. Irish Fus.

Place	Date	Hour	Summary of Events and Information	Remarks and references to Appendices
NOEUX-LES-MINES.	24th		Battalion remained in billets.	S.W.
				S.W.
"	25th		" " " "	S.W.
"	26th		" " " "	S.W.
"	27th		" " " "	S.W.
"	28th		" " " "	S.W.
"	29th		" " " "	S.W.
"	30th		" " " "	
"	31st		The Battalion relieved 6th Bn THE CONNAUGHT RAINGERS in the right subsection of the Puits 14 bis Sector. Companies occupied the following positions. D and A Company in the fire trenches from GORDON ALLEY (inclusive) to the first boyeau S. of RAILWAY ALLEY inclusive. The dividing line between these companies was ENGLISH ALLEY. C Company was in the Support line covering the whole front. B Company was in Reserve in RESERVE TRENCH and houses in the neighbourhood of NORTH STREET near RESERVE TRENCH. Battalion headquarters was in LOOS. The leading company left NOEUX-LES-MINES at 5pm. and the relief was complete at 12.20 am. 1st April.	S.W.

S. Watson Lt Col.
Comg 8th R. Irish Fusiliers.

2353 Wt. W2514/1454 700,000 5/15 D. D. & L. A.D.S.S./Forms/C. 2118.

Instructions regarding War Diaries and Intelligence Summaries are contained in F. S. Regs., Part II. and the Staff Manual respectively. Title pages will be prepared in manuscript.

1916

WAR DIARY
or
~~INTELLIGENCE SUMMARY.~~
(Erase heading not required.)

Army Form C. 2118.

XVI 49/16

8th Bn. R. IRISH FUSILIERS. Vol 3

Place	Date	Hour	Summary of Events and Information	Remarks and references to Appendices
LOOS	APRIL 1st		The companies were redistributed in the line as follows. D Company on the right from GORDON ALLEY (inclusive) to Bay 70 South of SCOTS ALLEY. C Company from Bay 71 to bay 101 South of ENGLISH ALLEY. A Company from bay 102 to bay 130 just South of RAILWAY ALLEY. Each of these companies held the fire trench with two platoons and had two platoons in the SUPPORT TRENCH. D Company remained in it former position.	S....
"	2nd		The Battalion was situated as above.	S....
"	3rd		The Battalion was relieved by 7th Bn. R. IRISH FUSILIERS. The relief started at 7.30 pm. and was completed by 4 am. 4th inst. As companies were relieved they marched back to PHILOSOPHE into billets to form the Brigade Reserve.	S....
PHILOSOPHE	4th		The Battalion remained in Brigade Reserve. Working parties were found for work on RAILWAY ALLEY.	S....
"	5th		Remained in Brigade Reserve.	S....
"	6th		The enemy bombarded the left sub-sector of the PUITS 14 BIS Sector and did some damage to ~~our~~ trenches. The bombardment lasted about one hour and was "intense". The Reserve was ordered to stand too. Companies started to move forward to the position of the Support Battalion in the neighbourhood of TENTH AVENUE at 6.30 pm. The Battalion relieved was 8th R. INNISKILLING FUSILIERS. Companies were situated as follows—. A Company ½ Company in 65 metre point Redoubt and ½ company in NORTHERN SAP REDOUBT. D Company in TENTH AVENUE with its left on POSEN ALLEY. B Company on the right of D Company in TENTH AVENUE. C Company in GUN TRENCH between RAILWAY ALLEY and POSEN ALLEY. Battalion Head Quarters at the junction of NORTHERN UP and OLD BRITISH LINE.	S....
NORTHERN UP	7th		Remained in Brigade Support. Large working parties found for work in immediate rear of left battalion.	S....

2353 Wt. W2544/1454 700,000 5/15 D. D. & L. A.D.S.S./Forms/C. 2118.

T3

Instructions regarding War Diaries and Intelligence Summaries are contained in F. S. Regs., Part II. and the Staff Manual respectively. Title pages will be prepared in manuscript.

WAR DIARY
or
~~INTELLIGENCE SUMMARY~~.
(Erase heading not required.)

Army Form C. 2118.

2

8th Bn R. IRISH FUSILIERS.

Place	Date	Hour	Summary of Events and Information	Remarks and references to Appendices
NORTHERN UP.	8th		Remained in Brigade Support.	S.W.
TENTH AVENUE	9th		Battalion Head Quarters moved to TENTH AVENUE half way between CHALK PIT ALLEY and NORTHERN UP. The Battalion moved up to take over the right sub section from 7th R. IRISH FUSILIERS. The leading company left the junction of RAILWAY ALLEY and TENTH AVENUE at 6.45 pm. Companies were situated as follows: B Company on the right, C Company in the centre and A Company on the left. D Company formed the Reserve and was distributed along RESERVE TRENCH instead of in houses. Relief was complete by 10.35 pm.	S.W.
LOOS.	10th		Battalion situated as above.	S.W.
"	11th		" " " " 2nd Lt B. J. START joined the battalion from 11th HUSSARS.	S.W.
"	12th		Relieved by 7th Bn R. Irish Rifles. The relief started at 7.30 pm and was complete 12.30 am. As companies were relieved they marched back to billets at MAZINGARBE being part of the Brigade in Divisional reserve.	S.W.
MAZINGARBE	13th		Remained in billets.	S.W.
"	14th		" " Started the training of bombers and parades for drill, rifle exercises and physical training.	S.W.
"	15th		As above. Instruction of wire entanglements undertaken.	S.W.
"	16th		Remained in billets.	S.W.
"	17th		" D Company's billet was shelled. Four casualties all slight.	S.W.
"	18th		G.O.C. 1st Army inspected all men considered unfit for service. Total number who paraded 74. All were passed unfit.	S.W.
"	19th		74 men referred to above were sent to 16th Infantry Base Depot.	S.W.

2353 Wt. W2544/1454 700,000 5/15 D. D. & L. A.D.S.S./Forms/C. 2118.

Instructions regarding War Diaries and Intelligence Summaries are contained in F. S. Regs., Part II. and the Staff Manual respectively. Title pages will be prepared in manuscript.

WAR DIARY
or
~~INTELLIGENCE SUMMARY~~.
(Erase heading not required.)

8th Bn R. IRISH FUS.

Army Form C. 2118.

3

Place	Date	Hour	Summary of Events and Information	Remarks and references to Appendices
MAZINGARBE	20th		The Battalion took over from 8th Bn MUNSTERS as battalion in Brigade support in the HULLOCH SECTOR. The positions of companies were as follows. – A Company in RESERVE TRENCH South of HAY ALLEY B Coy. in 10th AVENUE with it right on POSEN ALLEY. D Company in 10th AVENUE with its left on HULLOCH ROAD. C Company between B & D Company in 10th AVENUE finding the garrison of one platoon in LONE TREE REDOUBT. The relief started at 5.30pm and was finished by 9pm.	[illegible]
10th AVENUE.	21st		Battalion situated as above.	[illegible]
"	22nd		" " " "	[illegible]
"	23rd		" " " "	[illegible]
"	24th		Took over the left sub-sector of the HULLOCH SECTOR. The right ~~battalion~~ flank rested on HOLLY LANE and the left on STONE STREET. Companies were allotted frontages as under. B Company from HOLLY LANE to HAY ALLEY. D company HAY ALLEY to WINGSWAY. A Company from WINGSWAY to STONE STREET. C Company in RESERVE TRENCH between HAY ALLEY and STONE STREET. The defence of the craters were under special arrangements and was under command of MAJOR E.W.P. UNIACKE. The party for the defence of this area consisted of the bombers of C & D companies together with one officer and twenty four bombers from A & B companies. These bombers occupied the near lips of the craters and on the flanks of the craters as well as where communication trenches ran from the support trench to the fire trench. The fire trench immediately in rear of the craters was in a very bad condition owing to mining operations. The sandbags taken from the mines blocked the trench to a considerable extent. Battalion headquarters was in 9th AVENUE near HAY ALLEY.	
9th AVENUE	25th		The position was as above. Our lines were shelled by the enemy but not much damage was done. There was a certain exchange of rifle grenades.	[illegible]

Instructions regarding War Diaries and Intelligence Summaries are contained in F. S. Regs., Part II. and the Staff Manual respectively. Title pages will be prepared in manuscript.

WAR DIARY
or
INTELLIGENCE SUMMARY.
(Erase heading not required.)

Army Form C. 2118.

4

Place	Date	Hour	Summary of Events and Information	Remarks and references to Appendices
9th AVENUE	APRIL 26th		At 3.40 am. we fired two small mines South of MUNSTER CRATER and TRALEE CRATERS respectively. We occupied the near lips without any opposition from the enemy. It had been reported that a hostile mine was suspected between TRALEE CRATER and the crater just N of it. Acting on the advice of the tunnelling officer the front line between 6th AVENUE and CONNAUGHT LANE was evacuated in order to minimise casualties. TRALEE Crater was also left unoccupied. At about 3 pm. the whole of the front line trenches were cleared between FLY LANE and LEINSTER LANE in order to allow our 8" guns to fire on the enemy's front line trenches. The object of this was to destroy gas cylinders which had been reported in position to use against us. The shooting was good but no gas was discovered.	
			CAPTAIN E. R. COOKE killed in action while visiting the bombers in MUNSTER CRATER.	[illegible]
"	27th		At 5 am the enemy commenced an intense bombardment of our front, support, reserve and communication trenches. Light field guns were first employed and soon afterwards guns of all calibre joined in the bombardment. As regards the three companies occupying the front trenches and supports the shelling was chiefly confined to the support trenches and in consequence the officers commanding these companies decided to move their supports up into the firing line. This prevented many casualties.	
			At about 5.15 am. the enemy let off poisonous gas from opposite the right battalion of the HULLOCH SECTOR on a considerable front. At this time there was a gentle wind from the south east which was most favourable to the enemy. The gas was carried over the right half of our right company and also over the company in RESERVE TRENCH as well as battalion headquarters. At about 6.30 am another gas attack was started by the enemy and at 7.35 am. a message was received from O.C. D Company that the enemy had advanced into the craters and had penetrated our front line near 6th AVENUE where the line had been left unoccupied owing to the hostile mine being suspected. The bombing party posted at the junction of 6th AVENUE and the fire trench on discovering the presence of the enemy behaved most bravely. The party consisted of No 20979 Sergt P. J. McCAULEY and the following men. No 23108 Pte T. BURKE, No 21260 Pte A. LAVERY, No 20976 Pte T. O'NEILL, No 23154 Pte J. CAREY, and No 20677 Pte E. FINDON. They held back the enemy for a considerable time and	

Instructions regarding War Diaries and Intelligence Summaries are contained in F. S. Regs., Part II. and the Staff Manual respectively. Title pages will be prepared in manuscript.

WAR DIARY
or
INTELLIGENCE SUMMARY.
(Erase heading not required.)

8th Bn R. IRISH FUSILIERS

Army Form C. 2118.

5

Place	Date	Hour	Summary of Events and Information	Remarks and references to Appendices
			prevented the enemy working along our front line in a northerly direction. They were finally driven back slowly but only after Pte O'NEILL and Private CAREY had been killed and the remainder of the party had been wounded. At this time Captain G.W. EATON saw that the situation was serious so decided to bring up part of No 15 platoon to support the bombing party referred to above and placed his men in such a way on the high ground S of MUNSTER CRATER, forming a block behind the bombing party and at the same time commanding CONNAUGHT LANE so as to prevent the enemy advancing in that direction. While the enemy were advancing near the above mentioned place 2nd Lt J.A. CULLIMORE arrived at MUNSTER CRATER and found the enemy making an attack on this place. In spite of his not being a trained bomber he organized the bombers who were in this crater and drove off the enemy. The three men who were assisting him were No 23839 L/C. A FRANCE, No 23836 L/C M. RICHARDSON and No 23842 Pte H. MINSHALL.	
			At the time this was taking place MAJOR E.W.P. UNIACKE came along the fire trench from the direction of SMITH'S CRATER apparently alone. He found the enemy in possession of TRALEE crater. He returned to SMITH'S CRATER and obtained about three bombers and returned with them to bomb the enemy out of TRALEE and our front line. He continued to throw bombs with these three men and later sent orders for the bombers at the junction of the support line and 6th AVENUE and also at the junction of CONNAUGHT LANE and support line to bomb up to the front line. I consider the prompt action and splendid example shown by MAJOR UNIACKE contributed largely to the enemy being driven out of our front line. He was wounded twice but remained at his post until the enemy had been driven out and everything was quiet.	
			On the right front only one small party of the enemy advanced and were driven off by machine gun fire.	
			On the left front another small party advanced from their wire but when fired on those who were not hit retired. Four of this party are reported to have fallen.	
			The attached copy of the report gives fuller details	
			The casualties were as follows. 2nd Lt J.S. SWEETNAM, killed Major E.W.P. UNIACKE wounded, CAPT. N.G. ALEXANDER, wounded (at duty), Capt J.G. ANDREWS gassed + shock.	

2353 Wt. W2541/1454 700,000 5/15 D. D. & L. A.D.S.S./Forms/C. 2118.

Instructions regarding War Diaries and Intelligence Summaries are contained in F. S. Regs., Part II. and the Staff Manual respectively. Title pages will be prepared in manuscript.

WAR DIARY
or
INTELLIGENCE SUMMARY.
(Erase heading not required.)

8th Bn. R. IRISH FUS.

Army Form C. 2118.

6

Place	Date	Hour	Summary of Events and Information	Remarks and references to Appendices
			2nd Lt A CULLIMORE shock 2nd Lt. C. McSWEENEY wounded (at duty) 2nd Lt H. J. BARNARD, attached to Trench Mortars, wounded. Of the above Capt Andrews and 2nd Lt Cullimore remained at duty until the battalion was relieved on the following day. As regards other ranks it is difficulty to give exactly the figures for this date. The total casualties from midnight 26th–27th to 5 p.m. 29th were 25 killed, 45 wounded and 66 gassed. Of these it is known that 40 were gassed on 29th. At 7 p.m. it was reported that the enemy were discharging more gas but it was only in one place. At 10 p.m. the following telegram was received. "The army commander has telephoned to congratulate the 49th Infantry Brigade on their gallant conduct this morning. The divisional Commander wishes to say how proud he is of their behaviour."	[illegible]
9th AVENUE.	28th		The battalion was relieved by 7th Bn R. IRISH FUSILIERS, and became the brigade reserve at PHILOSOPHE WEST. Large working parties had to be detailed for this night and one of them was one Officer 4 N.C.Os. 40 men to clear the front line trenches where mining operations were being carried on.	[illegible]
PHILOSOPHE WEST.	29th		At 4 a.m. the gas alarm was given and the enemy started a heavy bombardment. PHILOSOPHE was also shelled with 8" shells but did not do much damage to the battalion owing to their fire being directed nearer the VERMELLES RAILWAY STATION. The gas was let off from in front of the HULLOCH SECTOR. The enemy were massing for the attack behind the CRATERS when the wind changed and blew their gas into their trenches. They evacuated their trenches on a front of 700 yards and suffered heavy casualties by our shrapnel. At 5.15 a.m. orders were received from the brigade to send two companies up to the VILLAGE LINE in case of a serious attack developing. A+B Companies moved off but the order was cancelled at 5.25 a.m. and both companies returned. At 5.40 a.m. the bombardment ceased. The working party mentioned above were caught by the gas when working in the trenches. This party was under 2nd Lt D. J. HENRY. Of the total of 45 only four were not gassed. Lt HENRY was amongst those gassed.	[illegible]

2353 Wt. W2544/1454 700,000 5/15 D. D. & L. A.D.S.S./Forms/C. 2118.

Instructions regarding War Diaries and Intelligence Summaries are contained in F. S. Regs., Part II. and the Staff Manual respectively. Title pages will be prepared in manuscript.

WAR DIARY
or
INTELLIGENCE SUMMARY.
8th Bn. R. IRISH FUS.

(*Erase heading not required.*)

Army Form C. 2118.

7.

Place	Date	Hour	Summary of Events and Information	Remarks and references to Appendices
PHILOSOPHE WEST	APRIL 30th		PHILOSOPHE was again shelled with 8" Shells. We suffered no casualties. A Company was detailed to occupy reserve trench in support of right Battalion in the HULLOCH SECTOR and to assist in burying the dead.	S.W.

S. Walcon[?]. Lt. Col.
Comdg 8th Bn. R. Irish Fus.

2353 Wt. W2544/1454 700,000 5/15 D. D. & L. A.D.S.S./Forms/C. 2118.

SECRET

Not to be taken beyond Bn H.Q.

SKETCH MAP OF HULLUCH CRATERS 18.4.16

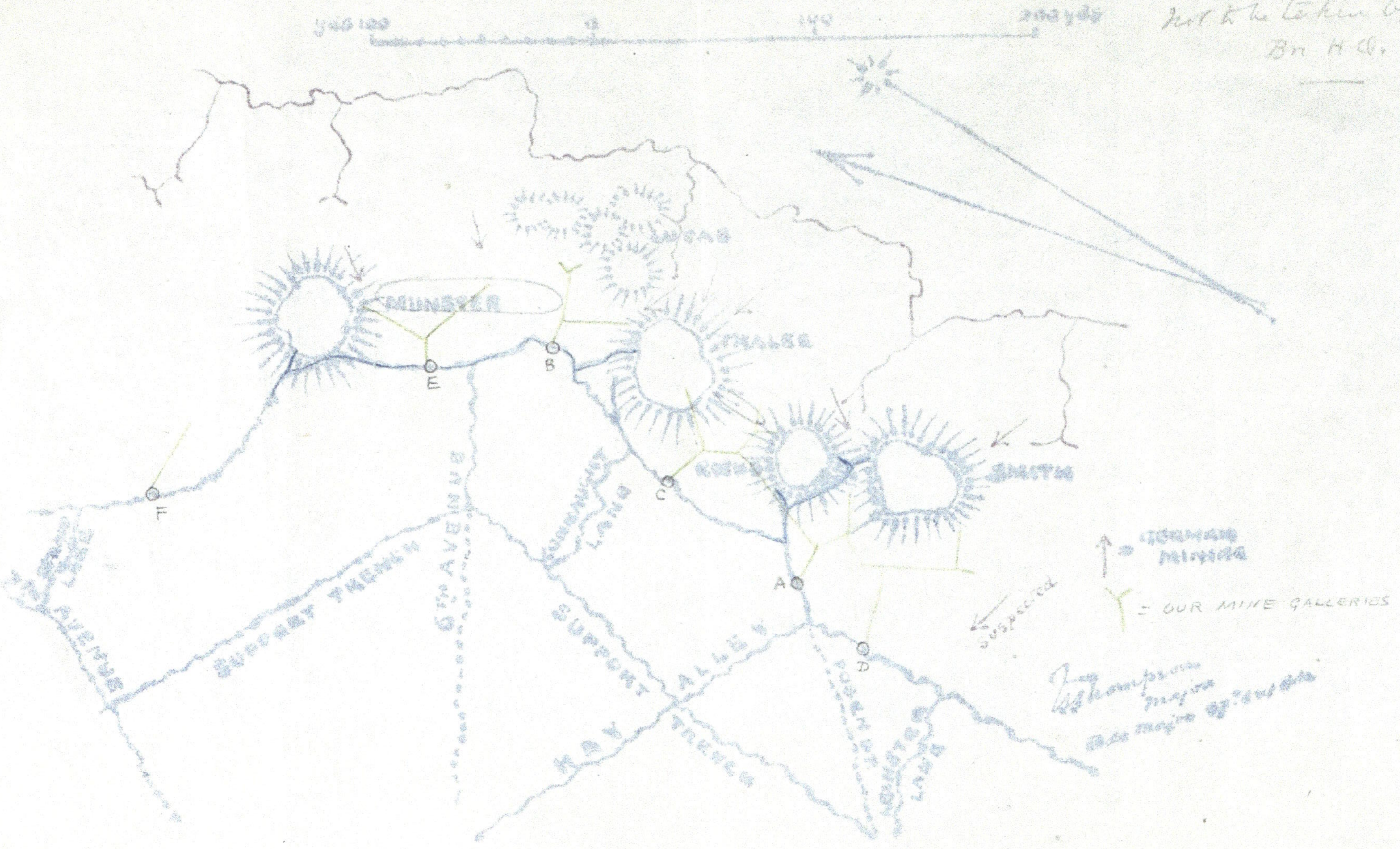

yds 100 0 100 200 yds

MUNSTER

SMITH

A

B

C

D

E

F

SUPPORT TRENCH

6th AVENUE

AVENUE

SUPPORT

ALLEY

KAY

TRENCH

POSEN ST.

LANE

↑ = GERMAN MINING

Y = OUR MINE GALLERIES

Suspected

Thompson
Major

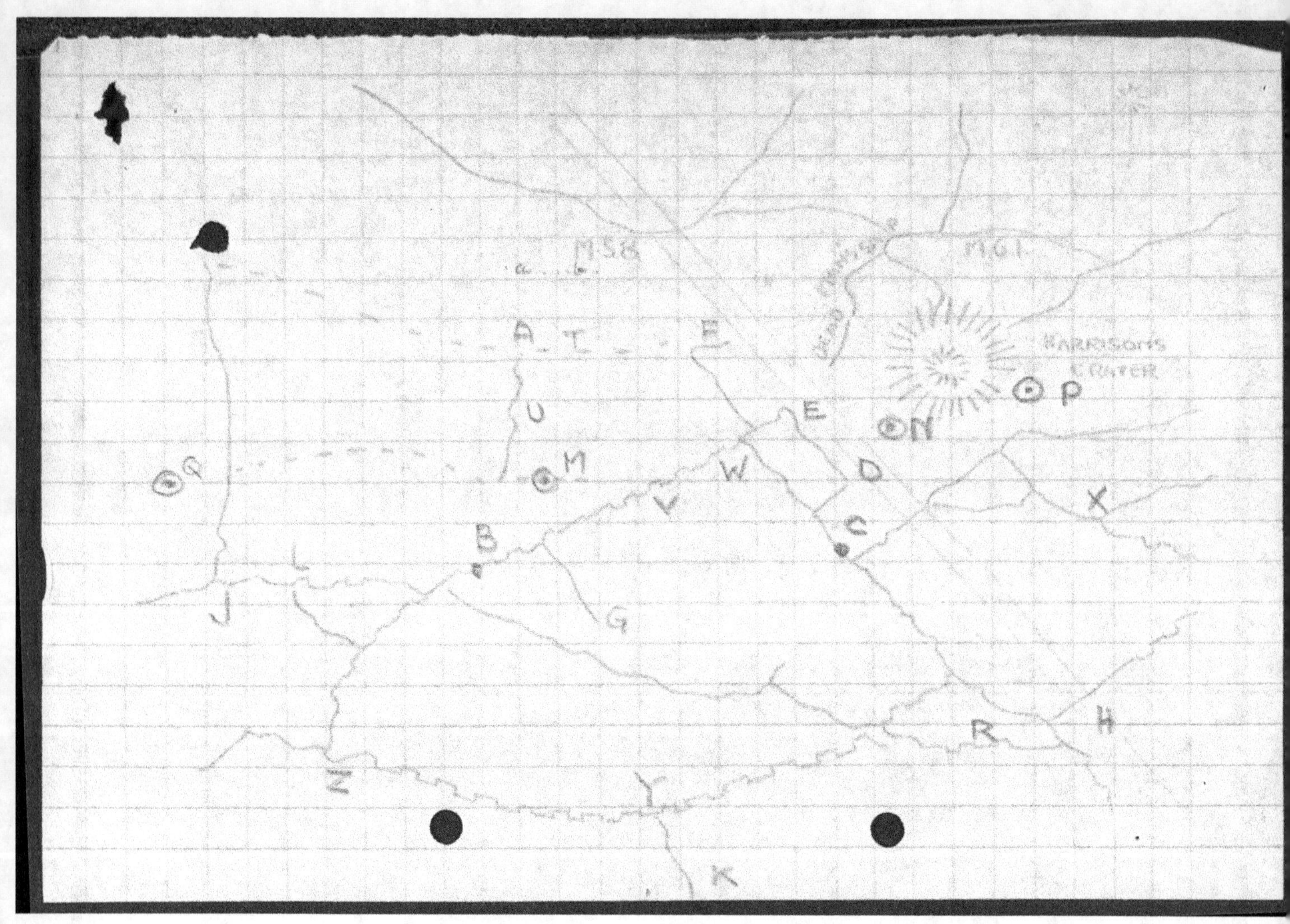

M58
M61
A
T
E
U
E
N
P
HARRISON'S
CRATER
Q
M
W
V
D
C
X
B
G
J
R
H
Z
Y
K

maintaining communication.

8. The following bombers worked very well indeed under 2nd LIEUT V.A. CULLIMORE ~~in the defence of MUNSTER CRATER mentioned on page 4~~. Stw.

No 23839 L/Cpl A FRANCE.
" 23836 " M. RICHARDSON.
" 23842 Pte. H. MINSHALL.

9. It is regretted that the casualties are larger in numbers than first reported. Up to the present the numbers are over 70.

and
work were. No 20617 L/C. C LAWRENCE and 22865 Private E CORR. these men were very actively employed in SMITH'S CRATER.

30. 4. 16.

[illegible] Lt Col.
Comdg 8th Bn R. Irish Fus.

W 316.

B

Head Quarters
49th Inf^y Bde.

Herewith report on raid carried out this morning.

At 1.15 am this morning two raiding parties, each consisting of two officers and 33 other ranks left our front line with the object of raiding the enemy's front line between M 5 d 8.3½ and M 6 c 1.5.

The left party was early in starting and bombs were thrown at 1.16 am. The right party at this time was not completely in position in order to rush forward. On seeing that the left party had advanced and were engaged with the enemy the officer in command of the right party ordered his men to advance.

Both parties found the enemy very much on the alert and their trenches strongly held.

As regards the right party ~~that~~ they found the wire much cut up but many loose pieces lying about which made it very difficult to get

B1

through. One officer and one NCO gained the hostile trench at M 5 d. 85. 43 and there met two of the enemy coming along the small trench into the front line. The front man was hit with a revolver bullet at 2 yards range and entirely collapsed. Five rounds were fired at the remaining man but the result is not known except that he fell.

Owing to the length of time taken in getting through the wire it was time to retire, the signal having been given, before the remainder of the party had got through.

Of this party two men were slightly wounded.

The left party met with greater success but at more cost. Ten of the party succeeded in entering the hostile trench at M 6 c 0. 5½ and worked right and left in the rectangular portion of the hostile trench and also along the sap running parallel to the LENS road.

Two dugouts are reported to have been bombed in the front line.

The wire in front of the hostile trenches

B2

was also very difficult in this part.
Details regarding the left party are difficult to gather owing to the two Officers both being wounded. Casualties in other ranks were six, all slight. The officers' wounds are serious. There are two men missing. All other wounded were brought in. The officer of the left party was brought in sometime after the recall signal, by Capt Eaton and others.
Nearly all casualties in the left party were caused by machine gun fire from the south side of HARRISON'S CRATER.

It is regretted that no prisoners or means of identification of the enemy were obtained.

Our ~~at~~ artillery barrage was good. The enemy's artillery fire was not heavy. His barrage was not deep. A noticeable feature was the number of "duds" in his 4.2s. He fired a few rounds behind Bn HQ the majority of which failed to explode.
The following is a time table of events.

B3

1.16 AM. Bombing started.
1.17 " Our guns opened fire.
1.18 " Red rocket fired by enemy.
1.18 " Enemy opened fire with artillery
1.20 " Green rocket fired by enemy.
1.21 " Hostile machine gun fire opened
1.33 " Enemy open artillery fire from a N.E. direction.
1.50 " Our guns ceased.
1.56 " Hostile artillery ceased.

There were no casualties from hostile artillery fire in front or support trenches

The enemy's artillery fire was badly aimed and chiefly fell behind our support line.

The enemy was the first to throw bombs.

The rapidity with which the enemy opened with bombs and artillery points to them being very much on the alert or even aware of the raid.

No machine gun opened fire from our right flank from the direction of the Long Sap at M 5 d Central.

11.7.16. [illegible] Lt Col
Comdg 8th R. Irish Fus.

C1

Further information obtained regarding raid carried out on 11.7.16.

Right party.

A patrol or wiring party of the enemy is believed to have been between their front trench and their wire when the raiding party started to rush. They bombed our men entangled in the wire but retired almost immediately.

One N.C.O. states he threw a bomb into a group of men who were trying to bring a machine gun into action. There was no machine gun fire from this point.

The front line trenches are reported to be about 6 feet deep.

One man reports that there is a kind of headcover over half the width of the trench.

At M 5 d 8½ 4¼ where the half dug trench enters the enemy's front line there is a ramp which would point to the half dug trench being used for communication to the Saps at M 5 d 7. 4¼

C 2

<u>Left Party.</u>

The enemy seen in the front line trenches at M 6 c 0.5/2 were wearing dark blue uniforms with steel helmets similar in shape to the French helmet. Others had soft round ~~knitted~~ caps.

The effect of these bombs was very local.

One man who entered the Sap at M 5 9/2 5/2 reports he threw box bombs at two Germans who ran down the Sap. These men were not carrying ~~any~~ rifles.

This Sap is about 5' 6" deep, is boarded but not revetted. The traverses were bad. It was wide enough at the top to allow free movement of arms and narrower at the bottom.

The Sap was very much damaged by our artillery and trench mortar fire and was knocked in places.

Judging from all reports the officers acted well and were not supported by the rank and file. The left party were unfortunate in having both officers wounded soon

C 3

after leaving our wire. Both these officers are unable to state what happened having only a very confused idea ~~of what happened~~ subsequent to their being wounded.

Captain GALVIN, after he was wounded attempted to regain our lines but had not sufficient strength. He was missed a short time after the recall signal had gone and a wounded man was seen by a sentry in the front line.

Lieut A.E. KINGHAN ~~of~~ the Lewis gun officer, on hearing that there was a wounded man lying out about 30 yards from our front trench, organised a covering party consisting of machine guns and two bombers, Cpl CAIRNS and Private McMULLAN. He then called on Lieut SARGINT (7th Bn R Irish Fus) Stokes mortar officer, to assist him in bringing in the wounded man. It was then discovered that the wounded man was Capt. GALVIN. While these two officers were bringing in Capt GALVIN they were joined by Capt

CH

EATON and Lt SPARKS. They succeeded in bringing him in in spite of a heavy hostile fire.

No 3107: Sergt J. MURPHY did good work in supporting Capt EATON in the night party.

S.E. Wilson Lt.Col.
Comdg 8th R. Irish Fus.

W 85.

Further report on the enemy's attack on the trenches occupied by 8th 13th R. IRISH FUSILIERS between HULLOCH ROAD G 12 d. and HOLLY LANE H 13 c. on 27th April 1916.

Reference map. 36c N W 3. Edition 6. Scale 1/10000 and attached sketch.

As already reported in my W 81, the enemy's bombardment started at 5 a.m. At this time the battalion was holding the line as follows – Three companies were holding the firing line and supports with special bombing parties occupying the craters in H 13 a and H 13 c under the command of MAJOR E.W.P. UNIACKE. One company was in RESERVE TRENCH and battalion headquarters in 9th AVENUE near its junction with HAY ALLEY.

It should be noted that owing to hostile mining being detected immediately north of TRALEE Crater that crater and the portion of the front line between 6th AVENUE and CONNAUGHT LANE was not held. This withdrawal from the front line was carried out in accordance with advice from the Tunnelling Officer.

This portion of the line was observed by means of patrols.

2. The statement in my former report that gas was not experienced by the three companies in the front line is not strictly accurate. The right Company was within the gas area to the extent of half its front.

3. The following information has been gathered as regards the action on the part of the three companies holding the fire trenches.

RIGHT COMPANY. (B Company under command of CAPTAIN N.G. ALEXANDER.)

The gas cloud prevented anything being seen of any hostile movement against the battalion on the right. When gas was detected helmets were adjusted with promptitude and all men warned. This action prevented any casualties occurring from gas with the exception of a few men who, subsequent to the attack, drank tainted water.

The only party of the enemy seen by this Company was on the South side of SMITH'S CRATER and numbered only five. On detecting them CAPTAIN ALEXANDER obtained a machine gun whose team had become casualties and in spite of not knowing how to handle the gun took it to SOUTHERN SAP and found a man who said he could work it and opened fire. One of the enemy was killed by the gun and another shot by revolver fire. The remainder of the ~~company~~ few withdrew. These bodies were both subsequently lost owing to their being covered up by shellfire.

Captain N.G. ALEXANDER remained with his company until the battalion was relieved in spite of his previously having had his finger shattered and receiving another shrapnel wound in his neck. He did good work in encouraging his men and set a fine example.

2nd LIEUT. C. MAC SWEENEY also showed great courage and coolness when under heavy shell fire and remained with his company until the battalion was relieved after having been wounded by shrapnel in the arm.

No 16657 acting Sergt T.H. JONES who was in command of No 1 Lewis gun remained with his gun the whole time during the gas and fired the gun himself.

The company commander states

that all ranks were most cheerful while under shell fire and performed their duties in a very satisfactory manner.

CENTRE COMPANY. (D Company under command of MAJOR T.H. BOARDMAN).

As already reported part of the front line was not occupied. 2nd LIEUT J.A CULLIMORE showed good initiative when the bombardment started by holding the left of the centre company's front line. He organised the bombers and held MUNSTER CRATER. This officer is not a trained bomber and was not told off for the defence of the crater.

A party, estimated at about 30, of the enemy advanced from the direction of LUCAS CRATER towards TRALEE to the unoccupied portion of our front line. CAPTAIN G.W EATON who saw that TRALEE was occupied by the enemy brought up part of No 15 platoon and occupied the high ground S. of MUNSTER CRATER thus forming a block and preventing the enemy moving north and at the same time commanding CONNAUGHT LANE.

The hostile party then withdrew from the neighbourhood of TRALEE

Two officers state definitely that they saw a hostile mine exploded at 6.10 a.m. but that no marked alteration in the configuration of the ground could be noticed afterwards. This mine is reported to be near SHAFT B. The R.E. officers employed in tunnelling cannot give any conformation of this and state that none of our shafts were damaged. As soon as the officer commanding the centre company, MAJOR T.H. BOARDMAN, came to the conclusion that this mine had been fired he re-occupied that portion of the front line between 6th AVENUE and CONNAUGHT LANE the enemy having found both flanks of the front trench blocked.

The O.C. centre company then decided to bring up his reserve platoon from RESERVE TRENCH. This platoon had been subjected to gas. The N.C.O. commanding this platoon, No. 7786 SERGT. F. CATLOW, who had been slightly gassed, brought up his platoon in very good style and in very quick time. This NCO has since been admitted to hospital suffering

from gas poisoning.
The Officer Commanding this company states that all officers, NCOs & men worked most cheerfully and well and he is ~~most~~ very pleased with their behaviour.

LEFT COMPANY. (A Company under CAPTAIN B.St.GALVIN.)

The only hostile party which left their front line trenches was a patrol of about ten strong who came out of a sap or listening post in front of their wire at H 13 a 1.9. They were engaged by Lewis Gun fire and rifle fire and four were seen to fall.

When our artillery started shelling ~~there~~ their front line it was observed that "knife rest" entanglements were thrown out of the front line trenches as if these rests had been removed from their own entanglements during the night in preparations for their attack.

This company was the first to send back word that the enemy were using gas. Telephone communica was broken with all companies very soon after the commencement of the bombardment. The officer Commanding the Company asked for a volunteer to go to Battalion Head Quarters with the message. No 18623 Private J. COSTIGAN volunteered. He was gassed but arrived with the message.

In this company, during the bombardment No 23564 Private S. CONNOR showed great resource in digging out men who had been ~~[illegible]~~ buried in the support line and dressing wounded. He rescued two comrades who were in a dugout which had been blown in on them, thus saving their lives. No 15207 Company Sergt Major T. O'NEILL showed great coolness and encouraged the men by his example.

RESERVE COMPANY (C Company under CAPTAIN E.M.H GREVILLE) This company was not employed actively during the day. They were subjected to two gas attacks and to very heavy shelling. An order was sent to the officer Commanding this Company owing to my having received a verbal report from a wounded man coming up the trenches, to reconnoitre the support line trench near HAY ALLEY and if found occupied by the enemy to counterattack with two platoons. He found this report to be unfounded.

He informs me that No 15214 L/Corporal T. KEITH volunteered to take messages to Bn Head Quarters, was very energetic in his work attending to wounded and also carried wounded to the aid post. No [illegible] Pte KINEY P was also most useful in the way of taking messages and patroling the communication trenches

CRATER PARTY (under MAJOR E.W.P. UNIACKE.) This party consisted of the bombers of the centre company, bombers of the reserve company and one Officer and 12 bombers from the flank Companies, as well as six headquarters bombers.

On the morning of the attack the bombers were posted as follows. One bombing post at MUNSTER CRATER, one post at junction of ~~CONNAUGHT LANE~~ 6th AVENUE and front line, one at junction of 6th AVENUE and Support line, one at junction of CONNAUGHT LANE + support line, one at Sap running to ROCHE and SMITHS

CRATERS. This last consisting of 14 men. As stated before TRALEE was unoccupied owing to the expected hostile mine. ~~At the time~~ When the enemy got into our front line at TRALEE the bombing post at the junction of 6th AVENUE and the fire trench started bombing the enemy and also two men got on the parapet and fired with rifles at the advancing enemy. This party made a gallant stand and were all killed or wounded. The N.C.O. in charge, No 20979 Sergt P.J. McCAULEY though wounded continued to fight and was finally supported by the party mentioned under the command of CAPT. EATON, vide page 4 and a party of miners under an officer whose name it is impossible to discover, after Sgt McCAULEY's party had been slowly driven back. I consider the behaviour of Sergt McCAULEY and this party most praiseworthy. The names of the remainder of the party are as follows.

No 23108 Private T BURKE.
No ~~2310~~ 21260 " A. LAVERY.
No 20976 " T. O'NEILL
No 23154 " J. CAREY.
No 20677 " E. FINDON.

At this time this was taking place MAJOR E.W.P. UNIACKE arrived from the direction of HAY ALLEY in the front line trench, apparently alone. He discovered the enemy in possession of TRALEE and immediately returned to SMITHS crater and collected about three bombers and returned at once to drive the enemy out of TRALEE and our front line which was unoccupied. He continued to throw bombs with these ^types^ men and later sent one man to order the bombers from the support line at 6th AVENUE and CONNAUGHT LANE to bomb up to the front line. This was done and the enemy driven out of the trenches. I consider that the prompt action and splendid example shown by MAJOR UNIACKE was the cause of the enemy being driven out of the occupation of our trench which he occupied for a very short period.

4. All officers who were in the front line trenches during the bombardment speak in the highest terms of the artillery fire. The burst of the Shrapnel was very well timed and the majority of the bullets appeared to strike the enemy's

front line. The heavier artillery was also most effective.

5. I should also like to bring to notice the good work done by LIEUT. G. BUCHANAN, R.A.M.C. medical officer in charge of the battalion. About seventy casualties passed through the aid post in one day all of which he attended to and all were evacuated by 3.30 a.m. the following morning.

6. Splendid work was done by Revd FATHER W. DOYLE, ~~C.F.~~ chaplain to the forces. Though gassed in the early part of the day he continued to work amongst the wounded and dead and his energy was unlimited. He paid frequent visits to the front line trenches and refused rest until forced to do so. Since the battalion came out of the trenches he has again visited the front line attending the wounded and burying the dead.

7. No [illegible] Sergt J. HOLTON, the signalling sergeant of the battalion was constantly at work and most attentive to his duties, repairing the lines and

49/16 XVI U.S.I. Vol 1/4

Army Form C. 2118.

Instructions regarding War Diaries and Intelligence Summaries are contained in F. S. Regs., Part II. and the Staff Manual respectively. Title pages will be prepared in manuscript.

WAR DIARY
or
~~INTELLIGENCE SUMMARY.~~ 8th Bn. R. IRISH FUSILIERS.

(Erase heading not required.)

Place	Date	Hour	Summary of Events and Information	Remarks and references to Appendices
	1916 MAY			
PHILOSOPHE WEST.	1st		The battalion, less A Company, remained in Brigade reserve.	S.
	2nd		The battalion relieved the 7th Bn. R. IRISH FUSILIERS in the left sub-sector of the HULLOCH SECTOR. Companies occupied the same positions as during 24th – 28th April. The relief was complete by about 1 pm. The enemy showed much less activity than when the battalion formerly occupied this line. The 16th DIVISIONAL CYCLISTS were attached to the Bn and occupied RESERVE TRENCH.	S.
9th AVENUE	3rd		At 1.30 am. a false gas alarm was passed along the line from the direction of LOOS. The day passed fairly quietly with the exception of shelling of our RESERVE TRENCH. A draft of 16 men joined the Battalion	S.
	4th		At 1.45 am. our bombers discovered a small party of the enemy on the far lip of SMITH'S CRATER. We attacked them with bombs and drove them out. The artillery assisted by clearing the far side of the crater. At 3 am. a very distinct shock was felt as if a mine had been fired. No firing resulted from either side. The following day it was discovered that this was a hostile camouflet. It did no damage to our galleries or trenches. At intervals during the day there were the usual exchange of rifle grenades and our trenches were shelled. ~~Two~~ Aerial torpedoes were used against our left.	S.
	5th		The usual exchange of rifle grenades and trench mortars at morning "Stand to" ~~[illegible]~~ At 5 pm. the enemy started an organised rifle grenade bombardment. Smoke bombs were also used but the wind was in the South. We replied but were unable to silence them. The enemy obtained a direct hit on a bomb store setting it alight. Our artillery retaliated along our whole front. The enemy's bombardment died down after about an hour. Sounds of mining were heard from the sap at SMITH'S CRATER. This was reported to the O.C. Tunnelling Company who reported there was no immediate danger. The enemy approached our SMITH'S CRATER during the night and were easily dealt with.	T.H.

T4

2353 Wt. W2544/1454 700,000 5/15 D. D. & L. A.D.S.S./Forms/C. 2118.

Instructions regarding War Diaries and Intelligence Summaries are contained in F. S. Regs., Part II. and the Staff Manual respectively. Title pages will be prepared in manuscript.

WAR DIARY ~~or~~ ~~INTELLIGENCE SUMMARY.~~

(Erase heading not required.)

Army Form C. 2118.

2

8th Bn. R. IRISH FUSILIERS

Place	Date	Hour	Summary of Events and Information	Remarks and references to Appendices
9th AVENUE	6th		At morning "Stand to" we bombarded the enemy's line with Stokes gun bombs and trench mortars, this preceded the usual bombardment with rifle grenades. The battalion was relieved by the 9th Bn R. MUNSTER FUSILIERS. The relief started at 11 am & was completed at 4 pm. The battalion marched to NOEUX-LES-MINES where they were accommodated in huts.	TMS
NOEUX-LES-MINES	7th		Remained in billets	
"	8th		" "	TMS
"	9th		" " MAJOR W. GARRARD and 2nd Lieut C. L. NAYLOR joined the Battalion	TMS
"	10th		Remained in billets Inspection by G.O.C. 49th Infantry Brigade	TMS
	11th		Remained in billets. The Battalion Stood to from 6.20 pm to 10 am 12.5.16	TMS.
	12th			
	13		Remained in billets 6 Officers 200 men working on LONDON ROAD	TMS.
	14		" " " " " 2nd Lieuts F.W. NELSON, F.A. NEWELL and H.J. LINFOOT joined the Battalion	TMS
	15		Remained in billets, 5 Officers 150 men working on LONDON ROAD	TMS.
	16		" "	
PHILOSOPHE EAST	17		The Battalion relieved the 8th Bn. R. MUNSTER FUSILIERS in PHILOSOPHE EAST. Relief completed at 5 pm. The Battalion became the Brigade Reserve. Captain H.R. KAVANAGH, Lieut W. SPARKS and 2nd Lieut C E W NEAT joined the Battalion. One platoon formed the garrison of LENS ROAD REDOUBT.	TMS
"	18th		Remained in Brigade reserve.	[illegible]
"	19th		" " " "	[illegible]
"	20th		" " " "	
LOOS.	21st		The battalion relieved the 7th Bn R. IRISH FUSILIERS in the left sub-sector of the LOOS sector. Companies were situated as follows. — C Company from HAYMARKET to DEAD MAN'S SAP. A Coy from DEAD MAN'S SAP	

2353 Wt. W2544/1454 700,000 5/15 D. D. & L. A.D.S.S./Forms/C. 2118.

Instructions regarding War Diaries and Intelligence Summaries are contained in F. S. Regs., Part II. and the Staff Manual respectively. Title pages will be prepared in manuscript.

WAR DIARY
or
~~INTELLIGENCE SUMMARY.~~

(Erase heading not required.)

8th R. IRISH FUSILIERS.

Army Form C. 2118.

3

Place	Date	Hour	Summary of Events and Information	Remarks and references to Appendices
LOOS	21st (continued)		to FIR STREET. B Coy from thence to NORTH STREET. D Coy was in reserve in ENCLOSURE. Bn H.Q was at G 35.d. central. The relief started at 8.30 pm. and was complete at 11.40 pm.	S.W.
"	22nd		A Company extended to its right as far as COPSE LANE in order to equalize the frontage held by Companies. One platoon of D Company was ordered to occupy REGENT STREET in support of B Coy whose line was too long to admit of sufficient men being available in support. A "strafe" with Stokes guns, rifle grenades, and Mills cups was organised by A Coy at evening "stand to". Fire was directed behind HARRISONS CRATER. The enemy's retaliation was weak and directed on DEAD MAN'S SAP. At about 10 pm. a hostile party of eight men appeared on the south side of HARRISON'S CRATER and when fired on three were seen to fall. A short time afterwards two men were seen by from DEAD MAN'S SAP dragging back a dead or wounded man.	S.W.
"	23rd		At 8.5 pm. the enemy exploded a camouflet between HARTS & HARRISONS craters which did very little damage to our trenches. Lieut G.P. BRYARS discovered that two miners were suffering from mine gas poisoning. He went to their assistance and was himself gassed. 2nd Lt F. A NEWELL, seeing what had happened went to his assistance, having put on his smoke helmet, and dragged him about 15 yards when a shell brought down some sandbags on top of Lt BRYARS legs. 2nd Lt NEWELL then went for assistance and was himself overcome by gas. ~~2nd Lt J A CULLIMORE was~~	S.W.
"	24th		2nd Lt J.A. CULLIMOIRE was killed in the early morning in DEAD MAN'S SAP (by a sniper). Lt. K.M. WALLACE was dangerously wounded and CAPT. G.W. EATON slightly wounded on the LOOS CRASSIER at about 2 am. A draft of 20 other ranks arrived and all were posted to "A" Coy. REGENT STREET was shelled by the enemy from about 3.30 to 4 pm. Some damage was done to our trenches.	S.W.
VILLAGE LINE	25th		The battalion was relieved by 7th Bn R. IRISH FUSILIERS and became battalion on Brigade Support. Companies were situated as follows. A Company in VILLAGE LINE, B Coy in cellars near LOOS post office. C Coy in cellars north of the LOOS CRASSIER and D Coy in the ENCLOSURE. The total casualties during the four days in the front line was 51.	S.W.

Instructions regarding War Diaries and Intelligence Summaries are contained in F. S. Regs., Part II. and the Staff Manual respectively. Title pages will be prepared in manuscript.

WAR DIARY
or
~~INTELLIGENCE SUMMARY.~~
(Erase heading not required.)

8th Bn. ROYAL IRISH FUSILIERS.

Army Form C. 2118.

4.

Place	Date	Hour	Summary of Events and Information	Remarks and references to Appendices
VILLAGE LINE	May 26th		Situated as on the evening of 25th.	S.W.
"	27th		A report was received during the afternoon that a German deserter stated that the enemy intended to attack somewhere on 1st Division front on the night of 28th-29th. B Company was moved up from the Post Office LOOS to the ENCLOSURE.	
E. WAY.	28th		Bn. H.Q. and A Company moved into E. WAY west of LOOS so as to be closer in case of attack on the brigade front.	S.W.
LOOS.	29th		The Battalion relieved 7th Bn. R. IRISH FUSILIERS in the right sub-sector of LOOS. All four Companies were in the fire trench owing to the likelihood of attack and the weakness of the battalion. The frontage of the battalion was about 1200 yards and the trench strength was 502. A Coy was on the right, D right centre, B left centre and C left. Two Companies 7th Bn were in the ENCLOSURE and attached as support to this battalion and to provide working parties.	S.W. / S.W.
LOOS	30th		The enemy fired a camouflet in the early morning. No damage was done to our trenches.	S.W.
LOOS	31st		At 10 am. we fired a mine on the enemy's side of HARTS CRATER. No damage was done to our trenches. At 12.30 pm. another mine was fired by us on the S.E. side of HARRISON'S CRATER. Only a very small crater was formed about 4 ft deep. Immediately after the explosion MAJOR W. GARRARD and six bombers advanced up to this mound from DEAD MAN'S SAP. They were exposed to rifle fire from the south west. They remained there about 10 minutes and then withdrew there being no advantage to be gained by remaining in this exposed position. 2nd Lt. C. McSWEENEY was wounded in the early morning. Lieut K.M. WALLACE died of wounds in hospital.	S.W.

S. Walton [?] Lt. Col.
Commanding 8th Bn. R. Irish Fusiliers.

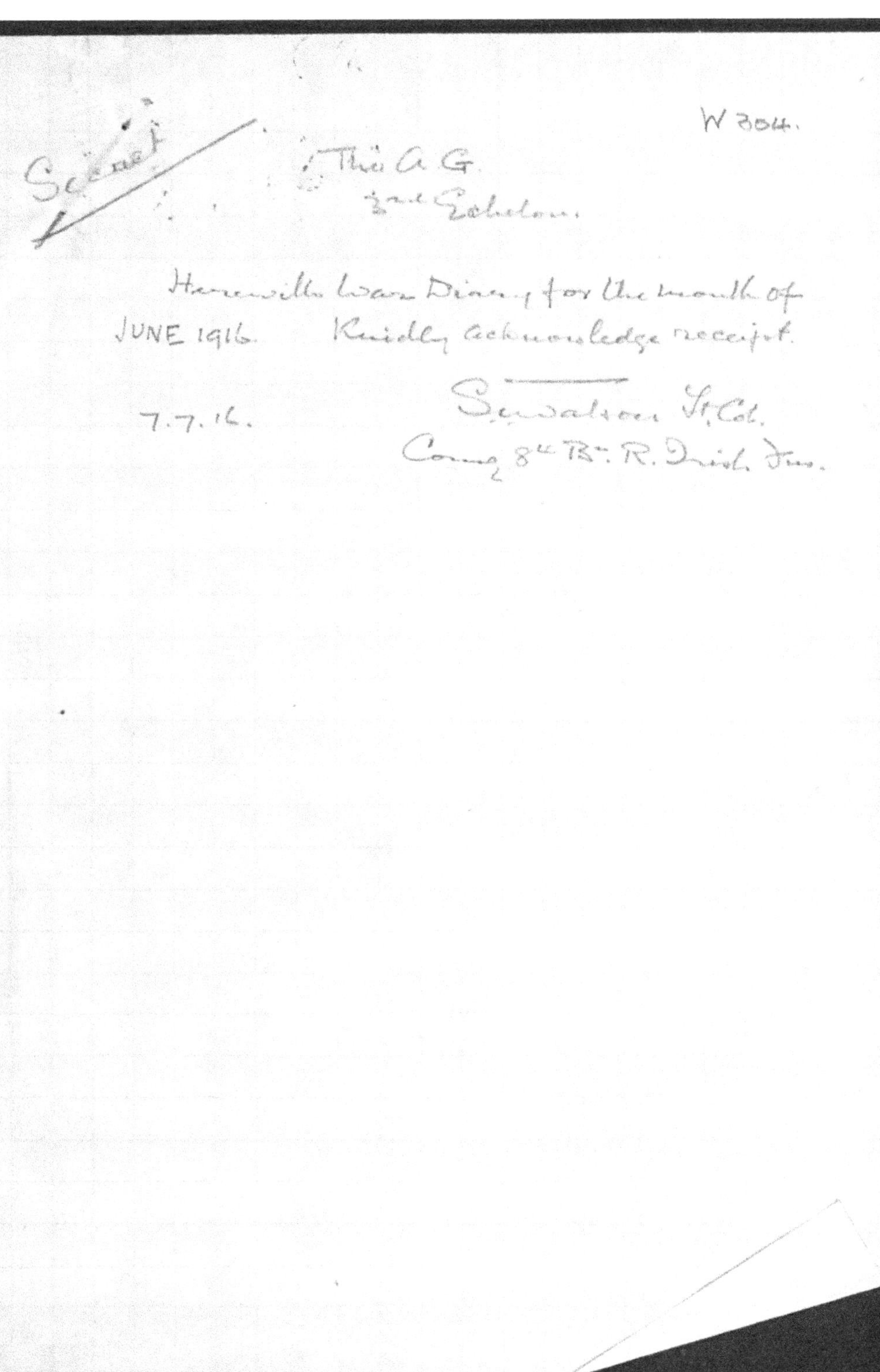

W 304.

Secret

The A G.
3rd Echelon.

Herewith War Diary for the month of JUNE 1916. Kindly acknowledge receipt.

7.7.16.

S. Walton Lt. Col.
Comm. 8th Bn. R. Irish Fus.

Instructions regarding War Diaries and Intelligence Summaries are contained in F. S. Regs., Part II. and the Staff Manual respectively. Title pages will be prepared in manuscript.

WAR DIARY
or
~~INTELLIGENCE SUMMARY.~~
(Erase heading not required.)

XVI

Army Form C. 2118.

June

8th Bn. R. IRISH FUSILIERS. Vol 5

Place	Date	Hour	Summary of Events and Information	Remarks and references to Appendices
LOOS	JUNE 1st		The Bn. was holding the line as on 31st ultimo. MAJOR W. GARRARD wounded.	
MAZINGARBE	2nd		The Battalion was relieved by 8th R. DUBLIN FUSILIERS. Relief was complete about 1am. on 2nd. Companies as relieved marched back to MAZINGARBE to billets. Owing to a hostile deserter having stated that attack was likely and owing to activity behind the hostile lines the Brigade in reserve was warned to turn out at one hour's notice by day and half hour's notice by night.	
"	3rd		Remained in reserve.	Sgd.
"	4th		" " " 1st Corps Commander presented medal ribbons to the following. No 20979 Sergt. P. J. McCAULEY (DCM) & No 20677 Pte E FINDON. Notification received that the following honours & rewards had been granted. MAJOR E.W.P. UNIACKE (DSO) 20979 Sergt P.J. McCAULEY DCM. The following were given the Military Medal 22108 Pte T. BURKE, No 21260 Pte A. LAVERY No 20677 Pte E. FINDON.	Sgd.
"	5th		Remained in reserve.	Sgd.
"	6th		" " " 1st Army Commander had ordered the parade of the Bn. for his inspection but the parade was cancelled owing to heavy rain.	Sgd.
"	7th		Remained in reserve.	Sgd.
	8th		" " " Notification received that four Military Medals had been awarded to the Bn. and the following were selected, their names having been previously submitted but no rewards granted. No 23839 Pte (L/Cpl) A. FRANCE, No 15135 Sergt. A. WARD, No 16814 Sergt J. HOLTON, No 18623 Pte J. COSTIGAN.	Sgd.
"	9th		Remained in reserve. 2nd Lt SHANE and a draft of 30 other ranks joined the Bn.	Sgd. Sgd.

2353 Wt. W2544/1454 700,000 5/15 D. D. & L. A.D.S.S./Forms/C. 2118.

Instructions regarding War Diaries and Intelligence Summaries are contained in F. S. Regs., Part II. and the Staff Manual respectively. Title pages will be prepared in manuscript.

Army Form C. 2118.

(2)

WAR DIARY
or
~~INTELLIGENCE SUMMARY.~~

(Erase heading not required.)

8th Bn. R. IRISH FUSILIERS.

Place	Date	Hour	Summary of Events and Information	Remarks and references to Appendices
RESERVE TRENCH	10th		Took over from 6th Bn CONNAUGHT RANGERS in the right sub-section of the 14 BIS section. Companies distributed as follows. D Coy ENGLISH ALLEY to BOYAU B Coy from there to BOYAU . A Coy from there to BOYAU 60. C Company in reserve with one platoon in FORREST TRENCH, one in MEATH TRENCH and remainder in RESERVE TRENCH. 2nd Lt P.H. FIGGIS joined the Bn.	[illegible]
"	11th		Front line bombarded with trench mortars and rifle grenades. Total casualties 9. Coy Sergt Major BRYAN killed. The following 2nd Lieuts joined the Bn: N. H. BIBLE. E.S. BIRD. C.L. PORTEOUS	[illegible]
"	12th		Situated as on 10th. A quiet day. One casualty.	[illegible]
"	13th		" " " " " " "	[illegible]
10th AVENUE	14th		Battalion was relieved by 7th Bn R. IRISH FUSILIERS. This battalion became the support battalion and occupied 10th AVENUE finding the garrisons of 65 METRE POINT and NORTHERN SAP REDOUBT.	[illegible]
"	15th		Remained in Brigade Support. 2nd Lt F.A MOODY + ~~P.H. FIGGIS~~ L.A. MARCHANT joined the Bn also 22 other ranks.	[illegible]
"	16th		" " " "	[illegible]
"	17th		" " " " The position of the Bn was changed in 10th AVENUE so that the left rested on VENDIN ALLEY and the right on NORTHERN SAP REDOUBT.	[illegible]
"	18th		In Brigade support as above.	[illegible]
"	19th		" " " "	[illegible]
RESERVE TRENCH	20th		Took over from 7th Bn R. IRISH FUSILIERS in the right sub-section of the 14 BIS section. Companies were situated as on 10th inst. Lieut G.P. BRYARS rejoined + 7 other ranks.	[illegible]
"	21st		Situated as above. Draft of 6 other ranks arrived.	[illegible]

2353 Wt. W2544/1454 700,000 5/15 D. D. & L. A.D.S.S./Forms/C. 2118.

Army Form C. 2118. (3)

Instructions regarding War Diaries and Intelligence Summaries are contained in F. S. Regs., Part II. and the Staff Manual respectively. Title pages will be prepared in manuscript.

WAR DIARY
or
~~INTELLIGENCE SUMMARY~~.
(Erase heading not required.)

8th Bn. R. IRISH FUSILIERS.

Hour, Date, Place	Summary of Events and Information	Remarks and references to Appendices
JUNE 22nd. RESERVE TRENCH.	Situated as on 21st.	
" 23rd. " "	" " " " At about 8.30 pm enemy shelled right of D Coy fairly heavily. This was part of the shelling which was directed against LOOS. Lieut C. L. PORTEOUS wounded.	S[illegible]
" 24th.	At 10 am. our trench mortars commenced the bombardment of the enemy's wire with a view to causing an opening for possible raids on the enemy's lines. They were supported by artillery. A noticeable feature of the day was the increase of shells fired by our own artillery after having saved for some months. The Bn was relieved during the afternoon and became battalion in Brigade Reserve. Head Quarters, A+D Coys were in PHILOSOPHE WEST and B+C Coys occupied that portion of 10th AVENUE between 65 METRE POINT and CHALK PIT ALLEY. On the night of 24th our Lewis gunners remained in the front line with 7th Bn R. IRISH FUSILIERS. During the night a strong hostile raiding party crept up to within a few yards of the front trenches. They were discovered and driven off by our Lewis gunners. Lieut A.E. KINGHAN did particularly good work and his name was forwarded by O.C. 7th Bn. R. IRISH FUSILIERS for reward. No 20102 L/C P. McALINDEN & 18388 Pte M. HARTE also did excellent work keeping their gun in action ~~and~~ until it was put out of action by a bomb. The former was severely wounded and the latter, who was also wounded carried the gun out of danger after it had been put out of action and he refused	

(4)

Army Form C. 2118.

Instructions regarding War Diaries and Intelligence Summaries are contained in F. S. Regs., Part II. and the Staff Manual respectively. Title pages will be prepared in manuscript.

WAR DIARY
or
INTELLIGENCE SUMMARY.
(Erase heading not required.)

8th Bn. R. IRISH FUSILIERS.

Hour, Date, Place	Summary of Events and Information	Remarks and references to Appendices
	to leave his gun until the enemy were driven off. 2nd Lt. H.B. REYNELL joined	S.W.
JUNE 25th. PHILOSOPHE WEST	The Bn. remained in Brigade Reserve.	S.W.
" 26th. NOEUX-LES-MINES	The Bn. was relieved at 3 p.m. by 8th Bn. R. DUBLIN FUSILIERS and marched to NOEUX-LES-MINES.	S.W.
" 27th " "	Remained in Divisional Reserve.	S.W.
" 28th " "	" " " " Draft of 8 other ranks received	S.W.
" 29th " "	" " " "	
" 30th " "	" " " "	

S. Watson Lt. Col.
Comg 8th Bn. R. Irish Fus.

(73989) ... H.&J.Ltd. Forms/C. 2118/10.

T.6

W A R   D I A R Y

8th (S) Battalion

Royal Irish Fus.

1st. July to 31st. July 1916.

VOLUME No. ~~X~~. 6

Instructions regarding War Diaries and Intelligence Summaries are contained in F. S. Regs., Part II. and the Staff Manual respectively. Title pages will be prepared in manuscript.

WAR DIARY
or
INTELLIGENCE SUMMARY.
(Erase heading not required.)

Army Form C. 2118.

8th Bn. R. IRISH FUSILIERS

(1)

Hour, Date, Place		Summary of Events and Information	Remarks and references to Appendices
JULY 1st	NOEUX LES MINES	Bn in Divisional Reserve.	[illegible]
" 2nd	" "	" " "	
" 3rd	PHILOSOPHE EAST.	The Bn relieved 6th R. IRISH REGT as battalion in brigade reserve. Companies were situated as follows. C Company in VILLAGE LINE South of RAILWAY ALLEY finding the garrison of one platoon in LENS ROAD REDOUBT. The remainder of the Bn in PHILOSOPHE EAST. Lt F. A. NEWELL rejoined.	[illegible]
" 4th	" "	Remained in Brigade Reserve. A draft of 41 other ranks received from the base. These men all belonged to the R. IRISH REGT	[illegible]
" 5th	" "	Remained in Brigade Reserve.	[illegible]
" 6th	" "	" " "	[illegible]
" 7th	LOOS.	The Bn took over from 7th Bn R. IRISH FUSILIERS in the right Sub section of the LOOS section. Companies were situated as follows. D Coy on the right from HAYMARKET to BOYAU 32. A Coy, right centre from thence to BOYAU 35. C Company, left centre as far as the sunken road and B Coy from thence to NORTH STREET.	[illegible]
" 8th	"	Situated as above. Intermittent shelling of our line by trench mortars and ~~small~~ aerial torpedoes. Some damage done to our trenches.	[illegible]

(73989) W4141—463. 400,000. 9/14. H.&J.Ltd. Forms/C. 2118/10.

2

Army Form C. 2118.

Instructions regarding War Diaries and Intelligence Summaries are contained in F. S. Regs., Part II. and the Staff Manual respectively. Title pages will be prepared in manuscript.

WAR DIARY
or
INTELLIGENCE SUMMARY.

(Erase heading not required.)

8th Bn R. IRISH FUSILIERS.

Hour, Date, Place		Summary of Events and Information	Remarks and references to Appendices
9th ~~JUNE~~ JULY 1916	LOOS.	Situated as on 8th.	S.J.W.
10th " "	"	" " " "	
11th " "	"	At ~~#~~ 1.15 am. a raid was carried out. The scheme for the raid is attached and marked A, A1, + A2. This raid had been practised when in Divisional Reserve against specially dug trenches. A copy of the report forwarded to Brigade Head Quarters after the raid is attached and marked B. B1, B2, + B3. Since the report was written the following information has been received. The wire in both places considerably delayed the forward rush to the enemy's trenches. Both Captain B. StJ. GALVIN, who was in command of the left party, and Lieut G.P. BRYARS, who was with the ~~#~~ left party, were both wounded within a very short time of leaving our front trenches. This did not prevent these two officers from pushing on and gaining the enemy's trenches. They were both wounded again and Capt. GALVIN fell when returning to our trenches and remained out on the LENS ROAD until his absence was discovered. Lieut A.E. KINGHAN, 2nd Lt. E.E. SERGINT (7th Bn R. IRISH FUSILIERS) 2nd Lt J.E. REA and CAPT. G.W. EATON went out and carried in CAPT. GALVIN. The officer in command of the right party was Capt G.W. EATON. He and No 21071 Sergt J. MURPHY were the only two who entered the hostile lines from the right party.	

Instructions regarding War Diaries and Intelligence Summaries are contained in F. S. Regs., Part II. and the Staff Manual respectively. Title pages will be prepared in manuscript.

WAR DIARY
or
INTELLIGENCE SUMMARY.
(Erase heading not required.)

Army Form C. 2118. 3

8th Bn. R IRISH FUSILIERS.

Hour, Date, Place	Summary of Events and Information	Remarks and references to Appendices
	The fact that both officers of the left party became casualties and the state of the hostile wire led to confusion. Further report marked C.C.2, C.3 + C.4 is attached.	
	The Battalion was relieved in the afternoon of 11th and became the Brigade support. Two companies and half the Lewis guns came under the orders of the right sub-section commander and were situated in the ENCLOSURE. These two companies were A + C. B + D companies and the remainder of the Lewis guns were under the left sub-section commander and were in PIP STREET and DUKE STREET respectively. Bn. H.Q moved to PHILOSOPHE EAST.	[illegible]
12th JULY 1916 PHILOSOPHE EAST.	Remained in Brigade Support.	[illegible]
13th " " "	" " " "	[illegible]
14th " " "	" " " "	[illegible]
15 " " "	" " " " Sergt Major DEXTER. R.MUNSTER FUS joined the Battalion	[illegible]
16th LOOS.	The Bn relieved the 7th Bn R IRISH FUSILIERS during the afternoon. Companies were situated as on 7th inst except that C Company became the left company and B the left centre. Sergt Major CALLACHER left the Bn for employment in ENGLAND.	[illegible]
17th " "	Situated as above.	[illegible]
18th " "	" " "	[illegible]

(73989) W4141—463. 400,000. 9/14. H.&J.Ltd. Forms/C. 2118/10.

Instructions regarding War Diaries and Intelligence Summaries are contained in F. S. Regs., Part II. and the Staff Manual respectively. Title pages will be prepared in manuscript.

WAR DIARY
or
INTELLIGENCE SUMMARY.
(Erase heading not required.)

Army Form C. 2118.

Hour, Date, Place	Summary of Events and Information	Remarks and references to Appendices
19th JULY 1916 LOOS	The Bn was relieved by 9th Bn R DUBLIN FUSILIERS, and proceeded to SOUTH HUTS, MAZINGARBE. A noticeable point during the last three days was his marked inactivity. Up to within five minutes of the relief being completed the total casualties for the three days was two other ranks wounded. During the four days 7th–11th JULY our casualties had been 42. The enemy shelled our trenches heavily for about 10 minutes while the relieved companies were marching out. He used 4.2s, light guns, and mortars. Our casualties were four other ranks.	S.W.
20th JULY 1916 MAZINGARBE.	Remained in billets	S.W.
21st " " FOSSE WAY.	The battalion relieved the 6/7th R. SCOTS FUSILIERS as the Bn in brigade reserve in the HULLOCH SECTION. A Coy was in 10th AVENUE South of HULLOCH ROAD. B Coy in O.B. 4. C Coy in O.B. 1. D Coy in CURLEY CRESCENT. Bn HdQrs was at the junction of FOSSE WAY + CURLEY CRESCENT.	S.W.
22nd " " " "	Situated as above.	S.W.
23rd " " " "	" " "	
24th " " " "	The Bn was relieved by 9th Bn. R. DUBLIN FUSILIERS and proceeded to SOUTH HUTS MAZINGARBE as part of the brigade in divisional reserve.	S.W.

(73989) W4141—463. 400,000. 9/14. H.&J.Ltd. Forms/C. 2118/10.

Instructions regarding War Diaries and Intelligence Summaries are contained in F. S. Regs., Part II. and the Staff Manual respectively. Title pages will be prepared in manuscript.

WAR DIARY
or
INTELLIGENCE SUMMARY.
(Erase heading not required.)

Army Form C. 2118.

Hour, Date, Place	Summary of Events and Information	Remarks and references to Appendices
25th JULY 1916 MAZINGARBE	Remained in divisional reserve. The following Officers' and NCOs' and men's names were submitted for reward as follows in connection with the raid on 11th inst. Capts GALVIN, EATON Lts KINGHAN A.E. and SARGINT (7th Bn) for military cross. Sergt MURPHY J.J for D.C.M. No 20529 L/C GARLAND 20930 L/C D. CAIRNS and 22860 Pte Mc GILL for military medal Lts BRYARS and SPARKS and No 3842 Pte D. McMULLEN for a divisional parchment certificate.	S.W.
26th " "	Remained in divisional reserve.	S.W.
27th " "	" " " "	
28th " "	" " " "	S.W.
29th " "	" " " " *	S.W.
30th " "	" " " "	
31st " RESERVE TRENCH. 14 BIS.	The Bn relieved the 6th Bn CONNAUGHT RANGERS in the right sub-section of the 14 BIS SECTION. Companies were situated as follows. A Coy in RESERVE TRENCH, D Coy on the right, B Coy in the centre, D Coy on the left.	S.W.
	* The following officers joined the Bn on 29th. 2nd Lts A.L. DOBBIN, J. LEONARD, L. SHORTLAND-BALL, H. SMYTH C. PICKETT, W. KEANE, C. LEWIS, R. PRESTON.	

S. Walcott Lt Col.
Comdg 8 R. Irish Fus.

Secret.

W 289

SCHEME FOR BATTALION RAID.

1 OBJECT. To inflict casualties on the enemy, capture prisoners, obtain identification, damage trench mortars & machine guns.

2 BOUNDARIES OF RAID. Shown on attached sketch. The map references are as follows:-

A.	M 5d 72·52.	D.	M 6C 10·47.
B.	M 5d 80·37.	E.	M 6C 03·53.
C.	M 6C 10·40.	F.	M 5d 95·60.

(Reference trench MAP LENS 36^c S.W.1.)

3. STRENGTH OF PARTY. 4 Officers, 12 N.C.O.s & 50 men. Supporting party 1 officer & 38.

4 DESCRIPTION of AREA TO BE RAIDED. The point marked G on attached sketch is thought to be an important place where damage could be inflicted. The rectangular system of trenches between C & F is believed to contain mine shafts. Photographs 2A 175 dated 17.5.16 gives the following information (surmised):-

Trench mortars at H & K.
machine gun at L.
3 dugouts between B & E.

The Trench south of G is unimportant. Sap A is probably joined to enemy's front line near B by means of a Russian sap. The junction of Sap F is also probably blinded. Information obtained thro' prisoners:-

machine guns are at M. N. P. Q.
Trench Mortars are at L & R.
Company H. Quarters at S.
Half-dug trenches exist between A & F, also between B & M.

5 PREPARATION. Artillery and trench mortars to cut wire at least two days before that fixed for the raid. Should it be found impossible, owing to the closeness of the two front-lines, to carry this out by means of artillery the wire should be cut by Bangalore torpedoes by the unit in the line. The points where wire is to be cut are T. U & E.

Stokes Guns & mortars to fire at intervals during the two previous days on the enemy's side of HART'S & HARRISONS CRATERS, and on enemy's line between these points.

6 METHOD OF ATTACK.

(a) One party consisting of 2 officers, 6 N.C.O.s & 25 men to raid area A B G. V. This party will be divided into the following groups and carry out the following tasks:-

Group I. Cross enemy's wire at T & U, enter sap A half way down & advance to A. Task:- to overcome enemy at A, capture prisoners if possible & 2 men to return with him at once to our front line. Remainder of party to hold Sap A & prevent attack from the west.

Group II. Cross enemy's wire at T, enter front line and form a block at B.

Group III. To enter enemy's front line at same place & raid trench G.

Group IV. To enter enemy's front line at same place but not to go further than V. all dugouts to be bombed.

(b). 2nd party consisting of 2 officers, 6 N.C.O.s & 25 men to enter enemy's trench at E & raid area F. E. D. C. W. This party will be divided into the following groups & carry out the following tasks:-

Group V. To enter enemy's sap F half way down & work towards F & to act in the same way as Group I as regards prisoners.

Group VI. To enter enemy's line at E & bomb towards W but not to pass that point.

SHEET II.

Group VII. To enter enemy's line at E, follow Group VI to W & then to bomb from W to C & establish a block at this point.

Group VIII. To enter enemy's line at E & bomb to D.

There will be no signal for these parties to rush the trenches.
No artillery to fire until the raiding party has reached the hostile trenches.
Barrage will be formed on the enemy's communication trenches.
Suggested points for barrage X.R.Y.Z.J. Stokes guns will fire on P.
Lewis guns to fire on X, L & J.
The supporting party will not leave their front line unless word is sent by O.C. raid to assist withdrawal.

7. TIME TABLE. At zero Nos I. II. III. & IV groups to be in position between a–b & nos V VI VII & VIII groups to be in DEAD MAN'S SAP.

At zero all these groups to rush to enemy's line.

0.2 Artillery barrage.
0.20 Raiders to return.
0.35 Artillery to cease fire.
} The zero will be notified later.

8. THE RETURN SIGNAL Three long blasts of a Strombus horn together with G's sounded on the bugle.

9. COUNTERSIGN. will be made known to every man prior to starting.

10. DRESS & EQUIPMENT. Bayonet men will have torches fixed to their rifles & 50 rounds of ammunition.

Bombers will carry 12 bombs & a bludgeon.
Carriers will carry 36 bombs & a bludgeon.
Bayonet men will carry rifles & bayonets fixed, 6 Mills & 3 P. bombs.
N.C.O's will be armed with revolvers & 24 rounds of ammunition.
Every third man will carry a pair of 'Shear' wire cutters.
All men will carry as little equipment as possible.
Each group will carry a new tracing tape the end of which will be fixed at the point of leaving our front line. These tapes will be unrolled on going across to show the best line of withdrawal. All means of identification will be removed before leaving our trenches. The only exception to this being that the identity discs will be retained but the name of the regiment scraped off by means of a knife.
All men will be warned before leaving that in the event of their being taken prisoner, they must not answer any questions regarding positions of machine guns, mortars or any military subject.
The only information they must give is their name & number (not the regiment or battalion).

2. 7. 16.

~~Signed~~ ?
S. [signature] Lt Col
Comdg 8th R. Irish Fus.

Vol 7

49/16

W A R D I A R Y.

8th Royal Irish Fusiliers

MONTH OF AUGUST, 1916.

VOLUME:- 7

Army Form C. 2118.

WAR DIARY
or
~~INTELLIGENCE~~ SUMMARY.
(Erase heading not required.)

Instructions regarding War Diaries and Intelligence Summaries are contained in F. S. Regs., Part II. and the Staff Manual respectively. Title pages will be prepared in manuscript.

8th Bn. R. IRISH. FUSILIERS.

Hour, Date, Place	Summary of Events and Information	Remarks and references to Appendices
1st August 1916. RESERVE TRENCH 14 BIS.	The Bn. was situated as on 31.7.16. namely D, B, C in the right, centre, and left of the front line and "A" Coy in reserve. C Coy in the neighbourhood of the CHALK PIT was worried considerably by heavy minenwerfers. Trenches were much damaged but casualties were very light. D Coy's support line was damaged by 5.9s.	Sig.
2nd Augt 1916. ditto.	Situated as above. Notification received that No 20529 L/C GARLAND, 20930 L/C D. CAIRNS and 22860 Pte McGILL have been awarded the MILITARY MEDAL. Divisional parchment Certificates were received for the following. Capts GALVIN + EATON Lt A.E. KINGHAN. and Sergt J.J. MURPHY in addition to those for the above mentioned men. The enemy was much quieter.	Sig.
3rd Augt 1916 ditto.	A ~~qu~~ quiet day. Lt + QrMr F.E. DOWNER joined the Bn.	
4th Augt. 1916. 10th AVENUE	The Bn was relieved by 7th Bn. R. IRISH FUSILIERS. The relief Commenced at 4.30 pm. and was complete by 6 pm. The Bn became the Brigade support. A Coy was attached to the 7th Bn and remained in RESERVE TRENCH. The casualties during the four days in the front line were five wounded. This was surprisingly light considering the activity of the hostile heavy trench mortars. A draft of 37 other ranks joined the Bn.	Sig.
5th Augt 1916. "	Remained in Brigade Support.	Sig.

(73989) W4141—463. 400,000. 9/14. H.&J.Ltd. Forms/C. 2118/10.

2

Army Form C. 2118.

WAR DIARY
or
~~INTELLIGENCE SUMMARY.~~
(Erase heading not required.)

Instructions regarding War Diaries and Intelligence Summaries are contained in F. S. Regs., Part II. and the Staff Manual respectively. Title pages will be prepared in manuscript.

8th Bn R. IRISH FUSILIERS.

Hour, Date, Place	Summary of Events and Information	Remarks and references to Appendices
6th AUGUST 1916 10th AVENUE	Remained in Bde. Support	[illegible]
7th " "	" " "	[illegible]
8th " RESERVE TRENCH.	Relieved the 7th Bn in the ~~left~~ front line and also relieved part of 7th Bn R. INNISKILLING FUSILIERS between POSEN ALLEY and boyau 61. The Bn front now extended from POSEN ALLEY on the left to Boyau 52. Companies were situated as follows. B Coy Boyau 52 - 56 (inclusive). D Coy Boyau 56 - 61 (exclusive) A Coy Boyau 61 - 64 (inclusive). C Coy in reserve finding one platoon in MEATH TRENCH.	[illegible]
9th " " "	Situated as above.	[illegible]
10th " " "	" " " Notification received that No Sergt J. J. MURPHY has been granted the Distinguished Conduct Medal.	[illegible]
11th	Draft of 5 other ranks joined the Bn. Situated as above. 2nd Lt. J. S. LEONARD wounded.	[illegible]
12th MAZINGARBE.	The Bn was relieved by 7th Bn. R. IRISH FUSILIERS and became the Brigade Reserve in NORTH HUTS, MAZINGARBE. Total casualties for the four days in the front line, one officer wounded and nine other ranks.	[illegible]
13th "	Remained in Brigade Reserve.	[illegible]
14th "	" " "	[illegible]

W4141—463. 400,000. 9/14. H.&J.Ltd. Forms/C. 2118/10.

Instructions regarding War Diaries and Intelligence Summaries are contained in F. S. Regs., Part II. and the Staff Manual respectively. Title pages will be prepared in manuscript.

WAR DIARY
or
INTELLIGENCE SUMMARY.
(Erase heading not required.)

Army Form C. 2118.

Hour, Date, Place	Summary of Events and Information	Remarks and references to Appendices
15th AUGt 1916 MAZINGARBE	Remained in Brigade Reserve. Draft of 10 other ranks joined	[illegible]
16th " " RESERVE TRENCH 14 BIS.	The Bn Relieved the 7th Bn R. IRISH FUSILIERS in the left Sub-Section 14 BIS. The three companies in the front line were C, D, A, from right to left. B. Coy was in reserve. Lt A.E. KINGHAN took over command of B Coy.	[illegible]
17th " " "	Situated as above. Notification received that Capt B. St J. GALVIN had been granted the Military Cross.	[illegible]
18th " " "	Situated as on 16th.	[illegible]
19th " " "	" " " "	[illegible]
20th " " 10th AVENUE	The Bn was relieved by 7th Bn R. IRISH FUSILIERS and became the Bn in Brigade Support. C. Coy was in gun trench and the remainder in 10th AVENUE. Total casualties in the four days was 7.	[illegible]
27st " "	Situated as above.	[illegible]
22nd " " "	" " "	[illegible]
23rd " " "	" " " 2nd Lt. W.A. DIXON joined the Bn	[illegible]
24th " " "	" " "	[illegible]
25th " HOUCHIN.	The Bn was relieved by the 6th Bn R. WARWICKS. After relief the Bn marched to HOUCHIN to be billeted. A draft of 65 other ranks joined from the CONNAUGHT RANGERS.	[illegible]
26th "	Marched to LAPUGNOY leaving HOUCHIN at 2.20 pm. and arrived at about 5.15 pm. The Battalion marched very	[illegible]

(2989) W4141—463. 400,000. 9/14. H.&J.Ltd. Forms/C. 2118/10.

Instructions regarding War Diaries and Intelligence Summaries are contained in F. S. Regs., Part II. and the Staff Manual respectively. Title pages will be prepared in manuscript.

WAR DIARY
or
INTELLIGENCE SUMMARY.
(Erase heading not required.)

Army Form C. 2118.

Hour, Date, Place	Summary of Events and Information	Remarks and references to Appendices
	well considering they had been in the line for 5 months without coming out for divisional rest.	S.W.
27th AUGUST 1916. LAPUGNOY	Remained in billets.	S.W.
28th " "	" " "	
29th " SAILLY-LE-SEC	The Bn was ordered to proceed to SAILLY-LE-SEC. The transport paraded at 1 am. and with A Company who acted as loading party proceeded to FOUCQEREIL Station. The remainder paraded at 3 am. The train left at about 6 am. and proceeded to LONGEAU near AMIENS which was reached at 2.30 pm. After detraining the Bn. marched via BLANGY-TRONVILLE — AUBIGNY — CORBIE-VAUX-SUR-SOMME to SAILLY-LE-SEC which place was reached at 10 pm. The Bn was billeted together in one farm.	S.W.
30th " " "	Remained in billets.	S.W.
31st " HAPPY VALLEY near BRAY.	The Bn left SAILLY-LE-SEC at 7.30 am. and marched to the HAPPY VALLEY which place was reached about 10.15 am. The accomodation consisted of tents and worked out to about 18 men per tent.	S.W.

S.W. Watson Lt. Col.
Comg 8 R. Irish Fusiliers

(73989) W4141—463. 400,000. 9/14. H.&J.Ltd. Forms/C. 2118/10.

WAR DIARY

8th Royal Irish Fusiliers

FOR MONTH OF SEPTEMBER, 1916.

VOLUME 8

Instructions regarding War Diaries and Intelligence Summaries are contained in F. S. Regs., Part II. and the Staff Manual respectively. Title pages will be prepared in manuscript.

WAR DIARY
or
INTELLIGENCE SUMMARY.
(*Erase heading not required.*)

Army Form C. 2118.

(1)

8th Bn R. IRISH FUSILIERS.

Place	Date	Hour	Summary of Events and Information	Remarks and references to Appendices
HAPPY VALLEY near BRAY.	Sept 1st		Remained in camp.	Sms
"	2nd		" " " MAJOR E.W.P. UNIACKE D.S.O. rejoined.	Sms
"	3rd		Moved to the CITIDAL at 8.15 a.m.	
	"	7.30 p.m.	Verbal orders received to move to BILLON FARM. That place was reached about 11 p.m. when instructions were given for the Battalion to move on to take up a position in CASEMENT TRENCH about 300x S. of BERNAFAY WOOD on the MARICOURT–LONGUEVAL road. All packs were left behind and only the trench strength of the Battalion moved on. 20 officers only were taken. The remainder of the Battalion remained at BILLON FARM.	
CASEMENT TRENCH.	4th	3 a.m.	Arrived in position from BILLON FARM.	Sms
		1 p.m.	Received orders to move up in close support of 95th Infantry Brigade to be available in case of hostile attack near LEUZE WOOD. The position of trenches to be occupied was A.5.d. The guide provided from 95th Bde led the Bn to the wrong place and our intended position was not reached until 7 p.m. No sooner was the Bn in position than the enemy shelled the trenches inflicting between 20 and 30 casualties. Permission was obtained to move the Bn which place was reached about 9.30 p.m. MAJOR E.W.P. UNIACKE D.S.O. was wounded. Operation orders of 95th Bde of 5th are attached marked A1 A2 - A3	
CHIMPANZEE TRENCH	5th	5 p.m.	Orders received to relieve 1st Bn DEVONS in LEUZE WOOD. On arrival at their Battalion H.Q an order was received for them to establish a line in front of the wood from T 21 a 4.9 to T.21.d.0.5. their front line then being T.21.c 3.7 to	Sms
LEUZE WOOD		8.30 p.m.	T 27.a.7.7. As this order arrived at the time relief was taking place the 8th R. IRISH FUSILIERS undertook to carry out this order. This line was established and trenches dug during the night. The position of companies is shown on the attached sketch marked B.	

2353 Wt. W2544/1454 700,000 5/15 D. D. & L. A.D.S.S./Forms/C. 2118.

Army Form C. 2118.

(2)

Instructions regarding War Diaries and Intelligence Summaries are contained in F. S. Regs., Part II. and the Staff Manual respectively. Title pages will be prepared in manuscript.

WAR DIARY
or
INTELLIGENCE SUMMARY.
(Erase heading not required.)

8th R. IRISH FUSILIERS.

Place	Date	Hour	Summary of Events and Information	Remarks and references to Appendices
LEUZE WOOD	5th		The position held by the Battalion was far from secure owing to it being a salient with the flanks very insecure. The right flank was entirely unsupported, the nearest troops being in T 27 c and the enemy holding a trench from about T 27.b.0.4 running in front of COMBLES and also from the first point parallel to the wood to about T. 21.d. central. The next regiment on our left extended from about T.20.d 7.7 to the west with a platoon joining the wood at about T 21.c.0.3. In front of the wood the enemy's line was about 100x north and parallel to our front line.	
		11.50pm	A report was received from O.C. "D" Coy that the battalion was in position and that touch had been obtained with the enemy.	
	6th	2.30am	~~At~~ A message was received from 95th Brigade that 15th Brigade were held up by wire and machine gun fire. This message was timed 8.30pm. on 5th. The message ordered a bombing party to bomb down trench running SE. from the wood at T 27 a. 7.6 in order to assist 15th Bde. This order was repeated to "B" Coy. At the same time a message was sent to A Coy to take special precautions for the protection of their right flank.	
			During the night our heavies directed their fire on the wood causing considerable casualties to the Battalion. This took place during the whole of 6th and four messages were sent for them to lengthen range. A reply was received that ~~none~~ no heavies attached to 5th Division were firing within 1800x of the front edge of the wood.	
		8.30am	On visiting the wood at 8.30am. it was found that the S.W end of the wood was being shelled and that the approach to the wood was under constant snipers fire which caused numerous casualties. ~~It~~	
		9am	It was decided not to move Bn H.Q forward into the wood owing to the insecure state of the position and the difficulty of maintaining communication with the Brigade from that forward position.	
		9.am	Rations arrived in the low ground in T.26.a. but owing to hostile barrage and snipers fire it was found impossible to get these up to the companies.	

2353 Wt. W2544/1454 700,000 5/15 D. D. & L. A.D.S.S./Forms/C. 2118.

Instructions regarding War Diaries and Intelligence Summaries are contained in F. S. Regs., Part II. and the Staff Manual respectively. Title pages will be prepared in manuscript.

WAR DIARY
or
INTELLIGENCE SUMMARY.
(Erase heading not required.)

Army Form C. 2118.

8th Bn R. IRISH FUS.

(3)

Place	Date	Hour	Summary of Events and Information	Remarks and references to Appendices
LEUZE WOOD	6th	10.30am	Operation orders were received from 1st LONDON SCOTTISH framed on orders issued by 95th Bde. The 95th Bde orders were never received and a copy was obtained from 1st LONDON SCOTTISH and was to the following effect. "REFORM and LOSK – (code names of 8th R. IRISH FUS. and 1st LONDON SCOTTISH BM 231 dated 6th. AAA. The French have reached the railway in COMBLES and the 95th Infy. Bde are understood to be through LEUZE WOOD AAA. In order to fill up the gap between us and the French the 15th Bde are sending up a battalion to work through LEUZE WOOD to S.W. end of BOULEAUX and then swing S.E. to join up with French and thus cut off a party of Germans with M.G. who held up their attack yesterday by M.G fire from W of COMBLES AAA. Push patrols into BOULEAUX WOOD and reconnoitre ground in order to secure a good jumping off place for this battalion aaa. Arrange guides to take them through LEUZE WOOD AAA. Cover this advance with Lewis and M.G. fire AAA. Report result of bombing down trench from T 27 a.8.7 southwards AAA. Can you see French on your right if possible try and get in touch with them by visual or patrol AAA Address REFORM repeat LOSK. FRAY 8.30am." The orders issued by the 1st LONDON SCOTTISH undertook all these orders with the exception of reconnoitring the ground as a jumping off point. It will be noticed that no hour was stated in 95th Bde orders for the arrival of this Bn in LEUZE WOOD.	
		11.55am	The following message was sent to Companies. — 1. The French have reached the railway at COMBLES. In order to fill up the gap caused by 15th Bde being held up by MG fire a Bn of that Bde is being sent through LEUZE WOOD to the N.E corner from which place they will advance towards COMBLES and join up with the French at the same time cutting off the enemy holding trenches running E and N.E from T 27 a.8.7. 2. A+B Coys REFORM will cover the advance of this Bn by rifle and L.G fire. 3. A+D Coys will push out patrols into BOULEAUX WOOD and reconnoitre ground in order	

2353 Wt. W2544/1454 700,000 5/15 D. D. & L. A.D.S.S./Forms/C. 2118.

Instructions regarding War Diaries and Intelligence Summaries are contained in F. S. Regs., Part II. and the Staff Manual respectively. Title pages will be prepared in manuscript.

WAR DIARY
or
INTELLIGENCE SUMMARY.
(*Erase heading not required.*)

Army Form C. 2118.

8th Bn R. IRISH FUSILIERS.

Place	Date	Hour	Summary of Events and Information	Remarks and references to Appendices
			to secure a good jumping off place for the Bn mentioned in para 1.	
			4. The LONDON SCOTTISH are finding a bombing party to work down trench at T 27 a. 8. 7. This Bn is also finding guides to lead the Bn of 15th Bde through LEUZE WOOD.	
			5. REFORM is establishing a signalling post at the S.W. edge of LEUZE WOOD to transmit messages to Bn H.Q and establish communication with the French.	
			6. The hour of the operations stated in para 1 has not been stated in any order received and will be notified as soon as known.	
			7. Acknowledge.	
			11.55 am. 6.9.16.	
			The Bn mentioned in 95th Bde never arrived in LEUZE WOOD up to the time this battalion was relieved.	
		~~10.30 am~~	~~A Small par~~ The signal post mentioned in para 5 was set up by Sergt HOLTON assisted by Ptes GAVAGHAN and JONES under heavy fire and continued to work for four hours ~~until~~ during heavy hostile fire until the daylight lamp was broken by shell fire. Touch was obtained with batteries in rear but not with the French.	
		10.30 am.	A hostile patrol entered the wood from the E side but were driven off by our men leaving 2 dead and 2 wounded.	
			The enemy was active during the whole morning especially from the direction of T. 20. b.	
		7.30 pm.	The enemy made an organised counter attack on the front line. His attack came from the direction of BOULEAUX WOOD and from the E side of the wood. He also attacked the N corner of the wood. Our front line trench was driven in on the second line running diagonally through the wood and that trench was attacked from the east. The Second line held the enemy back and finally drove him out of the wood and	

2353 Wt. W2544/1454 700,000 5/15 D. D. & L. A.D.S.S./Forms/C. 2118.

Instructions regarding War Diaries and Intelligence Summaries are contained in F. S. Regs., Part II. and the Staff Manual respectively. Title pages will be prepared in manuscript.

WAR DIARY
or
INTELLIGENCE SUMMARY.
(Erase heading not required.)

Army Form C. 2118.

(5)

Place	Date	Hour	Summary of Events and Information	Remarks and references to Appendices
			the front trench was reoccupied by patrols by 10pm. Owing to darkness it was difficult to estimate his numbers and his casualties but they must have been numerous as many dead and wounded were seen inside the wood whereas there must have been more on the front edge where hand to hand fighting was heavy. The total prisoners left in our hands was one warrant officer and twenty other ranks.	
		1030pm	The battalion was relieved by the 1st LONDON SCOTTISH.	
			Our casualties during the day were heavy and were as follows.	
			Officers, killed Capt. G.W. EATON MC. Capt T.G. FITZPATRICK, Lt. AE. KINGHAN 2nd Lt L. SHORLAND-BALL	
			Officers, wounded. Capt E.M. GREVILLE 2nd Lts. L. ALLMAN-MARCHANT, C.E.W. NEAT, N.H. BIBLE, A.L. DOBBYN.	
			Other ranks, killed 36. wounded 95, missing 40, missing believed prisoners 2.	
			Total. 173. (this includes 21 casualties on 4th + 5th).	
ARROW HEAD COPSE	7th.		After relief the Bn marched to trenches W of ARROW HEAD COPSE. The Bn remained in trenches in reserve.	[illegible]
"	8th.		" " " "	[illegible]
"	9th.		On this date the 4th Army renewed the attack at 4.45 pm. The Battalion orders for the attack are attached.	[illegible]
		8.30pm	A message was received stating the Bn was placed under the orders of G.O.C. 47th Infy. Bde.	
			About 9 pm. a verbal message was received from 47th Infy. Bde stating they had been checked, the 48th Bde had taken GINCHY, the 168th Bde had gone ahead and that there was probably a gap between 47th + 168th Bde. The Bn was ordered to go to	

Instructions regarding War Diaries and Intelligence Summaries are contained in F. S. Regs., Part II. and the Staff Manual respectively. Title pages will be prepared in manuscript.

WAR DIARY
or
INTELLIGENCE SUMMARY.
(Erase heading not required.)

Army Form C. 2118.

(6)

8th Bn R. IRISH FUSILIERS.

Place	Date	Hour	Summary of Events and Information	Remarks and references to Appendices
			~~Go to~~ cross roads T.20.c 2.4. to meet O.C. 6th R. IRISH. An attack by 1½ Bns of 168th Bde had been ordered to attack on the right so as to cut off the enemy. On arrival at T.20.c.2.4. it was found that O.C. 6th R. IRISH had been killed but the O.C. 8th MUNSTERS said there was probably a gap between the two brigades. It was decided to move up one company to fill this gap when it was discovered. On returning to the Battalion an officer of 168th Bde was met quite close to the Bn H.Q. of 8th MUNSTERS who stated that his brigade joined on to 47th Infy Bde. It was therefore decided to retain the Battalion in close support of 47th Bde in case the enemy should counter attack them or drive them in when the 1½ Battalions of 168th Bde attacked on the right. They occupied a trench on the south side of the cross roads at T.20.c.2.4.	[illegible]
near GUILLEMONT	10th	4am	The 47th Infy Bde was relieved by the Guards division. The Battalion marched back to BILLON FARM without coming into action.	[illegible]
BILLON FARM	11th	4pm.	Marched via MORLANCOURT to SALLY-LE-SEC which place was reached at 9.30pm.	[illegible]
SAILLY-LE-SEC	12th		Remained in billets and reorganised.	[illegible]
"	13th		" " " " "	[illegible]
"	14th		" " "	[illegible]
"	15th		The Battalion was inspected by the G.O.C. 49th Infy Bde at 11.30am. Special order of the day dated 13th Sept is attached. 2nd Lt E.J. McMILLAN joined.	[illegible]
"	16th		Remained in billets.	[illegible]
"	17th		" " "	[illegible]

2353 Wt. W2544/1454 700,000 5/15 D. D. & L. A.D.S.S./Forms/C. 2118.

Instructions regarding War Diaries and Intelligence Summaries are contained in F. S. Regs., Part II. and the Staff Manual respectively. Title pages will be prepared in manuscript.

WAR DIARY
or
INTELLIGENCE SUMMARY.
(Erase heading not required.)

Army Form C. 2118.

(7)

Place	Date	Hour	Summary of Events and Information	Remarks and references to Appendices
SAILLY-LE-SEC.	Sept. 18th		Marched to CORBIE. The infantry of the Division was conveyed by French motor buses to HALLENCOURT. The embussment was very slowly carried out and the journey was also slow. HALLENCOURT was reached at about 9 p.m.	[illegible]
HALLENCOURT (near ABBEVILLE)	19th		Remained in billets.	[illegible]
"	20th		" " "	[illegible]
"	21st		Marched to PONT REMY for entrainment at 10.50 p.m.	[illegible]
BAILLEUL	22nd		Arrived and detrained at about 7.30 a.m. Marched to the neighbourhood of WESTOUTRE and billeted there for the night.	[illegible]
WESTOUTRE	23rd		Paraded at 1.45 to march to KEMMEL in order to relieve 38th and 78th Battns CANADIANS the 16th DIVISION having received orders to take over from 4th Canadian DIVISION. The Bn formed to Brigade Support and was disposed as follows. "A" Coy in STRONG POINTS 8, 9 & 10. B Coys in STRONG POINTS 11 & 12. Head Quarters and C & D Coys were in KEMMEL CHATEAU.	[illegible]
KEMMEL	24th		Situated as above.	[illegible]
"	25th		" " "	[illegible]
"	26th		" " "	[illegible]
"	27th		The Bn relieved the 7th Bn INNISKILLINGS in the right front line. A Coy occupied STRONG POINTS 8 & 9. B Coy REGENT STREET dugouts C Coy left front line and D Coy right front line. Bn Head Quarters was in FORT VICTORIA.	
FORT VICTORIA	28th		Situated as above. 2nd Lieuts S. TURNER and G.N. BLENNERHASSET joined.	[illegible]
"	29th		" " "	[illegible]
"				[illegible]

2353 Wt. W2544/1454 700,000 5/15 D. D. & L. A.D.S.S./Forms/C. 2118.

Instructions regarding War Diaries and Intelligence Summaries are contained in F. S. Regs., Part II. and the Staff Manual respectively. Title pages will be prepared in manuscript.

WAR DIARY
or
~~INTELLIGENCE SUMMARY.~~

(Erase heading not required.)

Army Form C. 2118.

(8)

Place	Date	Hour	Summary of Events and Information	Remarks and references to Appendices
FORT VICTORIA	Sept 30th		Situated as on 29th	S.W.
			During the month the following Officers' N.C.Os' and men's names were submitted for "immediate reward":–	
			MILITARY CROSS. 2nd Lts B. J. START. C. L. NAYLOR. J. E. REA A. L. DOBBYN.	
			D.C.M. No 15636 Pte B. JONES; 16636 " T. GAVAGHAN; 16814 Serg't J. HOLTON; 5380 " RAFFERTY; 22711 Pte P. BEECHER; 9498 Sgt P. DOUGAN; 20817 Cpl C. LAWRENCE	
			MILITARY MEDAL No 20460 Pte N. BRENNAN; 16729 " P. SWEENEY; 21001 " J. BRANNEY; 23124 " T. COOMBES; 11406 " BOYNE; 20908 " GORMAN; No 23114 Pte W. CARTER; 14845 Sgt W. LAMBERT; 16656 " J. HORGAN; 23847 Pte H. PARTRIDGE; 14843 Cpl DUKE; 20941 Pte P. GRIBBEN	
			Of the above, notification was received on 30th that the following had been granted Military Medals. Sgt RAFFERTY, Sgt DOUGAN, + Pte BEECHER.	
			S. W. Watson, Lt Col. Comg 8 R. Irish Fus.	

2353 Wt. W2544/1454 700,000 5/15 D. D. & L. A.D.S.S./Forms/C. 2118.

SPECIAL ORDER OF THE DAY.

BY

BRIGADIER-GENERAL P. LEVESON - GOWER,
COMMANDING 49TH. INFANTRY BRIGADE, 16TH. DIVISION,

WEDNESDAY, 13TH. SEPTEMBER, 1916.

o-o-o-o-o-o-o-o-o-o-o-o-o-o-o-o-o-o-o-o-o-o-o-o-o-o-o-o-o-o-o-o-o-o-o-

The Brigadier wishes to express his admiration for the conduct and gallantry of all ranks of the 49th. Infantry Brigade during the recent operations, during which they have added greatly to the honour of their Regiments and Corps and also their Country. The discipline displayed and the bravery exhibited by all ranks was most marked.

The following has been received from 16th. Division :-

"General Wilson Commanding IV Corps wires Hearty congratulations "to 16 Div. from IV Corps. AAA

South African Brigade wires to 16 Division Hearty congratulations "on your success Ends".

(sd) L.B.Brierley, Captain,
Staff Captain, 49th. Inf. Brigade.

[illegible]

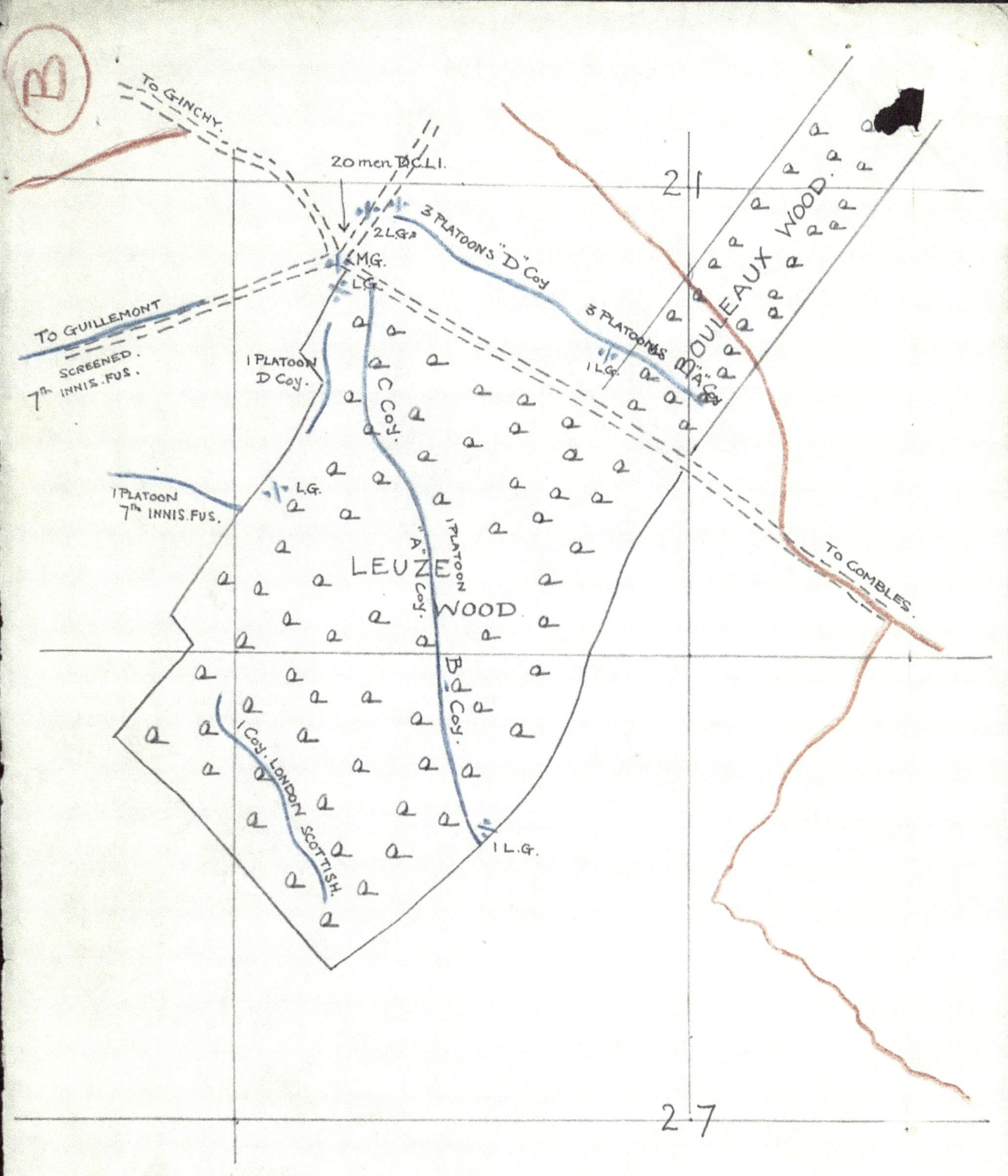

Distribution of Troops holding Leuze Wood at 8.30 a.m. 6.9.16.

Sides of squares = 500x.

Nearest troops on our right about 800x S. of wood.

Sw

8th R.Irish Fus.
--------------- W.412.

H.Qrs., 49th Inf. Bde.

Report on operations undertaken by the Btn. under my command between 7 th & 10th Sept. (in continuation of my W404).

7th Sept. Remained in trenches near ARROW HEAD COPSE.

8th Sept. Remained in trenches as above.

9th Sept. At about 8.30 p.m. a message was received to the effect that the Bn. was under orders of G.O.C. 47th Inf. Bde. An officer was sent to get communication with him on the telephone. At about 9 p.m. a verbal message was received from 47th Inf. Bde to the effect that the situation on the front of that Bde. was not clear, but it was believed that both brigades on the flanks had advanced whereas they were held up and that there was a gap in the line between 6th R. IRISH and the left Bn. of the brigade on the right.

I moved the battalion to ~~the~~ trenches near the cross roads T.20.c and went forward to consult with Colonel CURZON under whose orders I had been placed. I found that officer had been killed a short time before my arrival and that Colonel BROWN 8th Munsters was in command. He stated there was a gap in the line but was unable to give me information as to its extent or whereabouts and asked me to move up the Battalion to fill the gap. I said I would reconnoitre the gap and move one or more companies to fill the gap retaining the remainder in my hands. On leaving COL. BROWN'S H.Q. I found an officer of the LONDON SCOTTISH (the Division on our right who informed me that they joined the Inniskillings and that the latter regiment joined the 6th R.IRISH. It was then about midnight. I therefore decided to keep the Battalion where it was and to strengthen the trenches in case of hostile counter attack.

Col BROWN confirmed the message I had received from 47th Inf. Bde, as also did the officer of the LONDON SCOTTISH, that the division on our right was attacking across the front of 47th Inf. Bde., the enemy then being held in three sides of a square. This attack did not materialize during the period prior to relief.

The movements of the relieving unit was difficult to follow. No unit was relieving the battalion under my command and I therefore decided to remain in the ~~front line~~ the trenches until the GRENADIER GUARDS were in the front line. I withdrew the Battalion at 4 a.m.

During the time I was in these trenches a noticeable feature was the absence of larger shells than Whizzbangs sent over by the enemy.

3.35 p.m.
10.9.16

(Sd) S.- WATSON, Lt.Col.
Comdg. 8 R.Irish Fusiliers.

Copy No 7

W 406.

Secret.

Operation Order No 32

by

Lt.Col. S.T. WATSON Comdg 8 R. IRISH FUSILIERS.

Reference Map
GUILLEMONT Sheet 1/20000.

1/ The 4th Army will renew the attack on 9th Sept at an hour to be notified later.
XIV Corps is to capture the German position from T 27 b. 1.5½ – T. 21. d 5½ 2½ – Point 141.7 – the trench along the GINCHY-MORVAL road to trench junction T. 14 c. 5 4½ – T 14 a. 4. 2 and thence to road junction of trenches at T. 7 d. 4.0.
XV Corps will carry out a simultaneous operation on left of XIV Corps.

2/ The XIV Corps attack will be carried out by 56th Division on the right and 16th Div. on the left.
The dividing line between the 56th and 16th division will be from the GUILLEMONT – LEUZE WOOD road at T 20 d. 1.6. to trench junction at T 14 d 8½.4.
The dividing line between the 16th Division and 55th Division will be T 13 c. 6½. 1½. – T. 13. central — Trench junction T 7 d 4.0.

3/ The 16th Division attack will be carried out by 47th Inf. Bde. on right and

48th Inf. Bde on left.
Dividing line between brigades will be the GINCHY – WEDGWOOD road from present front line to T 20 a 1.6 (to 48th Inf. Bde) and thence the trench running to T 14 a 5. 4½ (to 47th Inf. Bde).

4. The objectives allotted to Brigades are as follows.

First Objective.

(a). 47th Inf. Bde. T 20 b 4½ 3½. – point where trench crosses GINCHY - LEUZE WOOD road at T 14 c 3½ 1½.

Second Objective

Trench junction at T 14 d 8½. 4 (exclusive) – point where trench crosses road at T 14 c 5. 4½ (inclusive)

(b). 48th Inf. Bde. First Objective

Point where trench crosses GINCHY – LEUZE WOOD road at T 14 c 3½ 1½ (exclusive) – road junction T 13 d. 7. 3½ – T 13 (Central).

Second Objective.

Point where trench crosses road at T 14 c 5. 4½ (exclusive) – T 14 a 4 2 – trench junction T. 7. d. 4 0.

5. At zero the 47th & 48th Inf. Bdes will advance to their first objectives and consolidate.

At zero plus 40 minutes they will advance to the 2nd objective and consolid

6. Strongpoints will be established at T 20 a.8.9., T14c(central) T14a 4.2. and T 7d.4.0.

7. The 49th Infy. Bde will be in divisional reserve.

8. 7th INNISKILLINGS will be in GUILLEMONT with Bn H.Q at T19c.9.4.

8th INNISKILLINGS will be in trenches between T.19b.0.3. and T19d.10.7. with ~~7th R IRISH FUSILIERS~~ Bn H.Q at T19a.9.8

7th R. IRISH FUSILIERS in old British line from the Gridiron to T20b8.9 with Bn HQ at T19c 2.4.

Bde H.Q will be in BERNAFAY WOOD S 28 b(central)

9. The Bn will not move from its present position unless orders are given to that effect for tactical purposes.

10. Dumps for water, ammunition, flares &c are being formed as follows. near ARROW HEAD COPSE, T19b.0.2 and T19d5.4

11. A forward brigade report centre will be at the Quarry at T19c.0.3

12. Contact aeroplanes will fly over the line. Should the Bn be ~~[illegible]~~ used as reinforcements to the front line Officers within 50 yards of the front

[illegible]

turn over

and at 6 a.m. or Sept 10th.

13. O.C. Companies will arrange to collect
sufficient am S.A.A. and bombs in the
the vacinity of their trenches to issue
an extra 100 rounds S.A.A. + two bombs
to each man should orders be given
to that effect.

14. Any prisoners will be taken to the
cage on the MONTUBAN – CARNOY road
at A.8.a.8.4. Receipts will be obtained
for prisoners and the escort will
return to the Battalion.

15. Should the enemy shell the present
position held by A Coy. the O.C. of that
company will arrange to occupy the
trench about 50 yards in rear of his
present position.

16. Two days rations have been issued
tonight. All ranks must be warned
to this effect. Water bottles must be
filled by 9 a.m. tomorrow and not used
unless orders are given to that effect.

17. Two guns of the 49th MGC are attached
to the Bn and will be accommodated
with A. Coy. In the event of these
guns being ordered to move forward
O.C. A Coy. will detail four
men to assist these guns to move

forward.

18 Should the Bn be moved forward O.C. Coys will send reports on the situation as frequently as possible.

19 Acknowledge.

8.9.16.

Capt & Adj.
8 R. Irish Fusiliers

Copy No 1 A. Coy.
" " 2 B Coy
" " 3 C Coy.
" " 4 D Coy.
" " 5. G.O.C. 49th Infy. Bde.
" " 6. M.G.O. 49th M.G. Coy.
" " 7 & 8 War Diary.

WAR DIARY
or
~~INTELLIGENCE SUMMARY.~~
(*Erase heading not required.*)

Instructions regarding War Diaries and Intelligence Summaries are contained in F. S. Regs., Part II. and the Staff Manual respectively. Title pages will be prepared in manuscript.

Army Form C. 2118.

(17)

8th Bn R. IRISH FUSILIERS

Place	Date	Hour	Summary of Events and Information	Remarks and references to Appendices
FORT VICTORIA near KEMMEL	Oct. 1st		Situated as on last day of September	
"	2nd		As above.	
"	3rd		The Bn was relieved by 7th Bn R. INNISKILLING FUSILIERS and became the battalion in Brigade reserve at KEMMEL SHELTERS.	
KEMMEL SHELTERS	4th		In brigade reserve.	
"	5th		" " " The following names were submitted for the New Years Honours list. MAJOR BOARDMAN Capt R.W KINGHAN, Capt FITZPATRICK (killed in action) Lt A.E. KINGHAN (killed in action) Lt CRILLY. Lt & Qr Mr DOWNER. Rev. Father DOYLE. ~~Coy S M KERR~~ C.S.M. BRIEN (killed in action) a/C.S.M. O'NEILL.	
"	6th		Remained in Brigade reserve.	
"	7th		" " " "	
"	8th		" " " "	
"	9th		The Bn relieved the 7th Bn R. INNISKILLING FUSILIERS in the right sub-section	
FORT VICTORIA near KEMMEL	10th		Situated as above.	
	11th		" " "	
"	12th		" " " ~~Lt Col. S.T. WATSON [illegible] command of 17th Bn Capt O'DONNELL [illegible] command of 1st Bn [illegible] REGT.~~	
"	13th		Situated as above. MAJOR T.H. BOARDMAN took over command of 8th R. INNISKILLING FUS vice Lt.Col. DALZELL-WALTON (killed in action) from 11th Sept 1916. (Bde order 1066 d/12.10.16)	

2353 Wt. W2544/1454 700,000 5/15 D. D. & L. A.D.S.S./Forms/C. 2118.

Instructions regarding War Diaries and Intelligence Summaries are contained in F. S. Regs., Part II. and the Staff Manual respectively. Title pages will be prepared in manuscript.

WAR DIARY

or

~~INTELLIGENCE SUMMARY.~~

(Erase heading not required.)

Army Form C. 2118.

8th Bn. R. IRISH FUSILIERS. (2)

Place	Date	Hour	Summary of Events and Information	Remarks and references to Appendices
FORT VICTORIA KEMMEL.	14th		Notification received that the following honours had been granted Lt. Col. S.T. WATSON a D.S.O. 2nd Lt C. L NAYLOR and 2nd Lt A.L. DOBBYN Military Cross. The Bn was relieved by 7th Bn. R. INNISKILLING FUS and became Divisional Reserve at LOCRE.	S.W.
LOCRE	15th		The Bn was amalgamated with 7th Bn. R. IRISH FUSILIERS under the title 7/8th R. IRISH FUS and under the temporary command of Capt T. F. O'DONNELL 7th Bn. Lt Col. WATSON was ordered to proceed to take over command of 1st Bn. The QUEENS.	S.W.
			S.T. Watson Lt. Col. Comg 8 R. Irish Fusiliers.	

2353 Wt. W2544/1454 700,000 5/15 D. D. & L. A.D.S.S./Forms/C. 2118.

7/8 (S) Battn. 'Royal Irish' Fusiliers

Instructions regarding War Diaries and Intelligence Summaries are contained in F. S. Regs., Part II. and the Staff Manual respectively. Title pages will be prepared in manuscript.

WAR DIARY
or
~~INTELLIGENCE SUMMARY.~~

October 1916

(Erase heading not required.)

Army Form C. 2118.

Place	Date	Hour	Summary of Events and Information	Remarks and references to Appendices
LOCRE	15th 10.16		The amalgamation of the 7 (S) Battn. and 8 (S) Battn ROYAL IRISH FUSILIERS commenced on 15' inst under the temporary command of CAPT T.F. O'DONNELL M C	W.H. Stitt
do	16.10.16		continued the amalgamation.	W.H.S.
KEMMEL SHELTERS	17.10.16		The Battn. moved to KEMMEL SHELTERS where it relieved the 2. ROYAL IRISH REGIMENT.	W.H.S.
do	18.10.16		Drill, training.	W.H.S.
do	19.10.16		do	W.H.S.
KEMMEL CHATEAU.	20.10.16		The Battn. relieved the 2nd. ROYAL IRISH REGIMENT in the left subsector on the 20' inst. during the afternoon. About 4PM our artillery fired several rounds at enemys front and support lines opposite N29.4. Enemy retaliated with about 20 minenwerfer and medium TM's.	W.H.S.
	21.10.16.		Our artillery and T.M's were active firing on hostile Support trench apparently with good effect. During the day enemy shelled S.P.10 with 5.9's. Nine shells including one dud fell doing considerable damage	W.H.S.

T.2134. Wt. W708–776. 500000. 4/15. Sir J. C. & S.

7/8 (S) Battn. Royal Irish Fusiliers

Instructions regarding War Diaries and Intelligence Summaries are contained in F. S. Regs., Part II. and the Staff Manual respectively. Title pages will be prepared in manuscript.

WAR DIARY

or

~~INTELLIGENCE SUMMARY.~~

(Erase heading not required.)

October 1916

Army Form C. 2118.

Place	Date	Hour	Summary of Events and Information	Remarks and references to Appendices
KEMMEL CHATEAU	22.10.16		Our artillery shelled enemy trenches during day. During the afternoon our T.M's were active.	W.H.S.
do	23.10.16		During night 22/23 our Lewis Guns swept enemys parapets and fired on working party. During the afternoon we shelled enemys lines with Stokes, 2" T.M. 18 pounders and Howitzers causing considerable damage, especially opposite N.30.3 and N.24.1. Enemy retaliated strongly.	W.H.S.
do	24.10.16		Our Lewis guns traversed enemys wire on night 23/24, dispersing a working party. The day passed remarkably quietly.	W.H.S.
do	25.10.16		There was an average amount of sniping and M.G. fire during the night. Our artillery and T.M's were active, especially on enemys wire.	W.H.S.
KEMMEL SHELTERS.	26.10.16		Our T.M's were very active cutting enemys wire opposite PECKHAM FARM. Enemy retaliated heavily with T.M's and minenwerfer. The 2 R IRISH REGT relieved this Battn in the left subsection. On relief the Battn moved to KEMMEL SHELTERS becoming Brigade Reserve.	W.H.S.
	27–31 10.16		Training in Bde Reserve. Bombing, sniping, Lewis Gun drill, and close order drill	W.H.S.

[signature] Lieut-Col
7/8 Battn. Royal Irish Fusiliers

T2134. Wt. W708—776. 500000. 4/15. Sir J. C. & S.

16 DIVISION

49 BDE

7/8th Bn Roy Ir. Fus.

~~Oct~~ 6. NOV 1916 – Feb 1918

DISBANDED FEB 1918

~~49 Bde H.Q.~~

2. J. L albris

W A R D I A R Y .

F O R

MONTH OF NOVEMBER, 1916.

VOLUME 2.

7/8th R. Irish Fusiliers.

Vol 10

7/8 (S) Battn. ROYAL IRISH FUSILIERS.

Instructions regarding War Diaries and Intelligence Summaries are contained in F. S. Regs., Part II. and the Staff Manual respectively. Title pages will be prepared in manuscript.

WAR DIARY
or
~~INTELLIGENCE SUMMARY.~~ November 1916.
(Erase heading not required.)

Army Form C. 2118.

Place	Date	Hour	Summary of Events and Information (Ref WYCHAETE map. sheet 28 S.W.)	Remarks and references to Appendices
KEMMEL SHELTERS	1.11.16		The Battn moved from KEMMEL SHELTERS. and relieved the 2. ROYAL IRISH REGT. in the left subsection of the RIGHT SECTOR during the afternoon. The evening passed quietly. Weather very wet. 2 Coys in front line.	W.H.S.
KEMMEL CHATEAU.	2.11.16		During night 1/2 enemy's snipers were very active. During the afternoon enemy T.M. were active. Our Stokes guns replied with 50 rounds silencing enemy	W.H.S.
	3.11.16		During the night a searchlight ~~silenced~~ swept our parapets. Our Lewis guns swept enemy parapet during the night. Situation very quiet during the ~~night~~ day	W.H.S.
	4.11.16		The morning passed quietly. T.M's were active on both sides. From 3.15 PM to 3.30 PM the whole Divisional Artillery and Corps Heavy Artillery bombarded the enemy's trenches in the neighbourhood of PETIT BOIS and MAEDELSTEDE FARM and behind these places. At the same time the T.M bombarded enemy's trenches opposite the whole Divisional Front. After this bombardment we changed the Coys round and ~~Co~~ held the front line with 1 Coy and 6 Lewis Guns. The evening was uneventful. 2 Lieut. W.M.A KEANE killed in action.	W.H.S.

T2134. Wt. W708—776. 500000. 4/15. Sir J. C. & S.

7/8 (S) Battn. ROYAL IRISH. FUSILIERS.

Instructions regarding War Diaries and Intelligence Summaries are contained in F. S. Regs., Part II. and the Staff Manual respectively. Title pages will be prepared in manuscript.

WAR DIARY
or
~~INTELLIGENCE SUMMARY.~~
(Erase heading not required.)

NOVEMBER 1916

Army Form C. 2118.

Place	Date	Hour	Summary of Events and Information (Ref. Maps WYCHAETE and sheet 28. S.W.)	Remarks and references to Appendices
KEMMEL CHATEAU.	5.11.16		The night 4/5 passed quietly. Enemy shelled KETCHEN AVENUE during the morning. Our T.M's were active during the day. The "strafe" carried out on 4" inst seems to have silenced enemy.	W.H.S.
	6.11.16		During the night our Lewis Guns fired on wiring parties. Enemy fired at S.P.10 doing some damage. Our artillery silenced the enemy. Usual amount of sniping.	W.H.S.
KEMMEL SHELTERS.	7.11.16		The morning passed quietly. The 2. Royal IRISH REGT. relieved the Battn. during the afternoon. On relief the moved to KEMMEL SHELTERS thus becoming Bde. Reserve	W.H.S
	8.11.16		Baths, cleaning, inspecting, re-equipping	W.H.S.
	9.11.16		do.	W.H.S.
	10.11.16		Training. etc	W.H.S.
	11.11.16		The Battn. was inspected by G.O.C 49. Inf Bde. Training continued in afternoon	W.H.S.
	12.11.16		Training	
KEMMEL CHATEAU	13.11.16		The Battn. relieved the 2. ROYAL IRISH REGIMENT in the left subsection on 13 inst. Dispositions as follows – A Coy and 2 platoons C Coy in front line. 2 platoons C Coy in SP.10. ~~2 platoons~~ B Coy YOUNG STREET. D Coy FORT REGINA and CHATEAU. The night passed quietly. Our Lewis Guns and snipers were active.	W.H.S.

2353 Wt. W2544/1454 700,000 5/15 D. D. & L. A.D.S.S./Forms/C. 2118.

7/8 (S) Battn ROYAL IRISH FUSILIERS

Instructions regarding War Diaries and Intelligence Summaries are contained in F. S. Regs., Part II. and the Staff Manual respectively. Title pages will be prepared in manuscript.

WAR DIARY
or
~~INTELLIGENCE SUMMARY.~~ NOVEMBER 1916
(Erase heading not required.)

Army Form C. 2118.

Place	Date	Hour	Summary of Events and Information	Remarks and references to Appendices
KEMMEL CHATEAU	14.11.16		Enemy seems to be very nervous; as he sends up a large number of very lights. Hostile anti-aircraft guns very active. The day passed quietly. Our snipers were active during night.	W.H.S
"	15.11.16		To the right of this Battn front between 11.30 AM and 12.30 PM our artillery and TM's bombarded enemys trenches. Retaliation was very feeble. On night 15/16 our patrols were active	W.H.S
"	16.11.16		About mid day hostile aerial torpedoes and TM's active. During the afternoon B Coy relieved A Coy and 2 platoons of C Coy from SP10 relieved the 2 platoons in front line. During the night hostile TM's retaliated on our front for raid carried out by 109 Bde	W.H.S
"	17.11.16.		The night 16/17 passed quietly. During the afternoon our TM's and artillery bombarded the enemys trenches opposite this Brigade, paying special attention to suspected T.M. emplacements. Enemys retaliation very slight.	W.H.S
"	18.11.16		During night 17/18 our Lewis Guns traversed enemys wire. Nothing unusual to report during the day. At night our patrols were active.	W.H.S
"	19.11.16		The morning passed quietly. During the afternoon the 2 ROYAL IRISH REGT. relieved this Battn. On relief, this ~~Bn~~ Battn. moved to KEMMEL SHELTERS	W.H.S

2353 Wt. W2544/1454 700,000 5/15 D. D. & L. A.D.S.S./Forms/C. 2118.

7/8 (S) BATTN. ROYAL IRISH. FUSILIERS.

Instructions regarding War Diaries and Intelligence Summaries are contained in F. S. Regs., Part II. and the Staff Manual respectively. Title pages will be prepared in manuscript.

WAR DIARY
or
~~INTELLIGENCE SUMMARY.~~
(Erase heading not required.)

NOVEMBER. 1916.

Army Form C. 2118.

Place	Date	Hour	Summary of Events and Information	Remarks and references to Appendices
KEMMEL SHELTERS.	20.11.16		Re-equipping and training. On 22nd. a route march took place	
	24.11.16		The Battn relieved the 2 ROYAL IRISH REGT in the left sub-section, right sector	W.H.S.
			About 10.0 P.M enemy bombarded our front line with TM's, rifle grenades, and field artillery. This appeared to be part of a "Straffe" which was directed chiefly against the Battn. on our right. The enemy appear to have brought up more artillery into this sector. Our artillery retaliated vigorously, silencing the enemy.	W.H.S.
KEMMEL CHATEAU	25.11.16		During the night 24/25 our Lewis Guns were active. The day passed quietly. There was a little sniping. Weather misty and damp.	W.H.S.
			There was a little T.M activity on both sides.	W.H.S.
	26.11.16		The day passed uneventfully. Considerable aerial activity on both sides as weather was very dry and atmosphere	
	27.11.16		clear. Our patrols were active at night.	W.H.S.
			Our aeroplanes were active but enemy's anti aircraft guns fired feebly. There was the	W.H.S.
	28.11.16		usual amount of Lewis and M.G fire at night.	
			Enemy snipers more active than usual. The day passed quietly.	W.H.S.
	29.11.16		During the afternoon the Battn. was relieved by the 2 ROYAL IRISH REGT. and on	
KEMMEL SHELTERS	30.11.16		relief being completed moved into Bde. Reserve at KEMMEL SHELTERS.	W.H.S.
			During the month the trenches occupied alternately by the 2 R IRISH REGT. and this Battn have been greatly improved, chiefly by drainage. A great amount of labour has been spent on KEMMEL SHELTERS with very good results. The enemy seem to have brought up more artillery to this area.	W.H.S.

[illegible signature] Lieut. Col
Commdg 7/8 (S) Battn. Royal Irish Fusiliers.

2/12/16

2353 Wt. W2544/1454 700,000 5/15 D. D. & L. A.D.S.S./Forms/C. 2118.

3 J.
A.M.

WAR DIARY FOR MONTH OF DECEMBER, 1916.

VOLUME 2

7/8th R. Irish Fusiliers

Vol XI

7/8th Battn. Royal Irish Fusiliers

Instructions regarding War Diaries and Intelligence Summaries are contained in F. S. Regs., Part II. and the Staff Manual respectively. Title pages will be prepared in manuscript.

WAR DIARY
or
~~INTELLIGENCE SUMMARY.~~
(Erase heading not required.)

DECEMBER. 1916.

Army Form C. 2118.

Place	Date	Hour	REF WYCHAETE map sheet 28 S.W. Summary of Events and Information	Remarks and references to Appendices
KEMMEL SHELTERS	1.12.16		Battn. in Bde Reserve.	W.H.S.
	1-6.12.16		Training special attention being paid to specialists.	
	4.12.16		The IX Corps front was reorganised with the result that the 16 Division took over the SPANBROEK Section from the 36. Div. on the night 5/6 Dec. The 49 INF BDE front was modified (vide map no. 1.)	W.H.S.
LA POLKA.	6.12.16		During the afternoon the Battn relieved the 2. R IRISH REGT in the left sub section. Battn Hdqrs. moved into DOCTORS HOUSE. LA POLKA. Distribution was as follows A Coy in Front line on Right. B. Coy (3 platoons) front line on left, 1 platoon in BROADWAY. C Coy 3 platoons S.P.11 + ALBERTA DUG-OUTS. 1 platoon FORT SASKATCHEWAN. D Coy 3 platoons YOUNG. ST, 1 platoon FORT. REGINA. During the relief the enemy were very active with T.M.s. Damage was done to our front line and to VIA CELLIA.	W.H.S.
"	7.12.16		During the night 6/7 our Lewis Guns dispersed 2 wiring parties. Between 5 P.M and 6 P.M enemy bombarded our front line VIA CELLIA and KETCHEN AV with heavy T.M.s Aerial Torpedoes and rifle grenades. We retaliated with artillery and Stokes guns.	W.H.S.
	8.12.16		About 3 P.M. enemy sent over a number of TM and aerial torpedoes against our left Coy. At 5 P.M. he opened a Strafe on our front line for 5 minutes. T.M. Aerial torpedoes and rifle grenades were employed and their M.G.s traversed our parapets.	W.H.S.
	9.12.16		During the night our Lewis guns were active and dispersed a working party. During the morning enemy sent over some 77 mm shells. Several direct hits were obtained on KETCHEN AV. causing the following casualties 2 O.R. killed 2 O.R. wounded	

7/8. ROYAL IRISH FUSILIERS

Instructions regarding War Diaries and Intelligence Summaries are contained in F. S. Regs., Part II. and the Staff Manual respectively. Title pages will be prepared in manuscript.

WAR DIARY
or
~~INTELLIGENCE SUMMARY.~~
(Erase heading not required.)

DECEMBER 1916

Army Form C. 2118.

Place	Date	Hour	Summary of Events and Information — REF maps 28 S.W. and WYTSHAETE	Remarks and references to Appendices
LA POLKA	9.12.16	(cont)	During the afternoon C and D companies relieved A and B Companies respectively in the front line. The evening passed quietly.	W.H.S.
"	10.12.16		Our snipers were active and claim a hit. Lewis Guns at night dispersed a hostile working party. During the afternoon our 6" and 9.2" Hows were active firing on enemys front and support lines	W.H.S.
"	11.12.16		The night 10/11 passed very quietly. At 2.22 PM our 2" TM's and Stokes Guns bombarded the enemys front line hoping to draw fire from the following hostile T.M's – HANNAH, IRENE, HAZEL. At 2.30 PM our artillery including 4.5" & 6" Hows. bombarded these T.M's. Enemys retaliation which consisted chiefly of artillery fire, was very strong.	W.H.S.
KEMMEL SHELTERS	12.12.16		The Battalion was relieved during the afternoon. B C and D Coys moved into KEMMEL SHELTERS. A Coy occupied KEMMEL ~~SHELTER~~ CHATEAU, and found the working parties for the Bde.	W.H.S.
"	13.12.16		Re-equipping etc. Training specialists etc.	W.H.S.
"	14.12.16			
"	15.12.16			
"	16.12.16			
	17.12.16			

T2134. Wt. W708–776. 500000. 4/15. Sir J. C. & S.

7/8 (S) Battn ROYAL IRISH FUSILIERS

Instructions regarding War Diaries and Intelligence Summaries are contained in F. S. Regs., Part II. and the Staff Manual respectively. Title pages will be prepared in manuscript.

WAR DIARY

or

~~INTELLIGENCE SUMMARY~~.

(*Erase heading not required.*)

DECEMBER. 1916

Army Form C. 2118.

Place	Date	Hour	Summary of Events and Information (Ref WYTSCHAETE map and 28 S.W.)	Remarks and references to Appendices
LA POLKA	18.12.16		The Battn relieved the 2. R. IRISH REGT in the left sub-section WYTSCHAETE SECTOR. Companies were distributed as follows Front line C Coy on right D Coy on left. A Coy ALBERTA DUGOUTS, S.P. 11, and FORT SASKATCHEWAN. B Coy YOUNG STREET and FORT REGINA	
			The afternoon passed quietly	W.H.S.
"	19.12.16		During the night our patrols were very active The day passed quietly.	W.H.S.
"	20.12.16		During the night 19/20 our patrols were very active. The day was very bright with the result that there was great aerial activity. Our heavies were active firing at enemys trenches to left of PETIT BOIS	W.H.S
"	21.12.16		Between 2.30 PM and 3.0 PM, our heavy T.M. was active firing at trenches in PETIT-BOIS and our artillery opened fire on SPANBROEKMOLEN to prevent enemy detecting position of heavy T.M. Enemys retaliation was heavy consisting of 77 mm. 4.2 Hows and T.M. A certain amount was directed on our front line, KETCHEN AV. and VIA GELLIA but the greater part was aimed at the Battn. on either flank	W.H.S
"	22.12.16		The night 21/22 passed quietly. Enemy appears to be nervous as he throws a few bombs into his own wire each night.	W.H.S

T.2134. Wt. W708—776. 500000. 4/15. Sir J. C. & S.

7/8 ROYAL IRISH FUSILIERS

Instructions regarding War Diaries and Intelligence Summaries are contained in F. S. Regs., Part II. and the Staff Manual respectively. Title pages will be prepared in manuscript.

WAR DIARY
or
~~INTELLIGENCE SUMMARY.~~
(Erase heading not required.)

DECEMBER 1916.

Army Form C. 2118.

Place	Date	Hour	Ref maps WYTSCHAETE SECTOR and 28 S.W. Summary of Events and Information	Remarks and references to Appendices
LA POLKA	23.12.16		The day passed quietly until 5.15 PM, when the enemy shelled the front line in the vicinity of VIA GELLIA and BROADWAY doing some damage	W.H.S.
LOCRE	24.12.16		During the forenoon the Battn. was relieved by the 2 R. IRISH. REGT. and on relief moved into DIVISIONAL RESERVE at DONCASTER HUTS, LOCRE	W.H.S.
"	25.12.16		Forenoon Church Parades, afternoon christmas dinners.	W.H.S.
"	26.12.16		Cleaning kit etc and bathing parades	W.H.S.
"	27.12.16		Training. During the afternoon a heavy bombardment was carried out on the enemy trenches opposite this Brigade Frontage, with T.M.s assisted by artillery. Great damage was done to enemys trenches. Retaliation was very feeble. 49 I.B. Order No 81. with amendments, attached	W.H. / W.H.S.
"	28.12.16		Training	W.H.S.
"	29.12.16		do	W.H.S.
"	30.12.16		The Battn. relieved the 2 R. IRISH REGT in the left subsection WYTSCHAETE SECTOR. C and D Coys were distributed in the front line. A + B Coys in support. Our Lewis guns were very active during the night firing at hostile working parties etc. The enemy front line appears to be badly damaged as the result of the bombardment on 27 inst.	W.H.S.

T2134. Wt. W708–776. 500000. 4/15. Sir J. C. & S.

7/8 (S) Battn. ROYAL IRISH FUSILIERS

Instructions regarding War Diaries and Intelligence Summaries are contained in F. S. Regs., Part II. and the Staff Manual respectively. Title pages will be prepared in manuscript.

WAR DIARY
or
~~INTELLIGENCE SUMMARY~~.
(Erase heading not required.)

DECEMBER 1916

Army Form C. 2118.

Place	Date	Hour	Summary of Events and Information (Reference Sheet 28 SW. and WYTSCHAETE SHEET.)	Remarks and references to Appendices
LA POLKA	31.12.16		Our artillery was very active during the day and especially up to midnight 31st	W.H.S.
			Total Strength of Battn on 31.12.16 officers. 37 O.R. 1054	
			Trench " " " officers 19. O.R. 698.	
			During the month a great amount of work has been carried out on improving and repairing the Battn frontage with very good results. The enemy appear to hold their front line very lightly and appear to be nervous. The enemy have brought more artillery into this area	W.H.S.

[signature] Lieut.-Col.

1/1/17. Commdg 7/8 (S) Battn. Royal Irish Fusiliers.

T2134. Wt. W708—776. 500000. 4/15. Sir J. C. & S.

Today is the anniversary of the landing of the 16th Division in FRANCE. The Divisional Commander wishes to express his appreciation of the spirit which has been shown by all ranks during the past year.

He feels that the Division has earned the right to adopt the motto which was granted by the King of FRANCE to the Irish Brigade which served in this country for a hundred years:- "Everywhere and always faithful".

With the record of the past, with the memory of our gallant dead, with this motto to live up to, and with our Trust in God, we can face the Future with confidence.

GOD SAVE THE KING.

W. B. Hickie,

Major-General,
Commanding 16th (Irish) Division.

December 18th, 1916.

Map No. 1

SECRET

SCALE :- 1: 10,000.

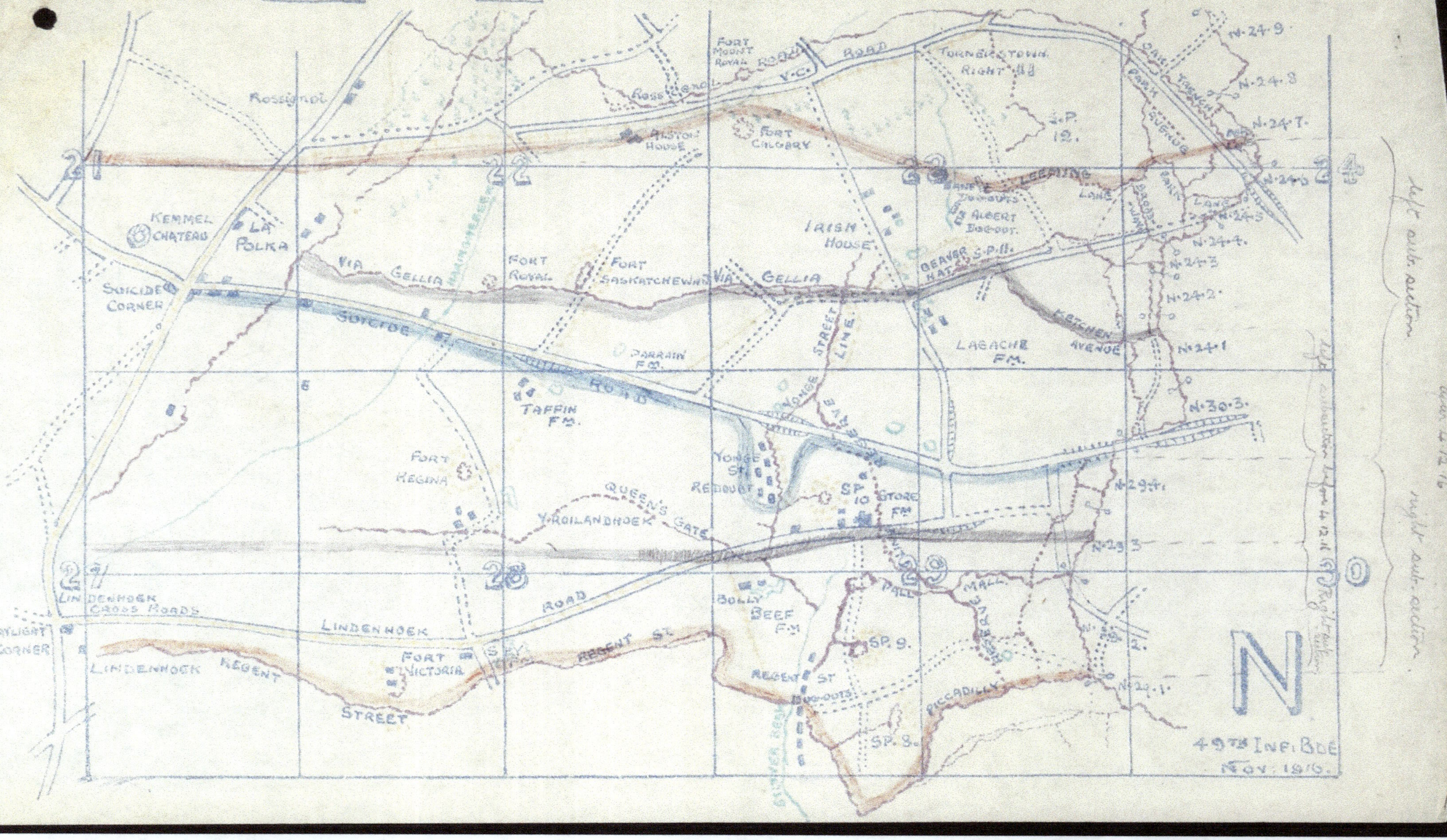

left sub-section

right sub-section

after 4.12.16

left subsection before 4.12.16

Right sub section

Rossignol
Fort Mount Royal
Ross Road
V.C. Road
Alston House
Fort Calgary
Torneistown Right
S.P. 12.
Oak Trench
Park Avenue
N.24.9
N.24.8
N.24.7.
N.24.5
N.24.4.
N.24.3
N.24.2.
N.24.1
N.30.3.
N.29.4.
N.29.3
Leaping Lane
Albert Dug-out.
Irish House
Kemmel Chateau
La Polka
Suicide Corner
Via Gellia
Fort Royal
Fort Saskatchewan
Beaver Hat
S.P. 11.
Kitchen Avenue
Lagache Fm.
Street Line
Suicide Road
Parrain Fm.
Taffin Fm.
Yonge St. Redoubt
S.P. 10
Store Fm.
Fort Regina
Queen's Gate
Vroilandhoek
Bully Beef Fm.
Pall Mall
S.P. 9.
S.P. 8.
Piccadilly
Regent St. Dug-outs
Lindenhoek Cross Roads
Daylight Corner
Lindenhoek Road
Lindenhoek Regent Street
Fort Victoria
Regent St.
21
22
23
24
27
28
29
30
N

49th Inf. Bde
Nov. 1916.

SECRET. Copy No...2........

49th Infantry Brigade Order No. 81 - 20-12-16.

****

1. A Trench Mortar Bombardment will take place on 26th December.

2. OBJECT.
To damage or destroy the enemy's front line system, especially his wire.

3. POINTS OF ATTACK.

"A" Group T.M's.....N.30.c.10.80 to N.30.a.30.15.
"B" Group T.M's.....N.30.a.30.15 to N.30.a.50.48.
"C" Group T.M's.....N.30.a.50.48 to N.30.a.65.85.
"D" Group T.M's.....N.30.a.65.85 to N.24.c.80.20.
"E" Group T.M's.....N.24.c.80.20 to N.24.c.85.54.

4. TIME TABLE.

Zero = . . 2-15 p.m.

Zero to Zero + 30 minutes	Fire by 2" T.M's as fast as possible. Stokes to fire 100 rounds in bursts.
Zero + 30 minutes. to Zero + 45 minutes.	Rest.
Zero + 45 minutes to Zero + 75 minutes.	Fire as before.

5. Troops will be withdrawn from front line only leaving some Lewis Guns, and a few groups of sentries.
The troops withdrawn will withdraw to Reserve Line, REGENT STREET & YONGE STREET DUGOUTS, who will replace a corresponding number withdrawn to FORT VICTORIA, FORT REGINA and FORT SASKATCHEWAN.

6. A Report Officer on telephone will be stationed at S.P.10 and S.P,11 to report on operations and enemy's fire direct to Brigade Headquarters.

7. Divisional Artillery to co-operate by firing on O.P's and enemys T.M. emplacements. Heavy Artillery to counter-battery if the enemy's Artillery open fire, and engage strong observation points.

8. Signal for commencement of Bombardment:-

1 RED ROCKET fired from Reserve Trench near Barricade, SUICIDE ROAD.

P. Leveson Gower
Brigadier General,
Commanding 49th Infantry Brigade.

Issued through Signals.

Copy No.			
1 to	8th R. Innis Fus.	6 to	O.C. Centre Group.
2	7/8th R. Irish Fus.	7	16th Division.
3	49th M.G. Coy	8	157th Field Coy,R.E.
4	49th T.M.B.	9	47th Inf.Bde.
5	7/16 T.M.B.	10	48th Inf.Bde.
		11	2nd Roy Irish Regt
		12	7th Roy Innis Fus

2nd R. Irish Regt.
7th R. Innis Fus.
8th R. Innis Fus.
7/8th R. Irish Fus.
49th M.G. Company.
49th T. M. B.
Z/16 T. M. B.
O.C. Centre Group.
16th Division.
157th Field Coy, R.E.
47th Inf. Bde.
48th Inf. Bde.

S E C R E T.

49th Infy Bde No. B.O. 81/2 - 22-12-16.

With reference to 49th Infantry Brigade Order No. 81 dated 20-12-16.

The Bombardment has been postponed until 27th December. All other details remain the same.

ACKNOWLEDGE.

[signature] Captain,

Brigade Major, 49th Infantry Brigade.

2nd R. Irish Regt.
7th R. Innis Fus.
8th R. Innis Fus.
7/8th R. Irish Fus.
49th M.G. Company.
49th T. M. B.
Z/16 T. M. B.
O.C. Centre Group.
16th Division.
157th Field Coy, R.E.
47th Infy Brigade.
48th Infy Brigade.

S E C R E T.

49th Infy Bde No. B.O.81/1 - 21-12-16.

Reference 49th Infantry Brigade Order No. 81 of 20-12-16, para 8 is now cancelled.

Watches will be synchronised on 26th instant with Brigade Headquarters at 8 a.m. and 12 a.m.

ACKNOWLEDGE.

Captain,

Brigade Major, 49th Infantry Brigade.

4. J.
g.D.

W A R   D I A R Y   for month of JANUARY, 1917.

VOLUME 11

1/8th Btn Rl. Irish Fusiliers

9d/12

7/8 (S) Battn ROYAL IRISH FUSILIERS

Instructions regarding War Diaries and Intelligence Summaries are contained in F. S. Regs., Part II. and the Staff Manual respectively. Title pages will be prepared in manuscript.

WAR DIARY
or
~~INTELLIGENCE SUMMARY.~~
(Erase heading not required.)

JANUARY 1917.

Army Form C. 2118.

Place	Date	Hour	Summary of Events and Information	Remarks and references to Appendices
			Ref sheet 28 S.W. WYTSCHAETE SHEET	
LA POLKA	1/1/17		During the night 31/1 our artillery fired short bursts at intervals at the German trenches. At 8.0 AM we bombarded the enemy's wire, front line and communication trenches, from N 30 a 42.72 to N 30 a 10.05 with 2" TM's and Stokes Guns. Our artillery cooperated by firing on O.P.s etc. Time table was as follows Zero to Zero + 15 Bombardment. Zero + 15 to Zero + 35 Rest. Zero + 35 to Zero + 50 Bombardment. The firing was accurate and considerable damage must have been done to the hostile trenches. Retaliation was slight. The remainder of the day passed quietly. The following is an extract from Supplement to London Gazette dated 1/1/17. Awarded the D.S.O. MAJOR (TEMP. LIEUT COL) WELDON K.C. Awarded the Military Cross TEMP. LIEUT STITT W.H. TEMP 2 LIEUT SARGINT E.E. Awarded the D.C.M. 15207 a/C.S.M. O'NEILL P.J., 13210 a/C.S.M. CRAIG. S., 18787 a/SGT. TIMMINS. The following were mentioned in despatches MAJOR (TEMP. LIEUT. COL.) WELDON K.C., TEMP. MAJOR BOARDMAN T.H. TEMP. CAPT FITZPATRICK T.G. (killed), TEMP. CAPT KINGHAN R.W., TEMP. LIEUT. KINGHAN A.E. (killed), 21380 L/Cpl NEALON P.	W.H.S.

T2134. Wt. W708—776. 500000. 4/15. Sir J. C. & S.

7/8 (S) Battn Royal Irish Fusiliers

Instructions regarding War Diaries and Intelligence Summaries are contained in F. S. Regs., Part II. and the Staff Manual respectively. Title pages will be prepared in manuscript.

WAR DIARY
or
~~INTELLIGENCE SUMMARY.~~
(*Erase heading not required.*)

Army Form C. 2118.

JANUARY 1917

Place	Date	Hour	Summary of Events and Information — Ref. maps 28 S.W. and WYTCHAETE Sheet.	Remarks and references to Appendices
LA POLKA ~~LOCRE~~	2/1/17		During the night 1/2 our patrols were extremely active. The enemy appear to remain chiefly in their support line and have very few sentries if any in their front line. Enemy's artillery was active during the day. Our artillery and Stokes Guns retaliated.	W.H.S.
do.	3/1/17		Our patrols on night 2/3 were very active. The situation was extremely quiet until about 2 PM when the enemy's artillery and TM's opened fire doing some damage to our front line and VIA GELLIA. About 8 P.M hostile TM's were very active.	W.H.S.
	4/1/17		The day was bright and there was considerable aerial activity. There was a small amount of T.M. fire on both sides. Our artillery was active firing well behind German front lines.	W.H.S.
	5/1/17		During the night our patrols were very active. The Battn. was relieved during the morning by the 2 R. I. REGT. and on relief moved into Divnl Reserve in LOCRE	W.H.S.
LOCRE	6/1/17		Cleaning up. Training etc.	W.H.S.
	7/1/17		do.	W.H.S.

T2134. Wt. W708—776. 500000. 4/15. Sir J. C. & S.

7/8 (S) Battn ROYAL IRISH FUSILIERS

Instructions regarding War Diaries and Intelligence Summaries are contained in F. S. Regs., Part II. and the Staff Manual respectively. Title pages will be prepared in manuscript.

WAR DIARY
or
~~INTELLIGENCE SUMMARY.~~ JANUARY. 1917

(Erase heading not required.)

Army Form C. 2118.

Place	Date	Hour	Summary of Events and Information (Ref. Maps 28 S.W and WYTSCHAETE sheets)	Remarks and references to Appendices
LOCRE	8/1/17		Training. Special attention being paid to Bombing and Bayonet Fighting	W.H.S.
	9/1/17		do	W.H.S.
	10/1/17		do.	W.H.S.
LA POLKA	11/1/17		The Battalion relieved the 2 R IRISH REGT in the left Subsection WYTSCHAETE SECTOR during the morning. Companies were distributed as follows:– C Coy Right Front Line, D Coy Left Front line. A Coy SP11 Alberta Dug-outs, FORT SASKATSCHEWAN B Coy YOUNG STREET and FORT REGINA. Hostile TM's were active during the afternoon doing considerable damage to VIA GELLIA.	W.H.S.
	12/1/17		The night passed quietly. Nothing to report during the day. Our artillery was active registering on enemy's trenches. While at Locre training was carried out for a raid which took place on 12 inst. Scheme orders and map are attached. The feint raid carried out on our right was successful as 2 prisoners were obtained. The scheme was carried out exactly as arranged with the exception that 2 instead of 4 parties were employed as only 2 gaps had been cut in the enemy's wire. The parties were ready formed up outside our wire at – 5 minutes and moved forward punctually at zero. Both parties were within 20 yds of their	W.H.S.

T2134. Wt. W708–776. 500000. 4/15. Sir J. C. & S.

7/8 (S) Battn ROYAL IRISH FUSILIERS

Instructions regarding War Diaries and Intelligence Summaries are contained in F. S. Regs., Part II. and the Staff Manual respectively. Title pages will be prepared in manuscript.

WAR DIARY
or
INTELLIGENCE SUMMARY.
(Erase heading not required.)

JANUARY 1917

Army Form C. 2118.

Place	Date	Hour	Ref maps 28SW and WYTSHAETE SECTOR — Summary of Events and Information	Remarks and references to Appendices
LA POLKA	12.1.17 (Cont)		objectives when our box barrage started and just as they charged for the gaps the enemy opened very heavy fire on his own front line with TMs, bombs and 77 mm. guns. The bombs were thrown from a trench in rear of, and within bombing range of enemys front line. The right party were driven back after reaching the enemys wire. The left party succeeded in entering the trench with 2 officers and about 8 men, but could not be supported owing to the intense fire. The trench or what was once a trench was knee deep in water. Only 6 of the enemy were encountered one of whom 2 LIEUT GERATY wounded and was in turn wounded by one of them before they made off. Owing to the extremely heavy fire, no progress could be made and only 4 of the above party succeeded in regaining our trenches. The left party returned to our trenches practically unmolested, but the right party were under schrapnel fire the whole way back. The enemy did not retaliate on our line until +15 minutes and practically everything fell behind our lines.	
			It is thought that the enemy does not hold his front line between N24C 7.1 and N24C 7½ 5½, but occupies a trench in rear of and within bombing distance	

T2134. Wt. W708—776. 500000. 4/15. Sir J. C. & S.

7/8 Royal Irish Fusiliers

Instructions regarding War Diaries and Intelligence Summaries are contained in F. S. Regs., Part II. and the Staff Manual respectively. Title pages will be prepared in manuscript.

WAR DIARY
or
~~INTELLIGENCE SUMMARY.~~
(Erase heading not required.)

JANUARY 1917

Army Form C. 2118.

Place	Date	Hour	Summary of Events and Information (Ref Maps 28 S W and WYTSCHAETE MAP)	Remarks and references to Appendices
LA POLKA	12.1.17 cont.		of his front line. The enemy's front line where the left party entered can hardly be said to exist as a trench being more in the form of a drain full of mud and water in which progress could be made only with the greatest difficulty.	
			Our casualties were 1 O.R. Killed 1 O.R. died of wounds 2LIEUT E J MACMILLAN and 5 O.R. missing. 2LIEUT T GERATY and 10 O.R. wounded.	W.H.S.
"	13.1.17		An intercompany relief took place commencing at 7.30 AM. There was slight artillery activity during the day	W.H.S.
	14.1.17		The were exceptionally quiet	W.H.S.
"	15.1.17		During the night 14/15 the enemy appeared to be very nervous as they bombed their own wire at intervals and their M.G. fire was above normal. During the morning the enemy sent over about 56 4.2's. These with the exception of 1 direct hit on our front line, did no damage.	W.H.S.
"	16.1.17		The day passed very quietly.	
"	17.1.17		The Battalion was relieved during the forenoon by the 2 R Irish Regt. and on relief moved into Bde Reserve in KEMMEL SHELTERS	W.H.S.

T2134. Wt. W708—776. 500000. 4/15. Sir J. C. & S.

7/8 (S) Battn. ROYAL IRISH FUSILIERS

WAR DIARY
or
~~INTELLIGENCE SUMMARY.~~ JANUARY 1917
(Erase heading not required.)

Army Form C. 2118.

Instructions regarding War Diaries and Intelligence Summaries are contained in F. S. Regs., Part II. and the Staff Manual respectively. Title pages will be prepared in manuscript.

Place	Date	Hour	Summary of Events and Information (Reference WYTSCHAETE SHEET and 28 S.W.)	Remarks and references to Appendices
MOUNT KEMMEL	18.1.17		Clothing and training.	W.H.S.
"	19.1.17		Bathing etc.	W.H.S.
"	20.1.17		Training	W.H.S.
"	21.1.17		Church Services in morning	W.H.S.
"	22.1.17		Training	W.H.S.
LA POLKA	23.1.17		The Battn relieved the 2 R. IRISH. REGT in the left Subsection WYTSCHAETE SECTOR during the morning. Companies were distributed as follows C Coy. Right Front line. D Coy left front line. A Coy S.P.11 Alberta Dugouts, Fort Saskatchewan, B. Coy. Young Street, Fort Regina. During the relief the enemy shelled junction PARK LANE and FRONT LINE doing damage to PARK LANE. During the afternoon there was a little T.M. activity on both sides.	W.H.S.
LA POLKA	24.1.17		The night passed very quietly. Considerable T.M. activity during the day	W.H.S.
"	25.1.17		At dawn our Lewis Gunners fired on party of enemy claiming several hits. The enemys front line appears to be blocked in places. Artillery were active on both sides.	W.H.S.
"	26.1.17		The morning passed very quietly. During the afternoon an intercompany relief took place. A Coy relieved C Coy and B Coy relieved D Coy.	W.H.S.

T2134. Wt. W708–776. 500000. 4/15. Sir J. C. & S.

7/8 Battn. ROYAL IRISH FUSILIERS

Instructions regarding War Diaries and Intelligence Summaries are contained in F. S. Regs., Part II. and the Staff Manual respectively. Title pages will be prepared in manuscript.

WAR DIARY
or
~~INTELLIGENCE~~ SUMMARY.
(Erase heading not required.)

JANUARY 1917.

Army Form C. 2118.

Place	Date	Hour	Summary of Events and Information (Reference maps 28 S.W. & WYTSCHAETE SHEET)	Remarks and references to Appendices
LA POLKA	27.1.17		The night 26/27 passed quietly. Nothing unusual occured during the day	W.H.S.
"	28.1.17		At 3 P.M. we carried out a short T.M. bombardment of 18 minutes duration on enemys wire and trenches between N 30 a 15 05 and N 30 a 45 35. Our fire appeared to be very accurate. Enemys retaliation was slight; being chiefly aimed at KETCHEN AVENUE.	W.H.S.
"	29.1.17		The front at present being held by the Division was reorganized as a two-Brigade front, with the result that the Battn. was relieved in the Left Subsection by portions of the following regiments 6 CONNAUGHT RANGERS, 1. R MUN. FUS, 7 R. IR RIFLES. The 49 INF. BDE moved into Divisional and Corps Reserve round LOCRE. This Battn. moved into CURRAGH CAMP	W.H.S.
CURRAGH CAMP.	30.1.17		Training	W.H.S.
	31.1.17		do.	W.H.S.

[signature] Major
Commdg. 7/8 S. Battn. ROYAL IRISH FUSILIERS

T2134. Wt. W708–776. 500000. 4/15. Sir J. C. & S.

5 J.

W A R D I A R Y.

FOR MONTH OF FEBRUARY, 1917.

VOLUME 5

UNIT:- 7/8th Irish Fusiliers

Vol 13

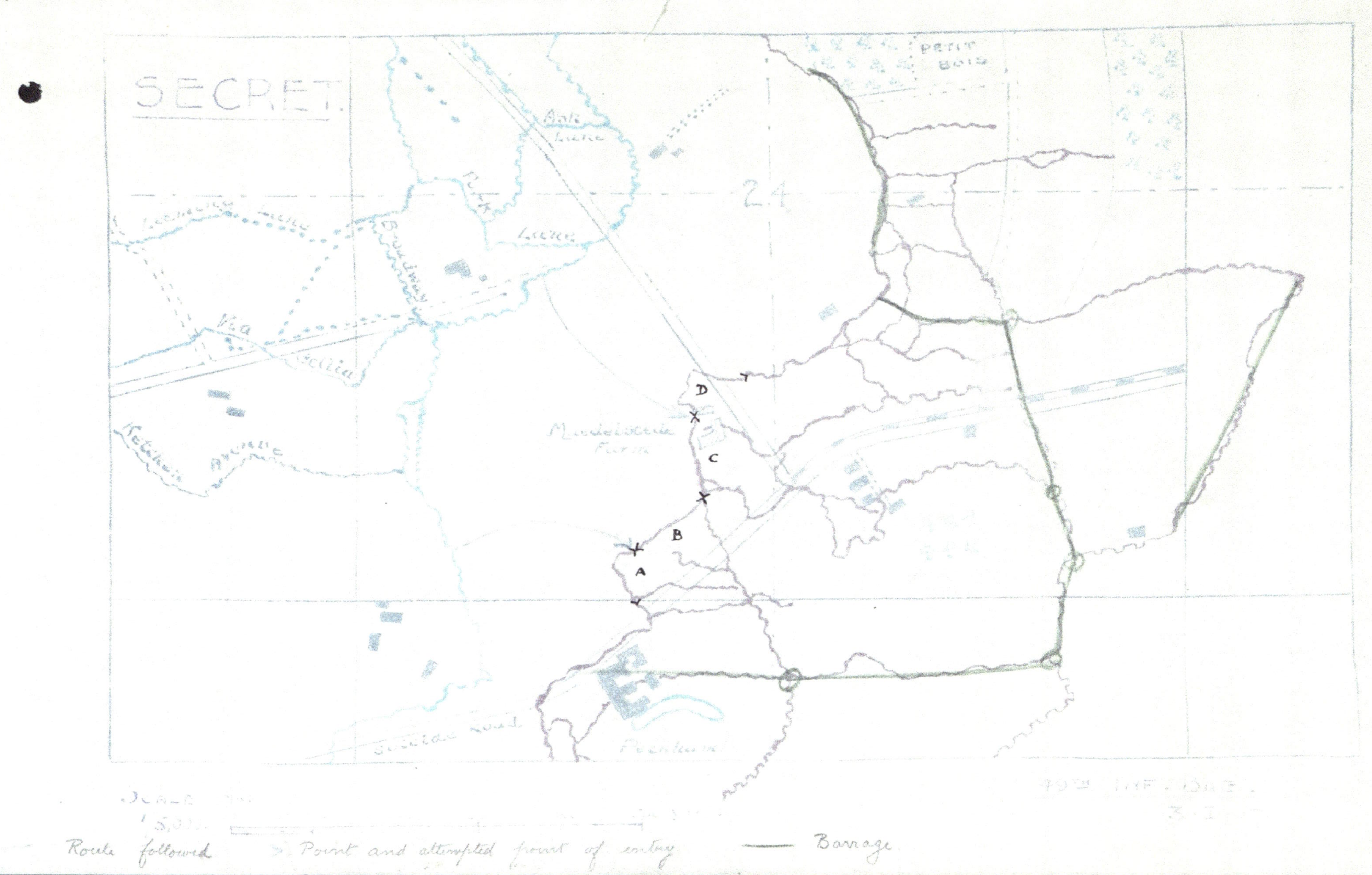
SECRET.
PETIT BOIS
24
Park
Lane
Broadway
Via
Gellia
Avenue
D
C
B
A
Route followed
Point and attempted point of entry
Barrage

ORDERS FOR RAID BY LIEUT.COL.K.C.WELDON,D.S.O.,COMMANDING 7/8th.ROYAL IRISH FUSILIERS.

SECRET.

Reference Map Attached.

DATE. 12.1.17
HOUR. 9.30 PM

STRENGTH OF PARTIES. Four parties as detailed below will raid the Enemy's Trenches between N.24.c.85.55.and N.30.a.6896.to a depth of approximately 280 yards N.24.d.27.55.to N.30.b.28.97 all parties moving to the attack at Zero.

No.I.Party under 2/Lieut.A.C.YOUNG........"C"Coy.
No.2.Party under 2/Lieut.J.D.BAKER........"C"Coy.
No.3.Party under 2/Lieut.E.J.MACMILLAN...."D"Coy.
No.4.Party under 2/Lieut.T.GERATY........."D"Coy.

Nos.1 & 2 parties under Capt.R.P.KNOWLES WITH Coy.Signallers will pass through our wire in Valley at N.24.c.3.1.and be ready formed up outside of it at minus 5.(five) minutes
Objective.No.1(One) Party ...A.See attached Map.
Objective No.2.(Two.)Party...B.See attached Map.
Nos.3.& 4 Parties under 2/Lieut.E.S.BIRD with Coy.Sigs.will pass through our wire where PARK LANE joins the FIRING LINE AND be ready formed up outside our wire at minus 5 minutes.
Objective.No.3.party......C.See attached Map.
Objective No.4.Party......D.See attached Map.

SUBDIVISIONS OF PARTIES. Nos.1.2.3.& 4 Parties will each consist of the following:-
1.(One.)Officer.
1.(One.)Senior N.C.O.
2.(Two.)Stretcher Bearers.
2.(Two.)Flagmen.
6.(Six.)Bombing squads of one N.C.O.and six men.(i.e.Two bayonet men,two bombers,two carriers.)

GUIDING TAPE. The rear squad of Nos.1 & 4 Parties will lay a tracing tape from the points of exit from our line to point of entry in Enemy's Line,both ends of which will be firmly secured

COUNTERSIGN. " WATERLOO. "

COMMUNICATIONS. The Battn.Signalling Officer will arrange for one line to communicate with officer i/c Nos.1 & 2 Parties from head of VIA GELLIA,and one line to communicate with officer i/c Nos.3 & 4 Parties from bomb proof dug out in Front Line N.of GLORY HOLE.
In the event of these wires being cut resort will be had to communication with special Signalling Lamp,the following CODE being employed in either case:-
I.........Have entered Enemy's Trenches.
2..........Bombs required.
3..........Prisoners taken.
4..........Raiders returning.

GAPS IN OUR WIRE. O.C."C"Coy.will be responsible that two gaps are cut in our wire as soon as it is dark on the night of......... at the following points and white flags placed in them to mark them
By the flagmen of No.I.Party at N.24.c.3.1.
By the flagmen of No.2.Party opposite where the Southern entrance to VIA GELLIA joins the FIRING LINE.
O.C."D"Coy.will be responsible that two gaps are cut as soon as it is dark on the night of.............at the following points and white flags placed in them to mark them.
By the flagmen of No.3.Party Fifty yards N.of BROADWAY.
By the flagmen of No.4.Party where PARK LANE joins FIRING LINE
All flagmen will be stationed at these gaps with megaphones to assist them in directing our men back into our trenches on their return.

IDENTIFICATION. It must be impressed on all ranks that it is most important to secure identification in the form of prisoners, portions of uniform,or papers taken from the bodies of any of the Enemy who may have been killed.Every man should carry his jack-knife for the purpose of cutting off shoulder straps,etc.

MEDICAL ARRANGEMENTS. Special instructions have been issued direct to Coys.for evacuation of Wounded.

POLICE. O.C."A"Coy.will arrange to police VIA GELLIA from Zero until

SECRET.

SCHEME FOR BATTALION RAID BY 7/8 R. IRISH FUS.

I. GENERAL IDEA. To raid Enemy's Front and Support Line Trenches between Lines running East and West, through N.24.c. 9.5., and N.30.A.7.8. to a depth of 300 yards with the object of securing prisoners and trophies and doing all possible damage to M.G. and T.M. emplacements etc. and ~~KMKMG~~ looking for Gas Cylinders, and if found bring one back if possible.

2 DATE. 12.1.17

HOUR. 9.30 PM

3. STRENGTH OF PARTY. Two Companies divided into four parties, each under one officer, the latter parties being sub-divided into bombing squads.

4. TIME. Time taken . 5(Five) minutes to cross.
Maximum time allowed in trenches 30(Thirty) minutes.

RETURN. All parties on returning must immediately report their arrival to O.C. Enterprise at Coy. H.Q. in VIA GELLIA.

6. DISTINGUISHING MARKS. Faces and hands will be blackened and countersign will be made known to everyone prior to raid.

7. DRESS AND EQUIPMENT. All officers will carry torches and revolvers, and bayonet men will carry torches fixed on their rifles. All bombers will carry eight bombs and shillelaghs, and all carriers will carry at least twelve bombs in a bucket and be armed with shillelaghs. Two pairs wire cutters per squad will be carried in addition to those attached to men's rifles and all N.C.Os. and men will wear side-arms.

8. FLAGMEN. The flagmen of Each of the four parties will leave white flags at the points where they ~~pass~~ cut through ~~HUN~~ our wire.

9. WATCHES. Watches will be synchronised FOUR hours before zero time at Coy H.Q. in VIA GELLIA, and checked again TWO hours before Zero.

10 COMMUNICATIONS. O.C. Enterprise, Lt. Col. K.C. WELDON, will be at NEW COY. H.Q. in VIA GELLIA, which will be in direct communication with the Artillery BDE. H.Q., and the two Coys. in the HUN Lines.

11. ACTION OF ARTILLERY. To form a box barrage round the area to be raided, marked RED on attached map, not to commence firing till the raiding party is in, i.e. plus 5 (five.) minutes and not to stop firing till the return of the raiding party.

12. ACTION OF T.Ms. & L.Gs. All Medium T.Ms., Stokes Guns and Vickers to fire on Communication Trenches leading to the area selected for raiding in(marked on attached map.)

13. FORWARD AID POST. The M.O. will arrange to form a forward Regtl. Aid Post at head of KITCHEN AVENUE in addition to his post near BEAVER HAT.

ACTION OF INFANTRY. At minus 5 (five) minutes the four parties of Infantry must be through their own wire ready formed up to move forward at Zero.

15. SIGNAL FOR WITHDRAWAL. Golden rain rocket fired from our Front Line top of VIA GELLIA.

Lieut. Colonel,
Commanding 7/8th. Royal Irish Fusiliers.

SHEET II.

POLICE. Continued. all wounded have beenevacuated from Dressing St Station in VIA GELLIA On no account are men to be allowed t to loiter round the Dressing station.

PRISONERS. All prisoners will be sent in first instance to officers i/c of "C" & "D" Coys. raiding parties who will retain them, bring them back with their parties when returning, and will hand them over to the Regtl. Police at Bn. H.Q. in VIA. GELLIA.

Lieut. Colonel, O.C. RAID.

NOTICE. A

At Zero ~~minus 10. (Ten.) minutes~~ 2 hours an intense bombardment with Artillery Stokes Guns, and 2" T.Ms." will take place on Enemy's Front opposite the Bn. on our right followed by a small raid by them at Zero. - 1 hour 55 minutes

7/8 (S) Battn. ROYAL IRISH FUSILIERS

WAR DIARY
or
~~INTELLIGENCE SUMMARY.~~
(Erase heading not required.)

FEBRUARY 1917

Army Form C. 2118.

Instructions regarding War Diaries and Intelligence Summaries are contained in F. S. Regs., Part II. and the Staff Manual respectively. Title pages will be prepared in manuscript.

Place	Date	Hour	Ref. maps 28.SW and WYTSCHAETE SHEET Summary of Events and Information	Remarks and references to Appendices
CURRAGH CAMP	1/2/17 -6/2/17		Training in CURRAGH CAMP while in Divisional and Corps Reserve.	W.H.S.
LA POLKA	6.2.17		The 49 Bde relieved the 47 Bde in the SPANBROEK SECTOR. This Battn relieved the 7. LEINSTER REGT in Bde Support. Battn Hdqrs DOCTORS HOUSE LA POLKA. B Coy 3 platoons LA POLKA FARM, 1 platoon FORT SASKATCHEWAN, D Coy 2 platoons YOUNG STREET 2 platoons FORT REGINA, A Coy FORT EDWARD, C Coy 1 platoon BEEHIVE DUGOUTS 1 platoon GALWAY DUGOUTS, 2 platoons COOKER FARM. B and D Coys came under the tactical command of the O.C. left sub section for tactical purposes and A and C Coys under the command of the O.C. Right sub section for tactical purposes.	W.H.S.
"	7.2.17		Nothing unusual to report	W.H.S.
"	8.2.17		do	W.H.S.
"	9.2.17		do	W.H.S.
NEWPORT DUGOUTS	10.2.17		The Battalion relieved the 2 R. IRISH REGT. in the RIGHT SECTOR SPANBROEK SECTOR just after dark. Boundaries of front are:- Right DURHAM ROAD (inclusive) N36c 85 80. left 1 firebay N of PICCADILLY (inclusive) N29 d. 82 50. The front is divided into 3	

T2134. Wt. W708–776. 500000. 4/15. Sir J. C. & S.

7/8 Battn ROYAL IRISH FUSILIERS

Instructions regarding War Diaries and Intelligence Summaries are contained in F. S. Regs., Part II. and the Staff Manual respectively. Title pages will be prepared in manuscript.

WAR DIARY
or
~~INTELLIGENCE SUMMARY.~~
(Erase heading not required.)

FEBRUARY, 1917

Army Form C. 2118.

Place	Date	Hour	Summary of Events and Information (Ref. Maps 28 S.W. and WYTSCHAETE SECTOR)	Remarks and references to Appendices
NEWPORT DUGOUTS	10.2.17 (cont)		sections viz. Left Section comprising PICCADILLY inclusive to REDAN AVENUE inclusive. Centre section REDAN AVENUE exclusive to left of break in line (approximately N 36.9 Right Sector. Right of break (approximately N36.6) to DURHAM ROAD. The trenches are in very bad repair, parapets low, and portion untenable by day.	W.H.S.
do.	11.2.17		The night 10/11 passed quietly. About 8.0 AM the enemy sent over a number of T.M's and rifle grenades. Our artillery and T.M's replied with good effect. Commencing at 3.7 PM we carried out a bombardment of the enemys trenches between Kingsway and Durham road, and N and S of PECKHAM, with artillery Heavy, Medium, and light T.M's fire. The bombardment last almost 1 hour and provoked hardly any retaliation.	W.H.S.
do	12.2.17		About 4.30 AM our Lewis Guns dispersed hostile wiring party. During the days our snipers were active and claim 3 hits. The day passed quietly	W.H.S.
do	13.2.17		Our Lewis were active during the night and at dawn, claiming several hits. About 11.30 AM enemy shelled S.P. 7 and vicinity with about 80 rounds of 4.2's and 5.9's No damage was done. Our T.M's retaliated along with the artillery. During the afternoon our T.M's were very active firing on enemys front and support lines.	W.H.S.

T2134. Wt. W708—776. 500000. 4/15. Sir J. C. & S.

7/8 (S.) Battn ROYAL IRISH FUSILIERS

WAR DIARY
or
~~INTELLIGENCE~~ SUMMARY.

(Erase heading not required.)

FEBRUARY 1917

Army Form C. 2118.

Instructions regarding War Diaries and Intelligence Summaries are contained in F. S. Regs., Part II. and the Staff Manual respectively. Title pages will be prepared in manuscript.

Place	Date	Hour	Summary of Events and Information (Ref maps 28 S.W. and WYTSCHAETE sectors.)	Remarks and references to Appendices
NEWPORT DUGOUTS	14/2/17		The Battalion was relieved in the Right Sub-section SPANBROEK SECTOR by the 7. LEINSTER REGT. and on relief marched to WAKEFIELD CAMP.	W.H.S.
WAKEFIELD CAMP.	15/2/17			
	16/2/17			
	17/2/17			
	18/2/17		Re-equipping training etc Special attention being paid to specialists	W.H.S.
	19/2/17			
	20/2/17			
	21/2/17			
	22/2/17		The Battalion relieved the 1. R. MUN. FUS in the Right Sub-section SPANBROEK SECTOR	W.H.S.
NEWPORT DUGOUTS	23/2/17		The night 22/23 passed quietly. The enemy bombed their own wire on several occasions. About 10.30 AM there was considerable TM activity on the right section. About 6.0 P.M. the enemy sent over some 4.2's and TM in the vicinity of PICCADILLY and ULSTER ROAD. Our TM's and artillery retaliated	W.H.S.

T2134. Wt. W708–776. 500000. 4/15. Sir J. C. & S.

7/8 (S) Battn ROYAL IRISH FUSILIERS

WAR DIARY
or
~~INTELLIGENCE SUMMARY.~~
(Erase heading not required.)

FEBRUARY 1917

Army Form C. 2118.

Instructions regarding War Diaries and Intelligence Summaries are contained in F. S. Regs., Part II. and the Staff Manual respectively. Title pages will be prepared in manuscript.

Place	Date	Hour	Ref 28 S.W. and WYTSCHAETE Maps Summary of Events and Information	Remarks and references to Appendices
NEWPORT DUGOUTS	24.2.17		The night 23/24 passed quietly. Enemy appears to be uneasy as he bombs his own wire frequently. Our patrols were active. About 6 P.M. enemy shelled ULSTER ROAD and S.P.7 with about 70 4.2's and 5.9's	W.H.S.
do	25.2.17		The night passed quietly. About 6 P.M. enemy shelled his own trenches at N.29.1. He sent up a green rocket and range was lengthened on to our front line. Very little damage was done. Our artillery were active, and replied very promptly and effectively to a hostile straffe about 3.30 P.M.	W.H.S.
do	26.2.17		The night 25/26 passed quietly. Our patrols were active. During the afternoon the Battn was relieved by the 2 R. IR. RECT. and on relief moved into Bde. Support 2 coys being behind under tactical command of 2 R. Ir. Regt. and 2 coys being behind and under tactical command of 8 R. INNIS. FUS. Battn Hdqrs. DOCTORS HOUSE	W.H.S.
DOCTORS HOUSE	27.2.17		Nothing unusual to report.	W.H.S.
	28.2.17		do	W.H.S.
			During the first 2 weeks of this month there was exceedingly heavy frost rendering repairs to trenches almost impossible.	

W.M. Weldon LIEUT. COL.
CMDG. 7/8 (S) BN. R. IRISH FUSILIERS.

T2134. Wt. W708—776. 500000. 4/15. Sir J. C. & S.

6. J.

W A R D I A R Y

FOR MONTH OF MARCH, 1917.

VOLUME 6

U N I T :- 7/8th Btn R. Irish Fusiliers

Vol. 14

7/8 ROYAL IRISH FUSILIERS

WAR DIARY
or
~~INTELLIGENCE~~ ~~SUMMARY~~.
(Erase heading not required.)

MARCH 1917

Army Form C. 2118.

Instructions regarding War Diaries and Intelligence Summaries are contained in F. S. Regs., Part II. and the Staff Manual respectively. Title pages will be prepared in manuscript.

Place	Date	Hour	Summary of Events and Information (Ref maps 28 S.W.)	Remarks and references to Appendices
DOCTORS HOUSE	1.3.17		Nothing unusual to report	G/F
	2.3.17		The 47th Infantry Brigade relieved the 49th Inf Bde in the SPANBROEK Sector. This Battalion was relieved by 7th Leinster Regt, in Brigade support. On relief the Battalion moved as follows:- A & B Coys to KEMMEL SHELTERS	
	[illegible]		C & D Coys to DONCASTER HUTS.	G/F
KEMMEL & LOCRE	3.3.17		Bathing. Re-equipping etc. Training.	G/F
	4.3.17		Training, special attention being paid to Specialists, and new formation of Companys.	G/F
	5.3.17		do	G/F
	6.3.17		do	G/F
	7.3.17		do	G/F
	8.3.17		do	G/F
	9.3.17		do	G/F
	10.3.17		do	G/F
	11.3.17		Sunday.	G/F
	12.3.17		Training. Carried out improvements on G.H.Q. 2nd Line.	G/F

T2134. Wt. W708—776. 500000. 4/15. Sir J. C. & S.

Instructions regarding War Diaries and Intelligence Summaries are contained in F. S. Regs., Part II. and the Staff Manual respectively. Title pages will be prepared in manuscript.

WAR DIARY
or
INTELLIGENCE SUMMARY.
(Erase heading not required.)

Army Form C. 2118.

MARCH 1917

Place	Date	Hour	Ref map. 28. S.W. Summary of Events and Information	Remarks and references to Appendices
KEMMEL & LOCRE	13.3.17		Training. Working parties on G.H.Q. 2nd Line.	G.F.
	14.3.17		do	G.F.
	15.3.17		do	G.F.
	16.3.17		Sunday. After Church Parade G.O.C. presented Parchment certificates.	G.F.
	17.3.17		St Patricks Day. Church Parade. Recreation.	G.F.
	18.3.17		Training.	G.F.
ROSSIGNOL	19.3.17		The 49th Infantry Bde relieved the 48th Infantry Bde in the VIERSTRAAT SECTION. This Battalion relieved portions of 2nd Dublin Fusiliers & 9th Dublin Fusiliers. Companies were distributed as follows:- A Coy 1 platoon FORT MOUNT ROYAL. 1 NCO 6 men FORT SASKATCHEWAN. remainder in LA POLKA FARM. B Coy. 1 Platoon in SANDBAG VILLA 1 platoon FORT HALIFAX, remainder in ROSSIGNOL. "C" Coy 2 Platoons S.P. 13. 2 Platoons VAN KEEP. "D" Coy 3 Platoons SIEGE FARM and 1 platoon SANDBAG VILLA.	G.F.
	20.3.17		Nothing unusual to report	G.F.
	21.3.17		do	G.F.
	22.3.17		do	G.F.

T2134. Wt. W708–776. 500000. 4/15. Sir J. C. & S.

Instructions regarding War Diaries and Intelligence Summaries are contained in F. S. Regs., Part II. and the Staff Manual respectively. Title pages will be prepared in manuscript.

WAR DIARY
or
INTELLIGENCE SUMMARY.
(Erase heading not required.)

Army Form C. 2118.

MARCH 1917

Place	Date	Hour	Summary of Events and Information	Remarks and references to Appendices
			Ref MAP 28 SW.	
HARLEY HOUSE	23.3.17		This Battalion relieved the 2nd Royal Irish Regt in the right sub section VIERSTRAAT SECTOR. Southern boundary VIA GELIA to KITCHEN AVE northern boundary, LARK LANE - VAN WAY ROSSIGNOL ROAD all inclusive. Companies were distributed as follows:- A Coy in SP 11 & ALBERTA dug outs. "B" Coy 2 platoons front line, 2 Platoons PARK AVE. "C" Coy 2 Platoons front line 2 Platoons BROADWAY. "D" Coy in SP 12, BANFF dug outs and TURNERSTOWN RIGHT. HQRS in HARLEY HOUSE.	G/F
	24.3.17		Our heavy artillery fired at enemys positions well behind front line.	G/F
	25.3.17		Commencing at 8 30 PM enemy sent over 3 to 5 77 MM shells at ½ hour intervals during the night, most of the shells fell near junction of PARK AVE & ROSSIGNOL Trench.	G/F
	26.3.17		Our stokes Guns and 2" TMs continued wire cutting, enemy retaliated on our our Right Bns front with 32.77 MM shells. During the night the enemy appeared nervous, sending up an unusual number of Very lights. At 4 AM enemy commenced a very heavy bombardment on Bde front on our ~~left~~ right, with heavies & TMs	G/F

T2134. Wt. W708-776. 500000. 4/15. Sir J. C. & S.

Instructions regarding War Diaries and Intelligence Summaries are contained in F. S. Regs., Part II. and the Staff Manual respectively. Title pages will be prepared in manuscript.

WAR DIARY
or
INTELLIGENCE SUMMARY.
(Erase heading not required.)

Army Form C. 2118.

MARCH 1917

Place	Date	Hour	Summary of Events and Information	Remarks and references to Appendices
HARLEY HOUSE	27.3.17		The "DUCHESS" fired 10 rounds, in the afternoon. Enemys wiring party dispersed by our Lewis Guns. At 5.AM our 18 pounders fired on working party in PETIT BOIS. Cries were distinctly heard. At hourly intervals enemy shelled HARLEY HOUSE, during the night. Enemy retaliated for our T.M.° fire with 3 salvoes of 5.9 & 4.2 getting 3 direct hits on CHINESE WALL.	G/F
	28.3.17		Our T.M.° continued to cut wire. Enemys minnenwerfer continued active during the day, getting one direct hit on mine shaft in PARK AVE	G/F
	29.3.17		This Battalion was relieved by the 2nd Royal Irish Regt, on relief the Battalion moved into BUTTERFLY FARM	G/F
	30.3.17		Cleaning clothes, washing equipment etc. ~~[illegible]~~ Working parties.	G/F
	31.3.17		Bathing. Cleaning. Working parties.	G/F

[signature] LIEUT. COL.
COMDG. 7/8 (S) BN. R. IRISH FUSILIERS

T.2134. Wt. W708—776. 500000. 4/15. Sir J. C. & S.

149/16 7.J. [illegible]

WAR DIARY FOR MONTH OF APRIL, 1917.

VOLUME:- 1

UNIT:- 1/8th R. Irish Fusiliers

8/15

7/8 (S) Battn Royal Irish Fusiliers

WAR DIARY
or
~~INTELLIGENCE SUMMARY.~~

(*Erase heading not required.*)

Army Form C. 2118.

Instructions regarding War Diaries and Intelligence Summaries are contained in F. S. Regs., Part II. and the Staff Manual respectively. Title pages will be prepared in manuscript.

APRIL 1917

Place	Date	Hour	Summary of Events and Information	Remarks and references to Appendices
DONCASTER	1.4.17		The Battalion was relieved in Brigade Reserve by the 6th Bn Connaught Rangers. The Battalion, on relief moved into DONCASTER HUTS.	G/F
	2.4.17		Carried out training under new formations. Coating & musketry	G/F
	3.4.17		do	G/F
	4.4.17		do	G/F
	5.4.17		do	G/F
	6.4.17		do	G/F
	7.4.17		The Battalion was inspected by Divisional Commander. The Battalion moved into KEMMEL SHELTERS and was relieved in DONCASTER HUTS by 2nd R. Irish Regt.	G/F
KEMMEL	8.4.17		Church Parade. Working parties	G/F
	9.4.17		Working parties.	G/F
	10.4.17		do	G/F
	11.4.17		do	G/F
	12.4.17		do	G/F

T2134. Wt. W708—776. 500000. 4/15. Sir J. C. & S.

7/8 Royal Irish Fusiliers

Instructions regarding War Diaries and Intelligence Summaries are contained in F. S. Regs., Part II. and the Staff Manual respectively. Title pages will be prepared in manuscript.

WAR DIARY
or
~~INTELLIGENCE SUMMARY.~~
(Erase heading not required.) APRIL 1917

Army Form C. 2118.

Place	Date	Hour	Summary of Events and Information	Remarks and references to Appendices
			Ref: MAP. 28 S.W. 1/20.000 HAZEBROUK 5.a. 1/100000	
KEMMEL SHELTERS	13.4.17		The 49th Infantry Brigade, commenced their march to the RECQUES area. Route :- BAILLEUL - STRAZELLE - PRADELLES. to HAZEBROUCK area. This Battalion left their "C" Company behind for working parties. The Battalion left KEMMEL SHELTERS at 8.AM and arrived in their Billets in the HAZEBROUCK area about 3.45 PM.	G/F
	14.4.17		The 49th Inf: Bde continued their march to the St OMER Area. This Battalion were billeted in WIZERNES for the night 14/15th. Route	G/F
	~~15.4.17~~		followed :- EBBLINGHAM - RENESCURE - ARQUES. Battalion reached billets at 2.30 PM.	
	15.4.17		The 49th Inf Bde concluded their march to the RECQUES area.	
TOURNEHEM.			This battalion arrived in their billets in TOURNEHEM at 3.45 PM. and were joined by their "C" Company, which arrived by Motor Lorries from LOCRE.	G/F
	16.4.17		Commenced training. Platoon training.	G/F
	17.4.17		Platoon training from 9AM to 1 P.M. Afternoon. Recreational training	G/F
	18.4.17		Very wet. Lectures and interior economy. "D" Company on range.	G/F
	19.4.17		Company Training. Firing on Range. Bayonet fighting etc.	G/F

T2134. Wt. W708—776. 500000. 4/15. Sir J. C. & S.

7/8th Royal Irish Fusiliers

Instructions regarding War Diaries and Intelligence Summaries are contained in F. S. Regs., Part II. and the Staff Manual respectively. Title pages will be prepared in manuscript.

WAR DIARY
or
~~INTELLIGENCE SUMMARY~~.
(Erase heading not required.) APRIL 1917

Army Form C. 2118.

Place	Date	Hour	Summary of Events and Information	Remarks and references to Appendices
TOURNEHEM	20.4.17		Company Training. Firing on Range. Bayonet Fighting etc.	G/J
	21.4.17		Company ~~in~~ Training in attack.	G/J
	22.4.17		Divine service. All specialists on parade. Lewis Gunners on Range.	G/J
	23.4.17		Battalion training in attack. Signallers carried out a signal scheme with Aeroplane	G/J
	24.4.17		The 49th Infantry Brigade ~~=~~ held "Assault at arms"	G/J
	25.4.17		Battalion training in the attack. Training Signallers with Contact aeroplane work.	G/J
	26.4.17		Brigade training, in attack.	
	27.4.17		do	
WIZERNES.	28.4.17		The 49 Inf Bde commenced their march back to the LOCRE area. This Battalion marched to WIZERNES ~~via~~ where it was billeted for the night 28/29.	W.H.S.
near HAZEBROUCK	29.4.17		March continued via ARQUES to HAZEBROUCK area where the same billets were occupied as on the march to the training area	W.H.S.
LOCRE.	30.4.17		The march was continued to the LOCRE area. The Brigade were inspected by the G.O.C IX Corps as they marched through BAILLEUL. The Battalion arrived at CURRAGH camp about 5.30 PM where the night 30/1 was spent.	W.H.S.

T2134. Wt. W708—776. 500000. 4/15. Sir J. C. & S.

7/8 (S) Battn. ROYAL IRISH FUSILIERS.

Instructions regarding War Diaries and Intelligence Summaries are contained in F. S. Regs., Part II. and the Staff Manual respectively. Title pages will be prepared in manuscript.

WAR DIARY
or
~~INTELLIGENCE SUMMARY.~~
(Erase heading not required.)

APRIL 1917.

Army Form C. 2118.

Place	Date	Hour	Summary of Events and Information	Remarks and references to Appendices
LOCRE			Weather. The weather during the first 2 weeks of April was cold and wet with snow. About the middle of the month the weather improved and towards the end was bright and Sunny	
			Strength The strength of the Battalion on the 30 inst. was officers 49 O.R 1087 These number include men on detachment.	
			The following officers joined the Battn. during the month of April :— LIEUT V. P. WARD. LIEUT D. H. W. KINGHAM. 2 LIEUTS. P. W. NELSON T. HOUSTON. C. E. W. NEATE G. C. WATSON.	
			CAPT. C. T. MACKERN was struck off the strength	W.K.S.
			[signature] Lieut-Col	
			1/5/17. Commdg 7/8 (S) Battn. ROYAL IRISH FUSILIERS	

T2134. Wt. W708—776. 500000. 4/15. Sir J. C. & S.

SECRET

Copy No. 10

Operation Orders. No. 41.

by

April 13th 1917.

Lieut. Colonel H. C. Wilson D.S.O.

Commanding Royal Irish Fusiliers

Map Reference HAZEBROUCK, Sheet 5A 1/100,000.

I. The 49 Inf Bde. will march to the ST OMER area tomorrow 14th inst.

II. Capt. T de C FALLE, with 3 Coy. Q.M. Sgts., Sgt. [illegible] & Armourer Sgt. on cycles will meet the STAFF CAPT. at the cross roads 500 yds. N.E. of last L in WALLON CAPPEL at 8.30 a.m. 3 Coys. horses to be at [illegible] at 7.45 a.m. 3 Coy. Q.M. Sgts., Sgt. [illegible] & Armourer Sgt. will meet Capt. FALLE at cross roads between "A" & "D" Coys. billets.

III. Route EBBLINGHEM – RENESCURE – ARQUES.

IV. The order of march will be Roy. Irish Fusrs. – "A" Royal Innis. Fusrs. – "A" Roy. Irish Regt. – 49 T. M. Bty. – Bde. Hd. Qrs. – "B" Royal Innis. Fusrs. – 49 M. G. Coy. Section Field Ambulance in rear of "B" Roy. Innis. Fus.

V. The Bn. will fall in & be ready to move off by 8.00 a.m. in the following order: H.Qrs. & [illegible] "B" Coy, [illegible] "D" Coy, "A" Coy, Lewis Gun Carts, Guard & Transport.

Hd. Qrs., "B" & "D" Coys. will fall in, head of column at cross roads between "A" & "D" Coys. billets.

"A" Coy. will fall in, head of Coy. at their cross roads ready to move off in rear of "D" Coy. as the column marches off towards WALLON CAPPEL.

Lewis Gun hand carts will fall in in rear of "A" Coy. under 2/Lieut. [illegible].

Transport will fall in in rear of "D" Coy. & follow on after "A" Coy.

VI. Lewis Gun Handcarts. The same sections will pull the handcarts.

VII. Officers kits & mess boxes to be stacked outside Hd. Qrs. by 7.30 a.m.

VIII. Officers horses to be sent by 8 a.m.

IX. One hours halt will be made for dinners at 11.00 a.m.

X. Brigade H. Q. will close at No. 62, RUE de la CLEF, HAZEBROUCK at 8.30 a.m. & will be billeted at Town Hall, ARQUES on arrival there.

XI. The Bn. will be billeted at WIZERNES.

XII. On arrival the Signalling Officer will send a guide to 144th Coy. A.S.C. ST MARTIN-au-LAERT to conduct back supply waggons to Q. M. Stores at WIZERNES.

XIII. Motor lorries will report to Bn. H.Qs at [illegible] p.m. on 14th inst & must be clear of starting point at cross [illegible] to 500 yds. N.E. of last L in WALLON CAPPEL [illegible] 7.00 a.m.

[illegible signature]

Lieut. & Adjutant.
Royal Irish Fusrs.

Issued through Signals.

Copy No. 1 A Coy
" 2. B "
" 3. D "
" 4 L.G.O.
" 5. M.O.
" 6 Signals

Copy No. 7. Q.M.
" " 8. T.O.
" " 9 2/Command
" " 10 C.O.
" 11 49 Inf. Bde.
" 12 Spare

Operation Orders No 39

by

Lieut. Colonel [illegible] D.S.O. [illegible]

Commanding [illegible] Royal Irish [illegible]

I The following move will take place on 7th April 1917

II Battn. H.Qrs., "A", "B" & "D" Coys. will move into KEMMEL SHELTERS.

"C" Coy. will move into [illegible] huts in BIRR BARRACKS.

III Bn. H.Qrs, "A", "B" & "D" Coys. will be [illegible] ready to move off at 2.0 p.m.

IV "C" Coy. will fall in at [illegible] p.m. and will pile arms, take off equipment and stand by. "C" Coy. will [illegible] [illegible] to BIRR BARRACKS at 4.0 p.m.

V All blankets will be rolled in tens and stacked in Company Stores by 12 noon.

VI All Officers kits, messes &c, will be stacked outside the Orderly Room by 12 noon. "C" Company's kits &c must be stacked separately. Each Company will send 1 mess cook and 1 servant as guard and loading party.

VII Lewis Gunners with their Guns &c will accompany their respective Companies

VIII The Transport Officer will arrange to have the necessary transport at DONCASTER HUTS at 12.15 p.m. He will arrange special transport for "C" Coy. to be sent to DONCASTER HUTS. Officers chargers to be [illegible] at [illegible] p.m. to their Companies

IX <u>Handing over</u> Major J. S. Crothers with [illegible] C.Q.M.S. will arrange to take over KEMMEL SHELTERS at 2. p.m. Q.M. will arrange to hand over DONCASTER HUTS at 2.0 p.m. O.C. "C" Coy. will detail an Officer with Coy. Q.M. Sgt. to report to [illegible] Reid [illegible] Inniskillings at BIRR BARRACKS at 2.15 p.m. to take over 1 Officers huts & 6 mens huts.

Sheet 2.

X. Cookers. "A", "B", & "D" Coys will have their dinners on arrival in KEMMEL SHELTERS. "C" Coy will have dinners at DONCASTER HUTS at 2.15 p.m. Cookers will be sent accordingly.

XI Movement Companies will move to KEMMEL SHELTERS in 3s, platoons at 200 yds interval.

XII Cleanliness Great care must be taken to hand over all huts and messes in a clean condition

XIII Arrival in Billets to be reported to Orderly Room

XIV Acknowledge.

[illegible signature]

Lieut & A/Adjutant

7/8th Royal Irish Fusiliers

Issued through Signals

Copy No. 1. ~~A Coy.~~
" 2. ~~B Coy~~
3 ~~C Coy~~
4. ~~D Coy~~
5. Q.M.
6. Transport.
7. R.S.M.
8. M.O.

Copy No. 9. Signals
10. ~~Lewis Gun Officer~~
11. 49th Inf Bde
12. 7 R. Innis Fusrs
~~13. 8 R. Innis Fusrs~~
~~14. 2 R. Irish Regt.~~
15. Spare
16. File

SECRET

Operation Orders No. 140. Copy No. 15
by
Lieut. Colonel H. [illegible] Weldon [illegible]
Commanding Royal Irish Fusiliers.

April 12th 1917.

Reference MAP 28 S.W. 1/20000
HAZEBROUCK 5A 1/100,000

I. The 49th Infantry Brigade will march to the RECQUES Area on the 13th, 14th & 15th inst.

II. The Brigade will be billetted in the HAZEBROUCK Area on the nights of the 13th/14th April.

III. The order of march will be 49th Inf. Bde. – Royal Irish Fusils – 7th Roy. Innis. Fusrs. – 2nd Roy. Irish Regt. – 49th T. M. Bty – 8th Roy. Innis. Fusrs. – 49th M.G. Coy.

13th April 1917.

IV. Route. LOCRE – BAILLEUL – STRAZEELE – PRADELLES.

V. Dinners. One hour's halt for dinners will be made when the head of the column reaches MEULENAEKER 1 mile S. of METEREN.

VI. The Bn. less "C" Coy. & 40 O.R.s will fall in ready to move off towards LOCRE at 8 a.m. in the following order H.Qs. & signallers, "A" Coy, "B" Coy, "D" Coy.

VII. Billetting. Capt. T. de C. FALLE with 3 Coy. Q.M. Sgts. & Sgt. Bird will meet the STAFF Capt. at road junction S.3.[illegible] at 8.30 a.m. on 13th inst. "C" Coy's horse will be sent to "A" Coy. at 7.45 a.m. Coy. Q.M. Sgts. of "A", "B" & "D" Coys. & Sgt. Bird on cycles will meet Capt. FALLE at Transport lines at 8.0 a.m.

VIII. Prisoners & Guard – Prisoners will rejoin their Coys. for the march and will be handed over to the guard on arrival.
The guard will march in rear of the column.

IX. Kits & Mess Boxes – Officers' kits & mess boxes will be stacked near the Headquarters Mess by 7.0 a.m.

X. Transport. [illegible] wagon, mess-cart & Maltese cart will be at H. Q's Mess at 7.0 a.m.
3 Limbers [illegible] for Lewis Guns will be loaded by 7.0 a.m.
The Transport will be ready to move off in rear of the Bn. by 8.25 a.m. on the LOCRE – KEMMEL road.
The Q.M. will be responsible for the [illegible] of wagons.
Officers' horses will be sent to their owners at 7.45 a.m.

XI. Lewis Gun Handcarts. "D" Coy. will [illegible] Lewis Gun Sections & "B" Coy. [illegible] the [illegible] Lewis Gun [illegible] carts in rear of "D" Coy. [illegible] only [illegible]
[illegible]

Sheet 2.

XII. Blankets. Blankets except those of "C" Coy. will be rolled in bundles of 20 and handed into Coy. stores by 7.0 a.m.
1 Motor Lorry will be outside Orderly Room at 7.15 a.m. Each Coy. will send over & load its own blankets. Sgt. Cooper will travel on the Lorry & be responsible for blankets.

XIII. "C" Coy. together with 200 7th Royal Innis. Fusrs. will remain in BIRR BARRACKS.
[illegible] men from "A" "B" & "D" Coys. will be temporarily attached to "C" Coy. They will take 1 blanket per man and day's rations. This party will remain behind for work and will remain in BIRR BARRACKS until the 15th inst.
On the 15th inst. the party will be taken in motor lorries to the RECQUES area. Details of lorries etc. notified later.

XIV. MAJOR O'DONNELL M.C. will stay behind and take command of 200 O.Rs. Royal Irish Fusiliers & 200 O.Rs. 7th Roy. Innis. Fusrs. remaining behind at BIRR BARRACKS. Capt. NEVILLE will hand over the Camp on 15th inst. & obtain usual receipt for [illegible].
No transport will be left for "C" Coy.
"C" Coy. cooker will accompany Bn. & O.C. "C" Coy. will arrange to draw from Q.M. the necessary dixies.

XV. MAJOR O'DONNELL M.C. will hand over KEMMEL SHELTERS to the Camp Warden and obtain the usual receipt. The [illegible] men per Coy. will remain behind under him if necessary to clean up the camp.

XVI. Bde. H.Qs will close at MONT ROUGE at 8.30 a.m.

XVII. The BAND will meet the Bn. at the Transport Lines.

XVIII. Mess Tins will be carried outside and under the Pack. Steel helmets to be worn.
The 2 Cooks per Coy. will parade in blue dungarees & march with the cookers.
The Bn. will march in threes & when marching at ease rifles will be slung.

XIX. The Bn. will march to attention with rifles slung on the right shoulder from BAILLEUL ASYLUM until clear of BAILLEUL.

XX. Acknowledge.

[signature]
Lieut. a/Adjutant,
Royal Irish Fusiliers.

Issued through Signals.

Copy No. 1. "A" Coy.
" 2. "B" "
" 3. "C" "
" 4. "D" "
" 5. Q.M.
" 6. Transport
" 7. R.S.M.
" 8. M.O.

Copy No. 9. Signals
10. [illegible]
11. [illegible]
12. [illegible]
13. [illegible]

SECRET.

Operation Orders No. 42.

Copy No. ...

by

April 14th. 17.

Lieut. Colonel H. C. Weldon D.S.O.

Commanding Royal Irish Fusiliers.

Map reference HAZEBROUCK 5A 1/100,000

I. The 49th. Inf. Bde. will march to the "Recques" area tomorrow 15 inst.

II. Route:- ST. MARTIN-au-LAERT — TILQUES – NORDAUSQUES

III. Starting Point:- Road junction 1 mile N. E. of WIZERNES

IV. Parade Order:- The Bn. will fall in & be ready to move off from the rendezvous at 6. 15 a. m. in the following order H. Qs. D Coy. BAND, A Coy., B Coy. L. G. Handcarts, Guard, Transport.

V. The head of the column will be on road running through first D of GONDARDENNE, ½ mile N.E. of WIZERNES.

VI. L. G. Handcarts:- Same pulling sections for L. G. Handcarts.

VII. Motor Lorries:- The Motor Lorries attached will remain at the Transport Lines for the night 14/15th. inst. The Transport Officer is responsible that they are despatched to TOURNEHEM at 8. 30 a. m.

VIII. Billetting Party:- The billetting party composed of Capt. [illegible], 3 Q.M.S. & Sgt. Bird will travel in the lorries to TOURNEHEM.

IX. On arrival at TOURNEHEM, the lorries must be immediately unloaded & the empty lorries instructed to report to H. Q. 49th. Inf. Bde. COCOVE CHATEAU one mile west of RECQUES.

X. Bn. H. Qs. will close at the Town Hall, ARQUES at 8. 30 a. m. & will open at COCOVE CHATEAU one mile West of RECQUES at 12 noon.

XI. Feet:- O.C. Coys. are responsible that every Platoon Commander inspects the feet of men in his platoon daily & [illegible] that every man washes his feet in cold water [illegible].

XII. Sick:- A motor ambulance will collect sick between [illegible] a. m. M. O's inspection at H. Q. Sigs. [illegible] a. m.

XIII. Officers' kits [illegible] boxes to be sent down to the Transport Lines by 8. 15 a. m. Any kits etc. not sent down by this hour [illegible]

XIV Dinner: One hour halt will be made for dinner at 12. 0 noon.

XV. Horses:- Officers' [illegible] be sent at 6. 30 a. m.

XVI. All blankets will be [illegible] to the transport lines [illegible] [illegible] be collected [illegible] company [illegible]

XVII Acknowledge

[illegible]

[illegible] Adjutant

[illegible] Irish Fusiliers.

SECRET

Operation Orders No. 44 Copy No 12

by

Lieut. Colonel A. C. Weldon D.S.O.

Commanding 7/8th Royal Irish Fusiliers.

April 27. 1917

I The 49th Infantry Brigade will march to the ARQUES AREA on 28th April. 1917.

II The Battalion will be billeted in WIZERNES on arrival.

III Route MOULLE —— ST. MARTIN-au-LAERT.

IV 2/Lieut. J.A. Moody with the 4. Coy Q.M. Sgts & Sergt Bird on cycles will rendezvous on the Square at 8.30. a.m. "B" Coys. horse will be sent there at that hour. The Battalion will occupy the same billeting area as before.

V Prisoners will rejoin the Coy. for the march and will be handed over to the N.C.O. i/c Guard on arrival. The Guard will march in rear of the column.

VI The Battalion will fall in on the Square in QUARTER COLUMN, Band on the right, ready to move off at 9.45. a.m. in the following order. "A" Coy, Band, "B" Coy, "C" Coy, "D" Coy, Lewis Gun handcarts.

VII The Transport will fall in on the road outside the Orderly Room, head of column ready to follow last Coy, at 9.45. a.m., Maltese Cart at 8.45. a.m. One hour's Halt will be made for dinners at 12.50 p.m.

VIII Officers' kits and mess boxes will be stacked separately outside Q.M. Stores by 8.30. a.m.

IX Blankets rolled in bundles of 20 and clearly labelled will be stacked by Companies outside the Q.M. Stores by 7.45. a.m.

X All Company Sanitary men will fall in under the Orderly Officer outside the Orderly Room at 9.45 a.m. They will remain behind to clear up billets, latrines &c. and will rejoin the Battalion as soon as possible. This in no way relieves O's. C. Coys. and Transport Officer from the responsibility of handing over the billets and lines in a perfectly clean and sanitary condition.

XI Captain P.R. Knowles will remain behind to hand over stores &c. to the incoming unit. "C" Coy's horse will remain behind for him.

Issued for Instructional Purposes only. Copy No....

SECRET.

Operation Orders. No. 43.
by.
Lieut. Colonel H. C. Weldon D.S.O. April 25th. 1917.
Commanding Royal Irish Fusiliers

I The X. Division in conjunction with Divisions on either flank will make an attack on enemy position on WYTSCHAETE. RIDGE on the 26th. April 1917.

II The X. Division will attack with two Brigades in the line and one Brigade in Reserve. The 49th. Infantry Brigade will attack on the left and the "Y" Infantry Brigade on the right. The "Z" Infantry Brigade will be in Reserve.

III The Boundaries between the 49th. Infantry and the Infantry Brigades on either flank are shewn in. RED on the attached map.

The Boundaries of Infantry Brigade on the left.

German Line at. P.5.d.60.55. — P.11.b.45.30. — P.11.do.60.65. — OBVIOUS AVENUE (exclusive) to P.17.b.20.60. — ESTAMINET P.17.b.60.05.

IV The Brigade Objectives are shewn on map attached:-
1.st. Objective in BLUE.
Final Objective in BLACK.

V The Battalion on the right, with the 7.th. R. Innis. Fusrs. on the left. will attack the 1.st. Objective. Boundary between the two Battalions marked in PURPLE.

VI The 2nd. Royal Irish Regt. will be in Brigade Reserve. After the first Objective has been captured and consolidated, the 2. Royal Irish Regt. will advance through 7/8. R. Irish Fusrs. and 7. R. Innis. Fusrs. and attack the Final Objective

VII Headquarters

Advanced Bde. H. Qrs. will be at P.5.a.80.70.
Reserve. Bde. H. Qrs. will be at. P.5.a.50.70.
Support. Battalion H.Q. will be at. P.5.a.20.50.
Left. Battalion H.Q. will be at. P.5.a.80.30.

VIII Battalion H. Qrs.

Battalion H. Qrs will be at. P.4.d.90.55.. When the 1.st Objective has been gained Battalion H.Q. will move up to BLACK. COT.

IX There will be four objectives to be attacked by the Battalion, marked on map by a series of dashes and the number of Objective

1st. Battalion Objective NAIL SUPPORT. TRENCH.
2nd. Battalion Objective GREEN LINE.
3rd Battalion Objective NANCY. DRIVE.
4th. Battalion Objective BLUE. LINE

(Contd.)

Sheet. 2.

X The Battalion will attack in four waves.
"A" Coy. on the right in two waves, supported by "C." Coy in two waves.

"B" Coy. on the left in two waves, supported by. "D" Coy. in two waves.

The Boundaries between Companies are marked by a thin pencil line.

XI "A" Coy. will form up in front line from P.4.d.70.60 to top of communication trench at P.5.C.30.65.

"B" Coy. will form up in front line at top of communication trench at. P.5.c.30.65. to P.5.c.65.85.
"C" and "D" Coys. will form up in Support Line behind the Companies they are supporting

XII Two Sections 8. R. Innis. Fusrs. will report to O's. C. "A" and "B" Coys. ~~at Zero — 1 hour~~, to act as "Moppers. Up" after 1. st. wave. Two Sections. 8. R. Innis. Fusrs. will report to O's. C. "C" and "D" Coys. ~~at Zero — 1 hour~~, to act as "Moppers Up" after 3rd. Wave.

O's. C. Coys. will each send 1. Guide to Battalion H.Qrs. at Zero — 3/4 hours to guide "Moppers. Up" to their Battle position

XIII "A" and "B" Coys' first waves will attack 1st & 2nd. Battn Objectives, dropping their "Moppers Up" at. 1st objective "A" and "B" Coys' second waves will occupy 1.st objective "C" and "D" Coys first wave will attack 3rd. & 4th. Battn. Objectives, dropping their "Moppers Up" at 3rd objective "C" and "D" Coys. second waves will occupy. 3rd. Battalion Objective. There will be a pause of 10 minutes at the line marked GREEN. to allow the attacks on either flank to get up, and a similar pause on the line marked. BROWN.

XIV The. O. C. Coy. 8. R. Innis. Fusrs, who are acting as "Moppers Up" will report to. Bn. H.Q. at Zero — 3/4 hour for instructions. The remaining sections will act as carrying parties for bombs and tools &c from the dump at P.11.A.9½. 6. to the BLUE. Objective, when it has been taken. They will follow the 4 th. wave after an interval.

All. "Moppers. Up" when they have cleared the trenches alloted to them, will return to Bde H. Qrs with their Lewis. Guns. at .P.5.A.80.70.. Carriers will remain behind on their alloted task

XV All positions will be consolidated as soon as captured

XII Strong points will be constructed by 8. R. Innis as marked on Sketch S. P's, "A", "B" and "C".

XVII O's. C. Companies will send 2 watches to Bn H. Q. to be synchronized at Zero — 1 hour.

XVIII Artillery

a. Bombardment of enemy's positions will take place on. V, W, X, Y. days.
The assault will take place Z. day at Zero hour.
The Heavy Artillery will bombard the crest of the Ridge and selected points. The Field Artillery will form a. Creeping Barrage along a line 100 yards short of the German Front line.
a. Standing Barrage on the German Support Trenches will move forward on succeeding lines and S. P's. as the Creeping Barrage progresses.
The Creeping Barrage will move forward at the rate of 100 yards in 4. minutes, pausing for 10. minutes, 150 yards beyond the GREEN line and then creep forward 150 yards beyond the BLUE line where it will remain, the rate of fire being slackened.
The Barrage will also pause for 10. minutes 150. yds. beyond the BROWN. LINE.

XIX Machine Guns. Two Vickers Guns will be attached to the Battalion for the attack. They will report at Bn. H. Qrs. for orders at P. 4. d. 90. 85. at Zero — 3/4 hour. Vickers' Guns will follow behind the 2nd Wave, one behind "A" Coy. on the right and one behind "B" Coy. on the left. They will remain behind the GREEN. LINE until the BLUE. LINE has been taken, when they will move up and support.

XX T. M's, 2" Stokes Mortars will be attached to the Battalion for the attack. They will report at Bn H. Qrs for orders at Zero — 3/4 hour. They will advance together behind the centre of the 2nd Wave and will remain behind the GREEN. Line, until the BLUE. LINE has been taken, when they will move up and support the BLUE LINE.

XXI a. Contact Aeroplane will fly over the area of attack from Zero hour to Zero + 2½ hours.
Flares will be lit by the leading platoons 50 yds. in front of their furthest positions at the following hours. or whenever the aeroplane asks for them by means of a succession of "A's on a Klaxon Horn

Sheet. 4.

XI (contd)
Horn or by a Very Light.

Zero plus. 40 minutes

Zero plus. 70. minutes

Zero for attack on Brigade Final Objective plus 20 minutes

Zero for attack on Brigade Final Objective plus 38 minutes

Each Platoon must carry at least. 7. flares.

XXII All troops to be in position by Zero — 30 minutes

XXIII Medical Arrangements.

A Regimental Aid Post will be established at P. 4. d. 9½. 9½. All Company stretcher bearers will report here to the M.O. at Zero — one hour. As soon as the BLUE. objective has been captured and held and the R.A.P. clear of the wounded, the M.O. will move forward to P. 11. a. 5. 7., if the enemy barrage permits. When he moves forward all Company Stretcher bearers. will be returned to their Companies.

XXIV Acknowledge. ✓

[signature]

Lieut & A/Adjutant
7/8 Royal Irish Fusiliers

Issued through Signals.

Copy. No. 1. "A" Coy
2. "B" Coy.
3. "C" Coy.
4. "D" Coy.
5. Q.M.
6. Transport
7. R.S.M.
8. M.O.
9. Signals.

Copy. No. 10. L. G. Officer
11. 49th Inf. Bde.
12. 2. R Irish Regt
13. 7. R Innis Fus.
14. 8. R Innis Fus
15. 49. T. M. Bty
16. 49. M. G. Coy
17. File
18. Spare.

Operation Orders No. 45. Copy No. ...

by

Lieut. Colonel [illegible] C. Weldon D.S.O.

Commanding 7/8th Royal Irish Fusiliers

I. The Battalion will march to the HAZEBROUCK AREA on the 29th inst and will be billeted in the same area village as on the march to the Training Area

II. Advance party consisting of Lieut Sparks, 4 C.Q.M. Sgts & Sgt Bird will rendezvous outside H.Q. mess at 7.30 a.m. with bicycles

III. Blankets & kits should be at Q.M. Stores by 8.30 a.m. Mess Cart will call at H.Q. mess before 8 a.m. to collect mess boxes. Motor lorries will be loaded and despatched soon to Level Crossing 600 yds. E. of Canal Bridge in ARQUES.

IV. The Brigade Order of March will be:-

7. R. Innis. Fusrs.

7/8. R. Irish Fusrs.

2. R. Irish Regt.

Battalion Order of March will be.

Drums.

Signallers

H.Qrs.

B. C. D. A. Coys.

Transport

V. Column will fall in with head at ROAD JUNCTION S. of S in WIZERNES facing E. ready to march off at 8.45 A.M. Coy Commanders will be careful to reckon the time required to reach the starting point as Coys should not be kept standing about after [illegible]

VI. The same arrangements as stated in yesterdays operation Orders will apply on leaving billets to-morrow under 2/Lieut. C.W. Pickett.

VII Acknowledge

Captain & Adjutant

7/8 Royal Irish Fusiliers

Copy No. 1 [illegible] ✓ Copy No. 6 C.O. ✓

2 [illegible] ✓ [illegible] Q.M.

3 [illegible] [illegible]

4 [illegible] [illegible]

[illegible] [illegible]

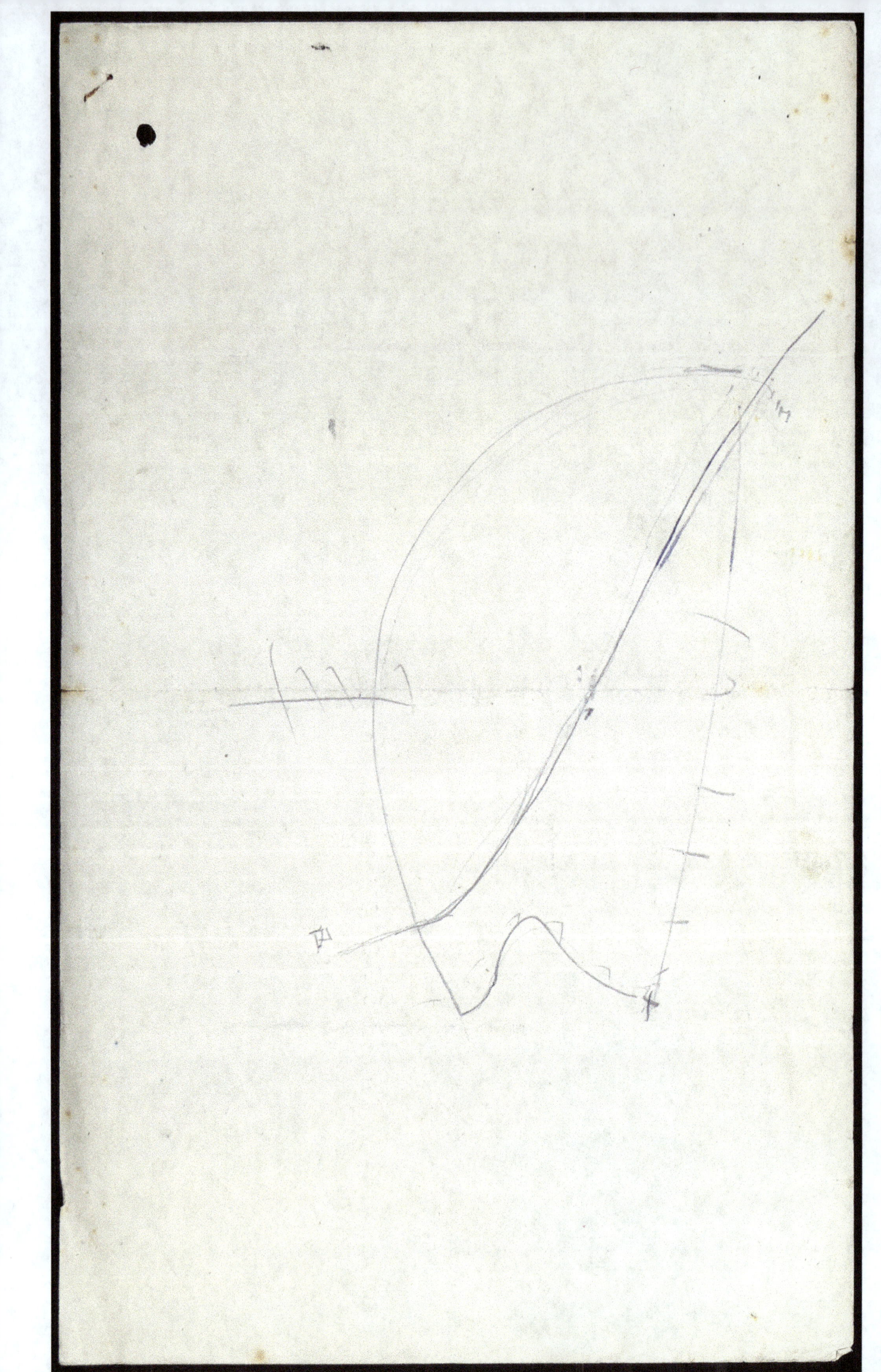

Sheet. 2.

XII "A" Coy. will provide 4 Lewis Gun Sections and "C" Coy. 2 Sections for pulling 6. Lewis Gun hand carts in rear of "D" Coy. Only packs may be put on the hand carts. Teams will report to 2/Lieut Waters at Orderly Room at 9.30. a.m.

XIII Acknowledge.

[illegible]

Lieut & A/Adjutant
7/8 Royal Irish Fusiliers

Issued through Signals

Copy No. 1. "A" Coy.
2. "B" Coy.
3. "C" Coy.
4. "D" Coy.
5. Q.M.
6. Transport
7. R.S.M.
8. M.O.
9. Signals

Copy No. 10. L. Gun Officer
11. 49th Inf. Bde.
12. Spare
13. File
14. War Diary

8 J. 9 D.

W A R D I A R Y :

------------oOo-----------

VOLUME:- 8

FOR MONTH OF MAY, 1917.

U N I T :- 7/8th Royal Irish Fusiliers.

9/16

7/8 (S) Battn ROYAL IRISH FUSILIERS

Instructions regarding War Diaries and Intelligence Summaries are contained in F. S. Regs., Part II. and the Staff Manual respectively. Title pages will be prepared in manuscript.

WAR DIARY
or
~~INTELLIGENCE SUMMARY.~~
(*Erase heading not required.*)

MAY 1917

Army Form C. 2118.

Place	Date	Hour	Summary of Events and Information (Ref. FRANCE Sheet 28 SW and 28 S.W.2)	Remarks and references to Appendices
RIDGE WOOD (N 5 a. b)	1.5.17 2.5.17 3.5.17 4.5.17		The 49 Inf Bde relieved the 56 Inf. Bde. in the DIEPENDAAL SECTOR on the 1st May 2 Battns in Front System, 1 Battn. Bde Support, 1 Battn Bde Reserve. This Battn was in Bde Support and relieved the 7 R. LANC. REGT in RIDGE WOOD. (N 5. a. 6) The 4 days passed quietly The weather was very warm and visibility high with the result that there was a large amount of aerial activity; and considerable artillery activity which was chiefly directed against back billets, roads etc.	W.H.S.
BRASSERIE (N.6.c.1.9)	5.5.17		The Battalion relieved the 2. R. IR. REGT in the left subsection DIEPENDAAL SECTOR during the night 5/6 (vide O.O. 48). The night 5/6 passed quietly	W.H.S.
	6.5.17.		The enemy artillery were active on this front commencing about 6.0 AM and firing intermittently until 11.0 AM with 77 mm and 4.2's. Targets engaged were New Reserve Trench and "BOIS CARRE". Our 18 pdrs and 4.2 Hows retaliated. During the day our heavies were active firing well behind the enemys lines. Visibility was high and aerial activity high. In the evening the enemy were very active shelling our back billets with 5.9's and 4.2's. Our 18 pdrs. 4.2's and heavies retaliated heavily	W.H.S.

T2134. Wt. W708-776. 500000. 4/15. Sir J. C. & S.

7/8 (A) Battn. ROYAL IRISH FUSILIERS **WAR DIARY** *or* ~~INTELLIGENCE~~ **SUMMARY.** MAY 1917.

Army Form C. 2118.

Instructions regarding War Diaries and Intelligence Summaries are contained in F. S. Regs., Part II. and the Staff Manual respectively. Title pages will be prepared in manuscript.

(Erase heading not required.)

Place	Date	Hour	Ref FRANCE sheets 28 S.W. and 28 S.W.2. Summary of Events and Information	Remarks and references to Appendices
BRASSERIE	7 8 17		The night 6/7 passed very quietly. About 6.15 AM the enemy shelled NEW RESERVE TRENCH and BOIS CARRÉ. Our artillery punished the enemy with 18 pdrs and 4.2's silencing him about 7.0 AM. Similar shelling took place between 8.30 AM and 10.0 AM. Our artillery were active during the day in punishment for hostile activity. About 11.30 AM one of our aeroplanes made a forced landing at N 5 b. central. As this spot was in view of the enemy, the enemy shelled the plane with shrapnel, 4.2's and 15 cm's considerably damaging the plane. Considerable work is going on in OBIT SUPPORT and OBSTRUCTION TRENCH. With the object of putting a stop to the enemy shelling our back areas at night, every gun and howitzer except 12" Hows, in the SECOND ARMY fired for 5 minutes at intense rate from 8.45 PM to 8.50 P.M. The enemy retaliated from 10.20 PM to 10.50 PM shelling Battn. Hdqrs, BRASSERIE and gun positions in rear. Another similar 5 minutes intense fire took place in the IX Corps area from 11.0 PM to 11.5 PM to which the enemy did not reply.	W.H.S.
"	8 8 17		The enemy again shelled NEW RESERVE TRENCH from 6.15 AM until about 7.0 AM. Our artillery fired an organized strafe for 5 minutes about 8.0 AM, to which	

T2134. Wt. W708–776. 500000. 4/15. Sir J. C. & S.

7/8 (S) Battn. ROYAL IRISH FUSILIERS

WAR DIARY
or
~~INTELLIGENCE SUMMARY~~.
(Erase heading not required.)

MAY 1917

Army Form C. 2118.

Instructions regarding War Diaries and Intelligence Summaries are contained in F. S. Regs., Part II. and the Staff Manual respectively. Title pages will be prepared in manuscript.

Place	Date	Hour	Summary of Events and Information	Remarks and references to Appendices
BRASSERIE.	8.5.17 (cont.)		the enemy did not reply. The enemys artillery was very active all morning. About noon they obtained a direct hit on Battn. Hdqrs. killing 6 men and wounding 2 and setting fire to a store. Intermittant artillery fire on both sides continued during the afternoon.	W.H.S.
	9.5.17		About 6.30 AM enemy artillery was very active firing at intervals on our trenches ~~from~~ with 10 cms 15 cms and 7.7 cm guns. This fire continued at intervals until about mid day. Our artillery fired on enemys trenches and at enemys battery positions. The enemy opened a heavy bombardment on the front of the Battn on the left about 7.5 PM in about 5 minutes this bombardment was extended to our front and a heavy bombardment maintained on FRONT LINE, NEW. RESERVE LINE and on the YPRES-VIERSTRAAT road for about 200x either side of the BRASSERIE. The S.O.S. signal was sent to the artillery who opened a very heavy bombardment on the front and support lines of the enemy. The enemys fire on front line consisted of 77 mm and Minenwerfer and on RESERVE TRENCH and in rear 77 mm, 10.5 cm and 15 cm. guns. Our artillery maintained the barrage until about 10.15 PM.	

T2134. Wt. W708–776. 500000. 4/15. Sir J. C. & S.

7/8 (S) Battn ROYAL IRISH FUSILIERS

Instructions regarding War Diaries and Intelligence Summaries are contained in F. S. Regs., Part II. and the Staff Manual respectively. Title pages will be prepared in manuscript.

WAR DIARY
or
~~INTELLIGENCE SUMMARY.~~
(Erase heading not required.)

MAY 1917.

Army Form C. 2118.

Place	Date	Hour	Summary of Events and Information (Ref map FRANCE 28 SW 2 and trench map attached.)	Remarks and references to Appendices
BRASSERIE	9.5.17		ably assisted by our Lewis and Vickers guns. The enemy's bombardment ceased about 10.5 PM. Considerable damage was done to our trenches and our casualties amounted to O R killed 3 wounded 13 It would seem that the enemy were about to raid but thanks to our barrage it did not materialize After 10.15 PM all was quiet. Shortly after the situation became normal the 7 S LANC RECT commenced to relieve the Battn. The Battn on relief moved to CARNARVON CAMP M 10 b 8.6 During the period 5-9/5/17 our casualties amounted to 1 off W. O.R Killed 10 wounded 18 wounded at duty 6.	W.H.S.
BUTTERFLY FARM	10.5.17		The 49. Inf Bde relieved the 47 Inf Bde in the VIERSTRAAT SECTOR The Battn. moved into Bde Reserve at BUTTERFLY FARM	W.H.S.
do	11.5.17		Training, squad drill etc	W.H.S.
	12.5.17		do	W.H.S.
	13.5.17		do	W.H.S.
YORK HOUSE N.16c.9.3.	14.5.17		The Battn relieved the 8 R INNIS FUS. in accordance with O.O. 50 attached, in the left sub-section VIERSTRAAT SECTOR The night 14/15 passed quietly. Our artillery fired during the night	W.H.S.
do.	15.5.17		During the forenoon our heavy artillery shelled "back areas". Our 18 pdrs carried	

7/8(S) Battn. ROYAL IRISH FUSILIERS

Instructions regarding War Diaries and Intelligence Summaries are contained in F. S. Regs., Part II. and the Staff Manual respectively. Title pages will be prepared in manuscript.

WAR DIARY
or
~~INTELLIGENCE SUMMARY.~~
(Erase heading not required.)

MAY 1917.

Army Form C. 2118.

Place	Date	Hour	Summary of Events and Information (Ref maps FRANCE Sheets 28 SW. Ed 5A and 28 SW 2 Ed. 5A and trench map.)	Remarks and references to Appendices
YORK HO.	15.5.17 (cont)		out wirecutting during the day. At 3PM our artillery (18 pdrs. 4.5 hows 6" hows and 8" hows) assisted by heavy, medium, and light T.M's carried out a bombardment of enemys lines and back areas. Good results were observed, considerable wire being destroyed and trench material being thrown up. During the morning the enemy shelled KEMMEL, DICKEBUSCH and HALLEBAST ROAD. Their retaliation to our bombardment was extremely feeble, the only reply to our bombardment being a few 77 mm. shells on N 29 b. and in vicinity of S.P. 13.	
YORK Ho.	16.5.7		Wirecutting was continued to-day by our artillery and 2" T.M's. Good results observed and about 70 yards of wire cut. Our Lewis Guns fired on these gaps where possible to keep them open. It was observed however that about 30 yds wire cut on 15.5.17 had been at once repaired during the night. The hostile inactivity (artillery, M.G, T.M and sniping) was very marked. His only retaliation being a few 10 cms on CHINESE WALL. Owing to unfavourable weather, our artillery only fired on gaps in the wire during the night.	W.R.S.
YORK Ho	17.5.7		Owing to rain and mist, little artillery activity during the morning. About 5.30 pm and onwards our field guns continued wire cutting. Our 60 pdrs fired with good effect on enemy trenches in PETIT BOIS, and heavier artillery on WYTSHAETE VILLAGE, and counter battery work. Our heavy fire	W.S.

T2134. Wt. W708–776. 500000. 4/15. Sir J. C. & S.

7/8th (S) Battn ROYAL IRISH FUSILIERS.

WAR DIARY
or
~~INTELLIGENCE SUMMARY.~~
(Erase heading not required.)

Instructions regarding War Diaries and Intelligence Summaries are contained in F. S. Regs., Part II. and the Staff Manual respectively. Title pages will be prepared in manuscript.

MAY 1917

Army Form C. 2118.

Ref. map FRANCE sheets 28 S.W. Ed. 5A and 28 SW 2. Ed. 5A and trench map.

Place	Date	Hour	Summary of Events and Information	Remarks and references to Appendices
YORK HSE	18/5/17		Wire cutting continued. Good work was done by the 18 pdrs who fired continuously throughout the day especially on UNNAMED WOOD and NAME SUPPORT. Retaliation was slight and the hostile artillery remained as inactive as previous days. About 9 am, an enemy aeroplane flew over our support line at about 200 ft high, but in spite of many hits from our Lewis gun fire, flew back over his own lines intact. At about 6.30 pm, one of our planes brought down a hostile kite balloon in flames behind the WYTSHAETE RIDGE. The Battn was relieved in the left sub-section VIERSTRAAT SECTOR by the 9th Battn. ROYAL IRISH RIFLES. The 49th Infantry Brigade was relieved by the 48th Infantry Brigade. On relief the brigade moved in Divisional Reserve in the neighbourhood of LOCRE, and the Battn moved into DONCASTER HUTS. This 6 days tour in the trenches was completed without a casualty in the Battn.	
DONCASTER HUTS	19/5/17		In Divisional Reserve. Provided working parties of 12 officers 450 O.R's.	
	20/5/17		" " " " "	
	21/5/17		" " " "	
	22/5/17		" " " "	WS
	23/5/17		" " " "	
	24/5/17		" " "	
	25/5/17		" " "	

T2134. Wt. W708—776. 500000. 4/15. Sir J. C. & S.

7/8th (S) Battn. ROYAL IRISH FUSILIERS

Instructions regarding War Diaries and Intelligence Summaries are contained in F. S. Regs., Part II. and the Staff Manual respectively. Title pages will be prepared in manuscript.

WAR DIARY
or
~~INTELLIGENCE~~ ~~SUMMARY~~.
(Erase heading not required.)

MAY 1917.

Army Form C. 2118.

Place	Date	Hour	Ref. Map FRANCE, Sheet 28. S.W. ... Summary of Events and Information	Remarks and references to Appendices
DONCASTER	26/5/17		In Divisional Reserve. Provided working parties of 10 Officers 400 men	
HUTS	27/5/17		" " " " " " " " . Several parties were sent back from the front line owing to heavy shell fire. Starting at 10.30 pm and at intervals throughout the night the enemy has shelled back areas & dumps with 5.9", ~~...~~ gas shells are reported. Transport lines in M.34 suffered severely.	
	28/5/17 29/5/17 30/5/17 31/5/17		In Divisional Reserve. Working parties continued. Hostile shelling of back areas, huts and ammunition dumps was systematically continued; in consequence, the huts occupied by the battn were vacated during the night. The principal gun used in this shelling is a 5.9" high velocity. The following officers and NCO's were mentioned in Sir. Douglas Haig's despatches:- Capt T de C FALLE, Capt G H L CLARKE, Capt A.C. SAXTON, 2/Lieut. T. GERATY. M.C. Sergt RANAHAN, No 20272, Pte. QUIGLEY. During this period in Divisional Reserve, there has been great activity behind our lines. The construction of roads has been pushed on, many guns of all calibres has been coming up, many ammunition dumps have been constructed & filled.	

[signature] LIEUT. COL.
COMDG. 7/8 (S) BN. R. IR. FUSILIERS

T2134. Wt. W708–776. 500000. 4/16. Sir J. C. & S.

9. J.

S. Abrahams

W A R   D I A R Y.

FOR MONTH OF JUNE, 1917.

V O L U M E :- 9.

UNIT:- 7/8th Battn. R. Irish Fusiliers

Jul 17

7/8th (S) Batt. ROYAL IRISH FUSILIERS

WAR DIARY
or
INTELLIGENCE SUMMARY.
(Erase heading not required.)

JUNE 1917

Army Form C. 2118.

Instructions regarding War Diaries and Intelligence Summaries are contained in F. S. Regs., Part II. and the Staff Manual respectively. Title pages will be prepared in manuscript.

Place	Date	Hour	Summary of Events and Information	Remarks and references to Appendices
			Ref. FRANCE 28 SW and 28 SW 2 [illegible] A Map attached.	
DONCASTER HUTS.	1.6.17		In Divisional Reserve. Provided working parties of 10 Officers and 350 O.R's. Considerable artillery activity heard but back areas have not been shelled by the enemy.	[illegible]
	2.6.17		Divisional Reserve. Providing same working parties. On the night 2/3rd June the 48th Infantry Brigade was relieved in the VIERSTRAAT SECTION by the 47th and the 49th Infantry Brigades. Brigade Headquarters moved to their battle position at the RIB. N 16 D 35 50. The Batt. remained in Brigade Reserve at DONCASTER HUTS.	[illegible]
	3.6.17		In Brigade Reserve. The first 4 sheets of Battalion Instructions for the Offensive were issued to all concerned. During the afternoon inter-company sports were held. At 3 pm an intense bombardment of the [illegible] front & back area took place, lasting about 1 hour. The retaliation was slight. At 12.30 am on the night 3rd/4th June a bombardment with OIL DRUMS was carried out on WYTSCHAETE WOOD, UNNAMED WOOD, GRAND BOIS. The illumination caused by the explosion of the drums lasted about 15 seconds & smouldering effects were observed for 15 minutes.	[illegible]
	4.6.17		In Brigade Reserve. The day was mostly occupied by inspections and issue of bomb-bags grenade bags, wire-cutters, field-glasses &c and in overhauling Lewis Guns. At 10.30 pm the 47th Infantry Brigade carried out a raid, entering the enemy trenches [illegible]	

T2134. Wt. W708–776. 500000. 4/15. Sir J. C. & S.

7/8th (S) Battn Royal Irish Fusiliers

WAR DIARY
or
INTELLIGENCE SUMMARY.
(Erase heading not required.)

June 1917

Army Form C. 2118.

2

Instructions regarding War Diaries and Intelligence Summaries are contained in F. S. Regs., Part II. and the Staff Manual respectively. Title pages will be prepared in manuscript.

Place	Date	Hour	Summary of Events and Information (Ref. FRANCE 28 SW & 28 S.W. 2. Ed. 5A)	Remarks and references to Appendices
DONCASTER HUTS	4/6/17 (contd)		N 24 a 87 62 to N 24 b 10 30. Sheets 8 and 9 of Battn Instructions for the offensive issued.	W.H.S.
"	5/6/17		On the night 4/5 a raid was carried out by the 47th Inf Bde. During the day our artillery shelled the enemys positions very heavily. The Battalion fell in at 9.0 PM and marched to the VIERSTRAAT SECTOR where it relieved the 8 R. INNIS. FUS just after the latter Battn had raided the enemys trenches, securing 4 prisoners. (vide B.O. No 1. dated 4.6.17) Relief was reported complete about 3.0 AM.	W.H.S.
S.P. 13	6.6.17		Our artillery fired continually during the day. Bombs etc were issued out to all ranks and final preparations made. At 10.0 PM our troops commenced moving to their assembly positions. Ladders were placed over trenches, positions prepared for climbing out of the trenches. Hot drinks were issued to the men. At midnight all ranks were reported in position in assembly positions.	W.H.S.

T2134. Wt. W708–776. 500000. 4/15. Sir J. C. & S.

7/8(S) Battn. ROYAL IRISH FUSILIERS 3

Army Form C. 2118.

WAR DIARY
or
~~INTELLIGENCE SUMMARY~~.
(Erase heading not required.)

JUNE 1917.

Instructions regarding War Diaries and Intelligence Summaries are contained in F. S. Regs., Part II. and the Staff Manual respectively. Title pages will be prepared in manuscript.

Place	Date	Hour	Summary of Events and Information (Ref. Maps sheets 28 SW and 28 SW 2 ~~Ed~~ 5A; Maps attached)	Remarks and references to Appendices
LOCRE	7/6/17.		From midnight until zero there was a normal ammount of shelling at 3 10AM it was still dark, ~~just~~ dawn was just creeping into the sky. The mines went off at zero and immediately the artillery opened gun fire and the M.G.'s etc opened fire. The mines in the PETIT BOIS SALIENT being so close to our trenches caused a little confusion, and the wind drove the gas towards our troops, with the result that 9 O.R. were slightly gassed. The Battalion climbed out of the trenches and set off in their various waves. a small amount of hostile fire was directed on our troops. The RED OBJECTIVE was reached well up to time and touch being obtained with Battalions on either flank and steps were taken to immediately consolidate the line. One machine gun offered considerable resistance firing from the N. edge of WYTSCHAETE WOOD, but this was rushed and captured by A Coy and is now in possession of this Battn. 'C' and 'D' Companies advanced in almost perfect order towards the BLUE LINE. This objective was taken well up to scheduled time and immediately consolidated in depth, and in touch with the	

7/8 (S) Battn. ROYAL IRISH FUSILIERS

WAR DIARY
or
~~INTELLIGENCE~~ SUMMARY.
(Erase heading not required.)

JUNE 1917.

Army Form C. 2118.

Instructions regarding War Diaries and Intelligence Summaries are contained in F. S. Regs., Part II. and the Staff Manual respectively. Title pages will be prepared in manuscript.

Place	Date	Hour	Summary of Events and Information (Ref maps sheets 28 S.W. and 28 S.W. 2 Ed 5A and maps attached)	Remarks and references to Appendices
LOCRE 7/6/17 continued			Battalions on our Right and Left. Later heavy fire was directed on this line by the enemy and a considerable number of casualties were suffered.	
			The cable laid in 'Z' passage from S.P.13, having been rendered useless by the subsidence of the passage resulting from the explosion of the mines, great difficulty was encountered in establishing the Battalion forward station at BLACK COT. This was eventually done by 4.50AM.	
			Battalion Hdqrs. moved from S.P. 13 at 5.5 AM and proceeded to the forward station at BLACK COT which was reached at 5.30AM, by which time communication had been established with all the Companies and Bde. Hdqrs.	
			The Battn. Forward Dump was established at BLACK COT and the carrying parties dumped stores, ammunition, L.C. drums etc there, and these were drawn by the Companies.	
			Four lines of trenches were consolidated. The RED LINE, the BLUE LINE, a line about 200x in front of the RED LINE and a similar line in front of the BLUE LINE. These were all consolidated in	

T2134. Wt. W708–776. 500000. 4/15. Sir J. C. & S.

7/8 (S) Battn. ROYAL IRISH FUSILIERS

WAR DIARY
or
~~INTELLIGENCE SUMMARY.~~
(Erase heading not required.)

JUNE 1917

Army Form C. 2118.

5

Instructions regarding War Diaries and Intelligence Summaries are contained in F. S. Regs., Part II. and the Staff Manual respectively. Title pages will be prepared in manuscript.

Place	Date	Hour	Summary of Events and Information	Remarks and references to Appendices
			Ref. Maps 28 SW and 28 SW 2 Ed 5A and maps attached.	
LOCRE	7.6.17 continued		depth.	
			The 2 R. IRISH RECT. passed through at 6.50 AM and captured the GREEN and BLACK LINES.	
			At 8 OAM 'B' Coy under 2 LIEUT V. J. LYNCH moved forward from the RED LINE in artillery formation and on arrival at the BLACK LINE extended into waves and passed through the 2 R IR. RECT. When contour 65 was reached a halt was made a small patrol was sent forward to reconnoitre SONNEN FARM. As a result of information received the company moved forward and occupied the FARM. On approaching LEG COPSE the company was held up with M.G. fire. Up to this time communication had not been established with the units on either flank. While the Lewis Guns swept the copse, a platoon moved round the right flank, and after a short but fierce fight, one M.G was captured and 30 prisoners taken, including an officer. This M.G is now in our possession.	
			Having cleared the COPSE, our patrols pushed forward and reported that posts of the GLOUSTERS were establishing themselves in front of	

T2134. Wt. W708–776. 500000. 4/15. Sir J. C. & S.

7/8 (S) Battn. ROYAL IRISH FUSILIERS

WAR DIARY
or
~~INTELLIGENCE~~ ~~SUMMARY.~~
(Erase heading not required.)

JUNE 1917

Army Form C. 2118.

6

Instructions regarding War Diaries and Intelligence Summaries are contained in F. S. Regs., Part II. and the Staff Manual respectively. Title pages will be prepared in manuscript.

Place	Date	Hour	Summary of Events and Information Ref. Maps 28SW, 28SW2 Ed. 5A and maps attached	Remarks and references to Appendices
LOCRE	7.6.17 (Cont.)		OOSTAVERNE WOOD. We continued this line of posts and later pushed our whole line forward to within 300x of OIL TRENCH. Up to this time no touch could be established with the troops on the R flank. It was then 2.30 P.M. at 3.15 PM a Battn of the R. DUB. FUS relieved this Coy. and pushed on to OIL TRENCH. Shortly afterwards a portion of the 33. INF BDE passed through and captured the OOSTAVERNE LINE. This Coy. during this advance to the MAUVE LINE captured 2 guns 2 MG's and 46 prisoners (including 2 officers), a canteen, and an artillery Group Hdqrs complete with telephones etc. The Vickers Guns and Stokes Guns rendered valuable assistance. The Tanks were not able to assist this Battalion very much. Water was brought up to BLACK COT on pack animals at 11.30 AM. The supply of Rations and Water was excellent throughout. When the BLUE LINE was captured, a forward dressing station was established in a shell hole at BLACK COT. Throughout the afternoon, the enemy fired intermittently, especially	

T2134. Wt. W708—776. 500000. 4/15. Sir J. C. & S.

7

7/8(10) Battn. ROYAL IRISH FUSILIERS

Army Form C. 2118.

WAR DIARY
or
INTELLIGENCE SUMMARY.

JUNE 1917.

(Erase heading not required.)

Instructions regarding War Diaries and Intelligence Summaries are contained in F. S. Regs., Part II. and the Staff Manual respectively. Title pages will be prepared in manuscript.

Place	Date	Hour	Summary of Events and Information	Remarks and references to Appendices
			Ref Maps 28 O W., 28 SW2 Ed. 5A and maps attached	
LOCRE	7.6.17 (cont)		in the vicinity of the HOSPICE. At 8 0 PM orders were received to withdraw to the vicinity of YORK ROAD where the Battn bivouaced in a field ready to move forward in case of a counter attack.	W.H.S
			Our casualties ammounted to officers killed 2 wounded 7. O.R. killed 20 died of wounds 5. missing 14 wounded 145 wounded at duty 2.	
			A large number of prisoners were captured and passed to the Divnl. Cage.	W.H.S
YORK. RD	8.6.17		Remained in vicinity of YORK ROAD	W.H.S
LOCRE	9.6.17		The Battn moved to TRALEE LINES "B".	W.H.S
	10.6.17		Supplied working parties for making roads from "No Mans Land" to WYTSCHAETE.	W.H.S
"	11.6.17		Resting. Cleaning up	W.H.S
	12.6.17		Bathing	W.H.S
MOOLENACKER	13.6.17		The Bde marched to the MERRIS AREA. This Battalion was billeted in farms in the vicinity of MOOLENACKER (B.O. No 3.).	W.H.S

T2134. Wt. W708–776 500000. 4/15. Sir J. C. & S.

7/8 (S) Battn. ROYAL IRISH FUSILIERS

Army Form C. 2118.

Instructions regarding War Diaries and Intelligence Summaries are contained in F. S. Regs., Part II. and the Staff Manual respectively. Title pages will be prepared in manuscript.

WAR DIARY
or
~~INTELLIGENCE~~ SUMMARY.
(Erase heading not required.)

JUNE. 1917

Place	Date	Hour	Summary of Events and Information — Ref map Sheet 27.	Remarks and references to Appendices
MOOLENACKER	14.6.17		Checking deficiencies re-equipping, cleaning up etc.	W.H.S.
"	15.6.17		do. close order drill. ~~Staff~~ Staff rides for junior officers. Instructing NCO's in map reading.	W.H.S.
"	16.6.17		ditto.	W.H.S.
CLARE CAMP	17.6.17		The Battn marched to CLARE CAMP ~~[illegible]~~ and were accommodated under canvas. The transport accompanied the Battn. (vide B.O. No 4 attached) Warning orders were received that the 16 Div. was to ~~the~~ relieve the 19' Division in the left section of the new 9' Corps front.	
MOOLENACKER	18.6.17		Orders were received about 12.15 AM the 49 Inf Bde would move back to the MERRIS AREA at 5.0 AM and occupy the same billets as occupied on 13 inst. Verbal instructions were issued and the Battn marched back to the neighbourhood of MOOLENACKER.	W.H.S.
MOOLENACKER	19.6.17		Warning orders were received that the 16 Division was being transferred from the IX Corps area to the Fifth army, and that the Division would move to the TILQUES SOUTH training area on the 20' inst. The G.O.C 49 Inf. Bde inspected the Battn. and expressed his satisfaction	

T2134. Wt. W708—776. 500000. 4/15. Sir J. C. & S.

7/8(0) Battn. ROYAL IRISH FUSILIERS

Army Form C. 2118.

Instructions regarding War Diaries and Intelligence Summaries are contained in F. S. Regs., Part II. and the Staff Manual respectively. Title pages will be prepared in manuscript.

WAR DIARY
or
~~INTELLIGENCE SUMMARY.~~
(Erase heading not required.)

JUNE 1917

Place	Date	Hour	Summary of Events and Information (Ref. Map. Sheets 27, 27A. S.E)	Remarks and references to Appendices
MOOLENACKER	19.6.17 cont		at the turn out of the men. The G.O.C. conveyed to the Battalion the congratulations of the Army Commander on their success on the 7th inst. The G.O.C. himself spoke very highly of the work done by the Battalion recently and their success on the 7th inst at the attack on the WYTSCHAETE - MESSINES ridge.	W.H.S.
Near STEENVOORDE	20.6.17		The Bde marched to and was billeted in the ECCKE area.	W.H.S.
	21.6.17		Company inspection, drill etc.	W.H.S.
BROXELLES area	22.6.17		The 49 Inf. Bde marched to the BROXELLES area. On the march the Bde were inspected by General PLUMER Commdg. 2nd Army. The G.O.C 2nd Army conveyed his congratulations to all ranks on their success on the 7th June. The Battn was in farms, some scattered.	W.H.S.
do	23.6.17		Training, inspections, lectures etc.	W.H.S.
	24.6.17		ditto	W.H.S.
	25.6.17		ditto	W.H.S.
	26.6.17		ditto.	W.H.S.
	27.6.17		ditto.	W.H.S.
do	28.6.17		ditto	W.H.S.
do	29.6.17		ditto	W.H.S.
CORMETTES	30.6.17		The Bde marched to the TILQUES SOUTH TRAINING AREA. The Battn was billeted in CORMETTES. LEULINE and AUDENTHUN.	W.H.S.

2353 Wt. W2544/1454 700,000 5/15 D. D. & L. A.D.S.S./Forms/C. 2118.

7/8 (S) Battn. ROYAL IRISH FUSILIERS

WAR DIARY
or
~~INTELLIGENCE SUMMARY~~.
(Erase heading not required.)

JUNE 1917

Army Form C. 2118.

Instructions regarding War Diaries and Intelligence Summaries are contained in F. S. Regs., Part II. and the Staff Manual respectively. Title pages will be prepared in manuscript.

Place	Date	Hour	Summary of Events and Information	Remarks and references to Appendices
CORMETTES	30.6.17		The following awards and promotions have been published during the month:– Extract from Field Marshal SIR DOUGLAS HAIG's despatch mentioning those soldiers who have rendered gallant service during recent operations:–	
			CAPT. T. de C FALLE, CAPT. ST. G.H.L. CLARKE, CAPT. A.C SAXTON, 2 LIEUT T. CERATY M.C., Sgt. P. RANAGHAN, 20272 Pte QUIGLEY.	
			M.C. awarded to 2 Lieut a/capt P. JOLLIFFE.	
			The Divisional Commander has awarded parchment certificates for devotion to duty and gallantry on the 7 June 1917 to the undermentioned officers and men	
			Major T.F. O'Donnell M.C. — R.S.M. Devlin D.	
			a/capt T. de C Falle — 17704 L/Sgt Dolan D.	
			2 Lieut W.H.H. Allen — 22138 Pte Ross W.	
			2 " G.T. Forbes — 21099 " Anderson M.	
			2 " P.H. Wray — 6837 " McIntyre W.	
			Capt C.F. Brady RAMC — 20958 " Murray W.	
			Lieut F.L. Crilly — 4916A " McGuire J.	
			2 " G.R. Attwood — 17032 L/Cpl Fanning	
			2 " C.L Henry. — 15944 Pte Davis J.	
			Lieut QM F.E. Downer — 19729 Grey F.	
			21103 Campbell P.	
			20911 Cunningham J.	
			Promotions	
			2 Lieut a/capt P JOLLIFFE M.C. relinquishes acting rank on 6/4/17.	
			To be acting Capts while Commdg Coys	
			2 Lieut P. JOLLIFFE M.C. 7.6.1917.	
			Lieut D.H.W. KINCHAN 18.5.1917.	
			CAPT T.F. O'Donnell M.C. promoted temp Major Extract London Gazette.	

[signature] LIEUT. COL.
COMDG. 7/8 (S) BN. R. IRISH FUSILIERS.

W.J. Statt

2353 Wt. W2544/1454 700,000 5/15 D. D. & L. A.D.S.S./Forms/C. 2118.

A

S E C R E T.　　　　　　　　　　　　　　C O P Y   N O..........

7/8th.(S)Battalion Royal Irish Fusiliers Orders No.I.

June 4th.1917.

Reference Maps FRANCE 28.S.W.2.Edition 5.A.

:-

1.INFORMATION.

The 7/8th.Royal Irish Fusiliers and the 7th.Royal Inniskilling Fusiliers will relieve the 8th.Royal Inniskilling Fusiliers on the night 5/6th. June 1917.

2.BOUNDARIES.

The Boundary on the left with the 7th.Royal Inniskilling Fusiliers will be:-

Front line at N.18.a.50.00.---Junction of CROWBAR TRENCH with SHANNON TRENCH-----Junction of CHOW STREET with SWATOW TRENCH---Junction of THE FOSSE with the VIERSTRAAT SWITCH.(SANDBAG VILLA to 7.R.Innis Fusrs.)

Boundary on right will be :-

LARK LANE---QUIP LANE to its Junction with VAN WAY---ROSSIGNOL ROAD,all exclusive.

3.DISPOSITIONS.

Battalion Headquarters S.P.13.Boundary between "A" and "B"Coys.will be Front Line at N.18.c.63.50.--Support Line at Junction of BIRR and FERMOY TRENCHES ---CHINESE WALL 100 yards S.of WATLING STREET.

"A"Company　One Platoon Front Line
ditto.　One Platoon FERMOY TRENCH.
ditto.　Two Platoons CHINESE WALL
Company Headquarters SHANNON TRENCH.

"B"Company.　One Platoon Front Line.
ditto.　One Platoon FERMOY and SHANNON TRENCHES.
ditto.　Two Platoons CHINESE WALL.
Company Headquarters SHANNON TRENCH.

"C"Company.　VIERSTRAAT SWITCH from ROSSIGNOL ROAD to DESTINET FARM

"D"Company.　VIERSTRAAT SWITCH from DESTINET FARM to FOSSE TRENCH.

4.ROUTE.

All movement will be by platoons at 200 yards interval.

Companies will move off by platoons as under.

1st.Platoon "A"Company at 9.30.p.m.
1st.Platoon "B"Coy.　at 9.40.p.m.
1st.Platoon "C"Coy.　at.9.50.p.m.
1st.Platoon "D"Coy.　at 10.0.p.m.
Headquarters 10.10.p.m.

Route to be followed-cross roads at M.22.d.9.5.thence by "A"and "D"Routes to YORK HOUSE.Thence by FOSSE C.T.The leading Platoon of "A"Coy.will be readyb to enter FOSSE C.T. at 11.30.p.m.

5.DRESS.

The Battalion will move into the trenches dressed and equipped as laid down in O.O.No.1.Para.11.Special care to be taken that all water bottles are full.

6.GRENADES etc.

All Platoons of "A"and "B"Coys.will send one N.C.O.forward to be at YORK HOUSE dump at 2.0.p.m.on the 5th.instato take over the complement of Bombs and Rifle Grenades.They must be provided with lists shewing the total number of Bombs and Rifle Grenades required by their platoons. Each Platoon will draw 96.Rifle Grenades.The Platoons of "A"and"B"Coys. will draw and issue their Grenades as they proceed to the trenches.On the morning of the 6th.inst."C"and "D"coy.and H.Qrs.will draw from the same dump their complement of bombs and rifle grenades.A certificate will be forwarded to Orderly Room by 6.0.p.m.the 6th.inst.stating this has been done.An Officer from "C"and "D"coys.should be present to draw the Grenades etc.and should have a list of their requirements.

(Continued on SHEET 2.)

SHEET. 2'

6. GRENADES etc. (Contd.)

All ranks should be warned that all bombs and Rifle Grenades issued at the Dump are already detonated.

Red Very Lights and Green Ground Flares will be issued to Companies by the R.S.M to morrow morning..

7. MEDICAL.

All Medical Stores will be stacked outside Orderly Room by 10.30 p.m. 4th. inst. The Maltese Cart will collect these and will take them to YORK HOUSE where a party to be detailed by the R.S.M. will put same on trucks and push xxxx to FOSSE AID POST.

This Maltese Cart as soon as it is off loaded will call at YORK HOUSE Bomb Stores and collect Red Very Lights and Flares which are to be handed over to the R.S.M. at DONCASTER HUTS.

8. LEWIS GUNS.

The Lewis Gun Magazines at the Q.M. Stores will be sent to YORK HOUSE in a limber to morrow night, so as to reach YORK HOUSE about midnight. From there they will be pushed on a trolley to S.P.13. where they will be stored under arrangements to be made by L.G. Officer.

9. KITS.

All packs and Officers' Kits will be ready stacked outside Orderly Room for removal by 12 noon.

Officers' Mess Kit will be stacked outside Orderly Room ready for removal by the Mess Cart at 8.30. p.m.

10. TRANSPORT.

Horses for H.Qrs. Officers, with mounted grooms will be at Orderly Room at 10.30 p.m.

The Transport Officer's attention is drawn to paras. 7, 8, 9.

11. BILLETS.

An Advance Party from the 8th. Royal Inniskilling Fusiliers will take over huts at 8.30. p.m.

12. RATIONS.

Arrangements for rations and water will be notified later.

13. ACKNOWLEDGE.

W.H. Stitt

June 4th. 1917

Captain & Adjutant.
7/8th. (S) Battalion Royal Irish Fusiliers

Issued through Signals. at 5.0. p.m.

Copy No. 1. "A" coy.	Copy No. 9. Intelligence Officer.
2. "B" Coy	10. Lewis Gun Officer.
3. "C" Coy.	11. 7th. R. Innis. Fusrs.
4. "D" Coy.	12. 8th. R. Innis. Fusrs.
5. M.O.	13. 49th. Infantry Brigade.
6. Q.M.	14. Spare.
7. T.O.	15. War Diary.
8. Signals.	16. File.

SECRET.   B   COPY. NO.......

OPERATION ORDERS. NO. /

REFERENCE MAPS. FRANCE 28. S.W. Ed. 5.a. and MAPS attached.   2 JUN 1917

0-0-0-0-0-0-0-0-0-0-0-0-0-0-0-0-0-0-0-0-0-0-0-0-0-0-0-0-0-0-0-0-0-0-0

I. GENERAL PLAN.

The attack on WYTSCHAETE RIDGE will be made by the 16th. Division with Divisions on either flank.

The attack by the 16th. Division will be made by:-

(a) 47. Infantry Brigade on the RIGHT.
(49th. Infantry Brigade on the LEFT.
48th. Infantry Brigade in RESERVE.

(b) The objectives allotted to the 7/8th. Royal Irish Fusiliers are:-
(1) NANCY SUPPORT marked on Map by a series of Red Dashes.
(2) RED LINE.
(3) NANCY DRIVE, marked on Map by series of Blue Dashes
(4) BLUE LINE.

(c) The Boundaries of the Battalion are:-
(1) With the 7th. Leinster Regiment onthe Right.:-
German Line at N.24.a.60.85.-----North Corner of PETIT BOIS. (N.24.b.4.9.) NORTH--WEST Corner BOIS DE WYTSCHAETE (N.24.b.75.80.)---South Corner of HOSPICE. This Boundary is marked on Map by broad YELLOW LINE.

(2) Left Boundary with the 7th. Royal Inniskilling Fusiliers is marked on Map with a PURPLE LINE and is as follows:-
N.17.b.80.00.----SHANNON TRENCH at N.18.a.32.00.----our Front Line at N.18.a.55.00.-----German Front Line at N.18.d.20.75.---along a line 30. yards South of NAIL DRIVE------Southern Corner of UNNAMED WOOD----O.13.c.80.15., 20. yards North of the Junction of OBVIOUS DRIVE and NANCY DRIVE. This Boundary is shewn in PURPLE.

TIME.

The following will be the times of Arrival and Departure from the various Coloured Lines.

RED LINE. Arrive Plus 0.35.
Depart. Plus 1.05.
BLUE LINE Arrive Plus 1.40.

2nd. Royal Irish Regiment will attack the Green and Black Lines passing through the BLUE LINE at Plus 3.40.

ATTACK.

The attack on the Red Line will be made by "A" Company on the Right "B" Company on the Left.

The Attack on the Blue Line will be by "C" Coy. on the Right and "D" Coy. on the Left.

Boundaries between Companies are:-
Between "A" and "B" Coys'. Point of Salient N.18.c.68.54.-----German Front Line at. N.18.d.27.18.----along a line running about 30 yards South of NAIL LANE to N.18.d.99.10.

Boundaries between "C" and "D" Coy. are:-
N.18.d.99.10.----along a line running North of NAME DRIVE to NORTH CORNER of HOSPICE (Inclusive to Right Coy.) at S.19.a.64.93.
Shewn on attached Map by Thin Pencil Line.

WAVES.

The Battalion will attack in four waves:-
"A" and "B" Coys first wave will occupy RED LINE.
"A" and "B" Coys second wave will occupy DOTTED RED LINE (NANCY SUPPORT)
"C" and "D" Coys. first wave will occupy BLUE LINE.
"C" and "D" Coys second wave will occupy DOTTED BLUE LINE.

(Continued on Sheet 2.)

S H E E T...2.

II. ASSEMBLY POSITIONS.

"A" Coy. in front line from N.18.c.48.25. to point of Salient at N.18.c.67.55. Boundary between Platoons will be Bay 29. (N.18.c.57.45.) inclusive to Left Platoon.

"B" Coy. in front line from Point of Salient at N.18.c.67.55. to N.18.a.55.00 (Bay.64. inclusive) Boundary between Platoons Bay 53. N.18.c.54.80.) inclusive to Left Platoon.

"C" Coy's. first wave in WREN WAY from N.18.c.20.00. to BIRR TRENCH.
"C" Coy's. second wave in FERMOY TRENCH from VAN KEEP to BIRR TRENCH.

"D" Coy's first wave in WREN WAY from BIRR TRENCH to CROWBAR TRENCH.
"D" Coy's. second wave in FERMOY TRENCH from BIRR TRENCH to CROWBAR TRENCH.

III. MOPPERS UP.

"D" Company of the 8th. Royal Inniskilling Fusiliers will be attached to the Battalion to act as "Moppers Up." This Coy. consists of three platoons.

PLATOON	STRENGTH.	COMMANDER	ATTACHED TO
(a) ½. No.13.	17.O.Ranks.	2/Lieut. Roulstone.	"A" Coy. 7/8th.
(b) ½. No.13.	17.O.Ranks.	ditto...	"B" Coy. 7/8th.
(c) ½. No.14.	17.O.Ranks.	2/Lieut. Palmgreen.	"D" Coy. 7/8th.
(d) ½. No.14.	17.O.Ranks.	ditto...	"C" Coy. 7/8th.
(e) No.15.	34.O.Ranks.	2/Lieut. FOLLEY.	"C" Coy. 7/8th.

(a) Party will "Mop.Up" dug outs at the junction of NAME SUPPORT and NAME DRIVE, NANCY SUPPORT. Assembly Point in front line behind "A" Coy.
(b) Party will "Mop Up" NANCY SUPPORT and along NAIL LANE up to and in BLACK COT. Assembly Point behind "B" Coy.
(c) Party will "Mop Up" dugouts round point O.13.c.72.15. Assembly Point in WREN WAY, N. of BIRR TRENCH behind "D" Coys. first wave.
(d) Party will "Mop Up" trench running S.E. from O.19.a.10.92. to dugouts at O.19.a.44.70.
(e) Party will go straight to HOSPICE. (d) and (e) Parties will assemble in WREN WAY, S. of BIRR TRENCH behind "C" Coy's first waves.

When these Parties have completed their tasks they will report the fact to the Companies to which they are attached and then to Battalion Headquarters.

IV. CARRYING PARTIES.

One Platoon of the 8th. Royal Inniskilling Fusiliers consisting of 35.O.Ranks under 2/Lieut. BROWN will act as carrying party. Assembly position in rear of Fourth Wave behind "D" Coy. in FERMOY TRENCH from BIRR TRENCH to CROWBAR TRENCH. This party will carry any material from Battalion Dump at Junction BIRR TRENCH with SHANNON TRENCH up to BLACK COT where dumps will be established, at least 20. yards apart under the R.S.M.

V. VICKERS GUNS.

The Two Vickers Guns under Lieut. A.G. MAY 49.M.Gun Co. will move behind the Fourth Wave, and will take up a favourable position in the neighbourhood of the BLACK COT from which to cover the advance on the BLUE LINE.
When the BLUE LINE has been taken, they will move forward to neighbourhood of the SOUTHERN BRICKSTACK, and assist in consolidating and in forming the Machine Gun Barrage for the attack on the GREEN and BLACK LINES.
They must be prepared to support the 3rd. and 4th. waves at any point in the attack on the BLUE LINE, either by filling gaps in the assaulting waves, or by putting a barrage on any strong point. The two guns will work conjointly.
Assembly Point will be in FERMOY TRENCH between BIRR TRENCH and CROWBAR TRENCH.

(Continued on Sheet 3.)

SHEET. 3.

VI. STOKES' GUNS.

Stokes' Guns under 2/Lieut. TAYLOR 4q.T.M.Bty. will move behind the 4th. Wave to the neighbourhood of BLACK COT and cover the advance of the 3rd. and 4th. Waves by firing on the HOSPICE, and on any STRONG POINTS or Machine Guns that may offer resistance or hold up the advance.
As soon as the BLUE LINE is taken, the Guns will be brought to a position in rear of NANCY DRIVE so as to help the consolidation of the BLUE LINE and the HOSPICE by firing on the STRONG POINT S.W. of the HOSPICE at O.19.b.10.60. The two guns will work conjointly. Assembly Trench will be FERMOY TRENCH between VAN KEEF and WATLING STREET H.Qrs. in a dugout at..............

VII. CONSOLIDATION.)
STRONG POINTS.)

All lines will be consolidated after capture. Strong Points will be constructed by the 157. Field. Co. R.E. to hold one Platoon and Vickers Gun.

RED POST ...O.13.c.15.90.
BLACK.......O.13.c.40.25.
OBVIOUS.....O.19.b.36.80.

As soon as the construction of a Strong Point is complete, the R.E. Officer in charge will report the fact to the Officer Commanding the Battalion in whose area the STRONG POINT is. In which case, a platoon of "A" or "B" Coys' may be detailed with its Lewis Gun to occupy the Strong Point.

VIII. POSITIONS OF HEADQUARTERS.

49th. Infantry Brigade Headquarters also Left Artillery Group H.Q.

THE RIB N.16.d.35.50.

7/8th. Royal Irish Fusiliers	S.P.13.
7th. Royal Inniskilling Fusiliers.	YUM YUM TRENCH (N.18.a.15.45.)
2nd. Royal Irish Regiment.	S.P.13.
8th. Royal Inniskilling Fusiliers.	THE FOSSE N.16.d.8.8.
49th. Machine Gun Company.	S.P.13.
49th. Trench Mortar Battery.	SWATOW TRENCH.
157 Field Company R.E.	THE RIB.

POSITIONS OF COMPANY HEADQUARTERS.

"A" Coy's H.Q. in a dugout front line at.................

"B" Coy's H.Q. in a dugout in front line at....................

"C" Coy's H.Q. in a dugout in FERMOY TRENCH at N.18.c.½.30.

"D" Coy's H.Q. in a dugout at Junction WATLING STREET and FERMOY TRENCH N.16.c.3.72. ? ? ? ? ?

Attached T.M's. in a dugout in FERMOY TRENCH at N.18.c.8.26.

Attached M.Guns in a dugout in WATLING STREET N.18.c.8.26.

H.Qrs. "Moppers Up" will be at Battalion Headquarters in S.P.13.
The Forward Command Post of the 2nd. Royal Irish Regiment for the attack on the BLACK LINE will be at Brigade Forward Station. The Brigade Forward Station will follow the last wave of the attack on the BLUE LINE and will be established about O.13.c.15.45.
When the BLACK LINE has been captured the Brigade Forward Station will move forward to O.19.b.75.85.

(Continued on Sheet 4.)

SHEET. 4.

IX. COMMUNICATION TRENCHES.

40th. Infantry Brigade are allotted Two Communication Trenches.
WATLING STREET. (In Trench.)

THE FOSSE. (Out Trench.)

As soon as possible after ZERO the following Communication Trenches will be made by the R.E. and Pioneers.
(a) THE FOSSE---BIRR TRENCH via NAME TRENCH ---NAME DRIVE to be used for out traffic.
(b) WATLING STREET----MAYO STREET via NAIL DRIVE. To be used for IN traffic.

The Communication Trenches connecting the CHINESE WALL LINE with the PARK LINE are allotted the BATTALION:-
THE FOSSE (To Be Constructed)
CHOW STREET............."B" and "D" Coys and "Moppers Up".
CORK TRENCH............"A" and "C" Coys. and "Moppers Up".
The Communication Trenches connecting the PARK LINE with the Front Line are allotted:-
BIRR TRENCH............"A" and "C" Coys and "Moppers Up"
CROWBAR TRENCH.........."B" and "D" Coys and "Moppers Up"

Two Overland Routes for Transport are being prepared.

(a) N.17.a.15.65.------N.17.a.50.70.-----N.17.b.00.80.---N.17.b.90.60. N.18.a.75.45.

(b) LAITERIE. N.16.d.48.10.---N.17.c.43.35;----N.17.c.80.10. NORTH of S.P.13.------by BIRR TRENCH.

X. DEFENSIVE FLANKS.

LATERAL COMMUNICATIONS.

Communication must be kept up with either flank. If it is found that any portion of a Company Line is more advanced than that on a flank, defensive flanks consisting of one or more Lewis Guns must be put out at once to cover the gap between the lines. In the same way, should the line on any Company's flank be more advanced, the Company is responsible that communication is established with the people on his flank and that the gap is covered with one or more Lewis Guns.

XI. DRESS.

All Officers will be dressed and equipped the same as the men. Sticks are not to be carried. Fighting Order for all ranks:-
(a) Clothing, Arms and entrenching tool as issued.
(b) Equipment as issued with the exception of the Pack.
Haversacks to be worn on the back except for Lewis Gunners and Rifle Bombers. who will carry it at the side
(c) Box Respirators and P.H. Helmets.
(d) [illegible]
(e) Iron Rations, unexpired portion of day's rations. Mess tin and Cover.
(f) 130 rounds of S.A.A. except Bombers!)signallers, runners.
Lewis Gunners and Rifle Bombers who carry 50 rounds. Carrying Parties 50 rounds S.A.A.
(g) Every men to carry two Mills' Bombs, one in each top pocket. These bombs will be collected into dumps as soon as the objective has been gained.
(h) Flares will be carried in the bottom pocket of the jacket.
NOTE. Machine Gun Coy., Trench Mortar Battery and Carrying Parties will not carry g. and h.
(i) Three Sandbags per man.
(j) One Water Bottle full of Cold Tea.
(k) Bombing Sections will carry:-
Bayonetman Six No.5. per man. (Mills')
Remainder of Section Twelve No.5. Grenades per man.
(l) Rifle Bombers will carry 12. Hales Grenades or 12 No.34. Grenades

(Continued on Sheet 5.)

SHEET. 5.

XI DRESS (Contd.)

(m) All Lewis Gun Sections will carry 30 Drums (All spare drums will be brought to BLACK COT DUMP by carrying party (vide para IV.)

XII. TIME.

In making references to times before or after which operations commence the following nomenclature will be adopted in future:-

(a) Referring to days.

"Z" Day is the day on which operations take place.
One day before "Z" Day................"Y" Day.
Two days before "Z" Day..............."X" Day.
Three days before "Z" Day............."W" Day.
Four days before "Z" Day.............."V" Day.
Five days before "Z" Day.............."U" Day.
Days before "U" Day will be referred to as "Z" minus 6, "Z" minus 7, "Z" minus 8. etc.

(b) Referring to hours on "Z" Day.

ZERO is the exact time at which operations will commence, and times will be designated in hours and minutes plus or minus from ZERO, even if they encroach on "Y" Day.

XIII. ZERO.

ZERO HOUR WILL BE.........3.10 AM.........................

"Z" DAY WILL BE ....7".........................JUNE 1917.

XIV. MAPS.

No marked Maps or any description of our lines are to be taken in advance of Battalion Headquarters by any Officer N.C.O. or man. Company Commanders are held responsible that these orders are made known to all ranks, and will return such maps to Orderly Room before going into the line, at the same time rendering a certificate, certifying that none of these maps remain in their possession.

XV. SIGNALLING.

(a) In order to prevent leakage of information and to ensure that other methods of information are practiced all communications by telephone except that mentioned in Sub-para (d) and messages sent on the buzzer will cease in advance of YORK ROAD until the hour of ZERO.

(b) The following methods of communication will be permitted in front of YORK ROAD.:-

PIGEONS.
VISUAL.
RUNNERS,
FULLERPHONES FOR "S.O.S" CALLS.
ROCKETS FOR "S.O.S." CALLS.

N.B.
ALL fullerphones in front of YORK ROAD will either be issued without hand sets, or have the microphones removed from the speaking circuits.

(c) Existing "S.O.S." Lines from Batteries to Companies are to be abolished; the Batteries are to be connected to Battalion Headquarters only.

(d) Companies in the Front Line will be connected to Battalion Headquarters Fullerphones only will be used on these lines and are not to be used except for "S.O.S" Calls.

(e) For Communication between Brigade Headquarters and the Headquarters of Battalions in the line, one telephone may be retained in each Battalion Commanders' Dugout.

(f) Until after ZERO hour no message will be sent by pigeon which contains anything in the address "TO" or "FROM", or in the body of the message, which would be of value if it fell into the hands of the enemy.

15.SIGNALLING (Continued)

(g) Two hours before ZERO,Companies will send one runner to Battalion H.Qrs.(S.P.13.)to report to Signal Officer.These runners will remain with Battalion Headquarters until the Battalion Forward Post is established in BLACK COT.

(h) Battalion Forward Post will be marked with a Blue and White Flag.

(i) As soon as Battalion Forward Post is established,all messages should be sent there

(j) Battalion Forward Post will move forward after fourth wave.

(k) CODE CALLS From ZERO hour onwards position calls (such as F.E.17) cease to exist and NAME CODES (A.K.,"B.K.," C.K.,D.K.,) will be used.
Companies will take call of Battalion followed by letters A,B,C,D, to denote the Company.
e.g. D.K.A. = "A"Coy.
D.K.B. = "B"Coy. and so on.

(l) Messages will be carried by all runners in the right hand breast pocket.

(m) In cases of important messages such as "Objectives have been taken" etc.Companies should send two runners,with a few minutes interval between them

XVI. MEDICAL.

The REGIMENTAL AID POST will be FOSSE N.17.d.2.3.Wounded will be collected and brought to Regimental Aid Post by Regimental Stretcher Bearers,Bandsmen,etc.and such others as may be detailed. Later,in the event of a successful advance,fresh Regimental Aid Posts will be improvised according to pre-arranged plan.
The carrying back from New to Old Regimental Aid Post will be done by Field Ambulance Personnel.
Advanced Dressing Stations will be at:-

KEMMEL	BREWERY	N.21.c.8.5.
LAITERIE		N.16.d.2.3.
PARRAIN FARM		N.28.b.70.95.

Walking wounded will proceed direct to BRULOOZE CORNER

XVII. CROSS COUNTRY TRACKS.

Cross Country Tracks as shewn on Maps already issued will be used by walking wounded,prisoners of war,reinforcements and horse transport as far as possible.

XVIII.BAYONETS.

It is most important that every precaution should be taken to prevent bayonets from flashing in thev moonlight,should there be a moon when units are moving to their places of assembly.

XIX. AIRCRAFT.

In the event of hostile aeroplanes flying over our lines to ascertain whether our trenches are more strongly manned than usual,all ranks will remain still and will not look up.Such Aeroplanes are to be dealt with by Anti-aircraft,Vickers or Lewis Guns.The Battalion Lewis Gun Officer will arrange for 4.L.G's to be maintained for this purpose.

XX.MINES.

All Mines on the 16th.Division Front will be exploded at ZERO hour If the explosion of any of the above mines has not taken place by ZERO plus 15 seconds,it is to be understood that it will not take place at all.
Danger Areas are being marked.Notice Boards will be put up in all Sub-ways.

XXI."S.O.S."

The S.O.S.Signal will remain,RED signal cartridges as at present.

XXII.NO MAN'S LAND.

In order to avoid casualties,the whole of the Infantry detailed for the assault of the RED and BLUE lines should get rapidly across "NO MAN'S LAND."As few troops as possible being left in the front and support lines.

SHEET. 7.

XXIII. DUMPS.

Dumps formed in the German Lines are to be marked with the following distinguishing marks (Lettering Black on White ground.)

12" × 12" — D.

XXIV. PRISONERS OF WAR.

A Divisional Collecting Station has been arranged at M.24.a.central Divisional Troops after troops to the collecting stations will be immediately marched back to their units. Prisoners are to be marched by cross country tracks and are to be kept off the road as far as possible. Sentries and Guards are not to talk to Prisoners.
Prisoners will receive ordinary rations only and soldiers are forbidden to give them tobacco, cigarettes or food.
Soldiers are on no account to take any buttons, caps or other articles from prisoners. Any German Documents etc. picked up are to be immediately sent to Battalion Headquarters.
Officer Prisoners to be kept separate from the men.
Escort should not exceed 20% of the number of prisoners.
It is the duty of the "Moppers Up" to take back Prisoners and not that of the Battalion carrying out the assault.
Carrying Parties returning for more stores and slightly wounded walking cases should be used where possible.

XXV. SUNRISE.

All Officers will carefully watch when the sun rises each morning, as the sun can be used as means of judging direction.

XXVI. WATER.

The R.E. will search for and open up the following sources of water supply:-

RED CHATEAU	N.18.b.80.20.
HOSPICE.	O.13.c.3.8.

On road N. of WYTSCHAETE CHURCH at O.19.b.20.35.
On no account will the water from the wells be drunk until passed fit to drink by the R.E.
60. Petrol Tins of Drinking Water arec being carried to the vicinity of O.13.c.15.45.,20 of these tins will be issued to this Battalion.

S E C R E T. COPY NO.......5

CONTINUATION OF OPERATION ORDERS NO.1. ISSUED ON /6/17.

SHEET 8.dated 4th./une.1917.

:-:

XXVII. OFFICERS.

The following Officers will accompany the Battalion:-

Lieut.Colonel.K.C.Weldon D.S.O.	Commanding..Officer
Major.T.F.O'Donnell M.C.	2nd.in Command.
Captain W.H.Stitt M.C.	Adjutant.
Lieutenant D.H.W.Kinghan	Lewis Gun Officer
2/Lieut. G.J.Forbes	Signalling Officer.
2/Lieut.J.B.Drea	Intelligence Officer

"A"Company.	"B"Company.
Captain T.de C.Falle.	Captain P.Jolliffe.
2/Lieut.H.B.Reymell.	2/Lieut.V.J.Lynch.
2/Lieut.G.R.Attwood.	2/Lieut.W.H.Waters.
2/Lieut.J.V.L.Mc Garry.	2/Lieut.C.W.Pickett.

"C"Company	"D"Company
2/Lieut.W.H.H.Allen	2/Lieut.F.A.Moody.
2/Lieut.P.H.Wray.	2/Lieut.S.Turner.
2/Lieut.M.Jestin.	2/Lieut.C.L.Henry.
2/Lieut.G.Coombes.	2/Lieut.J.P.H.Bell.

XXVIII. SMOKING.

When the Battalion is forming up and is formed up in the Assembly Trenches,no smoking is to be allowed.

XXIX. WIRE.

Each Company Commander is directly responsible that the wire in front of his assembly position is cut and that sufficient gaps exist.

XXX. LEWIS GUN MAGAZINES.

The Lewis Gun Officer will deliver 50 filled Lewis Gun Drums in tins to No.4.Main Brigade Dump at N.17.a.15.25.when instructed.The remaining 174 Drums in tins are to be delivered at Battalion Dump at Junction BIRR and FERMOY TRENCHES on Y/Z Day.

They will be handed over to the Bomb Store Keepers.All Magazines will be filled with "K" or "K.N" Ammunition .

XXXI. STORES.

Reference para.4.The following stores will be dumped at BLACK COT:- Picks,shovels,sandbags,rifle grenades,mills' No.5.Bombs,S.A.A., Lewis Gun Drums and S.O.S.Signals.

XXXII. BURIAL GROUNDS.

The following sites have been chosen as forward burial grounds, and will be used in case of severe losses in the line:-

"A"Cemetery N.17.d.5.7. (Near S.P.13.)

"B"Cemetery N.23.d.½.7½. (Near IRISH HOUSE.

Marks are being placed at these points.Burial Parties are being detailed under Divisional arrangements.

XXXIII. SYNCHRONIZATION.

Watches will be synchronized daily at 9.0.a.m.,12 noon and 6.0.pm.

XXXIV. FORWARD BRIGADE POST.

Brigade Forward Post will move to the corner of UNNAMED WOOD (O.13.c.15.45.)after our fourth wave.

XXXV. FORWARD BATTALION HEADQUARTERS

Battalion Headquarters will move forward to BLACK COT when the BLUE objective has been taken.

XXXVI. CONTACT PATROLS.

Aeroplanes for contact patrols will be R.E.8.Type.and will be specially marked by a black flap attached to the rear of each lower plane. One contact aeroplane will watch over WYTSCHAETE and the area N.of the village.

(Continued on Page 9.)

SHEET. 9.

XXXVI CONTACT PATROLS (Contd.)

Contact patrols will fly over the line and call for flares at the following hours and any hours subsequent to these hours at which special aeroplanes may be ordered. Troops will also be prepared to put out flares at any other time if the aeroplane calls for them:-

BY 7th. Royal Inniskilling Fusiliers and 7/8th. Royal Irish Fusiliers.)at ZERO plus 45.minutes ZERO plus 3.Hours.

BY. 2nd. Battn. The Royal Irish Regiment)at ZERO plus 4.hrs. 30 mins. ()at ZERO plus 5.hrs. 30.mins.

Aeroplanes will call for flares and Watson fans by sounding a CLAXON HORN and firing a "VERY" White Light or by giving either of these two signals.

Green Flares will be used. They should be lit in bunches of three about 30.yards apart.

Watson fans will be used in conjunction with flares. The fans should be turned over every two seconds and not quicker. The White side will be exposed to the aeroplane for two seconds, and the dark side for two seconds, and so on.

XXXVII. TANKS.

It must be impressed on all ranks in the Infantry that the tanks are there to assist their advance if possible, but they must never for a moment suppose that success depends on their presence. The men must never wait for the tanks, but must push on to their objective irrespective of xxxxxx whether they come up or not. There is a great danger of the attack being held up if this is not thoroughly realized by all ranks

XXXVIII. EMPLOYMENT OF TUNNELLING COMPANIES ON DUGOUTS AND ROADS.

A party of the 250 Tunnelling Company will reconnoitre captured dugouts as soon as the objective is reached.

This party will mark habitable dugouts with the number of men which can be accommodated in them, and will carry out repairs where necessary

XXXIX. CORRECTION.

Sheet 3. para. VI. Stokes' Guns. Line 7. for S.W. read S.E.

W.H. Stitt.

Captain & Adjutant.

7/8th. (S) Battalion Royal Irish Fusiliers.

Issued through Signals. at 7.30. p.m.

Copy No. 1. "A" Coy.	Copy No. 9. Medical Officer.
2. "B" Coy.	10. 49th. Infantry Brigade
3. "C" Coy.	11. 8th. R. Innis. Fusrs.
4. "D" Coy.	12. 7th. R. Innis. Fusrs.
5. Signals.	13. War Diary.
6. Transport Officer.	14. File.
7. Intelligence Officer.	15. 2/Lieut. Taylor 49. T.M.B.
8. Quartermaster.	16. Lieut. C. May. 49. M.G. Co.

SECRET

COPY NO............

B.K.Operation Order NO.2.

6.6.17.

Reference WYTSCHAETE SHEET 28.S.W.2 Edition 5.A.

:-:

I.ACTION ON THE CAPTURE OF THE BLACK LINE.

(a)The Black Line should be completely in our hands by ZERO plus 5.hours. On reaching the BLACK LINE "C.K." will push forward patrols to the protective barrage, which will be established 300 yards in advance of the BLACK LINE.

(b)The OOSTAVERNE LINE will be subjected to a heavy barrage from ZERO plus 5.hours, until the approach of our attacking Infantry, and a number of Field Guns will be brought forward into previously selected positions

II.ADVANCE ON THE MAUVE LINE.

(a)After the BLUE LINE has been captured by us at ZERO plus 5.hours 30 minutes the barrage will creep forward at the rate of 100 yards every 3.minutes and pile up on the line ROAD JUNCTION O.27.d.6.9.----O.21.Central----O.15.d.1.7.until ZERO plus 6.hours 30.minutes when it will cease unless recalled by the "S.O.S." Signal.

(b)At ZERO plus 5.hours 30.minutes. Cavalry Patrols will push forward within limits of the barrage, and the 36th., 16th., and 19th., Divisions will push forward strong patrols which will establish themselves on the line O.27.d.2.9.-----Rly.JUNCTION O.21.c.6.1.----OIL TRENCH---E. Side of OOSTAVERNE WOOD. This Line will be known as the MAUVE LINE. The portion of the MAUVE LINE allotted to the 16th.Division is from RLY.JUNCTION at O.21.c.6.1. on the Right (where it joins hands with the 36th.Division.) to JUNCTION of RLY and OIL TRENCH at O.21.a.2.8. on the left (where it joins hands with the 19th.Division)

(c)47th. and 49th. Infantry Brigades will each push forward two strong patrols of not less than 50 men each and accompanied by Lewis Guns, which will establish themselves on the MAUVE LINE. The boundary between brigades will be a straight line from the point of Junction between Brigades on the BLACK LINE (O.20.a.40.25.) to the S.end of EBG COPSE and thence along the WAMBEEK to the MAUVE LINE.

(d)It is the intention of the Divisional Commander as soon as circumstances permit to move forward troops from the 48th. Infantry Brigade in reserve to hold and ~~xxxxxxxxxx~~ and complete the consolidation of the MAUVE LINE within Divisional Boundaries, taking over the line from the patrols of the 47th. and 49th. Infantry Brigades, which will rejoin their Brigades.

(e)Four Sections of tanks with any others that can be rallied will co-operate in this advance, and in the subsequent advance to the OOSTAVERNE LINE.

III.TO CARRY OUT PLAN LAID DOWN IN PARA 2.

(a)O.C. "B" Coy. will after the BLUE LINE has been taken, form up his Company into four platoons of at least 32 men each with 8.Lewis Guns and additional Signallers. "A" Company will supply any deficiencies required in Officers, personnel and equipment to carry out on the advance from "C.K's" outpost line in front of the BLACK LINE TO THE MAUVE LINE where they will establish themselves in posts until relieved by the 48th. Infantry Brigade.

Arrangements must be made by O.C."B"Coy. to supply his Coy. with flares, S.A.A. and L.Gun Drums which can be drawn from Battalion Dump at BLACK COT.

This Company as soon as relieved by the 48th. Infantry Brigade, will move back to its original position in the RED LINE reporting its arrival at BLACK COT.

(b)A platoon of "C.K." will be in support SONEN FARM O.20.b.10.45. for the purpose of facilitating comminication and for taking over or assisting in collection of prisoners and passing them to the rear, and also to form a strong supporting point half way to the MAUVE LINE

IV.CAPTURED GUNS.

The following will be the policy of dealing with captured guns W. of the OOSTAVERNE LINE. Enemy's Guns which may be of use to us will be saved. The Gun Teams should be killed and the breech mechanism with any removable sight should be removed if necessary. Destruction by explosives is not to be resorted to unless it is evident that the OOSTAVERNE cannot be gained and held. In this case the Officer on the spot must use his own discretion as to destroying the guns. If the Guns are not going to be used by us, Parts removed will be returned to Battalion H.Qrs.

V.SMOKE CANDLES

Candles will not be used by the IXth. Corps on ZERO Day

SHEET 2.

VI. REPORTS.
To O.C. "D.K." at BLACK COT through O.C. "C.K." in OBVIOUS ALLEY about O.19.b.75.85.

VII. ACKNOWLEDGE.

W.H. Stitt.

Captain & Adjutant.
D.K.

Copy.No.1.O.C. "A" Coy.
3.O.C. "C" Coy.
Verbally to: Signalling Officer
2nd.in Command.
Lewis Gun Officer.

Copy.No.2.O.C. "B" Coy.
4.O.C. "D" Coy.
Intelligence Officer
2nd.R.Irish Regiment.

Issued through Signals at 6.30. p.m.

D

SECRET.

Copy No. 3....

49th Infantry Brigade Order No. 130 - 6-6-17.

1. GENERAL PLAN. (a) The 16th Division will in conjunction with Divisions on either flank attack the enemy's position on the WYTSCHAETE RIDGE on the 7th June, 1917.

(b) The Attack will be made in a series of Bounds, each bound is shown by coloured lines on Map A already issued :-

First bound	....	RED LINE.
Second Bound	....	BLUE LINE.
Third Bound	....	GREEN LINE.
Fourth Bound	....	BLACK LINE.
Fifth Bound	....	MAUVE LINE.

2. OBJECTIVES OF BRIGADES. The 47th Inf. Bde. on the right and the 49th Inf. Bde. on the left will attack up to and including the BLACK LINE and will push out strong patrols to the MAUVE LINE. The 48th Inf. Bde. will be in Divisional Reserve.

The Left Battalion of the 47th Inf. Bde. up to the BLUE LINE (inclusive) will be the 7th Leinster Regt., from the BLUE LINE to the BLACK LINE the 1st R. Munster Fus. The 47th Inf. Bde. will push out Strong patrols to the MAUVE LINE.

The 58th Inf. Bde. is attacking on the left of the 49th Inf. Bde. up to the GREEN LINE (inclusive). The right battalion of the 58th Inf. Bde. will be - Wiltshire Regt. up to the RED LINE and WELCH Regt. from the Red to the GREEN Line.

A Battalion of the 57th Inf. Bde. will be on the left of the 49th Inf. Bde. from the GREEN to the BLACK LINE.

3. BOUNDARIES. The Boundaries between the 49th Inf. Bde. and the Brigades on the right and left are as shown on Map A already issued.

4. TASKS OF BATTALIONS. The attack on the RED and BLUE LINES will be made by the 7/8th R. Irish Fus. on the right and the 7th R. Innis Fus. on the left.

The boundary between these two Battalions is shown in PURPLE on Map A already issued.

The RED LINE is to be captured at Zero plus 35 minutes. A halt of 30 minutes will be made on the RED LINE.

The BLUE LINE is to be captured at Zero plus 1 hour 40 minutes.

The attack on the GREEN and BLACK LINES will be made by the 2nd R. Irish Regt. who will leave the BLUE LINE at Zero plus 3 hours 40 minutes.

The GREEN LINE is to be captured at Zero plus 4 hours 10 minutes.

A halt of 10 minutes will be made on the GREEN LINE.

The BLACK LINE is to be captured at Zero plus 4 hours 40 minutes.

At Zero plus 5 hours 30 minutes one Company of the 7/8th R. Irish Fus., strength not less than 130 men with 6 Lewis Guns, will ~~push forward~~ and will establish posts on the MAUVE LINE from O.31.a.40.00 to O.31.a.30.75. and dig themselves in. Touch will be gained with similar patrols of the 47th Inf. Bde. and 19th Division.

x advance from the outpost line of the 2nd R Irish Regt. in front of the BLACK LINE

The 2nd R. Irish Regt. will send forward one platoon to establish a Supporting Post at SOHEM FARM, O.20.b.10.45 as soon as the Company of the 7/8th R. Irish Fus. has advanced East of the Farm.

Cavalry Patrols and Tanks will co-operate in the advance on the MAUVE LINE.

The O.C. 49th T.M.Battery will detail one of his Reserve mortars to accompany the Coy. of 7/8th R. Irish Fus. in the advance on the MAUVE LINE. They should report to O.C. 7/8th R. Irish Fus. immediately the BLUE LINE has been captured.

5. CONSOLIDATION. With the exception of the GREEN all objectives denoted by coloured lines will be consolidated as rapidly as possible after capture.

Strong Points will be constructed by 157th Field Coy, R.E.:-

RED POST at O.13.c.15.90.
BLACK POST at O.13.c.40.25.
OBVIOUS POST at O.19.b.30.80.

Garrisons of 1 platoon will be provided by Battalions in whose area they are when the R.E. Officer in charge reports the completion of the Strong Point.

The BLACK LINE will be wired by parties detailed by the 48th Inf. Bde. for the purpose under R.E. supervision.

6. ACTION OF MACHINE GUNS. Two guns of the 49th M.G.Company will be attached to each of the following Battalions :-

2nd R. Irish Regt.
7th R. Innis Fus.
7/8th R.Irish Fus.

The role of these guns will be :-

(a) To protect the assaulting battalion against counter attack during the assault.

(b) To assist in the consolidation of the BLUE and BLACK LINES by taking up positions from which they can cover those lines.

(c) To take advantage of good fleeting targets.

(d) To cover the front of any gap which may occur in our lines.

The Divisional Machine Guns will form a barrage 200 yards in front of the ARTILLERY Barrage and will lift in conformity with that barrage.

7. ACTION OF STOKES MORTARS. 2 Mortars of the 49th Trench Mortar Battery will be attached to each of the following Battalions :-

2nd R. Irish Regt.
7th R. Innis Fus.
7/8th R. Irish Fus.

They will assist Battalions in overcoming opposition as required. The remaining 2 Mortars will be kept in Reserve.

When the BLACK LINE has been captured the mortars attached to the 7th R. Innis Fus and 7/8th R. Irish Fus. will again come under the orders of the O.C. 49th Trench Mortar Battery.

8 MINES. At Zero Mines will be fired at the following places :-

(a) N.24.a.90.80.
(b) N.24.a.90.98.
(c) N.18.b.40.90.

The expected depths of the craters and heights which will be formed after the explosion has taken place are

PETIT BOIS MINES - 40 feet.
+ 19 feet.

It is advisable that no dugout should be occupied between Zero and Zero plus 15 seconds. If the explosion of any of the mines has not taken place by Zero plus 15 seconds it must be understood that it will not take place at all.

9.ACTION OF ARTILLERY. (i) The Divisional Artillery will form :-

(a) A Creeping Barrage) Covering the advance of
(b) A Standing Barrage) the Infantry.

(ii) The Creeping Barrage will lift off successive objectives to enable the Infantry to assault those objectives as shown on the Barrage Map already issued.

(iii) The 4.5" howitzers and the Medium and Heavy Howitzers will establish standing barrages in front of the 18-pdr standing barrage.

(iv) During the pauses on the RED, BLUE and GREEN LINES a protective barrage will be established 150 yards in front of our Infantry.

(v) The Protective Barrage in front of the BLACK LINE will be 300 yards in advance of our Infantry. The 2nd R.Irish Regt. will push out patrols as far as this barrage permits.

(vi) At Zero plus 5 hours 30 minutes the barrage will creep forward at the rate of 100 yards every 3 minutes and pile up on the line Road Junction O.27.d.6.9 - O.21.central - O.15.d.1.7 until Zero plus 6 hours 30 minutes when it will cease unless recalled by the S.O.S. Signal

10. TANKS. No. C Section (No. 2 Coy. "A" Battalion) is allotted to the 16th Division.

(a) One pair of tanks will have as their objective OBVIOUS TRENCH - NORTH HOUSE - BLACK LINE (System of trenches N.E. of WYTSCHAETE).

(b) A second pair of tanks will have as their objective OCCASION TRENCH - System of trenches to East of WYTSCHAETE - BLACK LINE at STEENZER CABARET and cutting.

11.COMMUNICATION. The Brigade Forward Station will advance from the CABLE HEAD in rear of the last wave of the leading assault Battalions and will be established about O.13.c.15.45. When the BLACK LINE has been captured communication will be extended forward to O.19.b.75.85.

Battalion Forward Posts. will be established as follows :-

7th R. Innis Fus. about O.13.c.00.55.
7/8th R.Irish Fus. about O.13.c.10.32.
2nd R.Irish Regt. about O.19.b.75.85.

The Forward Command Post of the 2nd R. Irish Regt. for the Attack on the BLACK LINE will be at the Brigade Forward Station O.13.c.15.45.

Unit Commanders are reminded of the importance of sending to Brigade H.Q. frequent reports on the situation and the attitude of the enemy.

Brigade Headquarters will remain at THE RIB.

The 58th Inf. Bde. Forward Station will be at O.13.a.73.60.

47th Inf. Bde. Forward Station will be at N.24.b.6.0. After the BLACK LINE has been captured it will be at O.19.b.3.1.

12 CONTACT AEROPLANES — Contact Aeroplanes (Type R.E.8) will fly over the line and call for flares at the following hours :-

Zero plus 45 minutes.
Zero plus 2 hours.
Zero plus 4 hours 20 minutes.
Zero plus 5 hours 20 minutes.
Zero plus 6 hours 30 minutes.
Zero plus 11 hours.

Flares and Watson Fans should be shown only by the leading troops. Troops will be prepared to light flares at other times when called for by the aeroplanes.

13. SYNCHRONIZATION. — All units will send a watch to Brigade H.Q. at 9 a.m. 12 noon, 6 p.m. and 11 p.m. daily until Zero hour.

14. S.O.S. SIGNAL. — The S.O.S. Signal will remain as at present, - RED Signal Cartridges.

15. ZERO HOUR. — Zero hour will be notified later.

16. BRIGADE PRISONERS CAGE. — The Brigade Prisoners Cage where all prisoners will be sent, will be at Brigade H.Q. THE RIB.

17. INSTRUCTIONS. — Instructions for the attack have been issued from time to time in 49TH INFANTRY BRIGADE INSTRUCTIONS for the OFFENSIVE. These Instructions are hereby brought into force.

18. ACKNOWLEDGE.

[signature] Captain,
Brigade Major, 49th Infantry Brigade.

Issued through Signals at 1.50 PM.

Copy No.			Copy No.	
1	to G. O. C.		11	to 58th Inf. Bde.
..	2	2nd R. Irish Regt.	12	57th Inf. Bde.
..	3	7th R. Innis Fus.	13	Left Group.
..	4	8th R. Innis Fus.	14	16th Div. Arty.
..	5	7/8th R. Irish Fus.	15	157th Field Coy, R.E.
..	6	49th M.G. Company.	16	11th Hants Pioneers.
..	7	49th T.M. Battery.	17	Bde. Intelligence Off.
..	8	16th Division	18-19	War Diary.
..	9	47th Inf. Bde.	20	File.
..	10	48th Inf. Bde.		

G/16/8
SECRET.
(Special) 1 : 10,000 MAP 8150/2.
OOSTTAVERNE LINE
DOTTED BLACK LINE
IX CORPS GREEN LINE
BLACK LINE
BLUE LINE
RED LINE
19th DIV.
16th DIV.
36th DIV.
Oosttaverne
Wambeke
Wytschaete
Vierstraat
CONVERSION TABLE
MINUTES — HOURS.
61 mins. = 1 hour 1 min.
62 2
64 4
65 5
67 7
69 9
70 10
71 11
72 12
73 13
77 17
82 22
85 25
90 30
91 31
100 40
104 44
105 45
108 48
110 50
113 53
115 55
116 56
118 58
119 59
120 = 2 hours 0 mins.
122 2
125 5
127 7
129 9
130 10
131 11
132 12
220 mins. = 3 hours 40 mins.
224 44
228 48
229 49
230 50
232 52
234 54
236 56
240 = 4 hours 0 mins.
244 4
245 5
246 6
248 8
249 9
250 10
255 15
264 24
272 32
275 35
280 40
284 44
286 46
288 48
300 = 5 hours 0 mins.
304 4
318 18
322 22
326 26
SECOND ARMY BARRAGE MAP.
June, 1917.
CORPS BOUNDARY
DIVISIONAL BOUNDARY
Scale 1:10,000

16th Div

F

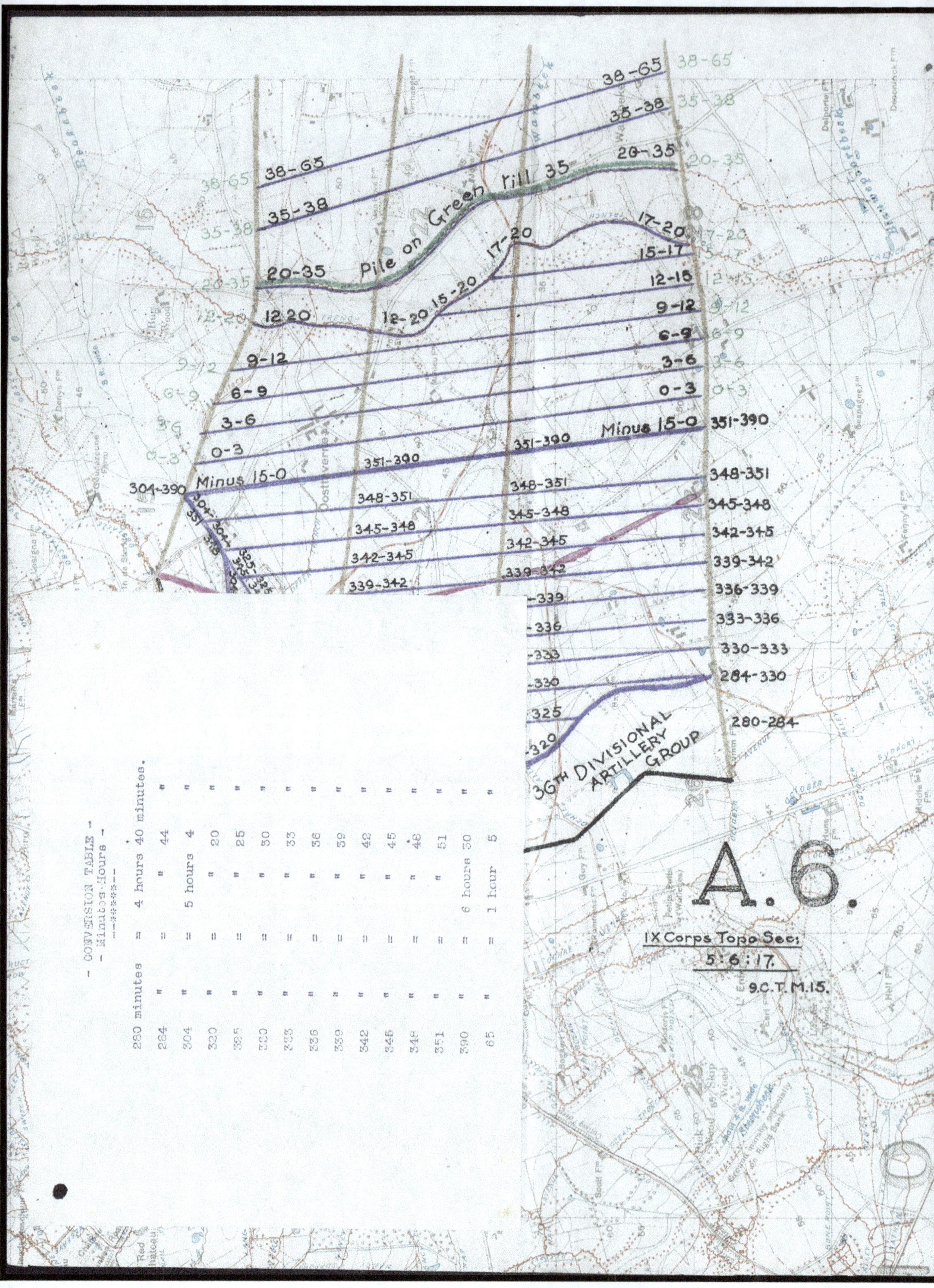

- CONVERSION TABLE -
- Minutes-Hours -

280 minutes	=	4 hours 40 minutes.
284 "	=	" 44 "
304 "	=	5 hours 4 "
320 "	=	" 20 "
325 "	=	" 25 "
330 "	=	" 30 "
333 "	=	" 33 "
336 "	=	" 36 "
339 "	=	" 39 "
342 "	=	" 42 "
345 "	=	" 45 "
348 "	=	" 48 "
351 "	=	" 51 "
390 "	=	6 hours 30 "
65 "	=	1 hour 5 "

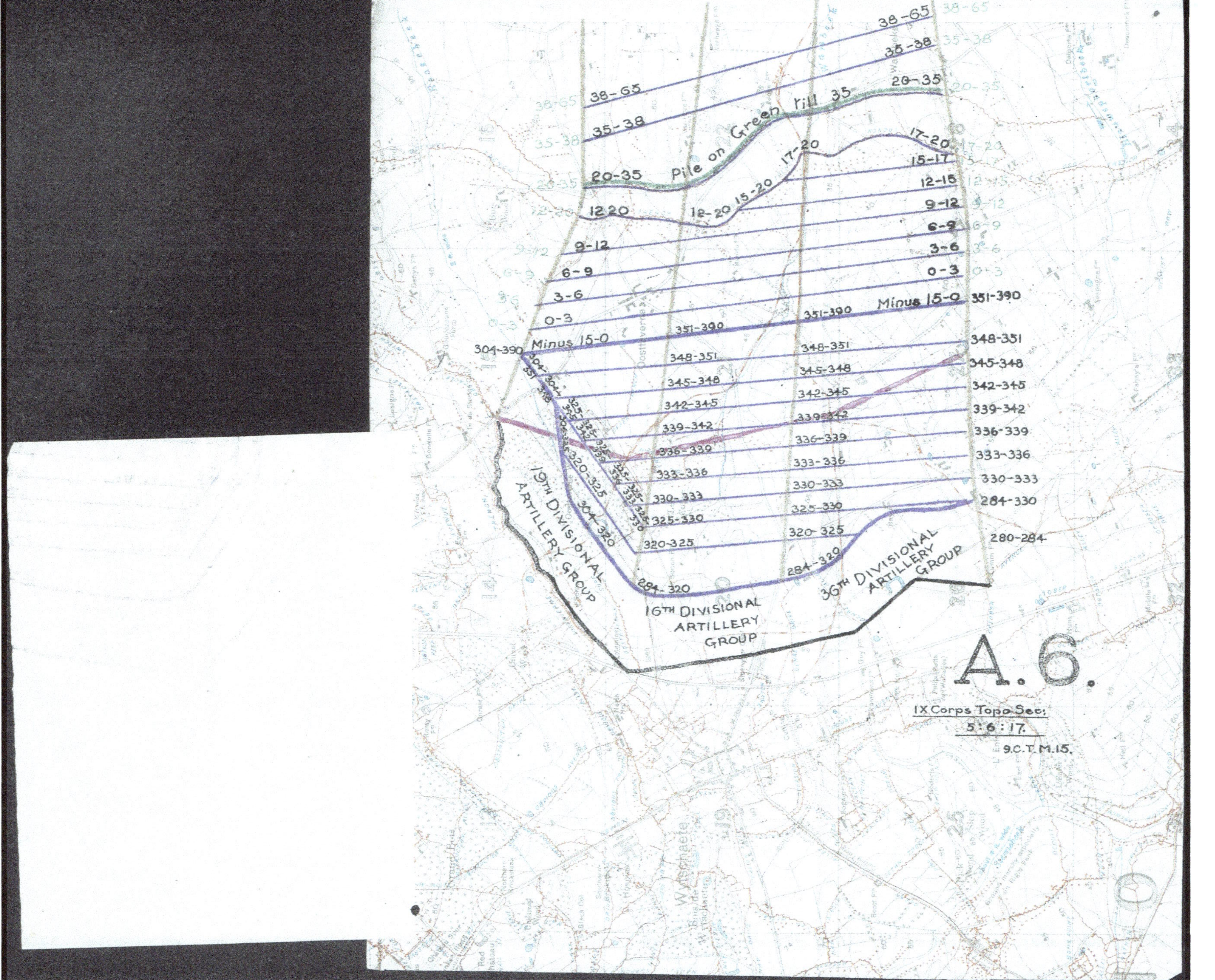
A.6.
IX Corps Topo Sec;
5:6:17.
9.C.T.M.15.
Pile on Green hill 35
19TH DIVISIONAL ARTILLERY GROUP
16TH DIVISIONAL ARTILLERY GROUP
36TH DIVISIONAL ARTILLERY GROUP
Minus 15-0
Wytschaete

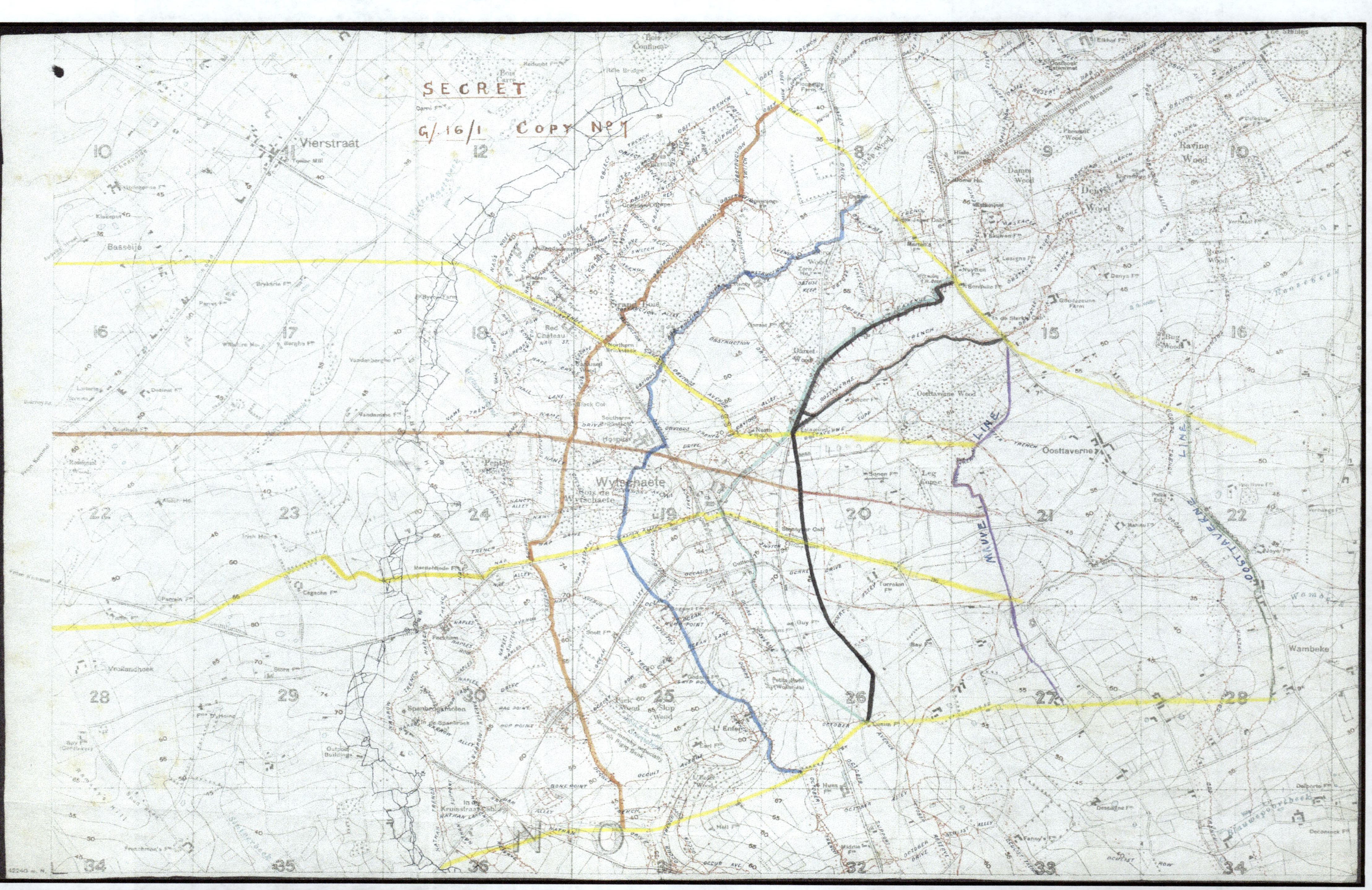

SECRET
G/16/1 COPY No 1
Vierstraat
Wytschaete
Oosttaverne Wood
Oosttaverne
Wambeke
MAUVE LINE
OOSTTAVERNE LINE
Ravine Wood
Damm Wood

Fab^e de faïence / Faïencerie	Pottery.
Ferme, F^me	Farm.
Filature, Fil^re	Spinning mill
Fonderie, Fond^ie	Foundry.
Fontaine, Font^ne	Spring, fountain.
Forêt	Forest
Forme de radoub	Dry dock.
Forge	Smithy.
Fosse	Mine, Pit.
Fossé	Moat, Ditch.
Four	Kiln.
.. à chaux	Lime-kiln

Marbrerie	Marble works.
Marais	Marsh.
Marais salant	Saltern, Salt marsh.
Marché	Market.
Mare	Pool.
Meule	Rick.
Minière	Mine.
Monastère	Monastery.
Moulin, M^in	Mill.
.. à vapeur	Steam mill.
Mur	Wall.
.. crénelé	Loop-holed wall.

.. d'aérage / .. ventilateur	Ventilating shaft.
.. de sondage	Boring.
Quai	Quay, Platform.
.. aux bestiaux	Cattle platform.
.. aux marchandises	Goods platform.
Raccordement	Junction.
Raffinerie	Refinery
.. de sucre	Sugar refinery
Râperie	Beet-root factory.

.. métallurgique	Metal works.
.. à agglomérés	Briquette factory.
Verrerie, Verr^ie	Glass works.
Viaduc	Viaduct
Vivier	Fish Pond.
Voie de chargement / .. .. déchargement / .. .. d'évitement / .. .. formation / .. .. manœuvre	Siding.
Zinguerie	Zinc works.

INDEX

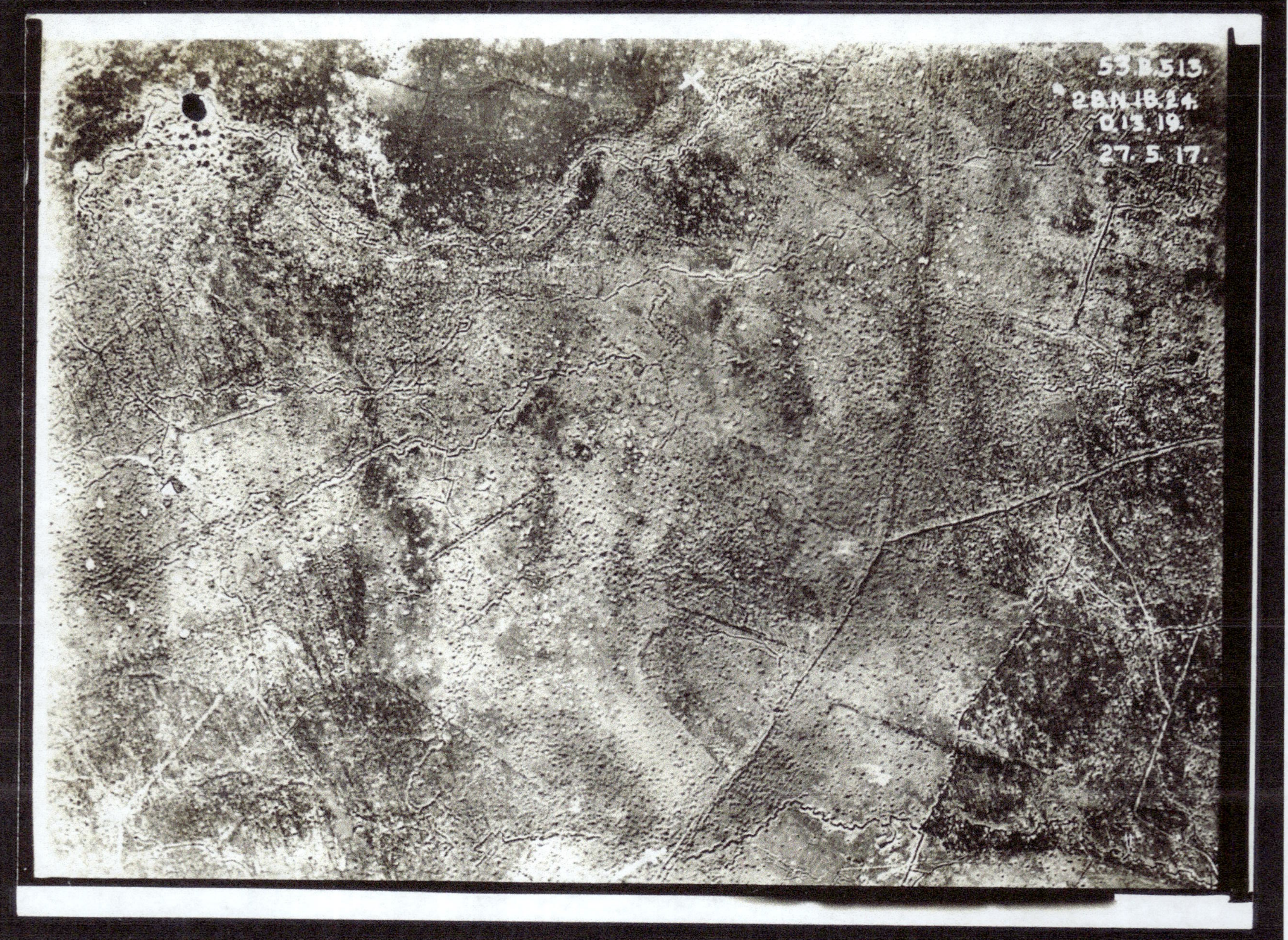
53.B.513.
28.N.18.24.
0.13.19.
27.5.17.

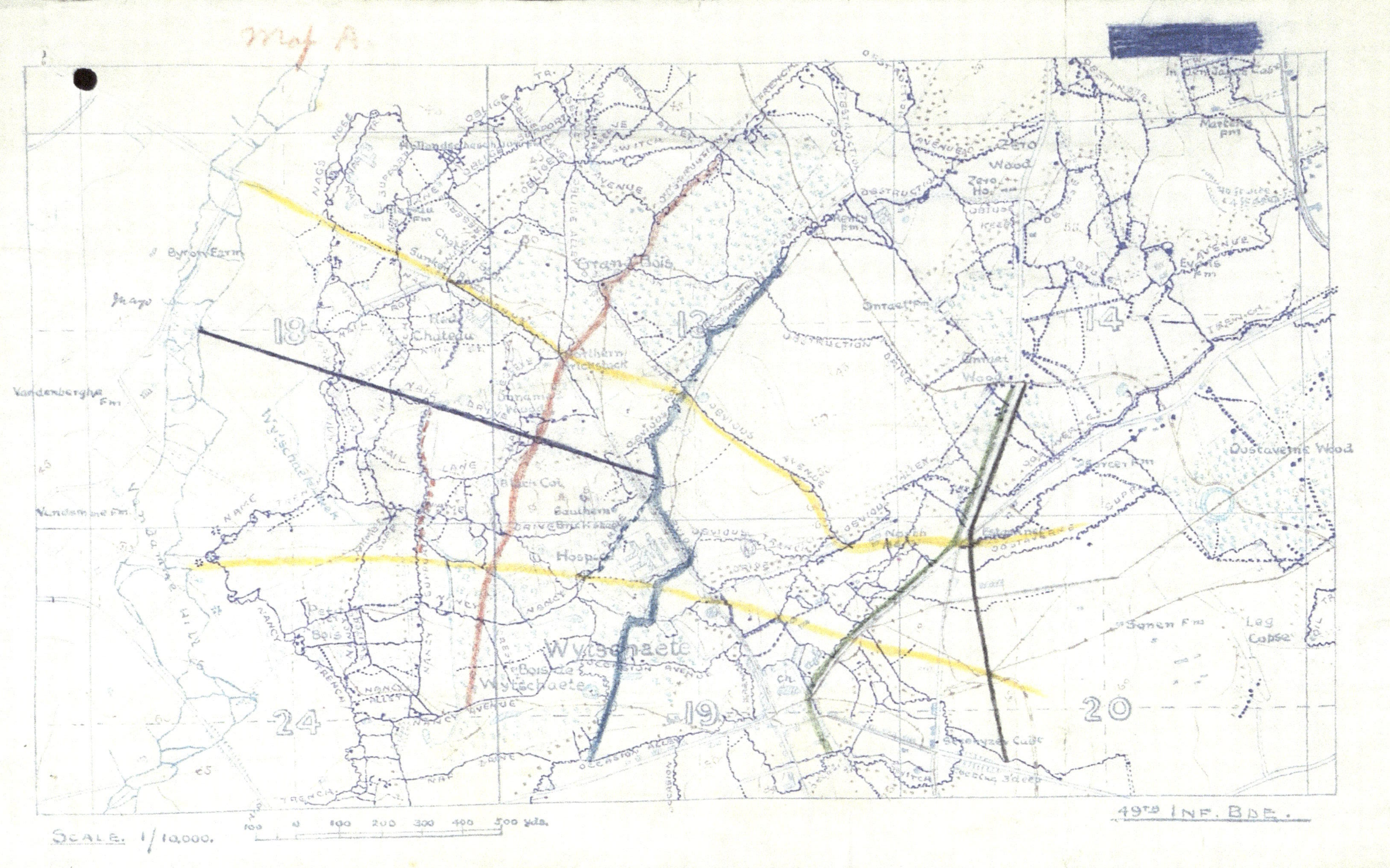

Map A
Grand Bois
Byron Farm
Vandenberghe Fm
Wytschaete
Bois de Wytschaete
Hospice
Zero Wood
Oostaverne Wood
Leg Copse
Sonen Fm
Unnamed Wood
18
13
14
19
20
24
SCALE. 1/10,000.
100 0 100 200 300 400 500 yds.
49th INF. BDE.

H

SECRET. Copy No.......4

49th Infantry Brigade Order No. 151 - 9-6-17.

1. The 49th Infantry Brigade will be withdrawn from the line today, 9th June.

2. Units will march to the LOCRE Area as follows :-

Brigade Headquarters.	LOCRE.
2nd R. Irish Regt.	BIRR BARRACKS.
7th R. Innis Fus.	WICKLOW LINES M.29.a.5.9.
8th R. Innis Fus.	DONCASTER HUTS.
7/8th R. Irish Fus.	TRALEE "B" LINES M.23.c.8.6.
49th T.M. Battery.	DONCASTER HUTS.
49th M.G. Company. (less 8 guns).	DONCASTER HUTS.

2. The 8 guns of the 49th M.G. Company now with 48th Inf. Bde. will remain under the orders of the G.O.C. 48th Inf. Bde.

3. Units will march via Route "E" - NUT ROAD - BUTTERFLY FARM. Leading platoons to pass junction of YORK ROAD and Route "E" at following hours :-

2nd R. Irish Regt.	1.30 p.m.
7/8th R. Irish Fus.	2.15 p.m.
7th R. Innis Fus.	3 p.m.
49th T.M. Battery.	
49th M.G. Company. (less 8 guns).	2.55 p.m.
8th R. Innis Fus.	3.35 p.m.

Movement will be by platoons at 200 yards interval.

4. Areas vacated will be left as clean as possible.

5. Arrival in billets will be reported to Bde Headquarters.

6. Bde. H.Q. will close at THE RIB at 2.30 p.m. and will open in LOCRE at 3.30 p.m.

7. ACKNOWLEDGE.

W.B. Willem Captain,
Brigade Major, 49th Infantry Brigade.

Issued through Signals at ..11.5 am

Copy No. 1 to 2nd R. Irish Regt.
.. 2 7th R. Innis Fus.
.. 3 8th R. Innis Fus.
.. 4 7/8th R. Irish Fus.
.. 5 49th M.G. Company.
.. 6 49th T.M. Battery.
.. 7 47th Inf. Bde.
.. 8 48th Inf. Bde.
.. 9 16th Div. (G).
.. 10 16th Div. (Q).
.. 11 Bde. Supply Officer.
.. 12 144th Coy, A.S.C.
.. 13 Staff Captain.
.. 14-15 War Diary.
.. 16 File.

12/6/17

7/8th. Battalion Royal Irish Fusiliers Order No. 3.

SECRET. COPY No. 6...

Reference MAPs 1/20,000 Sheet 28.S.W.& 1/40,000 Sheet 27.

:-

1. INFORMATION

The 49th. Infantry Brigade will march to the MERRIS AREA on the 13th. June.

2. STARTING POINTS AND ROUTE AND TIME.

Road and Track Junction at M.32.d.6.4.
Route. Track "A" as far as M.37.c.3.3.------CROIX de POPERINGHE------Road Junction M.26.d.2.3.---ST. JANS CAPPEL----SCAEKKEN---METEREN.
Headquarters will pass starting point at 7.15.a.m.

3. REVEILLE ETC.

Reveille at 4.30.a.m. Breakfasts at 5.0.a.m.

4. KITS etc.

All Officers' Kits will be loaded on G.S.Wagon in Officers' Lines before 5.40.a.m. Maltese Cart and Lewis Gun Limbers to be loaded before 5.50.a.m. All Wagons will leave Camp at 6.0.a.m. and proceed to Transport Lines to join remainder of Transport.

5. ADVANCE PARTY.

An Advance Party consisting of Lieut. W. Sparks, 4.C.Q.M.Sgts and Sergt. Bird on bicycles will meet Staff Captain at METEREN CHURCH at 6.30.a.m.

6. TRANSPORT.

Baggage Wagons will march with Units. Transport with Drums and Pioneers will move by road to CROIX de POPERINGHE and will join Battalion as it passes at about 8.15.a.m. Pioneers and Drums will fall in at head of Column, Transport at rear.
Officers' Horses will be at Camp by 6.45.a.m.

7. DISCIPLINE.

500 yards will be kept between Battalions and 50 yards between Companies. If a hostile Aeroplanes appears all ranks will remain still and not look up. Units will halt at 10 minutes before the hour and move off at each hour. Attention should be paid to the following points:-

1. Cleanliness of dress and equipment.
2. Steel Helmets to be worn and caps carried on the packs. On the Command "March to Attention" being given, every man will put on his Steel Helmet.
3. Each section of Fours to pay attention to their dressing.
4. Only brakesmen will march behind vehicles.
5. Cooks will be as clean as possible.
6. Mounted Officers' Packs will be carried on the G.S.Wagons
7. Water Bottles to be filled.

8. COOKING.

Tea will be cooked and consumed on route. Dinners will be eaten on arrival at destination.

9. LEWIS GUN HANDCARTS.

The Lewis Gun Hand carts will follow 50 yards in rear of "B" Company, followed by a guard xxx consisting of H.Qr. Guard and Police.

10. SICK.

The Crocks as detailed by the M.O. will fall in outside Orderly Room under 2/Lieut. J.B. Drea and move off at 5.15.a.m. Route same as laid down in para 2.

11. PARADE

The Battalion will fall in in Close Column of Companies facing Orderly Room at 6.45.a.m. ready to march off at 7.0.a.m. Order of March:- H.Qrs, "C" Coy. "D" Coy. "A" Coy. "B" Coy.

12. ARRIVAL.

Arrival in Billets to be reported to Battalion Headquarters.

13. MESSAGES.

To head of Column.

14. ACKNOWLEDGE

W H Stitt

Captain & Adjutant.
7/8th. (S) Battalion Royal Irish Fusiliers

ISSUED THROUGH SIGNALS AT 12.10.a.m. 13th. June 1917.

Copy No. 1. "A" Coy.
2. "B" Coy.
3. "C" Coy.
4. "D" Coy.
5. Q.M.
6. T.O.
7. L.G.O.

Copy No. 8. M.O.
9. H.Q. 49th. Infantry Brigade
10. Intelligence Officer
11. R.S.M.
12. Signals.
13. Lieut. Sparks.
14 & 15. War Diary & File.

J

SPECIAL ORDER

The 16th. Division has been relieved today.

For over eight months we have held our portion of the line in the SPANBROEK, VIERSTRAAT or DIEPENDAAL Sectors, and we can look back with pride and satisfaction to the record of those months. Neither rain or snow, or the heat of Summer has interfered with the constant work.

Long distances, wet roads, cold nights, shortage of fuel, hostile shelling, have all failed to damp the spirits of our men. With gun and howitzer, trench mortar, rifle, machine gun and bomb, and sometimes with bayonet, we have gradually worn down the boasting enemy; and two days ago, with small losses to the Division, we have completed this chapter of our history, by taking from him the Wood and Village of WYTSCHAETE, and the crest of the hill which means so much for future operations.

The Divisional Commander, in congratulating all Arms and all ranks of the Division on their victory of June 7th, thanks all the Officers, N.C.O's and Men under his Command for their loyalty and help, and for their bravery and skill in action.

Whatever new work lies before us, it will be tackled with the same endurance, the same cheerfulness and the same bravery; and again and again the Division and every man in it will justify the right to our motto "Everywhere and always Faithful".

W.B. Hickie,

Major-General,

June 9th. 1917. Commanding 16th. (Irish) Division.

K

 6/6/17

S E C R E T.

S P E C I A L   O R D E R.

The big day is very near.

All our preparations are complete, and the Divisional Commander wishes to express his appreciation, and his thanks, to all the Officers and Men who have worked so cheerfully, and so well.

The 16th. Division is fortunate in having had assigned to it the capture of the stronghold of WYTSCHAETE.

Every Officer and Man - Gunners, Sappers, Pioneers, R.A.M.C., A.S.C. and Infantrymen of historic Irish Regiments - knows what he has to do.

Let all do their best, as they have always done, continuing to show the same courage and devotion to duty which has characterized the 16th. (Irish) Division since it landed in France, and it will be our proud privilege to restore to Little Belguim, the "White Village", which has been in German hands for nearly three years.

W.B. Hickie,
Major-General,

June 5th. 1917. Commanding 16th. (Irish) Division.

L

CONFIDENTIAL
NOT TO BE ISSUED TO COMMANDERS OF LOWER RANK THAN BATTALION BATTERY AND FIELD COMPANY COMMANDERS AND NOT TO BE TAKEN INTO FRONT LINE TRENCHES

IXTH CORPS SUMMARY OF INTELLIGENCE
7th June, 1917.
(5 p.m.6/6/17 to 5 p.m. 7/5/17.) No.429.

PART I.
INFORMATION FROM OUR OWN FRONT.

1. OPERATIONS

At 3.10 a.m. an attack was launched against the enemy's positions between MOUNT SORREL (I.30.Central) and the River DOUVE, a front of about 10 miles. The attack has been successful along the whole front, and all objectives have been reached according to programme.

The line held on the IXth Corps front at 6 p.m. today is as shown on the attached map.

2. PRISONERS

Total number of prisoners admitted to Corps Cage during the last 24 hours up to 6 p.m. - 57 Officers and 1862 other ranks.

Total number of prisoners reported by Divisions about 2,500 including 1 Regimental Commander.

3. GENERAL INFORMATION FROM PRISONERS

The enemy has suffered very heavily in killed, wounded and prisoners, and a considerable amount of war material has been captured. It appears that our attack was not expected to take place for two or three days, and it was the enemy's intention to relieve all the troops which had been subjected to the heavy bombardment by fresh troops, more capable of withstanding an attack. The 40th Division who was holding the line opposite the southern portion of the Corps front were relieved on the nights 5th/6th and 6/7th. The relief was to have been completed on the morning of the 6th, but our fire on the back areas made it impossible to complete the relief, which was only carried out with heavy loss - one company alone having 20 killed and 25 wounded.

The 2nd Division were expecting to be relieved tonight (7th) by an unknown Division.

The loss of the WYTSCHAETE - MESSINES Ridge will be a great blow to the enemy. Prisoners state that the general feeling had been that the ridge would be held at all costs, firstly on account of its commanding position, and secondly owing to the heavy losses which had been sustained in its capture in 1914.

Prisoners are unable to account for the lack of support given them by the artillery, but are inclined to put it down to cowardice on the part of the German gunners. There appears to be a great lack of good feeling between the infantry and artillery. Our counter-battery work is reported to be very successful, and casualties caused to material are stated to have been on an average one gun per battery.

The mines which were exploded at Zero this morning appear to have had a considerable effect. One prisoner stated that practically the whole of his company was blown into the air by one mine.

/Prisoners . . .

Prisoners when captured were for the most part very hungry and thirsty, and quite satisfied to be captured.

4. UNITS IDENTIFIED

The order of battle was quickly established to be, North to South :-

44th I.R.	2nd Division.
33rd Fusiliers.	
4th Grenadiers.	
23rd Bav.I.R.	3rd Bav.Division.
17th Bav.I.R.	

In addition to the above, machine gunners were captured belonging to 388 Law.I.R. who had been moved down from the DIXMUDE Area, and had been put into COSTTAVERNE WOOD to cover a possible withdrawal of the guns behind.

Machine gunners of the 10th JAEGER ZU PFERDE werecaptured in WYTSCHAETE. These men belonged to the Divisional Cavalry of the 2nd Division, and had been moved up to strengthen the garrison of the WYTSCHAETE DEFENCES. One section only was in WYTSCHAETE, consisting of 3 guns.

5. LOSSES AND REINFORCEMENTS

The approximate strength of the enemy's troops on the IXth Corps front at Zero should have been about 5,500, including details and resting battalions. Out of this number about 2,500 have been captured, and undoubtedly the enemy have suffered heavily in killed and wounded both during bombardment and in to-days attack. It would appear therefore that 2nd Division as a fighting formation has practically ceased to exist. The same fate has befallen the 3rd Bavarian Division.

The enemy has a considerable number of divisions available for reinforcing the line.

The most probable reinforcements against the Corps front appear to be -

24th (Saxon) Division.
40th (Saxon) Division.
38th Division.
11th Division.

All the above are believed to be in the neighbourhood.

6. WEATHER FORECAST NOON TO NOON

Wind S, or S.W. 15-20 miles per hour, perhaps temporarily W. Probably light between S.E. and S.W. at night. Some local showers or thunderstorms at first. Probably mist at night and then fair and bright again. Very warm, becoming rather cooler. Visibility good, then indifferent, finally fair. Temperature 75-80 today, 70-75 tomorrow.

IXth Corps "I"
7th June, 1917.

A.E. GRASETT, Captain G.S.
for B.G.G.S. IXth Corps.

POSITIONS
THE FOLLOWING HOSTILE BATTERY /HAVE BEEN ACTIVE
OPPOSITE IX CORPS FRONT DURING PAST 24 HOURS.

P 13a 6343.
P 13a 7022.
P 13a 6000.
P 13b 1028.
P 13c 6280.
P 13c 7633. ?
P 13c 8649.
P 13c 4459.
P 13c 4303.

P 19a 6070.
P 19a 8380.
P 19a 9198.
P 19b 4199.
P 19c 0978.
P 19c 9581.
P 19d 1591.
P 19d 7749.
P 25b 2348.
P 25b 6768.
P 25c 4791.
P 26a 5015.
P 26a 6722.

O 28b 4060.
O 24a 3239.
O 24b 0346.
O 24d 9524.
O 24d 9142.
O 30c 7171.

- -: *** :- -

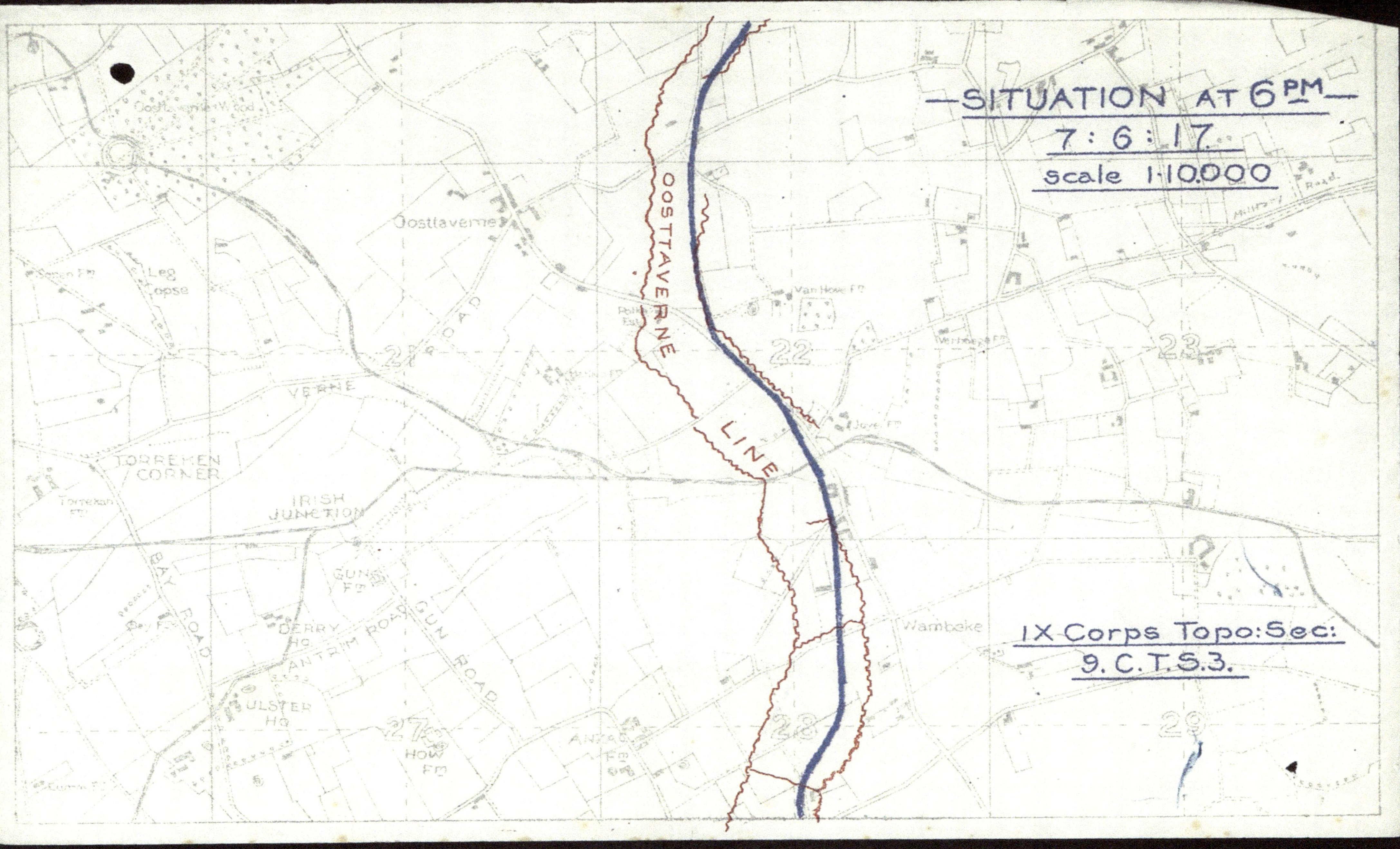
—SITUATION AT 6 PM—
7 : 6 : 17.
scale 1:10.000
IX Corps Topo: Sec:
9. C. T. S. 3.
OOSTTAVERNE LINE
Oosttaverne
Leg Copse
Van Hove Fm
Joye Fm
Wambeke
Military Road
TORREKEN CORNER
IRISH JUNCTION
VERNE
BAY ROAD
GUN ROAD
ANTRIM ROAD
DERRY Ho
ULSTER Ho
GUN Fm
How Fm
ANZAC Fm
22
23
27
28
29

M

- CONFIDENTIAL. -

NOT TO BE ISSUED TO COMMANDERS OF LOWER RANK THAN BATTALION BATTERY AND FIELD COMPANY COMMANDERS AND NOT TO BE TAKEN INTO FRONT LINE TRENCHES.

IX CORPS SUMMARY OF INTELLIGENCE. 8TH JUNE, 1917.

(5 p.m.7/5/17 to 5 p.m.8/5/17,.

No.430.

PART I
INFORMATION FROM OUR OWN FRONT.

--+++++++++++++++++++++++--

OPERATIONS. All gains made yesterday have been held, and the night passed comparatively quiet on the Corps Front. About 9 a.m. this morning, the enemy made an attack on our line west of JOYE FARM (O 22 d). The attack was repulsed with considerable loss to the enemy. Large parties concentrating in O 22 d were dispersed by our artillery and many were killed in attempting to retire.

ARTILLERY.

The general scheme for counter-battery work during the operations yesterday was to neutralize as many hostile batteries as possible and as soon as possible. A programme was arranged for As the conditions were favourable firing of gas shells if weather conditions were favourable 60-pdrs. and 4.5" fired gas shells up to a certain period when the wind became too strong when they/were stopped and the bombardment with H.E. and shrapnel continued. During the first period of the operation comparatively little hostile shelling was reported but as time went on the hostile fire became more intense. At 4 a.m. Zone calls were received and acted on and these continued throughout the day. The majority of these were in squares O 16, 17, 24, 30 and the P squares which showed that the enemy removed most of his guns from the forward areas during the day, and reinforced them by batteries brought up as a reserve. The Counter-batteries were firing continuously from dawn till late in the evening when there was a pause in the hostile activity.

On receipt of the S.O.S. call later in the evening the Counter-batteries replied vigorously.

MACHINE GUNS.

Machine gun positions from captured map. Some of these are shown as completed and others partially so. As the map is undated it is impossible to say whether work is complete.

O 18 d 10.15.
O 18 d 1. 1.

O 22 d 70.05.
O 22 d 73.05.

O 24 a 98.71.
O 24 c 87.05.
O 24 d 80.15.

O 28 b 43.08.
O 28 b 95.42.
O 28 b 98.35.
O 28 b 99.05.
O.36 a 37.85.
O.36 a 60.43.

O 28 d 67.93.
O 28 d 67.67.
O 28 d 97.76.

O 29 b 00.95.
O 29 b 05.43.
O 29 b 02.35.
O 29 b 83.47.

O 30 a 90.95.

O 30 b 67.25.
O 30 b 99.37.
O 30 c 32.10.
O 30 c 97.00.
O 30 d 60.87.
O 30 d 00.75.

/These points. . .

These points have been selected as suitable for M.G. positions and in some instances it may be assumed that actual emplacements already exist.

Positions are shown on the attached map.

PRISONERS.

Total number of prisoners passed through Corps Cage since 7th June up to 6 p.m. today.

Officers	62.
other ranks.	2632.
TOTAL.	2694.

These are composed as follows:-

2nd Division.

Units.	Officers.	O.R.
33rd F.R.	8	705.
4th Gren.R.	14	760.
44th I.R.	17	574.
10th Jaeger zu Pferde	1	8.
1st F.A.R.	1	7.
1st Pioneer Bn.	1	24.
Total	42	2078

40th Division.

104th I.R.	10	137.
32nd F.A.R.	-	3.
Total	10	140

24th Division.

139th I.R.	-	25.
133rd I.R.	-	1.
179th I.R.	-	1.
Total	-	27.

3rd Bavarian Division.

23rd Bav.I.R.	5	240.
17th " "	-	2.
18th " "		1.
Total	5	243.

35th Division.

176th I.R.	-	13.

1st Guard Res.Div.

64th R.I.R.	-	1.

19th Landwehr Div.

388th Landwehr I.R.	-	14.

7th Division.

393rd I.R.	-	3.

Pioneer Battalions.

4th	-	4.
25th	2	34.
14th	-	1.
19th	-	1.
24th	-	1.

/Foot . . .

	Units.	Officers.	O.R.
Foot Artillery Regiments.	12th	1.	7.
Field Artillery Regiments.	23rd	-	2.
	5th	-	4.
	7th Res.	-	2.
	93rd.	-	11.
Sanitäts Companies.	48th	-	8.
	602nd	1	13.
Nahkampf Battery.		-	2.
T.M.Units.		1	10.
Funkerklein Abteilungen.	65th	-	6
	62nd	-	7
	GRAND TOTAL.	62 officers.	2632 O.R.

Several hundreds still remain to come in.

INFORMATION OBTAINED FROM PRISONERS.

Artillery. Prisoners of the 7th and 12th Foot Artillery Regiments stated that almost all their guns had suffered from our counter-battery work during the last week. They were full of praise for our counter-battery work. They stated that what positions they had in front of the canal had been so badly damaged that the guns could no longer be used. They had not heard of guns being withdrawn to the east side of the canal. A prisoner of the 1st Field Artillery Regt. stated that his battery was in position in O 20. Two of their guns had been knocked out and also their O.P.

Miscellaneous. Prisoner of the 25th Pioneer Bn. stated that he left the ARRAS front a week ago. He knows that one company has come up here but does not know whether the whole battalion is in the neighbourhood.

Prisoner of the 10th Jaeger Zu Pferde belonged to a M.G. section attached to the 2nd Squadron. He knew the third squadron was in France, but knew nothing of the 1st Squadron. His section was armed with 3 Russian M.G.s. They had orders not to fire until we attacked. A RITTMEISTER of the 2nd Squadron, who was also captured, belongs to the squadron and not to the M.G. section.

Other Units. A reliable prisoner of the 1st Field Artillery Regiment stated that the artillery of the 1st Division (16th and 52nd Field Artillery Regiments), had been in position behind WYTSCHAETE for some weeks. He also stated that he had seen men of the 3rd Grenadiers Regiment near COMINES a few weeks ago.

He also said that the 11th Division was in the vicinity of WERVICQ. Another prisoner states that the whole of the 5th Army Corps is somewhere in the back area having been withdrawn from the Aisne after having suffered heavy losses.

GENERAL. Prisoners all agree that prior to our attack their organisations were entirely demolished. Our starvation fire on back areas all through the night with artillery and M.Gs. caused many casualties, and made supply of food and communication with the rear practically impossible. Their H.Qs. nearly all destroyed, and communications cut, with the result that there was no command.

IX Corps "I".
8th June, 1917.

A.E.GRASETT, Captain, for
B.G.G.S., IX Corps.

The M.M.G.Battery joined in the M.G.Barrage which had been ably planned by the C.M.G.O. under the direction of the General Staff.

The Cyclist Battalion could not be used as such on account of the broken nature of the ground, but their services were of the greatest value in the preparations beforehand.

The Miners and Tunnellers carried out their trying duties with a patience and fortitude worthy of the highest admiration. The whole of the units and special troops employed under the orders of the Chief Engineer worked with indefatigable energy for the success of the Corps which they may have the satisfaction of feeling was largely promoted by their exertions.

Among the non-combatant troops the ASC rendered throughout the most invaluable services, day and night, in all weathers, and under fire when necessary, in the supply of ammunition and food. The excellent control, supervision and maintenance of this essential service reflects the highest credit on all concerned.

The Army Medical Organization was designed and perfected in a most praiseworthy manner. It's units dealt most efficiently and rapidly, both on the Battle-Field and behind it, with the comparatively small numbers which, fortunately, the RAMC were called upon to handle.

The AOD dealt with the large masses of ammunition, clothing and equipment which pass through their accounts in a most efficient manner, while the other services, too numerous for specific mention, contributed in their several functions to the success of the troops.

The Corps Commander wishes to offer his most cordial congratulations to the IX Corps on its share in this brilliant victory for the British Army. Every officer and man in the Corps has the satisfaction of knowing that he personally helped in it's achievement, whether he belongs to the combatant troops who took an active part in the fighting, or to the non-combatant troops and services who performed their duties so efficiently and usefully. The Corps Commander wishes it to be known that he fully appreciates the value of the work done and that it was only the loyal co-operation of every single member of the Corps which ensured such a striking success.

J Percy.

Brigadier General.,
General Staff., IXth Corps.

15th June, 1917.

11th Division. (90)	285th A.T.Company R.E.	G.O.C. R.A.
16th Division. (90)	262nd Railway Coy.R.E.	IX Corps 'Q'.
19th Division. (90)	296th -do-	Chief Engineer (3)
36th Division (90)	No.3 Special Coy.,R.E.	A.D. Signals. (4)
IXth Corps H.A. (30)	'K' Special Coy .,R.E.	C.M.G.O.
53rd Sqdn: RFC. (3)	'O' -do-	A.P.M. (4)
No.5 K.B.Company. (2)	No. 27 Labour Group.	D.D.M.S. (3)
2/Bde:H.B..M.G.C. (3)	7th Labour Bn:	A.D. Ordnance. (3)
'A' Bn: -do- (3)	6th Labour Company.	D.A.D.P.S.
'B' Bn: -do- (3)	12th -do-	Field Cashier.
IX Corps Mtd Tps. (10)	19th -do-	S.M.T.O. (18)
IX Corps Schools. (3)	21st -do-	Chemical Adviser.
1st Entg: Bn. (6)	23rd -do-	D.A.D.L. (2)
8th Entg: Bn. (6)	84th -do-	Veterinary Officer.
175th Tun: Co.R.E.	94th -do-	Camp Commdt: (2)
250th Tun: Co.R.E	117th -do-	D.A.P.C.
1/Can:Tun: Co.R.E.	148th -do-	D.A.C.G.
136th A.T.Coy.R.E.	3rd West India Regt.	U.B.C.
167th A.T.Coy.R.E.	Intelligence.	French Mission.
No.8 Army Tramways Co.	335 Road Constn: Coy.	Belgian Mission.
	314th -do-	C.R.E. IX Corps Tps.

PLEASE DISTRIBUTE.

SECRET 7/8th. Royal Irish Fusiliers Order No.4. June 16th.1917

COPY NO.........

Reference Maps. Sheets 27. and 28.S.W.

-:-

1.INFORMATION.

The 49th. Infantry Brigade will move to CLARE CAMP on the 17th.June 1917

2.STARTING POINT AND TIME.

Where stream crosses roads at M.20.c.8.9.Drums will pass the starting point at 6.45.a.m.followed by H.Qrs."D"Coy."A"Coy."B"Coy."C"Coy.Lewis Gun Hand Carts,Guard consisting of H.Qrs.Guard and Police.Regimental Transport. Companies will march at 50 yards interval,Battalions at 500 yards interval. Pioneers will join H.Qrs.at starting point.

3.HALTS.

Units will halt at ten minutes to each hour and will march off at the hour.

4.PACKS.

All Packs will be stacked at Q.M.Stores to night.H.Qrs.and each Company being stacked separately.On off loading no packs will be issued without Q.M's sanction and the Q.M. will detail an N.C.O.to superintend the same.

5.DRESS.

Water Bottles will be full.Haversacks will be carried on back,water proof sheet under flap of haversack.Mess Tin hanging from straps or flap of haversack,steel helmets to be worn,caps should be handed in,inside the Packs.

6.REVEILLE ETC.

Reveille will be at 4.0.a.m.Breakfasts at 4.30.a.m.Sick.at 5.0.a.m.

7.CROCKS.

All crocks (same crocks as marched in advance to these billets)will be at Transport Lines at 5.15.a.m.2/Lieut.Drea will attend Sick Parade and collect such sick as the M.O.decides should go with crocks.2/Lieut Drea will march these to Transport Lines and pick up the others and then proceed to CLARE CAMP.

8.ADVANCE PARTY.

The four C.Q.MSgts.and Sergt.Bird.will meet Lieut.Sparks at Orderly Room at 6.15.a.m.They will proceed on bicycles to M.33.a.65.95.where they will meet the Staff Captain at 7.30.a.m.

9.SANITATION.

All Billets and surroundings must be left as clean as possible,H.Qrs.and Companies will leave their Sanitary Men behind.The Battalion Orderly Officer will collect these men at their respective billets when he is satisfied that the billets are clean.

10 DISCIPLINE.

There must be no drinking on the march.Dressing must be well kept.

11.COOKING.

Tea will be prepared in the Cookers on the march and will be ready for issue on arrival in camp.Dinners will be prepared later.

12 TRANSPORT.

A lorry will be at Brigade H.Qrs.at 6.0.a.m.for use of this Battalion & 2nd.Royal Irish Regiment.One Guide from 2nd.Royal Irish Regiment,and one from this Battalion to be detailed by Q.M.should meet there at 6.0.a.m. 2nd.Royal Irish Regiment will utilize the lorry for the first trip,this Battalion will utilize it for second trip and so on.The lorry may be used for as many trips as necessary.

2nd.in Command's Horse should be at Battalion H'Qrs.by 6.0.a.m.Company Commanders will pick up their horses as they pass the Transport Lines.

13.KITS.

Baggage wagons will accompany the Battalion.Maltese Cart should be at Battalion H.Qrs.by 5.15.a.m.All Officers Kits should be stacked outside their respective H.Qrs.by 5.15.a.m.The G.S.Wagon will then collect these and Orderly Room Boxes.Mess Cart will draw H.Qrs.Mess Box at 6.0.a.m. Company Mess Boxes will be placed on G.S.Wagon with Officers' Kits.Only bona fide Officers' Mess property will be taken.

14.REPORTS.

Reports to head of column.

15.LEWIS GUNS.

All Lewis Gun Drums etc.will be sent to Transport Lines and packed to night.The Lewis Gun Officer will superintend this.Lewis Gunners of "C" Company and two sections of "B"Company will draw thw handcarts.

16.ACKNOWLEDGE.

W.H. Stott.

Captain & Adjutant.

7/8th.(S)Battalion Royal Irish Fusiliers

S E C R E T.

S H E E T 2.

ISSUED THROUGH SIGNALS AT 9.0.p.m. 16th.June 1917

Copy NO. 1. "A" COY.
2. "B" Coy.
3. "C" Coy.
4. "D" Coy.
5. Q.M.
6. T.O.
7. L.G.O.

Copy.No.8. M.O.
9. H.Q. 49th. Infantry Brigade
10 Intelligence Officer
11. R.S.M.
12. Signals.
13. Lieut.Sparks.
14.& 15. War Diary and File.

7/8th. (S) Battalion Royal Irish Fusiliers Order No.8.
June 19th.1917

Q

COPY NO...15..

SECRET.

Reference Map Sheet 27 1/40,000

:-:

I. INFORMATION.
The 49th. Infantry Brigade is to leave the IX Corps Area to join the Fifth ARMY in the the TILQUES SOUTH Training Area.
The above move will be carried out in three stages as follows;-
20th. June to EECKE AREA.
21st. June to RENESCURE AREA.
22nd. June to TILQUES SOUTH TRAINING AREA.

II. MARCH.
To the EECKE AREA is about 4½ Miles. Starting Point ROAD JUNCTION W.34.b.8.6, ROUTE. Cross Roads W.17.d.1.3.----Cross Roads W.16.d.00.80 ---ROUGE CROIX----CAESTRE.
Order of March:- Drums, H.Qrs., "B", "C", "D", "A", Transport.
Companies etc. will be at starting point at 6.50.a.m. when a halt will be observed until 7.0.a.m. at which hour H.Qrs. will pass starting point. 50 yards will be maintained between Companies, 500 yards between Battalions. Normal halts will be observed.

III. SUPPLIES.
Supply railhead for 20th. June BAILLEUL.
Supply Railhead for 21st. June EBBLINGHAM

IV. ADVANCE PARTY.
Advance Party consisting of 4.C.Q.M.Sgts. and Sergt. Bird will be at Battalion H.Qrs. at 5.15.a.m. where they will report to Lieut. SPARKS. This Party will report to Staff Captain at CHURCH EECKE at 6.0.a.m.

V. REVEILLE ETC.
Reveille 5.0.a.m. Breakfast 5.30.a.m. Sick 5.45.a.m.
Dress for Sick marching Order.

VI. CROCKS.
The Crocks will Parade at Battalion H.Qrs. at 5.15.a.m. under 2/Lieut. J.B. DREA. Any Sick the M.O. may detail will accompany this party, they will march to CHURCH EECKE and wait there until a guide will report to 2/Lieut. J.B. DREA.

VII. SANITATION.
The H.Qrs. and Coy. Sanitary Men will remain behind under the Orderly Officer, who will visit the billets in turn and collect the sanitary men. This Party will march to Church EECKE and will wait there until a guide reports to the Officer.

VIII. DRESS.
Packs will be worn. Steel helmets on head, caps on back of Packs. 15 YUKON PACKS were issued to day, the men who carry these will carry all their equipment etc in them.

IX. TRANSPORT & KITS.
Officers' Valises and Mess Boxes will be stacked on road outside billets ready for removal at 5.45.a.m. Mess Cart and Maltese Cart will be at H.Qrs. at 6.0.a.m.

X. LEWIS GUNS.-
The Lewis Gun Limbers will be Packed to night.

XI. MEALS.
Tea will not be issued on arrival in camp. Dinners will be the first meal.

XII. REPORTS to head of column.

XIII. ACKNOWLEDGE.

W.H. Stitt.

Captain & Adjutant.
7/8th. (S) Battalion Royal Irish Fusiliers

Issued through Signals at 9.0.p.m. 19/6/17.

Copy No. 1. "A" Coy.	Copy No. 8. M.O.
2. "B" Coy.	9. H.Q. 49th. Infantry Brigade
3. "C" Coy.	10. Intelligence Officer.
4. "D" Coy.	11. R.S.M.
5. Q.M.	12. Signals.
6. T.O.	13. Lieut. SPARKS.
7. L.G.O.	14 & 15. War Diary & File.

16. Orderly Officer

R

7/8th.(S)Battalion Royal Irish Fusiliers Order No.7.

S E C R E T. Copy. NO........

JUNE 21st.1917

GGG::

I. INFORMATION.

The 49th.Infantry Brigade will march to the BROXELLES AREA on the 22nd.June.The Army Commander will inspect the Battalion as it marches through ZUYPTEENE.The Order of march is 2nd.R.Irish Regt. 6.R.Innis.Fusrs.7.R.Innis.Fusrs.7/8th.R.Irish Fusrs.

II MARCH.

Battalion Starting Point Road Junction P.18.a.5.1.Order of march Drums,H.Qrs.,"C","D","A","B".Regtl.Transport.500 yards will be maintained between Battalions,50 yards between Coys.H.Qrs.will pass starting point at 5.12.a.m.Route.SYLVESTRE--CAPPEL--ROAD JUNCTION P.14.a.5.5.--ROAD JUNCTION P.15.b.5.0.---cross roads O.12.d.4.9. OXPLAINE--BAVINCHOVE--ZUYTPEENE.Distance to BROXELLE 14½.miles.

III. ADVANCE PARTY.

An advance party consisting of Lieut.SPARKS,4.C.Q.M.Sgts.& Sgt.Bird, & Staff Sergt.Thursfield will leave Battalion H.Qrs.at 4.15.a.m. The T.O.will supply Lieut.Sparks with a horse.The remainder of the party will be supplied with cycles.This party will report to the Staff Captain at NOORDPEENE CHURCH at 6.0.a.m.

IV. TRANSPORT.

Officers' Kits and Coy.Mess Boxes will be ready for removal at 4.0.a.m."B"Coy.will carry their kits to the Transport Lines before 4.15.a.m.H.Qrs.Mess Cart & Maltese Cart will be at Battalion H.Qrs. at 4.30.a.m.Coy.Officers' will pick up their Horses at starting point.Baggage wagons will accompany units.All covers on vehicles must (be neatly tied down.

V. CROCKS.

The crocks will report to 2/Lieut.E.S.Bird at starting point at 4.0.a.m.

VI. REVEILLE etc.

Reveille 3.0.a.m.Breakfast 3.30.a.m.There will be no sick parade to morrow morning.

VII. DRESS.

FIGHTING ORDER.

VIII. MEALS.

Tea will be ready for issue on arrival in billets,dinners will be prepared later.

IX. SUPPLIES.

Supply railhead from 22nd.June inclusive will be ARNEKE.

X. ARRIVAL.

Companies will report their arrival in billets.

XI. ACKNOWLEDGE.

W.H. Stott
Captain & Adjutant.

Royal Irish Fusiliers

Issued through Signals at 5.50.p.m. 21/6/17.

Copy No.1. "A"Coy.	Copy No.9. L.G.O.
2. "B"Coy.	10. Lieut.SPARKS,
3. "C"Coy.	11. 2/Lieut.E.S.BIRD.
4. "D"Coy.	12. 49th.Inf.Bde.
5. "Q.M.	13. R.S.M.
6. T.O.	14. War Diary.
7. M.O.	15. File.
8. Signals.	16. Spare.

SECRET. Copy.No........

7/8th.(S)BATTALION ROYAL IRISH FUSILIERS ORDER NO.8.
June 29th.1917.
Reference Maps 1/40,000 Sheet 27. 1/100,000 HAZEBROUCK 5.A.
1/20,000 Sheet 27 A. S.E.

;;;

I. INFORMATION
The Battalion will march to the TATINGHAM AREA on 30th.June 1917 and will be billeted in CORMETTE,LEULINE,and AUDENTHUN.

II. STARTING POINT.
Cross roads M.6.a.7.9. Time, 6.10.a.m. Order of March,Drums,H.Qrs., "D"Coy.,"A"COy.,"B"Coy.,"C"Coy.,Guard,Regtl.Transport.,
Route:Road Junction G.33.a.8.3.---St.MOMELIN---St.OMER,---St MARTIN.

III. DRESS.
Fighting Order,Steel Helmets to be worn.

IV. PACKS"OFFICERS' KITS etc.
Packs and Practice grenades will be collected and taken to the Q.M. All Packs will be clearly marked with the Regtl.No.,Rank,Name and Coy, these will be taken to Q.M.Stores to night.They will be brought on by Motor Lorry to morrow.All Officers' valises will be collected by limbers at 4.0.a.m.and taken to Q.M.Stores where they will be packed on G.S. Wagon.Mess Cart will be at Battalion H.Qrs.at 5.30.a.m.It will join the Transport at Starting Point.Maltese Cart should be packed to night ready for removal in the morning.

V. LEWIS GUNS.
Lewis Gun Limbers will be packed to night.

VI. SANITATION.
All billets will be left clean,and all latrines filled in.Box latrines will be emptied and left standing.All Tins will be buried.

VII. CROCKS?
All crocks as selected by the M.O.will parade under 2/Lieut.H.B.Reynell at BUYSSCHEURE CHURCH M.6.a.9.4. at 5.0.a.m.

VIII. ADVANCE PARTY.
The advance party left to day.They will meet the Battalion,Crocks,lorry etc.Cross Roads ½ mile W.of S in St.MARTIN (Ref.HAZEBROUCK Map)

IX. MEALS.
Tea will be issued at a halt during the march.

X. REPORTS.
Reports to head of Column.

XI. ACKNOWLEDGE.

W.H. Stitt.
CAPTAIN & ADJUTANT.

7/8th.(S)BATTALION ROYAL IRISH FUSILIERS.

Issued through Signals at p.m.

Copy No.1.	"A"Coy.	Copy No.9.	L.G.O.
2.	"B"Coy.	10.	2/Lieut.H.B.Reynell.
3.	"C"Coy.	11.	49th.Inf.Bde.
4.	"D"Coy.	12.	R.S.M.
5.	Q.M.	13.	Spare.
6.	T.O.	14.	File.
7.	M.O.	15)	War Diary.
8.	Signals.	16)	

10.J. 9.D

49/76

WAR DIARY.

FOR MONTH OF JULY, 1917.

VOLUME :- 10

UNIT :- 1/8th Royal Irish Fusiliers.

8/18

7/8 (S) Battalion ROYAL IRISH FUSILIERS

WAR DIARY
or
~~INTELLIGENCE SUMMARY.~~

(Erase heading not required.)

JULY 1917

Army Form C. 2118.

Instructions regarding War Diaries and Intelligence Summaries are contained in F. S. Regs., Part II. and the Staff Manual respectively. Title pages will be prepared in manuscript.

Place	Date	Hour	Summary of Events and Information	Remarks and references to Appendices
			Ref. maps 1/20,000 Sheet 27A S.E. 1/100000 HAZEBROUCK 1/20000 Sheet 27.	
CORMETTES	1.7.17		Morning church parades, evening Company Training.	W.H.S.
	2.7.17		Battalion attack, on open Warfare lines.	W.H.S.
	3.7.17		Outpost Schemes. Each Company took up positions for night outposts.	W.H.S.
	4.7.17		Battalion practised for Bde. Attack to be carried out on the 6th inst.	W.H.S.
	5.7.17		Musketry. Every man fired 3 practices. (a) 5 rounds application lying at 300x yds. 2nd class elementary target. (b) ditto 10 rounds rapid. (c) same as (a)	W.H.S.
	6/7/17		The Bde carried out an attack, for training purposes vide O.O. No 9. attached	W.H.S.
	7/7/17		The Bde. again carried out the same attack. The only difference being that tanks co-operated. The Corps and Divisional Commanders expressed their satisfaction at the excellent manner in which the attack was carried out	W.H.S.
RUBROUCK	8/7/17		The Bde. marched to the RUBROUCK area. This Battn. was billeted in RUBROUCK and vicinity	W.H.S.
WINNEZEELE	9/7/17		The Bde. marched to the WINNEZEELE area and was accommodated under canvas.	W.H.S.
	10/7/17		Divine Service. Cleaning equipment. Checking equipment and necessaries and trench stores.	W.H.S.
	11/7/17		Training. Arms drill, Squad drill. Training of specialists. Parades for N.C.O's. Lecture for officers etc.	W.H.S.

2353 Wt. W2544/1454 700,000 5/15 D. D. & L. A.D.S.S./Forms/C. 2118.

7/8 (O) Battn. ROYAL IRISH FUSILIERS **WAR DIARY** *or* ~~INTELLIGENCE SUMMARY.~~ JULY 1917

(*Erase heading not required.*)

Army Form C. 2118.

Instructions regarding War Diaries and Intelligence Summaries are contained in F. S. Regs., Part II. and the Staff Manual respectively. Title pages will be prepared in manuscript.

Place	Date	Hour	Summary of Events and Information (Ref sheet 1/40000 Sheet 27, 1/20000 28 N.W.)	Remarks and references to Appendices
WINNEZEELE	12.7.17		Inspections. Training of specialists. Special Instruction for NCO's etc	W.H.S.
"	13.7.17		Inspections. Training in fire and movement. Sports in evening	W.H.S.
"	14.7.17		Marched to STEENVORDE training area. Practised fire and movement. Reinforcing by sections and man by man. Judging distance.	W.H.S.
"	15.7.17		Divine Service	W.H.S.
"	16.7.17		Training. Deploy from column of route into artillery formation. Training of specialists	W.H.S.
"	17.7.17		ditto	
"	18.7.17		ditto.	W.H.S.
"	19.7.17		ditto. Bde sports in afternoon at which this Battalion won the Bde Championship.	W.H.S.
"	20.7.17.		Presentation of medal ribbons by Major General Hickie	W.H.S.
"	21.7.17		Attack on Training area	W.H.S.
"	22.7.17		Bde Attack on Training area	W.H.S.
	23.7.17		Inspection specialists training.	W.H.S.
	24.7.17		" " " Range finding practice for NCO's	WS
	25.7.17		" " "	
	26.7.17		The 49th Inf. Bde marched to WATOU No 2 area. The Battn was billeted in area L.14. central	WS.

2353 Wt. W2544/1454 700,000 5/15 D. D. & L. A.D.S.S./Forms/C. 2118.

7/8th (S) Battn. ROYAL IRISH FUSILIERS

WAR DIARY

or

~~INTELLIGENCE SUMMARY~~.

(Erase heading not required.)

Army Form C. 2118.

Instructions regarding War Diaries and Intelligence Summaries are contained in F. S. Regs., Part II. and the Staff Manual respectively. Title pages will be prepared in manuscript.

Place	Date	Hour	Summary of Events and Information	Remarks and references to Appendices
WATAU AREA No 2	27.7.17		"A" & "B" Coys rejoined the Battn from the YPRES area in motor buses. In their work on roads in that area the following casualties were sustained. 1 Officer gassed. 4 O.R killed. 3 O.R. died of wounds. 32 wounded. Model of XIXth Corps front visited. Refitting of clothes.	WS.
	28.7.17		Refitting & baths. Orders for Offensive issued to those concerned	WS.
	29.7.17		Church parades. Brigadier 49th Inf. Bde presented parchment certificates. The following are awards made during the month.	
			Legion d'Honneur (Croix d'Officier). Lt Col. K.C. Weldon DSO.	
			Military Cross. 2/Lieut V. J. Lynch	
			D.C.M. No 14850, Sgt Young H.	
			Bar to Military Medal. 16814, Sgt Nolan J.	
			Military Medal. 16636. Sgt Morgan J. 21220. Pte Maguire T. 21411. " McCready E. 15434. L/Cpl McCandless R. 20962. Cpl McCurley R. 21304. Pte Linnott T. 18314. " Kelly J.	
			Parchment Certificates :- Major T F O'Donnell MC, A/Capt T de C Falle, 2/Lieut W H Allen, 2/Lieut G J Forbes, Capt C F Brady RAMC, Lieut F L Smilly, 2/Lieut G R Attwood, 2/Lieut C L Henry, 2/Lieut P H Wray, 2/Lieut W H Waters, Lt & Qm F E Hanmer, 2/Lieut V J Lynch MC.	WS

2353 Wt. W2544/1454 700,000 5/15 D. D. & L. A.D.S.S./Forms/C. 2118.

1/8th (S) Battn ROYAL IRISH FUSILIERS

WAR DIARY
or
~~INTELLIGENCE SUMMARY.~~
(Erase heading not required.)

Army Form C. 2118.

Instructions regarding War Diaries and Intelligence Summaries are contained in F. S. Regs., Part II. and the Staff Manual respectively. Title pages will be prepared in manuscript.

Sheet 28. N.W. 1/20,000.

Place	Date	Hour	Summary of Events and Information	Remarks and references to Appendices
WATAU	29/7/17 (cont)		Parchment certificates (contd):– 18140. R.S.M. Devlin — 16656. Sgt. Horgan J. — 17032 L/Cpl. Jammy P 22138 Pte Ross W. — 9411 Pte. McCready E — 19729. Pte Grey F 6837. " McIntyre W. — 21220 " Maguire T. — 20911 " Cunningham J. 40164. " McGurk J — 6932 " Walker Wm. — 16818. Sgt. Holvan 15944 " Dawes J — 17704 L/Sgt. Dolan B — 20962. Cpl. McCawley. 21103 " Campbell P.J — 21099 Pte. Anderson W — 18314 Pte Kelly 14850 Sgt. Young — 20958. " Murray W. — 21304 " Sinnott T	W3
BRANHOEK No 1. AREA.	30/7/17.		The 49th Inf. Bdge moved to the BRANDHOEK No 1 Area on the night 30/31st July. The Battn was camped at QUERY CAMP on arrival. During the period in this camp the battn was at 2 hrs. notice to move to a forward assembly position near VLAMERTINGHE.	
	31/7/17.		Bombs &c. were issued in the morning. At 7 pm, a warning order was received from 49th I.B to be ready to move up to assembly position in H.10. At 9 pm, the battn moved up & stopped the night in a field. At 10.30 am. 1/7/17, the battn marched back to QUERY CAMP & remained at 2 hrs notice. At 3.50 am, the offensive commenced. The weather was fine but dull during the day, but towards midnight, it commenced a steady downpour which continued throughout the day.	W3

[signature] Lieut. Col.
Comdg. 1/8th (S) Bn. Rl. Irish Fus.

The attached Instructions are issued to you today, they are not complete and will be added to from time to time.

Lieut. & A/Adjutant.
7/8th. Royal Irish Fusiliers.

28th. July. 1917.

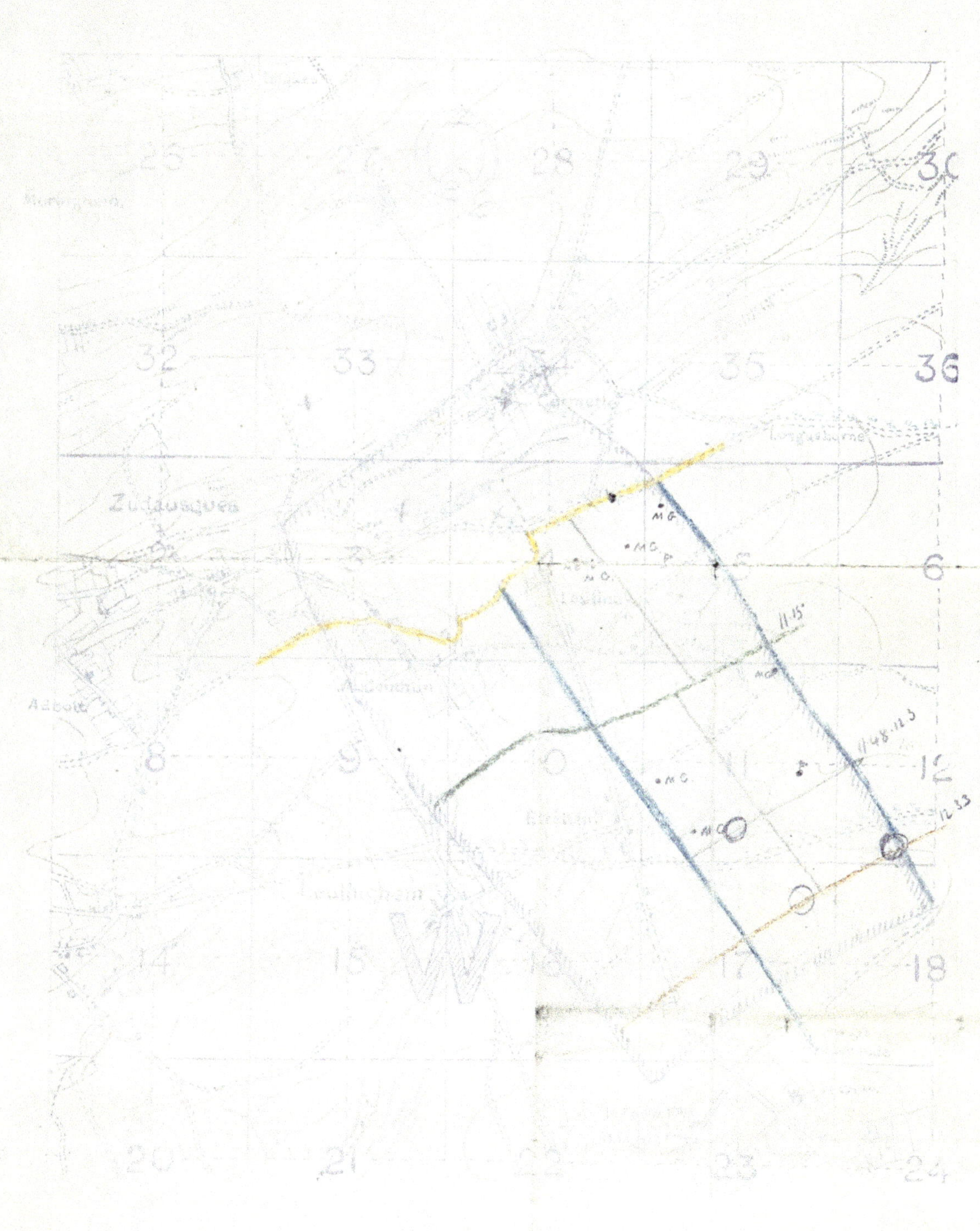

27
28
29
30
32
33
35
36
Zudausques
6
11.15
11.48-12.3
12
12.33
14
15
17
18
20
21
22
23
24

SHEET. 2.

15. From the time of arrival in QUERY CAMP, all movement in the vicinity of huts, camps or bivouacs is to be restricted to a minimum Special attention is to be paid to the screening of lights.

16. Brigade H.Qrs. will close at L.13 Central at 10.0.p.m. and ~~QXXXX~~ open at RED ROSE CAMP H.2.c.2.7. on arrival.

17. ACKNOWLEDGE

JULY 30th.1917

Lieutenant & A/Adjutant.

7/8th.(S)Battalion Royal Irish Fusiliers.

Issued through Signals at p.m. 30th/7/17.

Copy No.1.	"A"Coy.	Copy.No.8.	M.O.
2.	"B"Coy.	9.	H.Q.49.Inf.Bde.
3.	"C"Coy.	10.	Signals.
4.	"D"Coy.	11.	R.S.M.
5.	Q.M.	12	File
6.	T.O.	13	War Diary
7.	L.G.O.	14.	Spare.

SECRET.   JULY 29th.1917   COPY NO. 12

7/8th.(S)Battalion Royal Irish Fusiliers Order No.16.

Reference Map Sheet 28.N.W. 1/40,000.
Sheet 37. 1/10,000

::

1. With reference to "INSTRUCTIONS FOR THE OFFENSIVE "the 49th.Inf. Bde.will move to BRANDHOEK No.1.AREA on Night 30th/31st.JULY 1917.

2. The Battalion on arrival will be camped at XXXXX QUERY CAMP, G.6.a.8.2. Transport will be Brigaded in lines at G.1.c.1.8.

3. Order of March, Drums, Bn. H.Qrs., "A", "B", "D", "C", Guard & Transport. Head of Column will pass Road Junction L.14.b.4.5. at 11.45.p.m.

4. Route: L.11.b.8.8. --- L.6.c.9.4. --- GRAND PLACE, POPERINGHE ---Main YPRES ROAD. DISTANCE. about 6½ Miles.

5. Movement. East of L.6.c.50., 200 yards will be maintained between Companies and between the rear Coy. and Transport. Communicating Files will be sent out by Coys. to the Preceding Coy. The Signalling Officer will arrange to mark the head and tail of the column with lamps.

6. ADVANCE PARTY. 4.C.Q.M.Sgts., Sgt.Bird and one N.C.O. to be detailed by the Q.M. will report at Orderly Room at 9.0.a.m. to morrow. Signalling Officer will arrange to provide as many bicycles as possible. 2/Lieut. H.J.LINFOOT will proceed and take over QUERY CAMP on morning of 30th.inst.

7. Handing Over The Q.M. will arrange to hand over to the Camp Warden.

8. DRESS Fighting Order. It is suggested that every two sandbags be tied together and that men take turns at relieving each other. No article is to be put into the sandbag that would be required should the Battalion go into action. Waterbottles must be filled.

9. Officers' Kits. All Officers' Kits, Mess Boxes will be stacked outside Orderly Room at 8.30.p.m.

10. SANITATION Every effort must be made to have the Camp and Transport Lines cleaned up before dark on 30th.inst as no rear Party will be left.

12. TRANSPORT The following vehicles will remain in QUERY CAMP and the horses sent to the Transport Lines.
Cookers   Water Carts   L.Gun Limbers   Maltese Cart.

13. Party left behind A list of names of men to be left behind when the Battalion moves into the line has been issued to all concerned. This Party will parade at 11.30.p.m. outside the Orderly Room under C.S.M.KERR and will be billetted separately.

14. The Battalion will hold itself in readiness to move at two hours' notice to the front line. In the event of such action, Officers and men on receipt of orders will fall in in Fighting Order, sandbags and kits will be stacked outside Coy. Stores and left in charge of the Coy.Q.M.S. It is suggested that Officers sort their kits at once. Tarpaulins will be issued to cover dumps of Kit &c. left behind.

SECRET. COPY NO.....9.......

7/8th.S.Bn.R.IRISH FUSILIERS, Order No.15, 25.7.17.

Reference Map Sheet 27 1/40,000.

-:-

1. INFORMATION. The 49 Inf.Bde.less 113 Field Ambulance will march to WATOU No.1 Area, on the 26th.July.

2. SITUATION. The Battalion will be billetted near L.14, Central.

3. ADVANCE PARTY. The billetting party left here this afternoon.

4. MOVE. The Battalion will fall in on their respective parade grounds ready to move off through the gate at South corner of the Camp at 6.20 a.m.

ROUTE. Cross Roads J.12.b.8.7. _ WATOU _ Cross Roads in K.12.c. distance about 7 miles.

ORDER OF MARCH. DRUMS, "Headquarters, "D"Coy., "C"Coy., Transport.

5. DRESS. Fighting Order. Packs will be carried, containing Water-proof sheet, cleaning gear, iron rations, one pair of socks, mess tin and cover.

Great coat, havresac, etc. will be put into a sandbag and stacked in separate piles outside the Q.M.Stores by 6 a.m. Sandbags will be clearly marked with Regt.No., Rank, Name, Platoon and Company. Steel helmets will be worn and all water bottles must be full.

6. TRANSPORT. A lorry is allotted to the Battalion and will be available for as many trips as necessary.

7. OFFICERS' Kits etc. All Officers' valises and Mess Boxes will be stacked outside Orderly Room at 5.30 a.m.

8. CROCKS. The crocks and one sanitary man per Coy. will be left behind under the Orderly Officer to clean up the Camp. This does not relieve the Officers concerned from the responsibility of leaving their lines perfectly clean.

9. RAILHEAD AND RE-FILLING POINT. Railhead on the 26th. Inst. will be WIPPENHOEK (L.28.c.) Re-filling point will be L.9.b.3.4.

10. TIME TABLE. Reveille 4.30 a.m., Breakfast 5.30 a.m., Sick Parade 3.30. p.m. 25th. Inst.

11. MARCH DISCIPLINE. The strictest attention is to be paid to March Discipline. The attention of Os.C.Coys. and Transport Officer is drawn to the recent Divisional Letter sent out.

12. ARRIVAL. Hot tea will be served out on arrival.

13. ACKNOWLEDGE.

Lieut. a/Adjutant,
7/8th.S.Bn.R.IRISH FUSILIERS.

Issued through Regt. Signals at .... 25.7.17.

No.1........"C"Coy.	No.2."D"Coy.
No.3........O.C.Signals.	No.4...L.G.Officer.
No.5........Transport Officer.	No.6...Quartermaster.
No.7........49th.Inf.Bde.	No.8...R.S.M.
Nos.9 & 10..War Diary.	No.11..File.

No.12. Medical Officer.

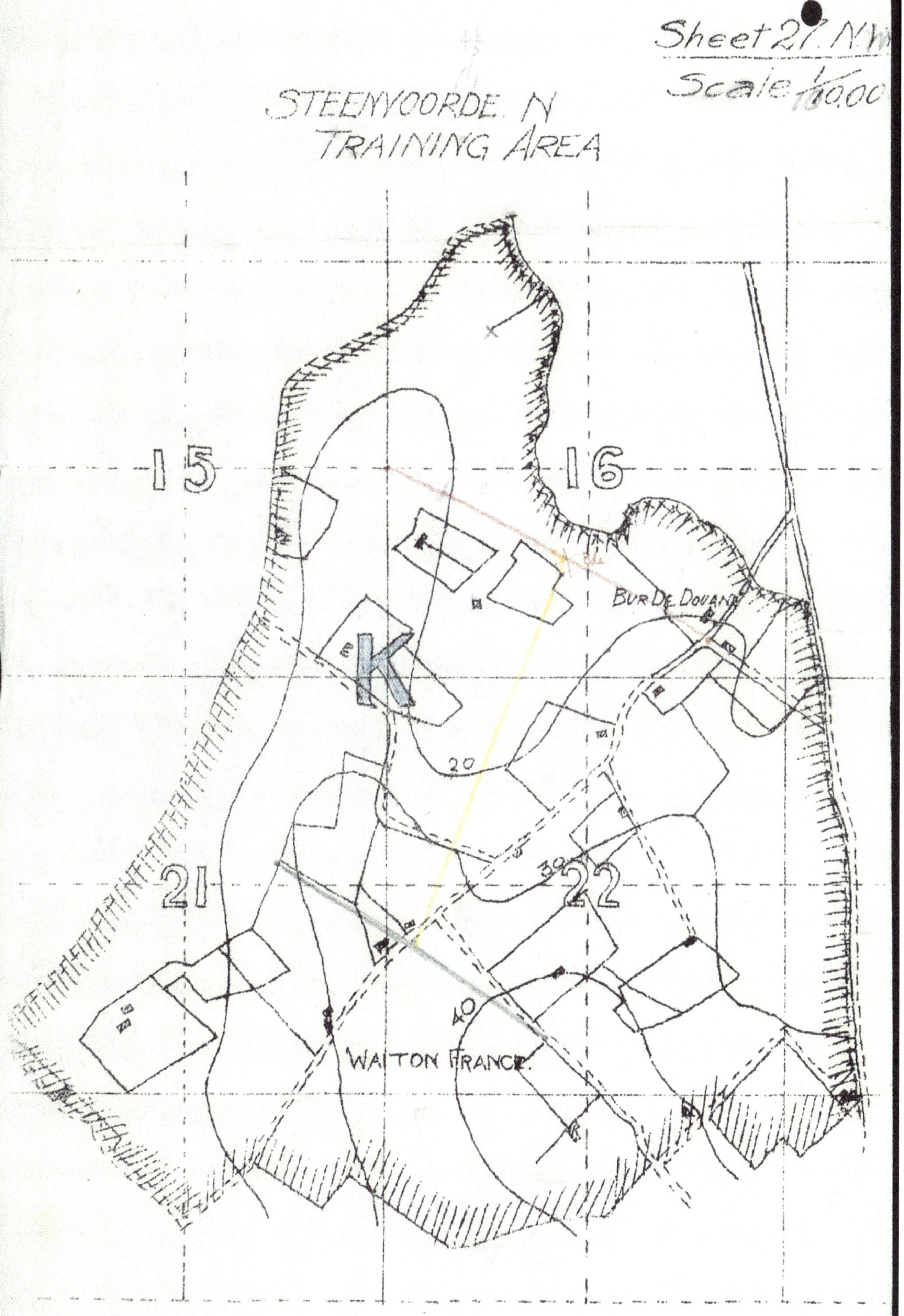

Sheet 27 N.W.

Scale 1/10.000

STEENVOORDE N
TRAINING AREA

15

16

K

BUR DE DOUANE

20

30

21

22

40

WAITON FRANCE

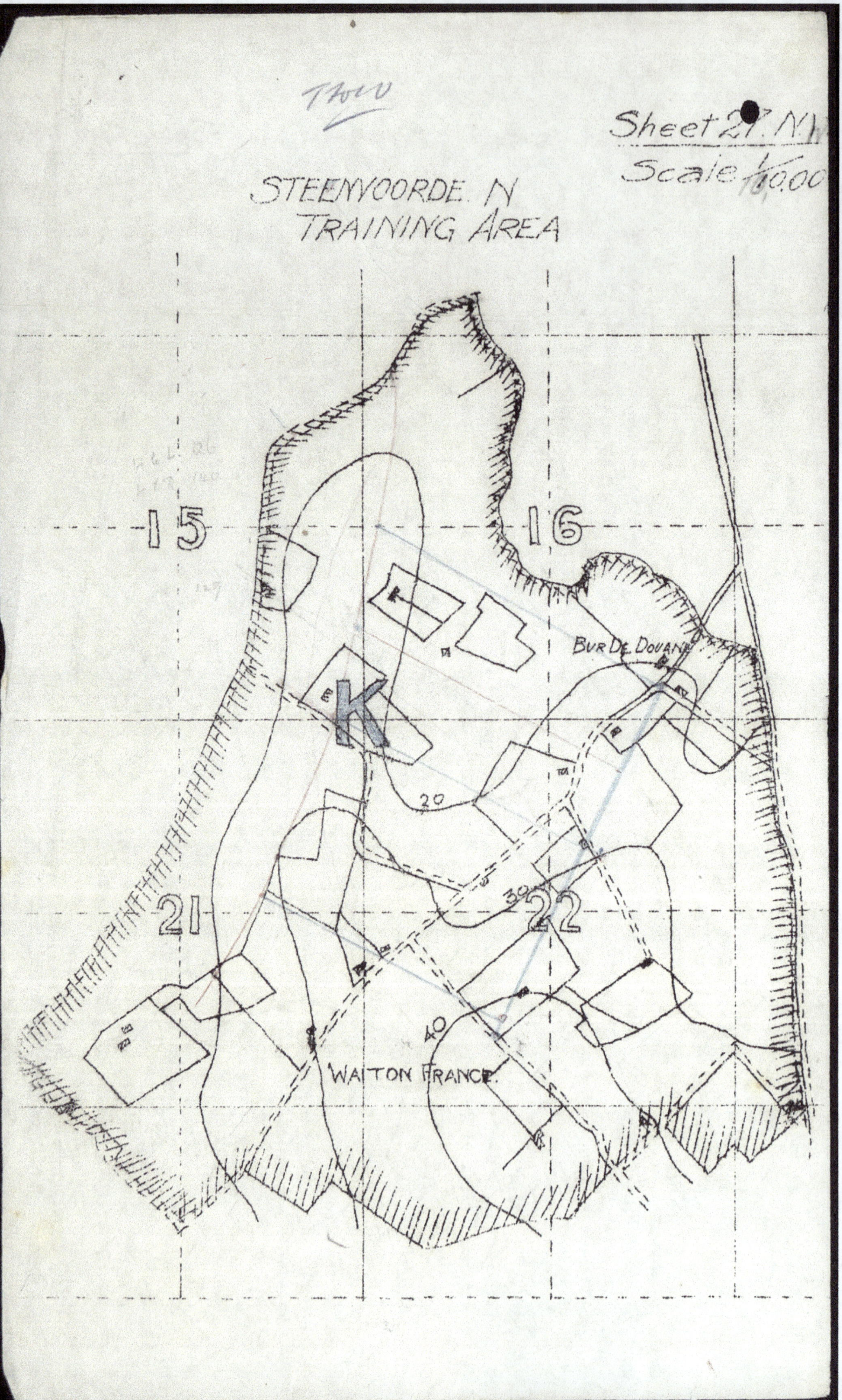

STEENVOORDE N TRAINING AREA

Sheet 27. N.W.

Scale 1/10.000

15

16

K

BUR DE DOUANE

20

30

21

22

40

WAITON FRANCE

49th IMB No. B.M.C. I/104
20th July 1917.

ALLOTMENT OF TRAINING AND SPORTS FIELD.

Hours.		July 22nd.	July 23rd.	July 24th.	July 25th	July 26th
8 a.m. to 12 noon.	Training.	2nd R. Irish Regt.	7th R. Innis Fus.	7/8th R. Irish Fus.	8th R. Innis Fus.	2nd R. Irish Regt.
12 noon to 4 p.m.	Training.	7/8th R. Irish Fus.	8th R. Innis Fus	2nd R. Irish Regt.	7th R. Innis Fus.	7/8th R.Irish Fus.
4 p.m. to 8.30 pm.	Recreation.	7/8th R.Irish Fus.	8th R. Innis Fus.	2nd R. Irish Regt.	7th R. Innis Fus.	7/8th R.Irish Fus.

The STEENVORDE North Training Area may be used by the 7th and 8th R. Innis Fus on the afternoon of the 22nd July. On the other days this area is not allotted to the Brigade.

Captain,

Brigade Major, 49th Infantry Brigade.

A

TO BE READ IN CONJUNCTION WITH O.O.No.9.DATED 5/6/17.

It must be understood that the GREEN and BROWN LINES do not represent lines of trenches, they are tactical objectives chosen by the Higher Command. Compass bearings should be used to direct the advance.

The 16th. Divisional Coy. will represent the enemy, and will man M.G. Emplacements, S.P.'s etc. They will be supplied with blank ammunition. H.G's. will be represented by tins containing stones being rattled. The Massed Drums of the Brigade will represent the Barrage. The Q.M. will detail the Drums to report to the Bde. Intelligence Officer at Road Junction W.4.c.9.9. at 8.30.a.m. on the 6th. inst. Yukon Packs have been asked for and if available will be issued on a scale of One per Platoon. Ten Shovels & Two Picks will be carried on each Pack. These will be drawn from the Regtl. Reserve of Tools. Should Yukon Packs be issued each Company will draw direct from Transport Officer 40 Shovels and 8 Picks. These must be handed in by 6.0.p.m. the 6th. inst.

W.H. Stott.

July 5th. 1917. Captain & Adjutant.

7/8th. (S) Battalion Royal Irish Fusiliers.

B

7/8th. ROYAL IRISH FUSILIERS BATTALION ORDER NO. 10.

SECRET JULY 7th. 1917 COPY NO......

Reference 1/20,000 Sheet 27. A., S. E.
1/40,000 Sheet 27.
1/100,000 HAZEBROUCK 5. A.

::

Ø I. INFORMATION.

The 49th. Infantry Brigade will march to the RUBROUCK AREA on July 8th. On the 9th. inst. the Brigade will move from the RUBROUCK to the WINNIZEELE AREA. Detailed Orders will be issued later for the march on the 9th. July.

II. STARTING POINT, ROUTE &c.

Starting Point Road Junction Q. 35. d. 8. 3. at 6. 10. a. m.
Route, St MARTIN-au-LAERT----St OMER---St MOMELIN---BROXEELE--RUBROUCK.
Order of March. Drums, H. Qrs., "A", "B", "C", & "D" Regtl. Transport.

III. SANITATION.

All Billets must be left clean. Care should be taken to ensure that no equipment is left behind. All latrines should be filled in.

IV. PACKS, DRESS &c.

All Packs clearly labelled should be sent to Q.M. Stores this evening. Dress will be Fighting Order. Steel Helmets will be worn.

V. TRANSPORT.

Baggage Wagons will accompany the Battalion. Three Motor Lorries will be shared by this Battalion and the 8th. Royal Inniskilling Fusiliers. Q.M. will leave a loading party. These Lorries will report at Battalion H. Qrs. at 7. 0. a. m. on 8th. inst. Signalling Officer will detail two Orderlies to meet the Lorries at Battalion H. Qrs. take them to Q. M. Stores and accompany them to RUBROUCK. These Lorries are not to be used for more than one journey. Lewis Gun Limbers will be packed to night. Officers' Kits from "B", "C", and "D" Companies will be carried to Q. M. Stores and dumped by 5. 0. a. m. Transport Officer will detail the Mess Cart to collect Officers' Kits at Battalion H. Qrs. and at "A" Company at 4. 30. a. m. The Mess Cart will take these Kits to Transport Lines and will then return to Battn. H. Qrs. for H. Qrs. Mess Boxes. Company Mess Boxes will as far as possible be sent with valises. The remaining portion will be placed on the Kitchens, Maltese Cart will be loaded to night ready for removal in the morning.

VI. CROCKS.

All Crocks will meet 2/Lieut. A. C. YOUNG at Road Junction Q. 35. d. 8. 3. at 7. 0. a. m. They will then proceed direct to RUBROUCK. These could assist with Sanitary Arrangements.

VII. BILLETS.

Companies will report arrival in Billets, and state Map Reference of Company H. Qrs. A List should be sent to Battalion H. Qrs. before 3. 0. p. m. 8th. inst. shewing billets occupied in RUBROUCK AREA and number of Officer, men and horses in each.

VIII. ACKNOWLEDGE.

W. H. Satt

CAPTAIN & ADJUTANT.

7/8th. (S) BATTALION ROYAL IRISH FUSILIERS

Issued through Signals at p. m.

Copy No. 1. "A" Coy.
2. "B" Coy.
3. "C" Coy.
4. "D" Coy.
5. Q. M.
6. T. O.
7. L. G. O.

Copy No. 8. M. O.
9. H. Q. 49. Inf. Bde.
10. Intelligence Officer.
11. 2/Lieut. A. C. YOUNG.
12. Signals
13. R. S. M.
14. War Diary.

Copy No. 15. File Copy No. 16. Spare.

C.

7/8th.(S)Battalion ROYAL IRISH FUSILIERS ORDER No.11.

SECRET JULY 8th.1917 COPY NO.........

Reference Map 1/20,000 Sheet 27.

!!!

I. INFORMATION.
The 49th.Infantry Brigade will march to the WINNEZEELE AREA to morrow the 9th.inst.

II. STARTING POINT TIME &c.
Starting Point Road Junction H.4.a.30.30.Head of Column to pass Starting Point at 5.25.a.m.Route via-Road Junction B.29.d.7.7.---WORMHOUDT--Road Junction C.17.a.5.8.--KIEKENPUT--LOOGEHOEK. Order of March.Drums,H.Qrs.,"B"Coy.,"C"Coy.,"D"Coy.,"A"Coy.,Guard, Regimental Transport.Approximate distance of march from Starting Point 10.miles.

III. SANITATION
All Billets must be left clean.

IV. CROCKS.
The Crocks will meet 2/Lieut.C.W.PICKETT at Road Junction H.4.a.30.30. at 7.0.a.m.

V. KITS.
All Officers' Kits will be ready for collection by 3.45 a.m.All possible Mess Kit.should be sent with Officers' valises.Remainder should be placed on Field Cookers.The Mess Cart will collect Kits at H.Qrs.at 3.45.a.m.and take same to Transport Lines.The Mess Cart will then return to Battalion H.Qrs.for H.Qrs.Mess Box.A Limber should be sent to Battalion H.Qrs.at 9.0.p.m. to night to collect Orderly Room Boxes &c.

VI. DRESS.
Fighting Order,Steel Helmets to be worn.

VII. TRANSPORT.
The Transport Officer's attention is drawn to Para V.

VIII. ACKNOWLEDGE.

Captain & Adjutant.
7/8th.(S)Battalion Royal Irish Fusiliers

Issued through Signals at 5.45 p.m.

Copy No.1.	"A"Coy.	Copy No.9.	H.Q.49th.Inf.Bde.
2.	"B"Coy.	10.	Intelligence Officer
3.	"C"Coy.	11.	2/Lieut.C.W.PICKETT.
4.	"D"Coy.	12.	Signals.
5.	Q.M.	13.	R.S.M.
6.	T.O.	14.	War Diary.
7.	L.G.O.	15.	File.
8.	M.O.	16.	Spare.

D

SECRET JULY 11th.1917 COPY NO.........

7/8th.(S)Battalion Royal Irish Fusiliers Order No.12.
Reference Map Sheet 27. 1/40,000

::

I. INFORMATION.
The 49th.Infantry Brigade in WINNEZEELE AREA will be in Corps Reserve from 10/7/17.and will be prepared to move in buses or Lorries, Transport by march,to the vicinity of YPRES at Four Hours notice.

II. ACTION ON RECEIPT OF ORDERS.
On Orders being received,the Battalion,less Transport,Drums,Q.M. Details and Surplus Officers and men will move to the undermentioned positions ready to get into Buses and Lorries,They will fall in on the Right hand side of the Road,facing North,and as clear of the road as possible.

III. DRESS.
Dress Marching Order with Packs and Steel Helmets.Troops will carry 150 rounds S.A.A.per manwith the exception of Lewis Gunners, Bombers,Scouts,Signallers and Runners who will carry 50 rounds per man (Vide S.S.135 Page 59.)Water Bottles to be filled.The unexpended portion of the day's rations will be carried.Also Iron Rations.

IV. POSITION OF EMBUSSING.
On WINNEZEELE --WATOU ROAD facing North. Brigade H.Qrs.will halt with head on forked roads just West of DROGLANDT.J.12.b. Head of this Battalion Fifty yards in rear of Brigade H.Qrs. Route to WINNEZEELE--WATOU ROAD via NORTHERN Entrance to Camp--- Cross Roads J.6.c.--Cross Roads J.12.a.

V. SANITATION
All Latrines etc to be filled in with exception of one to be left for Transport,Q.M.Control etc.which will be filled in by them before leaving.

W.H. Still

Captain & Adjutant.

7/8th.(S)Battalion Royal Irish Fusiliers

Issued through Signals at p.m.

Copy No.1. "A"Coy.
2. "B"Coy.
3. "C"Coy
4. "D"Coy.
5. L.G.O.
6. Q.M.
7. T.O.
15. Signals.
16. R.S.M.

Copy No.8. M.O.
9. Intelligence Officer.
10. C.O.
11. File.
12. War Diary
13. 49th.Inf.Bde.
14. 7th.R.Innis.Fusrs.
17. Spare.

O.C. "A" Coy.
"B" Coy.
"C" Coy.
"D" Coy.
Lewis Gun Officer.
Transport Officer
Medical Officer
Quartermaster
Spare
File
War Diary.

SECRET.

Herewith Copy No. ..13..... of "Instructions for the Offensive"

The role of the 49th. Infantry Brigade in the next offensive is uncertain, and these instructions contain information regarding the probable front, ways of approach etc.

Please acknowledge receipt.

[signature]

JULY 27th. 1917

Lieut. & A/Adjutant.

7/8th. (S) Battalion Royal Irish Fusiliers

INSTRUCTIONS FOR THE OFFENSIVE NO. 3.   COPY NO.......

REFERENCE MAPS ATTACHED "A"&"B" 28.N.W.,28.N.E.
St.JULIEN 1/10=000   ZONNEBEKE 1/10=000.

::

1. GENERAL PLAN.

Offensive operations on a large scale in which the XIX Corps is to take Part, will shortly commence.

2. ENEMY DISPOSITIONS.

The German lines opposite the XIX Corps Front are held by:-

One Regiment 17th.Div.100 yards S. of YPRES--ROULERS RLY.to C.29.d.2.9.

One Regiment 233rd.Div.from C.29.d.2.9. to about C.23.b.6.1.

The Disposition of each Regiment is:-

One Battalion Front Line System. (1st.Line.)
One Battalion STUTZPUNKT Line (2nd.Line.)
One Battalion GHELUVELT--LANGEMARCK Line (3rd.Line.)

3. GENERAL PLAN OF ATTACK. There are 3 Objectives

BLUE LINE   1st.Line System.
BLACK LINE   2nd.Line System.
GREEN LINE   3rd.Line System.

The Attack will take place on "Z" Day.

4. DISPOSITION.

(a) The Order of Attack from North to South is:-

55th.Division supported by 36th.Division
15th.Division supported by 16th.Division.
8th.Division supported by 25th.Division.

(b) The 15th.Division will attack with :-

46th.Brigade on the left.
44th.Brigade on the Right.
45th.Brigade in support.

Boundaries between 55th. and 15th.Divisions are shewn on attached Map "A"

(c) On Y/Z Night the 16th.Division will move to the BRANDHOEK AREA.
Divisional H.Qrs. POPERINGHE (G.1.d.5.1.)
49th.INFANTRY BRIGADE, Red Rose Camp.(H.3.c.3.7.)
7/8th.ROYAL IRISH FUSILIERS QUERY CAMP (G.6.a.8.3.
Whilst in BRANDHOEK AREA the 49th.Infantry Brigade will be held in readiness to move at two hours'notice.

5. PROBABLE ROLE OF DIVISION.

As far as possible the 16th.Division will be used to support the 15th.Division.

When the 16th.Division finally relieves the 15th.Division,the 48th. and 49th.Infantry Brigades will relieve the Right and Left sections of the 15th.Division respectively.

47th.Infantry Brigade will be in reserve.

S H E E T. 3.

No.6. HEADQUARTERS OF 15th. DIVISION at ZERO.

15th. DIVISION H.Q. H.7.c.9.5.
44th. Infantry Brigade I.4.d.6.0.
46th. Infantry Brigade. I.5.a.1.7.
45th. Infantry Brigade. I.8.d.3.7.

Map "B" attached shews the Trench System at present held by the 15th. Division and overland Tracks.

7. ARTILLERY.

(a) The Creeping Barrage, which opens on enemy front line at ZERO., will advance 100 yards in 4. minutes.

(b) "S.O.S." In case of an "S.O.S." Signal being received the Batteries concerned will fire on their S.O.S. Lines for ten minutes and cease fire at the end of this period unless the signal is repeated or orders are received from their respective Divisions

8. COMMUNICATION TRENCHES.

There are four main Communication Trenches in the 15th. Division Sector.

East and West Lanes	OUT.
PICCADILLY	IN.
HAYMARKET.	IN.
CURZON STREET.	OUT.

After ZERO, PICCADILLY and HAYMARKET will if necessary be carried forward by the R.E. to join up with ICE and IBERIA LANES in the present GERMAN LINES.

9. TRACKS. (Shewn on Map "B".

(a) Tracks "C" and "F" might be used to bring up Infantry should GORDON's TRACK be shelled heavily. These tracks are not passable by wheeled traffic and would be difficult for Infantry after heavy rain.
All these tracks (No.1 --- 5. "C" & "F") should be reconnoitred before using them, although they are marked on the ground.
This applies especially to "C" and "F" Tracks.

(b) After ZERO hour the following tracks will be carried forward into the captured positions :-

(a) By the 15th. DIVISIONAL ENGINEERS.

Two tracks wide enough for guns and horsed transport.
(I) From I.5.d.5.4. through BILL COTTAGE and D.26.a.7.4. to LOSTIN FARM.
To be marked with White Posts marked with one stroke.

(II) From I.5.b.1.4. through BAVARIA HOUSE to DELVA FARM.
To be marked with White Posts marked with two strokes.

(b) By 55th. DIVISIONAL ENGINEERS.

(I) No.5. Track (For Pack Transport) to be carried forward from OXFORD ROAD to the BLUE, and subsequently the BLACK LINE.

(II) Two other forward tracks will also be marked out.

10. (c) ROADS and TRAFFIC CIRCUITS.

(a) After ZERO hour the circuits on forward roads, together with others further east, will gradually come into force as the necessary repairs are completed.

(b) Pending the issue of further instructions the following have been issued by 15th. Division:-

(I) The POTIJZE -- YPRES road may be used as a forward road for clearing existing dumps.

11. (Contd.)

(II) Vehicles are not to halt on the YPRES -- POTIJZE road. They will draw off the road if a halt is required.

12. At 5.0.p.m. on "Z"plus 1.day,further instructions as to Traffic Circuits will come into force.A Map shewing these further circuits will come into force.A map shewing these ~~xxxxxxx~~ further circuits will be issued later to all concerned.

13. DRESS.

The following will be worn by all ranks during the forthcoming operations :-

FIGHTING ORDER.

(a) Clothing,arms and entrenching tools as issued.
(b) Equipment as issued,packs worn on the back.
(c) Box Respirators and P.H.Helmets.
(d) Iron Rations,unexpended portion of the day's rations,mess tin and cover,Field Dressing.
(e) Waterproof Sheets.
(f) Riflemen 170 rounds S.A.A.,2.Mills' Bombs.
(g) Lewis Gunners 50.rounds S.A.A.,4.Lewis Gun Drums.
(h) Bombers 100 rounds S.A.A.,6.Mills' Bombs.
(i) Rifle bombers,100 rounds S.A.A.,6.Rifle Grenades.
(j) Signallers,50.rounds S.A.A.
(k) The Personnel of Coy.and Platoon H.Q.will carry 50 rounds S.AAA. and 18."P"Bombs.The "P"Bombs to be distributed as Company Commanders think fit
(l) Personnel of Battalion and Coy.H.Qrs.will carry Very Pistols & ammunition and 6."S"O"S"Rifle Grenades per Headquarters.
(m) Every man will carry two sandbags.

All Officers will wear men's equipment and will carry Map,Binocular Prismatic Compass and Watch.

14. CONSOLIDATION.

The following arrangements for Engineer work and consolidation have been made by the two attacking divisions.

15th.DIVISION.

(a) Infantry Brigades are responsible for the consolidation of objectives gained.

(b) Captured Engineer material is to be utilized in the consolidation of the position anr information where it is to found is to be given to Battalions by R.E.Personnel carrying out the reconnaissances.

(c) After the capture of the GREEN LINE ,an R.E.Stores Dump will be established as far forward as possible.When the position of this dump has been decided,the C.R.E.will inform Infantry Brigades.

(d) The following work will be carried out under C.R.E's orders
(I)Open up the POTIJZE--- FREZENBERG Road,making it fit for Artillery and limbered wagons.
(II) Open up the two forward tracks mentioned in Para 9.(a) Nos.1.& 2.
(III)If required to do so,prolong PICCADILLY and HAYMARKET TRENCHES to join up with ICE and IBERIA LANES.
(IV) Construct Strong Points at the following places.

D.26.a.7.2.
D.20.c.7.3.
D.26.a.5.9.

No.14. CONSOLIDATION (Contd.)

55th. DIVISION.

(e) The following work will be carried out by the 55th. Divisional Engineers and Pioneers.

(1) Open up the SAINT JEAN -- GREVINSTAFEL road.

(2) Carry forward No.5.Track from OXFORD ROAD to the BLACK LINE.

(3) Mark out two other forward tracks.

(4) Construct Supporting Points (as distinguished from Strong Points made by the Infantry) at about the following places.

C.18.c.50,85.
C.24 C.23.a.90,60.
D.10.c.65.60.
D.7.d.65.50.
D.7.d.60.30.
D.13.b.75.00.
D.14.c.55,20.

The Garrison of each of these Supporting Points will be one Machine Gun, One Lewis Gun and half Platoon Infantry.

15. PACK TRANSPORT.

The Brigade Transport is organised in sections of 24 Pack animals each. Special Instructions have been issued to those concerned. One Section under the Transport Officer has been allotted to the Battalion.

On the Brigade advancing to the attack the following loads will be carried:-

1st. Load. "A","B","C" and "D" Sections will each carry:-

7. animals -- water -- 8. tins each = 112 gallons.
4. animals -- L.G. Drums -- 32 each = 128 drums.
6. animals -- S.A.A., rifle oil and flannelette = 12,000 etc.
7. animals -- Picks and shovels.
(4. carrying 32 shovels each) = 144 shovels
(2. carrying 24 Picks each.) " - &
(1. carrying 12 Picks & 16. shovels.) 60 Picks.

This allows 32 shovels per Coy.
12 Picks per Coy.
16 shovels Bn.H.Qrs.
12. Picks Bn.H.Qrs.

2nd. LOAD

1 animal carrying V.LIGHTS = 3. boxes. 1" & 1 Box 1½".
4. animals carrying shovels = 32. per Coy.
7. animals carrying water = 112 Gallons.
4. animals carrying L.G. Drums. = 128 Drums.
4. animals each carrying 4 coils Wire & 12 Screw Pickets.) 16 Coils Wire.) 48 Screw Pickets.
3. carrying S.A.A. = 6,000 rounds
1. carrying Rifle Bombs = 8 - Boxes.

3rd. LOAD This will be notified later.

In addition to the above, an emergency Pack section of 9. animals will be formed under the Quartermaster for ration carrying when the Brigade Pack Coy. is not available.

These loads will be dumped near Bn.H.Qrs., when any load has been dumped, the fact is to be reported to Bn H.Q. before the Sections move off.

16. DUMPS.

All salvage will be dumped at a Regimental Dump near Battalion H.Qrs. The Brigade will then be notified of its position and will be responsible for its removal.

SHEET.. 5.

17. MEDICAL ARRANGEMENTS.

(a) Behind the 15th. Division.

REGIMENTAL AID POSTS.: Two behind CAMBRIDGE ROAD.

COLLECTING STATIONS.: MENIN ROAD (I.9.d.4.6.) POTIJZE CHATEAU.

ADVANCED DRESSING STATIONS.: KRUISSTRAAT (H.24.a.5.9.) PRISON YPRES.

MAIN DRESSING STATION BRANDHOEK (G.12.b.8.6.)

CORPS WALKING WOUNDED COLLECTING STATION VLAMERTINGHE MILL (H.8.a.9.8.)

(b) Regimental Stretcher Bearers assisted by R.A.M.C. Bearers will clear to R.A.P's.

(c) Walking wounded will be guided by directing signs skirting the North and South sides of YPRES to the Corps Walking Wounded Collecting Station, where busses will take them to the C.C.S. BUSSES will also pick up walking wounded near BELGIAN CORNER.

(d) As the advance takes place, new collecting posts will be selected, possibly at FREZENBERG and BRIDGE HOUSE, and evacuation will take place from these posts.

18. STRAGGLERS.

A Brigade line of Stragglers Posts will be established, under the orders of the A.P.M. 16th. Division.
Each Post will be in possession of Drinking water, spare gas helmets Iron Rations, Field Dressings, picks and shovels, and will have means of giving a hot meal to stragglers before returning them to 1st. line transports.

19. PRISONERS

(a) Cages are established at.
Corps Cage:- H.7.d.3.7.
RIGHT DIVISION. ECOLE I.9.c.5.3.
The route for prisoners from Right Divisional Cage to Corps Cage is --- Track S. of YPRES to CANAL BRIDGE I.13.c.7.5. -- track through H.18.b. and c., H.17.b. and a., H.16.b., H.15.b. and a., H.8.d. and c., to H.7.d.
The representative of the A.P.M. at the Divisional Cage will give a receipt to fighting troops for all prisoners taken over.

(b) Fighting troops who capture prisoners are to immediately search all Officers and to take away from them all documents, which are then to be placed in an empty sandbag and sent with the escort to the Divisional Cage. Special attention should be paid to pockets in back skirt of tunics and back of trousers. Personal belongings and decorations should not be removed.

20 SIGNALLING.

(a) Telephone system. Field Cable.
It must be impressed on all ranks that the supply of cable is very limited and unnecessary waste must be avoided. Units must not use their Mobile Equipment except in a case of emergency, and the fact that it has been used should be reported at once. Metallic Circuits only are to be laid. If an earth circuit has to be employed fuller-phone must be used

(b) VISUAL.
German Visual Stations are reported at D.8.c.65.57., D.20.a.65.80. D.20.c.30.40., D.25.c.50.62., D.12.a.45.00., (Sheet 28.N.E.)
These points are almost certain to make good O.P's and Brigades should attempt to use them in their communications.

(c) PIGEONS.
During operations "PRACTICE MESSAGES MUST NOT BE SENT" even when birds have to be released without operation messages.

(d) AEROPLANES
Troops will signal to aeroplanes by flares and WATSON FANS (latter if procurable) and by ground panels from Battalion And Brigade H.Qrs. Aeroplanes will signal by lamps, KLAXON HORNS and Very Lights.

SHEET.... 6.

20. SIGNALLING

(e) TANKS.

Tanks signal to Infantry by means of Red, Green, and White Discs (No. 2. Edition of Tank Signals will be used).
Infantry may signal to tanks by making use of the Signal Tank one of which will operate on each Divisional Front. These are easily recognised by being of the old Pattern without guns but carrying a wireless mast on the roof

(f) LATERAL COMMUNICATIONS

When in the line Units must establish communication with Units on either flank, either by telephone, visual or runner. Bde. H.Q. must be linked up laterally by Bde. Signals at the first opportunity

(g) Two message dogs have been allotted to the 55th. Division. All ranks should be warned that dogs carrying message pouches on their collars are not to be detained, except for the purpose of having the messages read by an Officer.

(h) ROCKETS.

An issue of message carrying rockets is being made. This rocket carrier has a range of 1200Ø yards, whistles during its flight and burns a magnesium flare. It is very accurate in direction and fairly accurate in range. Each Company H.Q. will carry a proportion of these rockets, 6 rockets and one firing tube will be carried by one man, the whole bundle weighing about 20 lbs. It should not be fired too close to a H.Qrs. The Brigade-Signal Officer will issue instructions for firing them

(i) MISCELLANEOUS.

A forward Signal Station should be clearly and properly marked so that it may not be "MOPPED UP" in case the Signal Party has pushed on ahead of the Moppers Up. Operators and linesmen must be instructed not to call up continuously on lines that are apparently down. The lines may perhaps be earthed and this calling will jam the power buzzer. Calls must be made for a short time only, say. one minute in every four.
As the enemy will be falling back on positions more or less prepared the ordinary precautions of trench warfare against overhearing must be enforced at the earliest possible moment.
It is again impressed on all Units that it is their duty to get into communication with the Brigade Forward Station with all possible speed and that they are responsible for the maintenance of that communication.

21. WATER SUPPLY EAST OF POPERINGHE.

The initial water points in the forward area for the supply of drinking water are located as follows :-
(Sheet 28.) Water Carts, water tank lorries, and water bottles will be able to refill at these points

Tank No.4.	at G.7.d.9.5.	yielding daily	7,400	gallons.
" No.5.	" G.3.c.7.2.	" " "	25,250	gallons.
" No.6.	" G.15.b.3.6.	" " "	11,700	gallons.
" No.9.	" H.14.a.9.6.	" " "	7,000	gallons.
" No.11.	" G.10.c.4.9.	" " "	15,500	gallons.
" No.14.	" H.8.b.9.9.	" " "	5,000	gallons.
" No.14.A.	H.8.d.8.3.	" " "	3.200.	gallons.
" 14.B.	H.3.c.3.5.	" " "	3,200	gallons.
" No.32.	" G.12.c.5.1.	" " "	4.000	gallons.
" No.48.	" G.12.a.9.9.	" " "	5,000	gallons.

The first forward water point will be established for Operations just off the road West of existing pumping house near the swimming bath in the N. East Corner of YPRES. It is hoped to establish the second forward water point on the St. JEAN --- WIELTJE Road West of WIELTJE. Tank Lorries, water carts, and water bottles will be able to be filled at both refilling points when completed.

SHEET. 7.

21. WATER SUPPLY.
As soon as the second forward water point is completed the tank lorries will work forward to a third forward water point.

22. HORSE WATER SUPPLY.
The location of the shallow wells are.
BRANHOEK AREA NO.1.

G.5.c.4.9.
G.5.d.4.7.
G.6.c.4.3.
G.13.a.9.9.
G.10.b.1.4.
G.11.a.8.3.
H.7.a.4.8.

The wells ~~xxx~~ will be fitted with pumps and troughs and can water 40 horses at a time.

23. WATER SUPPLY WEST OF POPERINGHE.
No.74 Water Point for Water Bottles, water carts and Tank Lorries is at L.11.a.6.5.
Lorry fed reservoirs have been built at L.17.d.10.4.in WATOU AREA No.2.and at J.10.b.2.3. in WINNEZEELE AREA No.2.
Thesex will be kept filled by the section of No.2.Water Column Horses are not to be watered direct reservoir tanks or pits. Division will erect sufficient watering troughs in the vicinity of Horse lines into which the water is to be pumped. An Officer ,or, in exceptional cases when no Officer is available, a warrant officer or senior N.C.O. will be in charge of every watering Parade.
Men are to dismount when horses are being watered and bits removed. Watering troughs will be so arranged that horses are not taken along or across main roads to water. Horses are not to be taken along tram lines to water, railway lines, or through fields where railway lines are in process of construction. Horses are not to be allowed to drink until water troughs are full.
In the event of an advance all sources of drinking water must be tested before use by the Medical Officer of Units. Sentries and warning notices must be posted on suspected water supplies and samples sent in at once to the mobile laboratory for conformation.
Notice boards labelled (A) DRINKABLE or (B) POISONOUS. will be erected at all sources of water supply tested during an advance.

SHEET 8.

24. CONTACT AEROPLANES.

(a) Two Contact Patrol Aeroplanes, one to each of the two attacking Divisions, will be detailed by No.21 Squadron, R.F.C.

(b) These Contact Aeroplanes will be marked with a BLACK PLAQUE projecting the right lower wing, thus

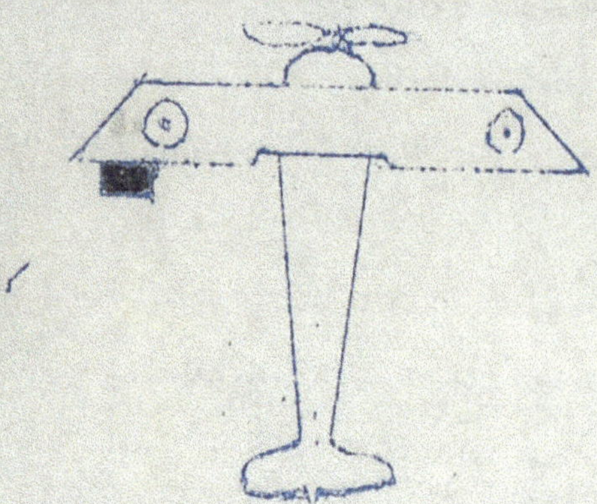

PLAQUE AS SEEN FROM BELOW.

(c) In Signalling to Aeroplanes, Infantry will follow the instructions laid down in S.S.135, Appendix B. Paras 4 & 5.

(d) The following means will be used to shew the most advanced position of the Infantry:-
(1) WHITE FLARES.
(2) WATSON FANS (If Available.)

(e) Flares will be lit by Infantry in the front line.
(1) When called for by the Contanct Patrol Aeroplanes by means of KLAXON HORNS and Very Lights. This call will, if the attack proceeds as arranged only be made at times when the Infantry are believed to have reached the BLUE, BLACK, and GREEN LINES.
(2) When the Infantry consider it advisable to make known the position of their front line.

(f) Dropping Stations for 15th. Divisional H.Qrs. will be notified later

JULY 28th.1917

Lieutenant & A/Adjutant

7/8th. (S) Battalion Royal Irish Fusiliers

APPENDIX "A" TO BE READ IN CONJUNCTION WITH PARA 7.

TIME TABLE OF ATTACK.

SERIAL NO.	TIME	ACTION OF ARTILLERY	ACTION OF INFANTRY.
1.	00.00.	Barrage put down on enemy front line.	Infantry leave their trenches and advance to the assault.
2.	plus 00.06.	Barrage lifts off enemy front line and advances at rate of 100 yards in 4 minutes	Infantry assault and capture enemy front system of trenches.
3.	plus 00.54 R. 00.42 C. 00.42 L.	Protective barrage formed 300 yards in front of BLUE LINE	Infantry halt and consolidate on BLUE LINE.
4.	plus 01.15.	Barrage put down on ~~whole~~ whole front of attack.	~~Infantry~~ Infantry assemble close under barrage in readiness to advance
5.	plus 01.39 R. 01.33 C & L.	Barrage lifts and advances at rate of 100 yards in 4 mins.	Infantry advance and capture enemy second line system (STUTZPUNKT LINE)
6.	plus 02.06.R. 02.15.C. 01.59.L,	Protective Barrage formed 500 yards in front of BLACK LINE	Infantry halt and consolidate on BLACK LINE.
7	plus, 06.20.	Barrage put down on whole Corps front.	Infantry assemble close under barrage and prepare to advance.
8.	plus. 06.28.	Barrage lifts and advances at the rate of 100 yards in 4 mins.	Infantry advance and capture the GHELUVELT LANGEMARCK.LINE
9.	plus 07.36.R. 07.38.C. 07.28.L.	Protective barrage formed 500 yards in front of GREEN LINE	Infantry halt and consolidate on GREEN LINE
10.	plus. 08.30.	Protective Barrage ceases on whole Corps Front.	

R. = On Right Corps Boundary

C. = On Divisional Boundary

L = On Left Corps Boundary

JULY 28th.1917

XIXth CORPS.

← 2,800 yds. →

55th Div. — 15th Div — 8th Div.

15th Div: 46th Bde. 45th Bde. / 44th Bde.

36th Div. — 16th Div. — 25 Div

16th Div: 49th Bde 48th Bde / 47th Bde

DISPOSITION ON Z DAY.

SHEET No. 8.

INSTRUCTIONS FOR THE OFFENSIVE.

35. MAPS TO BE CARRIED.

Every Officer in the attack is to be in possession of the following maps :-

(a) The 1/10,000 FREZENBERG map of the XIX th.Corps Front, Edition 2. An issue of this sheet has alrady been made.

(b) The latest Edition of each of the following Sheets of the 1/10,000 map.

ST JULIEN.
ZONNEBEKE
ZILLEBEKE.
WESTROOSEBEKE.

All these sheets have already been issued.

(c) The Barrage Maps of operations in which they are actually engaged. These will be issued as soon as received.

(d) An adequate number of Message Forms with maps on the back. These will be issued as soon as they are received.

36. "S.O.S." SIGNALS.

(a) The present S.O.S. Signal on the Fifth Army Front is a succession of "S.O.S."Rifle Rockets each bursting into two RED and two GREEN Lights simultaneously,until the Artillery comply.

(b) No alternative S.O.S.Signal to the above is to be used.

(c) In the event of circumstances requiring a change of "S.O.S"Signal, the new "S.O.S"Signal will probably be made with VERY coloured Signal Cartridges.
If therefore the Division relieves another Division in the line,the number of coloured VERY Lights taken over is to be checked carefully and steps should be taken to make good any deficiencies. As much notice as possible will be given of any proposed change in the "S.O.S"Signal.

(d) Company Commanders will select if possible,a position for sending up "S.O.S" Signals so that the Signals are visible in rear.

37. ALLOTMENT OF TANKS.

(a) The 3rd.Brigade,Heavy Branch Machine Gun Corps is attached to the XIX Corps for operations.
"C"Battalion is allotted to the 15th.Division.
One Company of each Battalion will be in Corps Reserve. Of these No.8,Company ("C"Battalion) will be prepared to co - operate with the 16th.Division and will be located on "Z"Day at OOSTHOEK WOOD (A.34.)

(b) ACTION
Two Companies will be employed on each Divisional Front against the BLACK LINE and two Companies against the GREEN LINE.
In the event of the 15th.Division advancing beyond the GREEN LINE with a view to consolidating a line East of it,No.4.Section,No.D. Company,"C"Battalion will co - operate and will remain with the Infantry until 4.0.a.m.on "Z" plus One day as a support.

No. 27. ALLOTMENT OF TANKS Contd.

(c) SIGNAL COMMUNICATIONS.

Infantry will signal to TANKS in accordance with Instructions contained in "TANK COLOURED DISC and LIGHT CODE " 2nd. Edition.

No other Signals will be used from TANKS to INFANTRY except the following which must be learnt by heart.

RED and GREEN DISCS = "HAVE REACHED OBJECTIVE"
RED,RED and RED. DISCS = "BROKEN DOWN "
RED,WHITE and WHITE DISCA = "NO ENEMY IN SIGHT.

(d) RALLYING FLAGS.

Tanks Section Commanders will use Rallying Flags two feet square with the number or Section on them,Colour as under

"C"Battalion GREEN.

28. PRISONERS

All Prisoners will be at once sent back to the Brigade Cage. They can only be utilised on their way back if they volunteer, to assist their own or our wounded.

28. ACTION IN CASE OF NON-SUCCESS OF 15th.DIVISION AT ANY OBJECTIVE.

(a) Refers to action which would take place if the 15th.Division fails as a whole.

(b) Refers to action which would be taken if the 15th.Division failed to advance beyond the BLACK LINE.

In the event of "A"

It will benecessary to establish Brigade H.Qrs.at HILL COTTAGES, and concentrate the Brigade for attack in our own lines,and in the Parts of the German Lines taken,and carry on the attack as arranged for by the Division or Corps.The Concentration will have to take place by night, as the advance in front of YPRES unless covered by an attack from the Front Lines,would entail heavy loss.

In the event of "B"

Brigade H.Qrs.will be established at HILL COTTAGES unless a good Brigade Forward Station has been established by the BLUE LINE.The Brigade would relieve 15th.Division and be disposed :-

LEFT BATTALION. From D.19.c.90.90. to D.19.d.00.10.
H.Q. About SQUARE FARM or C.30.b.~~55~~.60. 45.
RIGHT BATTALION. From D.19.d.00.10. to D.25.b.00.20.
H.Q. C.30.d.35.75.

SUPPORT BATTALIONS.

In BLUE LINE and GERMAN FRONT SYSTEM.
Dividing Line. C.30.d.10.70. -- ODER HOUSE.
Left Battalion H.Q.) NEW COTTAGE
Right Battalion H.Q.) DUGOUTS.
and reconnoitre for more forward ones.

MACHINE GUN COMPANY H.Q. HILL COTTAGES.
4 Guns on line FREZENBERG --- GREY RUIN --
4 Guns on Line LOW FARM -- POMMERN CASTLE.

T.M. Battery H.Q. I.6.a.30.95.
2 Guns each forward Battalion.

IN THE EVENT OF "C" Which refers to normal action if the 15th Division ~~succeeds~~ attack

Would relieve in depth by two Battalions supported by two Battalions side by side.The position of,not only Brigade H.Q. but Battalion H.Q.would a good deal depend on the existing H.Qrs.when we take over,and also on the intended line of buried or other Signal Route.The following two lines might be taken for this route:-

SHEET. 11.

"A"	"B"
MILL COTTAGES C.30.d.35.65.	MILL COTTAGES. C.30.d.35.65.
LOW FARM	LOW FARM.
BORRY FARM	BECK HOUSE
COFFEE FARM	DELVA FARM
VAN ISAACKEERE FARM	DOCHY FARM
BOURDEAUX FARM	OTTO FARM
	BOETHOEK FARM

(a) would be the most central route for the Division and would
Probably be the one to be adopted.

(b) would be the best for command Purposes of this Brigade.

Roads for relief by night would be the VELORENHOOK road or Track I.5,a.~~3c~~ to DELVA FARM.

II. ARRANGEMENTS FOR RELIEF ON GREEN LINE.

Brigade H.Qrs. C.30.d.35.75.

Brigade Forward Station D.25.b.35.75.

Left Battalion from D.14.d.30.40. (on road.)
to
D.20.b.35.70.

Battalion H.Qrs, Dugouts behind DELVA FARM

RIGHT BATTALION. from D.20.b.35.70. to D.20.d.30.90.

Battalion H.Qrs, COFFEE FARM D.20.c.1.1.

Left and Right Support Battalions will hold BLACK LINE and BLUE LINE in depth back to old German Front Line.

DIVIDING LINE. D.19.d.00.10. -- C.30.d.10.75.

H.Q. Left Battalion C.30.b.45.60.

H.Q. Right Battalion LOW FARM

T.M. Battery H.Q. GREY RUIN: Two Guns each forward Battalion.

III. If wee relieve the RED LINE

Bde. H.Qrs. Behind DELVA FARM or COFFEE FARM.

Bde. Forward Station OTTO FARM or EAST of it.

Left Battalion GRAVENSTAFEL Cross Roads to D.15.b.90.80.
H.Q. OTTO FARM

Right Battalion D.15.b.90.80. to D.16.a.65.25.
H.Q. at DOCHY FARM or VAN ISAACKERE FARM

Right and Left Support Battalions
BLACK and GREEN LINES.

Dividing LINE D.19.d.10.80. -- D.20.b.35.70.

Left Battalion H.Q. DELVA FARM.

Right Battalion H.Q. COFFEE FARM

T.M. BATTERY. H.Q. near DELVA FARM.

JULY 20th. 1917.

Lieutenant & A/Adjutant.

7/8th. (S) Battalion The Royal Irish Fusiliers

APPENDIX "B" TO BE READ IN CONJUNCTION WITH MAP "C"

No. on Map.	NAME	POSITION	CONTENTS.
1.	Q.A.A.	H.7.d.6.9.	EXPLOSIVES, LIGHTS
2.	Q.A.B.	I.3.d.4.4.	ditto.
3.	A.R.A.	I.10.a.4.3.	ditto.
4.	A.R.A.	I.9.d.3.8.	ditto.
5.	A.R.B.	I.5.d.7.0.	ditto
6.	A.R.C.	I.6.c.9.7.	ditto
7.	A.R.D.	J.1.a.Central.	ditto.
8.	M.V.A.	I.4.a.7.0.	ditto.
9.	M.V.B.	I.5.a.4.1.	ditto.
10.	M.V.C.	I.5.a.3.4.	ditto.
11.	M.V.D.	C.30.c.9.7.	ditto.
12.	B.M.D.	In H.17.	S.A.A., Grenades & T.M.Ammn.
13.	C.A.A.	I.M.5.d.2.2.	S.A.A., Grenades, T.M.Ammn. & Explosives.
14.	C.A.B.	I.6.b.3.8.	S.A.A., Grenades etc.
15.	C.A.C.	D.25.c.8.5.	S.A.A. Grebades, Stokes etc.
16.	C.A.D.	D.19.d.1.5.	S.A.A., Grenades & Stokes Ammn.
17.	C.A.E.	I.20.a.9.3.	S.A.A., Grenades & Stokes Ammn.

The above dumps will be formed by the 15th. Division.

JULY 29th.1917

Lieutenant & A/Adjutant

7/8th. (S) Battalion Royal Irish Fusiliers

SECRET COPY NO.........

SHEET 13.
OF
INSTRUCTIONS FOR THE OFFENSIVE.

29. REPORTING OF CASUALTIES.
Company, Platoon, and Section Commanders must take with them into action a roll of all N.C.O's and men under their Command. This will be carried in the Right Breast Pocket in order that, in the event of a casualty, it is known where it can be found,
A Roll Call should be made as soon as possible after heavy fighting.
Casualty reports are of two kinds ;(a) Casualty wires. (b) Nominal Rolls.

(a) CASUALTY WIRES
(1) ACCURATE DAILY WIRE. Sent at a fixed hour whether fighting is in Progress or not.
(2) APPROXIMATE. (or estimated) Wire. Shewing approximate casualties sustained during heavy fighting, and sent in addition to the accurate daily wire.

(b) NOMINAL ROLLS. Shewing killed, wounded and missing.

APPROXIMATE CASUALTY WIRES.
(Not to effect the sending of the accurate daily wire.)
(a) Approximate (or estimated) casualties will be reported in "Phases" and each wire will include all casualties since the commencement of the "Phase" whether Previously reported on an accurate daily wire, approximate wire, or not at all. In other words, during any "Phase" each wire is cumulative and includes all losses since the commencement of that "Phase", and under no circumstances will the word "additional" be used.
(b) The "PHASE" commenced at MIDNIGHT 25th/26th. July 1917 and approximate wires will commence "Total estimated casualties from 26th July, until the commencement of a later "PHASE" is notified, when the date is amended as necessary.
No distinction is drawn in approximate wires between Killed, wounded and missing.
The Words "OFFICERS" and "O. RANKS" will not be used; the two categories being separated by the word "AND" e.g. "2 and 49" means "Two Officers and 49 O. Ranks" "4 and Nil" means "4 Officer and No O. Ranks"
The Prescribed code names of Units will be used.

Every effort should be made to send an approximate casualty wire so as to reach Battalion H.Qrs by 2.0.p.m. each day. If further heavy casualties occur during the night another wire should be sent so as to reach Battalion H.Qrs. by 8.0.a.m.

MISCELLANEOUS.-
MISSING CASUALTIES -- When Fifty or more of any one Unit are reported "MISSING" in an accurate daily wire, a brief statement should be sent with the wire of the circumstances under which they became missing. Casualty wires must not be delayed if this report is not to hand. When Personnel are reported as "MISSING" and are afterwards accounted for, this information should be forwarded so that reports may be rectified.
For the purposes of "Accurate Casualty Wires" -- "KILLED" includes all those who died before they have been taken over by the Medical Authorities. If the latter take over a case alive, the return should be wounded. Should death take place subsequently it is the duty of the MEDICAL AUTHORITIES to report the fact. The expression "died of Wounds" or "Since died of Wounds." should not appear in a casualty wire.

JULY 30th. 1917

Lieutenant & A/Adjutant.

7/8th. (S) Battalion The Royal Irish Fusiliers

SECRET. E Copy No. Spare

7/8th.S.Bn.R.IRISH FUSILIERS,ORDER NO.14.13.7.17.

Reference Map Sheet 27 1/40.000.
Sheet 28.N.W.1/20000.

-:-

1. INFORMATION. "A" and B" Coys.will be detached from the Battalion from to-morrow the 14th. Inst. in order to find the following parties for work on roads.

(1) Party of two hundred men with complement of Officers and N.C.Os. for work under C.R.E.15 DIVISION. To be located in camp H.16.c, to report en route at H.Q., 15th, DIVISION. (H.7.c.7.4.)

(2) Party of one hundred men with complement of Officers and N.C.Os. for work under C.R.E.55th.DIVISION. To be located in Camp A (H.1.d.9.9.) To report to O.C.Camp for accommodation.

2. MOVE. "A"Coy. plus one Officer and 50 men of "B"Coy.will be accommodated in Camp at H.16.c. "B"Coy. less one Officer and 50 men will be located in Camp A(H.1.d.9.9.) Each Coy. will proceed as under :- number of lorries 6 (To take 150.) Each Coy.will embus at DROGLANDT CROSS ROADS (J.12.b) and debus at BRANDHOEK. "A"Coy.will embus at 7-a.m. "B"Coy.will embus at 2 p.m.

"A"Coy. on arrival at BRANDHOEK will proceed to and report to H.Q.15th.DIVISION vide para.1. "B"Coy. on arrival at BRANDHOEK will send one Officer and 50 men to report to H.Q.15th.DIVISION, (vide para 1 & 2) and will then follow "A"Coy. Remainder of "B"Coy. will proceed direct to Camp "A"(H.1.d.9.9.)

3. TRANSPORT. The transport as detailed below will move as soon as the Supply Wagons report at this Camp. Route via WATOU and SWITCH ROAD, N. of POPERINGHE. On arrival at BRANDHOEK the cooker and L.G.Limber for "A"Coy.will proceed direct to "A"Coy.H.16.c. The remainder of the Transport will proceed direct to "B"Coy.at H.1.d.9.9. where it will be accommodated . One Supply Wagon for rations and Officers' Kits, 2 Cookers, 2 L.G.Limbers, 1 Tool Limber, 1 Water Cart 2 Officers' Chargers, The Transport Officer will proceed with the Transport. He will rejoin the remainder of the Battn. on the 15th. Inst.

4. RATIONS. Rations for consumption on the 15th.Inst.will be drawn by the Supply Wagon from 104 Coy.A.S.C. Rations for consumption on and after the 15th.Inst.will be supplied by the DIVISIONS to which the parties are attached. "A"Coy. will arrange for men to carry unconsumed portion of current day's ration as their Cooker will not reach its destination until about 4 p.m. "B"Coy.will arrange for dinners to be cooked and eaten before embussing.

5. OFFICERS' KITS. All officers' kits must be stacked outside Q.M.STORES before 9 a.m.14th.Inst.

6. COMMAND. Capt.D.H.W.KINGHAN will command these parties while on detachment.

7. COMMUNICATION. Each Coy.will send one cycle orderly with the transport.

8. .... ACKNOWLEDGE.

W H Stitt

Capt.& Adjutant,
7/8th.R.IRISH FUSILIERS..

Issued through Signals at p.m.

Copy No.1.& 2. "A"Coy.	Copy No.3 & 4. "B"Coy.
" " 5.Signalling Officer.	" " 6. L.G.Officer.
" " 7.Transport Officer.	" " 8. Quartermaster.
" " 9. 49th.Inf.Bde.	" " 10. R.S.M.
" " 11 & 12 War Diary.	" " 13. File.

ISSUED FOR TRAINING PURPOSES ONLY.

SECRET July 5th.1917 COPY NO........

7/8th.R.Irish Fusiliers Operation Orders No.9.
Reference Map 1/20,000 Sheet 37 A.S.E.

I. INFORMATION

(a) The 49th.Infantry Brigade will,in conjunction with Brigades on either flank continue the attack from the YELLOW LINE on the 6th.July 1917.The attack will be made in two bounds,these bounds are shewn by coloured lines on Map "A"

(b) This First Bound GREEN LINE
Second Bound BROWN LINE.

(b) This Battalion will continue the attack from the GREEN LINE to the BROWN LINE in conjunction with the 7.R.Innis.Fusrs on our Right and the 10th.Kings Liver Pills on our left.

II BOUNDARIES.

The Boundaries between Battalions will be as shewn on attached Map "A" The Boundaries between Companies will be a line drawn down the centre of the Battalion Frontage.

III. FORMATION OF ATTACK.

Two Battalions of this Brigade will commence the attack from the YELLOW LINE on the GREEN LINE at NEW ZERO HOUR.The GREEN LINE is to be captured at New Zero plus 56 minutes.This Battalion will advance from the GREEN LINE at New Zero plus 1 hour 45 minutes vide Para 1 (b) The Battalion will attack in four waves at 100 yards interval.Each wave consisting of 2 lines."A"Coy.on the Right "B"Coy.on the left will find the first two waves.The second two waves will be found by "C"Coy. on the Right and "D"Coy.on the Left.
The Battalion will proceed to the YELLOW LINE in Artillery Formation, when "A"and "B"Companies will form into wave formation."C"and "D"Coys. will form into wave formation just before reaching the GREEN LINE.

IV. ACTION OF ARTILLERY.

The Artillery Barrage will lift at the rate of 100 yards in 4 minutes as shewn on attached Barrage Map "A".
During the pause on the GREEN LINE a protective barrage will be formed 300 yards in advance of the Infantry.This Barrage will cease at NEW ZERO HOUR plus 3 hours 20 minutes.
Between the GREEN LINE AND the BROWN LINE the Barrage will pause for 15 minutes along line W.12.c.15.05. to W.16.b.1.1.

V. OBJECTIVES

"A"and "B"Coys. will advance as close up to the Barrage as possible. The first wave will halt and consolidate along a line as close up to the Barrage as possible when it halts for the pause.The second wave will halt and consolidate about 300 yards in rear of the first wave.

As soon as the Barrage lifts "C"and "D"Coys. will pass through "A"& "B"Coys. and follow as close up to the Barrage as possible.
The 3rd.wave (1st wave of "C"&"D"Coys.) will halt and consolidate on BROWN LINE..The 4th.wave will halt and consolidate 300 yards in rear of the 3rd.wave

VI. ACTION OF STOKES MORTARS.

Two Stokes Mortars of the 49th.T.M.Bty will be attached to this Battn. They will follow the second wave and on the first wave reaching their objective will place their guns in position ready to support them.
On the 3rd and 4th waves passing through,these guns will follow behind the 4th.wave,and on the BROWN LINE being reached the guns should be placed in such a position as will give most support to the Coys.
"O.C."A"Coy.will detail 12 men to report to "O.C.T.M.Bty Detachment, attached to this Battalion ,at the place of Assembly.

VII. ACTION OF MACHINE GUNS.

All M.G. Barrages will move in conformity with the Artillery Creeping barrage and will be 300 yards in front of the Artillery Creeping Barrage. When the BROWN LINE has been captured two guns will be moved up to that line for direct fire and fleeting targets.

All M.G's on the GREEN LINES will be given "S.O.S" Lines in case of a counter-attack on the BROWN LINE.

VIII. COMMUNICATION and BATTALION H.Qrs.

Advanced Brigade H.Qrs. will be at Q.34.d.5.1. The Brigade Forward Station will advance from the YELLOW LINE in rear of the leading assault Battn. and will be established about W.4.d.9.8. On this Battalion moving forward from the GREEN LINE the Brigade FORWARD STATION will move forward and will be established about W.11. central.

Battalion Forward Posts will be as follows:-

8th. Royal Inniskilling Fusiliers about W.5.c.3.9.

7/8th. Royal Irish Fusiliers about W.11.d.6.9.

The Forward Command Post of this Battalion will be the Battalion Forward Post of the 8. Royal Inniskilling Fusiliers until communication with this Battalion Forward Post has been established. Battalion H.Qrs. however will not move forward to the Battalikn Forward Post until the BROWN LINE has been captured. Personnel for establishing Battalion F Forward Post will follow the 4th. Wave.

IX CONTACT AEROPLANE.

A Contact Aeroplane (Type) will fly over the line and call for flares at following hours;

NEW ZERO plus 56 minutes. NEW ZERO Plus 3 hours 3 minutes.

Flares will be lit only by the leading troops. Troops will be prepared to light flares at other times when called for by the aeroplane. Flares will be called for by the Aeroplane by a succession of "A's" on a KLAXON HORN and a WHITE SIGNAL CARTRIDGE.

X. "S.O.S."

The "S.O.S." Signal will be RED SIGNAL CARTRIDGES.

XI. TRANSPORT.

The Brigade Pack Transport Coy. will be assembled at Q.34.c.5.1. at 9.0.a.m on 6th. inst, and will await the orders of the Staff Captain. The Brigade Pack Transport Company will be represented by the Battalion Pack Mules of each Battalion under the Command of Lieut. REID 7.R. Innis. Fusrs. Water only will be carried by our Battalion. S.A.A., Mills' Bombs, and Rifle Grenades will be carried by other sections of the Brigade Coy.

XII. ASSEMBLY POSITION.

The Battalion will form up in Artillery Formation facing SOUTH about Q.34.a.1.1. at 6.45.a.m on the 6th. inst.

XIII. WATERS

Water Bottles will be carried full.

XIV. RATIONS.

The Iron Ration will be carried.

XV. DRESS.

Fighting Order as laide down in S.S.135.

XVI. PRISONERS

All Prisoners will be sent to W.4.b.3.9.

XVII. SYNCHRONIZATION

Watches will be synchronised with a watch to be taken round about 8.0.p.m. on the 5th. inst. and again at about 9.15.a.m. on the 6th. inst.

XVIII. ZERO HOUR.

New Zero hour will be 9.30.a.m.

XIX. CONSOLIDATION.

All Objectives will be consolidated in reality as soon as taken. Patrols should immediately be sent out as far as the barrage permits.

XX ACKNOWLEDGE.

W.H. Stott.

Captain & Adjutant.
7/8th. (S) Battalion Royal Irish Fusiliers

PROGRAMME of TRAINING for "C" and "D" Companies for Period 19th. July to 25th. July 1917

::

Thursday 19th. July 1917

7.30.a.m. Adjutant's Parade, Inspection etc.
9.0.a.m. to 10.30.a.m. Company Inspection, Bayonet Fighting and Training of Specialists.
3.0.p.m. to 4.0.p.m. Forming Artillery Formation and Extended Order from Column of Route.

Friday 20th. July 1917

7.30.a.m. Adjutant's-Parade Inspection etc.
8.0.a.m. to 3.0.p.m. Disinfecting Clothing; Company not disinfecting Clothing, Gas Drill and Bayonet Fighting.

Saturday 21st. July 1917

7.30.a.m. Adjutant's Parade Inspection etc.
9.0.a.m. to 10.15.a.m. One Company Fire and Movement, One Company Specialist Training.
10.45.a.m. to 12 noon. Ditto reversed.

Sunday 22nd. July 1917

Divine Services, Iron Ration Inspection etc.

Monday 23rd. July 1917

7.30.a.m. Adjutant's Parade Inspection etc.
9.0.a.m. to 10.15.a.m.) One Company Box Respirator Drill and Intensive Digging. One Company attacking a STRONG POINT.
10.45.a.m. to 12 noon. Ditto Reversed.
2.30.p.m. Lecture for all Officers.

Tuesday 24th. July 1917

7.30.a.m. Adjutant's Parade Inspection etc.
9.0.a.m. to 10.0.a.m. Company Inspection, Judging Distance, Musketry Exercises etc.
10.30.a.m. to 12 noon. Specialist Training.
12 noon. Lecture for all N.C.O's on Discipline.
2.30.p.m. Staff Ride for Officers.

Wednesday 25th. July 1917

7.30.a.m. Adjutant's Parade, Inspection etc.
9.0.a.m. to 10.30.a.m. One Company Fire Movement, Passing through Gaps etc. One Company Physical Training, Fire Orders and Judging distance.
10.30.a.m. to 12 noon. Ditto reversed.

Recreational Training will be carried out each afternoon.

W.H. Stitt

Captain & Adjutant.

7/8th. (S) Battalion Royal Irish Fusiliers.

Issued through Signals at 3.0. p.m.

Copy No.1. "A"Coy.
2. "B"Coy.
3. "C"Coy.
4. "D"Coy.
5. Q.M.
6. T.O.
7. L.G.O.
8.M.O.

Copy No.9. 2nd.in Command.
10. 49th.Inf.Bde.
11. 49.T.M.Bty.
12.7.R.Innis.Fusrs.
13.8.R.Innis.Fusrs.
14. War Diary
15. File.
16. Spare.

49/16

War Diary
of
7/8th R. Irish Fus.
for
August 1917.

11 J.

49/16

WAR DIARY.

FOR MONTH OF AUGUST, 1917.

VOLUME......11......

UNIT 7/8th Royal Irish Fusiliers

9/19

7/8th (S) Battn. ROYAL IRISH FUSILIERS

WAR DIARY
or
INTELLIGENCE SUMMARY.
(*Erase heading not required.*)

AUGUST 1917

Army Form C. 2118.

Instructions regarding War Diaries and Intelligence Summaries are contained in F. S. Regs., Part II. and the Staff Manual respectively. Title pages will be prepared in manuscript.

Place	Date	Hour	Summary of Events and Information	Remarks and references to Appendices
			Ref. Map. BELGIUM. Sheet 28 NW 1/20,000	
QUERY CAMP G.6.A.7.4	1/8/17		On the night of the 31st July/1st Aug. the battn was moved up to an assembly position in H.10.D. At 10.30 am the Brigade moved back to the BRANDHOEK AREA; the battn was camped at QUERY CAMP under 1 hrs. notice	WS.
"	2/8/17		Remained in camp. At about 3 am an order was received to move early that morning to a position east of YPRES. This was cancelled at about 3.30 am.	
ECOLE	3/8/17		The 49th Inf. Bdge moved up in support of the 47th Inf Bdge. The 16th Division relieved the 15th Division in the Right sector of the XIX Corps front. The battn was billeted the ECOLE & School Hse.	WS.
	4/8/17		Remained in Divisional Support. Between 12 midnight and 4 am the ECOLE and neighbourhood was heavily shelled with heavy guns. An armour piercing shell was also used. The weather, which since the evening after the offensive commenced had been very unfavourable to all operations, commenced to clear. The roads and country tracks were in an extremely bad condition with mud	WS
"	5/8/17		The 49th Inf. Bdge relieved the Left section 47th Inf. Bdge in the front line. The battn was relieved by the 7th R. Irish Rifles at 6 pm. On relief the battn moved back to Brigade Reserve at "A" Camp H.16.A.4.8. During the afternoon, our air service profited by the change of weather & carried out reconnaissances and registration shoots. At about 10 pm a violent drum fire commenced on the right and lasted for over 1½ hrs.	WS
VLAMERTINGHE	6/8/17		The 48th & 49th Inf Bdges. relieved the 47th Inf. Bde. in the front line on the night 5/6th August. (see 5/8/17) Battn remained in Brigade Reserve. Cleaning up, checking deficiencies &c.	
	7/8/17		The Battn relieved the 2nd R. IRISH REGT in support. The relief commenced at 12 midnight. Few	

2353 Wt. W2544/1454 700,000 5/15 D. D. & L. A.D.S.S./Forms/C. 2118.

7/8th (S) Battn ROYAL IRISH FUSILIERS

Instructions regarding War Diaries and Intelligence Summaries are contained in F. S. Regs., Part II, and the Staff Manual respectively. Title pages will be prepared in manuscript.

WAR DIARY
or
~~INTELLIGENCE SUMMARY~~.
(*Erase heading not required.*)

AUGUST 1917.

Army Form C. 2118.

Place	Date	Hour	Summary of Events and Information	Remarks and references to Appendices
			Map Ref. Sheet 28 N.W. 1/20,000 Map attached. X.	
VERLORENHOEK	8/8/17	(contd)	casualties were sustained during the relief in spite of a gas shell bombardment on the road past POTIZE CHATEAU. Bn. H Q was situated at I.6 a 2 8. 2 companies on the right and 2 on the left of FREZENBERG Rd, near BAVARIA HO. During the day the enemy intermittently shelled our trenches with 4.2" & 5.9", aided by observation from aeroplanes at a low altitude. At 10 pm the enemy sent up his SOS (two green & two red flares), & put a heavy barrage on our trenches. The situation became normal at 10.30 pm. At 9 pm our front line put up an SOS, apparently in mistake. Our Artillery fired on their SOS lines for 10 minutes.	WS
	9/8/17		The enemy was extremely active throughout the day, shelling our two right companies, Bn. H Q's, BAVARIA HO, & the FRENBERG Rd. 3 enemy planes flew up & down our lines at 5 am as the result of this reconnaissance seemed to account for the heavy fire during the day.	WS
	10/8/17		Enemy aerial activity continued, especially in the afternoon when over 20 aeroplanes were over our lines. During the early morning, his shell fire became intense. At about 2 am. our artillery opened up heavily on our right, but no action followed on our front. The situation did not become normal until about 4.30 am. The Battn relieved the 7th R Innis. Fus in the front line, relief starting at about 12 midnight. During the relief, hostile shelling was slight. Bn H Q was at SQUARE Fm. A line was run out to Regtl Centre Way.	

D. D. & L., London, E.C. (A7883) Wt. W803/M1672 350,000 4/17 Sch. 52a Forms/C/2118/14

7/8th (S) Battn ROYAL IRISH FUSILIERS

Instructions regarding War Diaries and Intelligence Summaries are contained in F. S. Regs., Part II, and the Staff Manual respectively. Title pages will be prepared in manuscript.

WAR DIARY

~~INTELLIGENCE SUMMARY.~~

(Erase heading not required.)

AUGUST 1917

Army Form C. 2118.

Place	Date	Hour	Summary of Events and Information (Ref. Map. Sheet 28. NW 1/20000, Attached Map. X)	Remarks and references to Appendices
SQUARE Fm	11/8/17		Our aeroplanes were active during the day & observation was excellent. There was a marked decrease in the hostile shelling throughout the day. This was especially marked as his activity on previous days had been incessant & heavy. He did not fire on our front lines. Our artillery was active during the day on the ridge in vicinity of IBERIAN FARM. One of our planes came down under control at about 5 pm near APPLE Fm.	
			The battn was relieved in the front line by the 6th R. Irish Regt. Relief commenced at 11 pm & was complete at 3·30 am owing to guides losing their way in the dark. On relief the battn moved to camp at H·16 a 4·9.	
			The total casualties during the 4 day tour was.	
			Officers. 2/Lieut. E. S. Bird killed; Capt. KINGHAN. D.H.W, 2/Lieuts. McGARRY, TOWELL, McMONAGLE wounded; Capts FFORDE & SARGINT wounded at Duty.	
			O.R. 14 killed, 66 wounded, 18 missing.	WS.
			Capt. E. E. SARGINT. M.C. was recommended for a bar to his M.C. for excellent work & gallantry in remaining with his company when wounded & when all his Coy. H.Q. were either wounded or killed.	
			A congratulatory message from the OC. 9th GORDONS, with reference to the	

D. D. & L., London, E.C. (A7883) Wt. W803/M1672 350,000 4/17 Sch. 52a Forms/C/2118/14

1/8th (S) Battn ROYAL IRISH FUSILIERS

WAR DIARY or ~~INTELLIGENCE SUMMARY~~. AUGUST 1917

Army Form C. 2118.

Instructions regarding War Diaries and Intelligence Summaries are contained in F. S. Regs., Part II. and the Staff Manual respectively. Title pages will be prepared in manuscript.

(Erase heading not required.)

Place	Date	Hour	Summary of Events and Information	Remarks and references to Appendices
			Ref Map 28 N.W. 1/20,000 – Barrage Map attached. – FREZENBERG " "	
H.16.a.9.4	12/8/17		the good work of the 2 companies detached as working parties near YPRES	WS
"	13/8/17		remained in Brigade reserve.	WS
	14/8/17		Order No 4, Instructions for the offensive, were issued. Day spent in completing to scale of bombs, flares &c.	WS
	15/8/17		The Battn moved up to their assembly position. H.Q. at SQUARE FARM. Motor lorries took the battn as far as the Square, YPRES.	WS
	16/8/17		All companies were in position by 3 am. At 4.45 am the 16th Division with divisions on either flank attacked the enemy position ~~from [illegible]~~. The battn supported the attack & acted as 'moppers up' and carrying party to the assaulting battns. "B" Coy under Capt V.J. Lynch, M.C. supported the 7th R. Innis. Fus; "C" Coy under 2/Lieut. E.L. HENRY supported the right attack ~~[illegible]~~ by the 8th R. Innis. Fus; "D" Coy under Capt E.E. SARGINT, M.C. attacked BECK Ho; "A" Coy under Capt E.H. FFORDE acted as carrying party.	
			Heavy shell fire continued throughout the night, and at 4.45 am the barrage commenced. At 5 am, BECK Ho. was captured by "D" Coy with slight casualties, and the left attack was progressing favourably. At 5.50 am, OC "D" Coy reported that BORRY FARM had not yet been taken & that the sniping and machine gun fire from this farm was holding up	

D. D. & L., London, E.C. (A7883) Wt. W803/M1672 350,000 4/17 Sch. 52a Forms/C/2118/14

1/8th (S) Battn ROYAL IRISH FUSILIERS

AUGUST 1917

Army Form C. 2118.

Instructions regarding War Diaries and Intelligence Summaries are contained in F. S. Regs., Part II. and the Staff Manual respectively. Title pages will be prepared in manuscript.

WAR DIARY
or
INTELLIGENCE SUMMARY.
(Erase heading not required.)

Place	Date	Hour	Summary of Events and Information	Remarks and references to Appendices
	16/8/17	(cont'd)	the whole right attack. He proposed to try and work round the flanks. The attempt failed. In the meantime the left attack was pressed on as far as DELVA FM., whilst the right flank of this attack became more and more exposed. No news was received from "C" Coy during this action. At 6.50 am. O.C. 'B' Coy reported that his platoons had reached their various objectives and were digging in behind the 9th R Innis Fus. It was at about 9 am that the Division on our left began to waver and it was reported they had been driven back by a counter-attack. BORRY FARM still held out & was causing heavy casualties to the left attack by heavy enfilade M.G. fire. At 8.40 am. O.C. 'B' Coy reported that the 9th R Innis Fus had, on finding both flanks exposed, retired to a line 200 yds EAST of IBERIAN, & that the situation was critical. From this point the situation became obscure. The enemy delivered a heavy counter-attack on the left flank of the 9th R. Innis Fus and our line was driven back to the original front line system on the BLACK LINE. At one time during the morning the situation became critical owing to the general confusion caused by the retirement and the fact that nearly every officer in the brigade front line had become a casualty. Our artillery & M.G. barrage caused great losses to the enemy & smashed up any further attempts on his part to advance.	

D. D. & L., London, E.C.
(A7883) Wt. W803/M1672 350,000 4/17 Sch. 52a Forms/C/2118/14

7/8th (S) Battn ROYAL IRISH FUSILIERS

Instructions regarding War Diaries and Intelligence Summaries are contained in F. S. Regs., Part II. and the Staff Manual respectively. Title pages will be prepared in manuscript.

WAR DIARY
or
INTELLIGENCE SUMMARY.
(Erase heading not required.)

AUGUST 1917

Army Form C. 2118.

Place	Date	Hour	Summary of Events and Information	Remarks and references to Appendices
			Ref. attached signal communication map.	
			SIGNALS. The signal communications arranged for are shown on the attached map. The wireless on the top of SQUARE FARM was broken ½ hr. after zero hour. The power buzzer could send but could obtain no answer from the receiving station owing to the great number of messages sent by neighbouring stations which were too close. Air lines were useless in the enemy barrage. In consequence during the whole action pigeons & runners only could be used, & this meant that Bde H.Q. often received some important message 4 to 5 hours from the time of sending. The Bde. Forward Stn left SQUARE Fm at zero but no communication was established with them. The Battn Signal Officer, 2/Lieut. Forbes, went forward to IBERIAN at 4 am but owing to heavy casualties arrived there with about 4 men. Visual stations could not be established.	
			CASUALTIES. Our casualties during the action on the 16th August were:-	
			Officers. 3 killed 7 wounded 3 missing	
			O.R's. 21 killed 105 " 90 "	
			Evacuations were carried out throughout the day from SQUARE Fm to BAVARIA Ho.	
			Splendid work was done during the day by company stretcher bearers who continued to carry men from the front line to the dressing station in spite of M.G. fire. Enemy snipers apparently respected them while working.	WH

D. D. & L., London, E.C. (A7883) Wt. W807/M1672 350,000 4/17 Sch. 52a Forms/C/2118/14

1/8th (S) Battn ROYAL IRISH FUSILIERS

Army Form C. 2118.

WAR DIARY or ~~INTELLIGENCE SUMMARY.~~

AUGUST 1917

Instructions regarding War Diaries and Intelligence Summaries are contained in F. S. Regs., Part II, and the Staff Manual respectively. Title pages will be prepared in manuscript.

(Erase heading not required.)

Place	Date	Hour	Summary of Events and Information	Remarks and references to Appendices
			Maps attached. Sheet 28. N.W. 1/20,000. Sheet 27	
			Owing to the heavy casualties sustained by the attacking battns, the 6th CONNAUGHT Rangers took over the whole of the brigade front at about 12 midnight.	
CAMBRIDGE Rd	17/8/17		On relief the battn moved into the old British support line in CAMBRIDGE Rd. During the day, about 30 men rejoined from other regiments of the brigade.	
			The 15th Division relieved the 16th Division on 18/19th August. At 9.30 pm, the battn moved off via YPRES to H.17.a.1.8.	
H.17.a.1.8	18/8/17		The 49th Inf Bde embussed at VLAMERTINGHE at 6pm & arrived in WATOU No C Area. The battn on arrival was billeted near K.17.b. Lt Col K.C. Weldon D.S.O. returned to the battn after acting as Brigadier during the action.	
H.17.a.1.8	19/8/17		Usual parades, change of clothing &c., organising companies and checking deficiencies. Capt [illegible] M.C. arrived. Lieuts Sparks, Turnbull, Downie proceeded on leave. 2nd Lieut [illegible]	
K.17.b	20/8/17		Batt marched to Ecke Area. Moved off 4.15 p.m. Billeted [illegible] 2.15 [illegible]	
Ecke	21/8/17		Checking casualty lists & correcting rolls for entraining on the next day.	
Ecke	22/8/17		The Batt marched off at 8.15 a.m. to Bavinchove Station via St Sylvestre & Cassel. Entrained by 11.45 a.m. Train left 12.30 p.m. Arrived at Miraumont 8.15 p.m. Arrived at Camp [illegible] Achiet le Petit [illegible]	

D. D. & L., London, E.C. (A7883) Wt. W809/M1672 350,000 4/17 Sch. 52a Forms/C/2118/14

7/8 ROYAL IRISH FUSILIERS

AUGUST 1917

Army Form C. 2118.

Instructions regarding War Diaries and Intelligence Summaries are contained in F. S. Regs., Part II, and the Staff Manual respectively. Title pages will be prepared in manuscript.

WAR DIARY
or
~~INTELLIGENCE SUMMARY~~.
(Erase heading not required.)

Place	Date	Hour	Summary of Events and Information	Remarks and references to Appendices
	22/8/17		on Bucquoy Road about 9 p.m	
Achiet le Petit	23/8/17		Re-organised Companies & inspections. Deficiencies of kit.	
"	24/8/17		Company Training of Specialists. Afternoon Baths.	
"	25/8/17		Company Training. Afternoon Swimming at Achiet le Grand. Inter Coy football matches. change of clothing.	
"	26/8/17		Church Parade, in the morning. The afternoon was spent by having: Guard mounting competitions, and Platoon competitions.	Halt
	27/8/17		Company training. Training of specialists. Lewis Gunners on Range.	
	28/8/17		The 16th Division (less artillery) relieves the 21st Div (less artillery) in the line in the VI Corps ~~front~~ Centre sector. The 47th & 48th Brigades take over the Right & Left sections respectively. The 49th Bde. will be in Bde reserve. The 49th Bde moved to the Reserve Bde area.	
			This Battalion left HENHAM CAMP. ACHIET-LE-PETIT. at 10.20 A.M. and marched to HAMLINCOURT, arriving at Camp about 12.30. P.M. Camp situated at (S.23. c. 4. 3. Ref. map 51.B.)	Halt

D. D. & L., London, E.C. (A7883) Wt. W803/M1672 350,000 4/17 Sch. 52a Forms/C/2118/14

Instructions regarding War Diaries and Intelligence Summaries are contained in F. S. Regs., Part II. and the Staff Manual respectively. Title pages will be prepared in manuscript.

WAR DIARY
or
INTELLIGENCE SUMMARY.
(Erase heading not required.)

AUGUST 1917

Army Form C. 2118.

Place	Date	Hour	Summary of Events and Information	Remarks and references to Appendices
HAMLINCOURT	29/8/17		Company training. Bayonet fighting. Bombing etc.	G/4
do	30/8/17		do.	G/4
do	31/8/17		do.	G/4

[illegible signature] Lt. Col.
Comdg. [illegible]

D. D. & L., London, E.C.
(A7883) Wt. W807/M1672 350,000 4/17 Sch. 52a Forms/C2118/14

SECRET
CREEPING BARRAGE MAP
T.B.56
St Julien
Winnipeg
Vinzig
Schuler Fm.
Hindu Cott
Nile
Hanebeek
Kansas Cross
Somme
Keir Fm.
Gallipoli
Bank Fm.
Toronto
Riverside
Fokker Fm.
The Gravenstafel Switch
Boetleer
S' Gravenstafel
Otto Fm.
Dochy Fm.
Van Isackere Fm.
Zonnebeke
Beck House
Zevenkote
Bremen Redoubt
Vampir
Windmill Cabt
Zonnebeke
Potsdam
+2hrs 50min
+2hrs. 50m
+5
+10
+15
+20
+25
+30
+35
+40
+45
+50
+55
+60
+65
+70
+75
+80
+85
+90
+95
+100
+105
+110
+115
Protective

1:10 000
REFERENCE
New trenches
Dugouts
Tracks
New Wire
Machine Guns
R.1.
7-8-17
EDITION 2.
APPROXIMATE BRITISH FRONT LINE
8/9
Scale 1:10,000.
5TH FIELD SURVEY COY, RE (1328)
27-7-17. No2 Advanced Section A.P.& S.S.

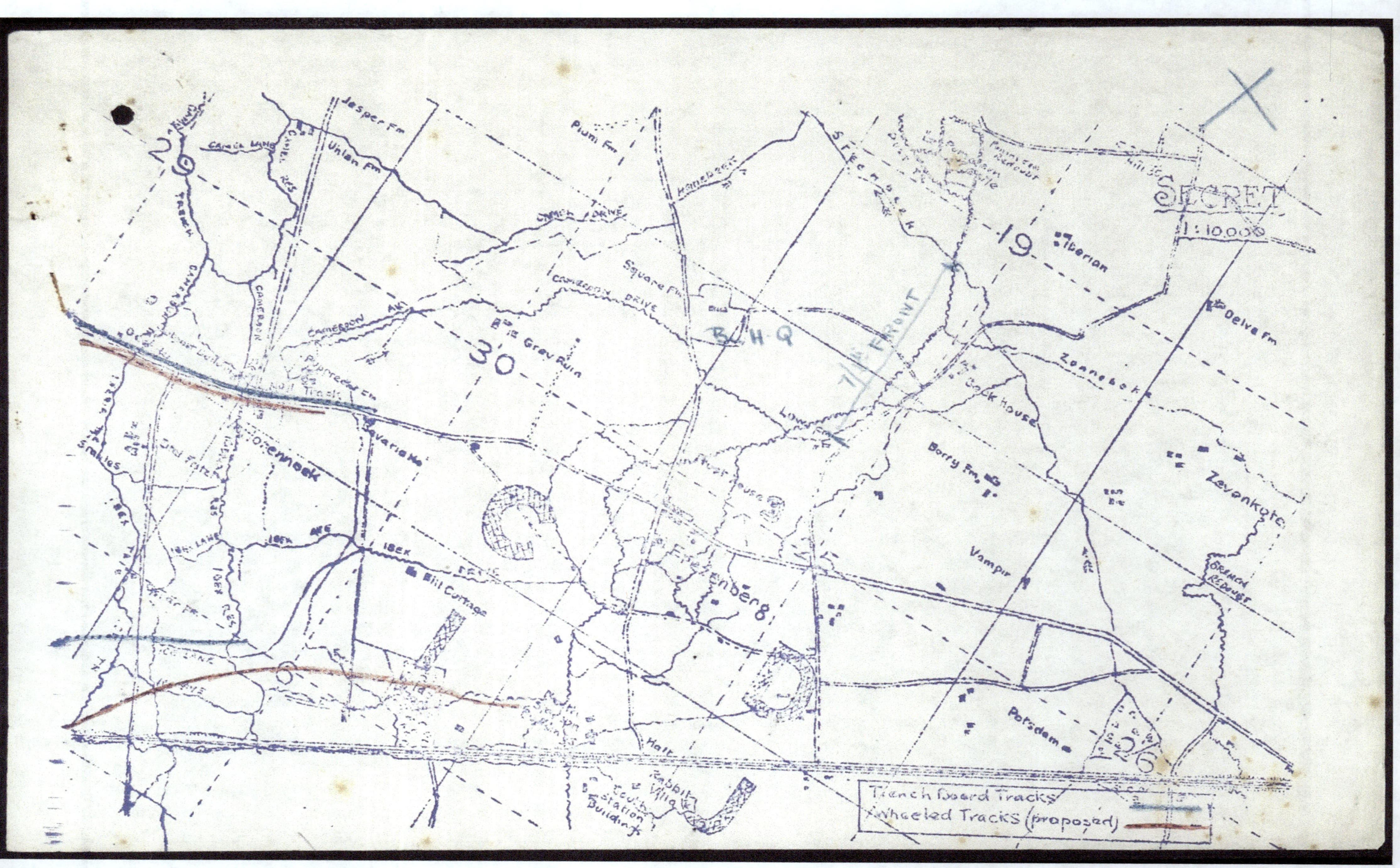
SECRET
1:10,000
Trench Board Tracks
Wheeled Tracks (proposed)
Jasper Fm
Uhlan Fm
Plum Fm
Hanebeek
Steenbeek
Iberian
Delve Fm
Zonnebeke
Beck House
Borry Fm
Zevenkote
French Redoubt
Vampir
Potsdam
Frezenberg
Square Fm
Cameron Drive
B.H.Q
Gray Ruin
Low Fm
Hill Cottage
Ibex
Halt
Rabbit Villa
South Station Buildings
19
29
30
26

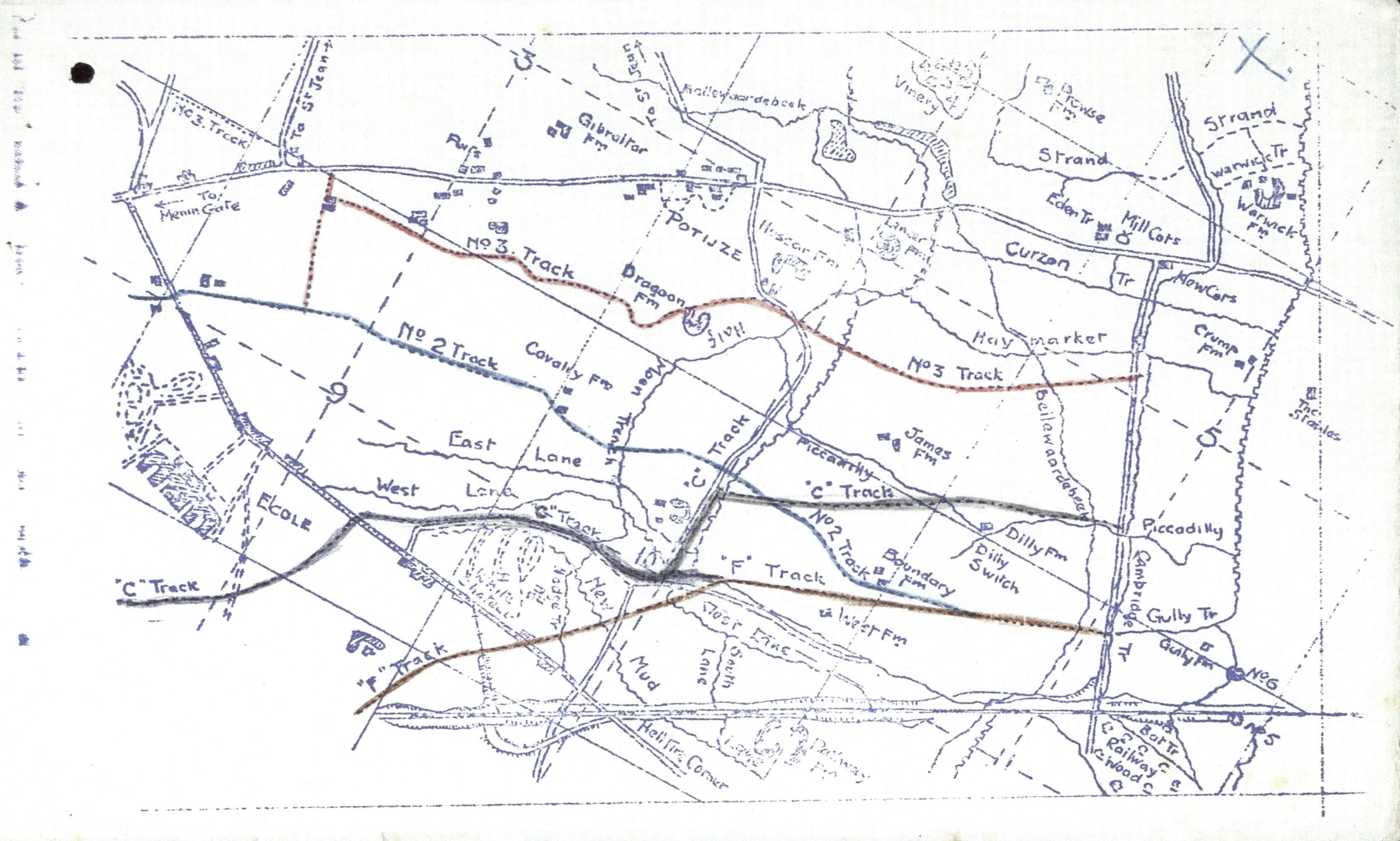

To St Jean
To St Jean
Gibraltar Fm
Ruft
Beilewaardebeek
Vimery
Frowse Fm
Strand
Strand
Warwick Tr
Warwick Fm
No 3. Track
To Menin Gate
Potijze
Eden Tr
Mill Cots
Curzon
Tr
New Cots
No 3. Track
Dragoon Fm
Hill
Haymarket
Crump Fm
No 3 Track
The Stables
No 2 Track
Cavalry Fm
Moen Trench
"C" Track
James Fm
Piccadilly
Beilewaardebeek
5
6
East Lane
West Lane
"C" Track
Ecole
"C" Track
No 2 Track
Piccadilly
Dilly Fm
Dilly Switch
Boundary Fm
"F" Track
Cambridge Tr
Gully Tr
"C" Track
Hodge Tr
New
White Chateau
West Lane
West Fm
Gully Fm
No 6
"F" Track
Mud
South Lane
Hell Fire Corner
Railway Fm
Bur Tr
Railway Wood
No 5

H.Q.
16TH DIVISION.
No. E.S. 1283
Date 9.8.17

HEADQUARTERS,
15th DIVISION.
[illegible] AUG 1917
Reg. No. 132

Confidential

H. Q.

15th Division

May I please be allowed to bring to your notice the very fine work done by the detachment of the 7/8 Royal Irish Fusiliers who were attached to us for work on GORDON ROAD.

The way they stuck to their work and carried the slabs night after night under heavy shell fire, up to the scene of work, was the subject of our greatest admiration.

They were always anxious to help in every way and never once failed to do everything that was wanted in spite of, at times, heavy casualties.

Without their splendid assistance the road could never have been finished in time.

T G Taylor Lt Col

Comdg 9th Gordon Highlanders (P)

4.8.17.

2. 15th.Div.No.132/G.b. 6.8.17.

16th. Division.

I have very much pleasure in forwarding the above report.

H. F. Thuillier

Major General.
Commanding 15th.(Scottish) Division.

3

49th Infty Bde. 16th Div. No. E.S. 1283/2.

I need not say how gratified I am to receive this acknowledgement of the fine work which has once again been done by this Battalion.

Please convey to them my appreciation.

W. B. Hickie Maj. Gen.
Comdg 16th (Irish) Division

Aug 9th 1917.

To the

O.C. 7/8 Royal Irish Fus.

I have great pleasure in forwarding the attached complimentary report on the fine work done by the detachment from your Battalion.

Very many congratulations

R Leveson Gower Brig Gen
49th I.B.

10/8/17

War Diary.

War Diary

Herewith Copy No. 12 of Operation Orders No. 4. They are not complete and will probably have to be amended as information is received on several points.

Please acknowledge.

August 14th. 1917

Lieut & A/Adjutant.

7/8th (S) Battalion The Royal Irish Fusiliers

SECRET. AUGUST 14th.1917 COPY NO..12..........

OPERATION ORDERS No. 4.
BY.
Lieut.Colonel. H.C.WELDON D.S.O.Comdg Royal Irish Fusiliers

::

PROVISIONAL ORDERS FOR THE ATTACK.

1. GENERAL PLAN

The 16th.Division ,in conjunction with Divisions on either flank,will attack the enemy's positions on a date to be notified later.
The attack will be made in two bounds,each bound is shewn by coloured lines on Map "A"

First Bound GREEN LINE
Second Bound DOTTED RED LINE.

2. OBJECTIVES OF BRIGADES

The 16th.Division will attack with:-
48th.Infantry Brigade (plus 1 Battalion) on the Right.
49th.Infantry Brigade (plus 1 Battalion) on the Left.
47th.Infantry Brigade (less 3 Battalions) in reserve.
Left Battalion 48th.Infantry Brigade will be 2nd.R.DUBLIN FUSILIERS.
Right Battalion 108 Infantry Brigade will be 9th.R.IRISH FUSILIERS.

3. BOUNDARIES.

The Boundaries between the 49th.Infantry Brigade and the Bde.on either flank are as follows :-

Boundary with 48th.Infantry Brigade.
D.25.a.75.05. -- where DOTTED RED LINE crosses the ZONNEBEKE STREAM.

Boundary with 108th.Infantry Brigade.
D.19.c.7.8. -- D.19.b.70.50. -- D.14.d.20.40.

These boundaries are shewn in BLUE on Map "A"

4. TASKS OF BATTALIONS.

The attack on the GREEN and DOTTED RED LINES will be made by the 7th. Royal Inniskilling Fusiliers on the Left and the 8th.Royal Inniskilling Fusiliers on the Right.
Boundary between Battalions is shewn in BLACK on Map "A"
The GREEN LINE is to be captured at ZERO PLUS..........
There will be a pause of 20 minutes on the GREEN LINE.
The DOTTED RED LINE is to be captured at ZERO PLUS ....
As soon as the DOTTED RED LINE has been captured a line of posts will be pushed out as far as the barrage premits.

The 7/8th.Battalion Royal Irish Fusiliers will support the attack and will find "MOPPERS UP" and Carrying Parties as under.

(a) "C"Company (2/Lieut.C.L.HENRY.)
No.10:.Platoon (2/LIEUT.A.C.YOUNG.)to Mop Up BORRY FARM and hold it as a Supporting Point
No..11...Platoon (2/LIEUT. W.A.) These two platoons will Mop Up
No..12:..Platoon (DIXON.) ZEVENCOTE and hold it as a Supporting Point.
No..9.. Platoon (2/LT.G.COOMBES.) to Mop Up COFFEE FARM,D.20.c.15.15.
and then join the two platoons at ZEVENCOTE.
These 4 Platoons will move into position on Y/Z Night and will advance in rear of the last wave of the 8.R.Inniskilling Fusiliers.

Continued on Page 2.

SHEET 2. (Para 4. continued)

(b). "B"Company Captain V.J.LYNCH M.C.
No...8..Platoon (2/LT.C.W.PICKETT) to Mop Up DELVA FARM and will join the Platoon at IBERIAN when the H.Q.7th.R.Innis.Fusrs moves to DELVA FARM.
No...6..Platoon (2/LT. DICKSON) to form a Supporting Point about D.19.d.80.80.
The above two platoons will advance ~~with~~ in rear of the first wave of the 7th.Royal Inniskilling Fusiliers (Right Half Battalion)

(c) No..7...Platoon ( )to Mop Up IBERIAN and the dugouts in the vicinity and form a Supporting Point there.
No..5...Platoon( )One to Mop Up and hold as a Supporting Point the clump of trees at D.19.b.70.35.
The above two Platoons to advance in rear of the 1st wave of the 7th. R Innis Fusrs. (Left Half Battalion)
"B"Company will move into position on Y/Z Night.

(d) "D"Company (Captain E.E.SARGINT M.C.)
This Company will assemble in the Front Line from D.25.a.80.90 to D.19.c.80.30.
At ZERO hour,this Company will advance and capture BECK HOUSE,and the ground as far East as the Stream,reform and on receipt of orders from Battalion H.Qrs,move to IBERIAN in support.

(e) "A"Company.(Captain E.H.FFORDE)
This Company will provide Carrying Parties as under :-
No..1..Platoon (2/LT.POWELL) and No...2.Platoon (2/LT.SHEPPARD)will carry to COFFEE FARM.
No.3.Platoon (~~2/Lieut.~~ Capt.OLIVER) and No 4.Platoon (Sgt.TIMMINS)
will carry to DELVA FARM.
Nos.1.& 2.Platoons on completion of their tasks will join the Company at ZEVENCOTE.
Nos.3.&.4.Platoons on completion of their tasks will join the two Coys.at IBERIAN.
"A"coy.will move into position on Y/Z Night

5. LOADS.

	COMPOSITION OF LOAD.	WHERE PICKED UP.
1st.LOAD		
2nd.LOAD.		
3rd.LOAD.		

The Officer or N.C.O i/c of any carrying party,when he has completed his journey will report the fact at the Battalion H.Qrs.of the Unit for which he is carrying and will on no account leave without obtaining the written authority of the O.C.to do so.
A detail of loads will be issued for the first three journeys,but if necessary more journeys will be made.The first load on YUKON PACKS will be picked up as they march past MILL COT.The number of YUKON PACKS available will be......

6. All Companies will remain under the orders of the O.C.7/8th.R.Irish Fusiliers

SHEET. 3.

7. ASSEMBLY POSITIONS.

On Y/Z Night the Battalion moves into Assembly Positions. The order of march on leaving Camp at H.16.a.4.9. will be

Battalion H.Qrs.
"D"Company.
"A"Company.
"B"Company.
"C"Company

"D"Company 7/8th.Royal Irish Fusiliers will relieve "C"Coy.7th.R.Innis. Fusrs. in the front line from D.25.a.80.90. to D.19.c.80.30. Four guides will be sent to BAVARIA HOUSE.

"A"Coy.7/8th.R.Irish Fusiliers will move to an assembly position in rear of "D"Coy.
No.1 & 2.Platoons on the Right
3.&.4.Platoons on the Left.
No guides will be sent for this Company.

"B"Company 7/8th.Royal Irish Fusiliers will move to assembly positions:
Nos. 5 & 7 Platoons to form up behind the 1st.wave of the 7.R.Innis. Fusrs.Left Half Battalion
Nos. 6 & 8. Platoons to form up behind the 1st wave of the 7.R.Innis. Fusrs Right Battalion.
4 Guides will be sent to BAVARIA HOUSE.

"C"Company 7/8th.Royal Irish Fusiliers will form up behind the 1st. wave of the 8th.Royal Inniskilling Fusiliers.
4 Guides will be sent to BAVARIA HOUSE.

8. RATIONS.

Rations for "Z"Day will be issued to eac[h m]an on the afternoon of "Y"Day and will be carried up on the man

9. SHOVELS.

On moving into Assembly Positions "B" ,"C" and "D"Coys' will take shovels from the Transport Lines on a scale of one every other man. No picks will be taken

10. LEWIS GUNS.

The Four Lewis Guns of "A"Coy. will be attached :-
(a) Two to the 7.Royal Inniskilling Fusiliers
(b) Two to the 8th.Royal Inniskilling Fusiliers
Only two men with a bag of spare parts and 5 filled drums will accompany each Gun.
(a) These two guns will proceed to SQUARE FARM with Battalion H.Qrs.
(b) These two Guns will proceed with "D"Coy.O.C."D"Coy will arrange to hand them over to O.C.8.R.Innis.Fusrs. at LOW FARM.

11. MOPPING UP.

The 7th and 8th.Royal Inniskilling Fusiliers are responsible for Mopping Up all ground in their areas in front of DELVA FARM and ZEVENCOTE.The 7/8th.Royal Irish Fusiliers are responsible for Mopping Up in rear of DELVA FARM and ZEVENCOTE (inclusive)

12 CONSOLIDATION.

The RED DOTTED LINE and all Supporting Points held by the 7/8th.Royal Irish Fusiliers will be consolidated as soon as possible after capture. The R.E.will work under the direction of the C.R.E.16th.Division, and will erect wire on the GHELUVELT -- LANGEMARCK LINE when captured.They will also prepare certain positions for defence in vicinity of DELVA FARM and IBERIAN.

---

13. MACHINE GUNS

The Machine Guns will be under the direction of the Divisional Machine Gun Officer.
12 Guns of the 49th.M.Gun Coy. will assist in the Machine Gun Barrage which will be 800 yards in advance of the Artillery Creeping Barrage and will lift in conformity with that Barrage.
Two Guns will move in rear of the attacking Infantry to a position in vicinity of DELVA FARM and 2 Guns will move to a position near Hill 37. (D.20.a.)

14. ACTION OF STOKES MORTARS.

Two Stokes' Mortars will be attached to each assaulting Battalion. They will move in rear of the last wave, and will assist the Infantry to overcome opposition as required. The remaining 4 Mortars will be left at Brigade Headquarters.

15 ACTION OF ARTILLERY

The Divisional Artillery will form a Creeping Barrage covering the advance of the Infantry. At ZERO HOUR the Barrage will be put down 300 yards in advance of our present front line; BECK HOUSE will be specially dealt with. The first lift will take place at ZERO plus 5. minutes, and it will then proceed forward at the rate of 100 yards in 5 minutes.
During the 20 minutes pause on the GREEN LINE a protective barrage will be maintained 200 yards in advance of the Infantry.
After the capture of the DOTTED RED LINE a standing barrage will be established 300 yards in advance of it for aperiod of one hour, after which it will cease unless recalled by the "S.O.S." Signal.

16. COMMUNICATIONS.

BRIGADE H.QRS. will remain at MILL CCT.
The Bde. Forward Station will advance behind the last wave of the leading Assaulting Battalions, and will be established in the vicinity of IBERIAN.
Battalion Forward Posts will be established as follows:-

7th. Royal Inniskilling Fusiliers DELVA FARM
8th. Royal Inniskilling Fusiliers COFFEE FARM (D.20.c.2.2.)
7/8th. Royal Irish Fusiliers IBERIAN.

Battalion H.Qrs will not move forward to these positions until Communication has been established with them.
As many pairs of Pigeons as available will be issued to the Battalion half of these will be sent to the Battalion Forward Post.
Runner Relay Posts will be established at :-

(a) IBERIAN
(b) SQUARE FARM
(c) BAVARIA HOUSE.
(d) BRIGADE H.Qrs.

Runners should not be used unless all other means of Communication fail.
The Brigade Forward Station of the 48th. Infantry Brigade will be at VAMPIR.
The Brigade Forward Station of the 108th. Infantry Brigade will be at ....
The Brigade Visual Station and O.P. will be at C.29.d.8.7.

17. CONTACT AEROPLANES.

One Contact Aeroplane (Type..........) and One Protective Aeroplane will be in the air over the 16th. Division and 36th. Division Areas from ZERO HOUR onwards. Flares will be lit and WATSON FANS will be shown by the leading troops at the following hours.

The leading troops will be prepared to light flares and show WATSON Fans at other times if asked for by the aeroplane

SHEET....5.

No.18.S.O.S.SIGNAL.
The "S.O.S" will be GREEN SIGNAL CARTRIDGES.

19.PRISONERS
All prisoners will be sent to BECK HOUSE, where they will be ~~xxxx~~ collected by the 2nd. The Royal Irish Regt. and sent down in batches to the Brigade Prisoners Cage at Brigade H.Qrs.
Only one man to every ten prisoners will be sent down.

20 .ZERO HOUR.
ZERO HOUR will be notified later.

21. TANKS.ACTION OF.
One Section of Tanks, from "C"Battalion, Tank Corps, has been allotted to the 16th.Division. These tanks will not be available unless the weather conditions improve. In any case they are only likely to arrive behind the Infantry in time to act as "Moppers Up." In cases where isolated positions continue to hold out.

22. SYNCHRONIZATION.
The Signal Officer will arrange to send a watch to Bde.H.Qrs.at 6.0.P.m.daily for synchronization and will send same round to all Officers daily.

23. HEADQUARTERS
The disposition of all Headquarters is as shewn on attached plan.

24. ACKNOWLEDGE.

August 14th.1917 — Lieutenant & A/Adjutant.

7/8th.(S)Battalion The Royal Irish Fusiliers

ISSUED THROUGH SIGNALS AT 5·30 P.M.

COPY NO.1.	"A"Coy.	Copy.No.10.	Transport Officer.
2.	"B"Coy.	11.	War Diary
3.	"C"Coy.	12.	War Diary.
4.	"D"Coy.	13.	49th.Infantry Brigade.
5.	Lewis Gun Officer	14.	7.R.Innis.Fusrs
6.	Intelligence Officer	15.	8.R.Innis Fusrs.
7.	Signalling Officer.	16.	2.The R.Irish Regt.
8.	Medical Officer.	17.	Spare.
9.	Quartermaster	18.	O.C.Echelon "B"

Copy No.20.File.

War Diary

SECRET

COPY NO. ....

Reference Operation Orders No.4. Copy.No.........issued to day please note the following amendments.

Para 10. LEWIS GUNS.

(a) For "D" Coy. in both places read "C" Company

Para 4. TASKS OF BATTALIONS.

(a) The 4 Platoons of "C" Coy will advance in rear of the first wave of the 8th. R. Innis. Fusrs. and not as previously stated.

Para 5. Add.
Unless further instructions are issued in the meantime, the loads for the 2nd. and 3rd journeys and any subsequent journeys will be drawn from the R.E. Dump at SIX TREES DUMP. It is possible that forward dumps may be established at SQUARE FARM and LOW FARM for respective Battalions.

26 WATER (Extra Paragraph.)
A forward WATER TANK will be established at C.30.d.5.5.

[signature]

August 14th. 1917 Lieutenant & A/Adjutant.

7/8th. (S) Battalion The Royal Irish Fusiliers

7/8th.(S)Battalion The Royal Irish Fusiliers Order No.18. Aug.17/17

War Diary

S E C R E T. COPY NO. 16.

1. The Battalion will move to Assembly Positions as laid down in Operation Orders No.4. of 14.8.17. on the 15th inst.

2. The Battalion will form up in Quarters Column facing the [struck out] Road on the SOUTH Side of the Camp, in the following order :-
Battalion H.Qrs. in front. "D"Coy., "A"Coy., "B"Coy.& "C"Coy. Companies will be formed up ready to embus at 9.0.p.m.

3. All Lewis Guns etc. will be carried by the men. The Lewis Gun Officer will ensure that two guns of "A"Coy. are sent to Battalion H.Qrs., SQUARE FARM. O.C. "C"Coy. will be responsible that the other two guns are taken to H.Q. 8th. Royal Inniskilling Fusiliers, LOW FARM. Lewis Guns will be carried up by the teams from MENIN GATE.

4. Officers' Kits and spare Mess Kit will be stacked outside Bn.H.Q. at 8.30. p.m. If it is raining they will be stacked inside the house. All Mess Sand Bags will be taken in the Busses.

5. The Transport Officer will arrange to send 56 Petrol Tins to be dumped by the side of the road at I.5.a.8.9. by 10.30.p.m. C.Q.M. Sgt. of "B"Coy. will remain in charge of this dump, and will issue three tins to each platoon and eight to Bn.H.Q. as they march East. This water will be carried up to Assembly Positions and should be made into Dumps there, so that Coys. can send to these dumps should they require water during the day. All mens' Sand bags will be stacked in Coy. Dumps near the road by 8.0.p.m. Bn.H.Q. will also form a dump. Bivouacs will be pitched so as to afford cover should it be wet.

6. Guides. Four Guides from 7.R.Innis.Fusrs. for "D"Coy.7/8th.R.Irish Fusrs. will be at BAVARIA HOUSE at 11.0.p.m.
Four Guides from 7.R.Innis.Fusrs for "B"Coy.7/8th.R.Irish Fusrs. will be at BAVARIA HOUSE at [struck out] 11.0.pm
Four Guides from 8.R.Innis Fusrs. for "C"Coy.7/8th.R.Irish Fusrs will be at BAVARIA HOUSE at 11.0.p.m.

7. Maps of our own lines are not to be taken into Assembly Positions.
8. The importance of absolute silence and absence of light during the assembly should be impressed on all ranks.
9. All Companies must be in position by 2.30.a.m. O's.C."Coys. will report to Bn.H.Q. immediately that all Platoons are in Assembly Positions.
10. SHOVELS. Reference Para.9. Operation Orders No.4. The Transport Officer will arrange to dump 80 Shovels outside the Camp at 9.0.a.m.
~~"A"Coy. will draw 21.~~ "B"Coy. will draw 24. "C"Coy. will draw 24.
"D"Coy. will draw 28. Battalion H.Qrs. will draw 4.
11. MEDICAL.
The Medical Officer will arrange to have his stores carried from MENIN GATE.
Aid Posts in the forthcoming operations will be established :-
Regimental Aid Post SQUARE FARM
Aid Post at LOW FARM
" " " DELVA FARM
" " " BAVARIA HOUSE.

12. ACKNOWLEDGE.

August 14th.1917

[illegible] for Lieutenant & A/Adjutant.
7/8th.(S)Battalion The Royal Irish Fusiliers

Issued through Signals at 10.0.p.m.

Copy No.1. "A"Coy.
2. "B"Coy.
3. "C"Coy.
4. "D"Coy.
5. Quartermaster
6. Transport Officer.
7. Medical Officer
15 & 16. WAR DIARY.

Copy No.8. R.S.M.
9. Signalling Officer
10. Lewis Gun Officer
11. Intelligence Officer
12. O.C."B"Echelon.
13. H.Q.49.Inf.Bde.
14. File

12. J.

G.D.

WAR DIARY.

FOR MONTH OF SEPTEMBER, 1917.

VOLUME 12

UNIT:- 7/8th Btn Ro Irish Fuslrs.

9/1 20

9th Royal Irish Fusiliers — SEPTEMBER : 1917

Army Form C. 2118.

Instructions regarding War Diaries and Intelligence Summaries are contained in F. S. Regs., Part II. and the Staff Manual respectively. Title pages will be prepared in manuscript.

WAR DIARY
or
INTELLIGENCE SUMMARY.
(Erase heading not required.)

Place	Date	Hour	Summary of Events and Information	Remarks and references to Appendices
	SEPTEMBER			
	1		Church parades.	O/C.
ARMAGH	2		Battalion Sports commencing 4.45 pm G.O.C's inspection in morning	
CAMP S23 C. 5.0			Lieut V. P. WARD rejoined the Battn	O/C.
LEFT SUPPORT FONTAINES SECTOR	3		49th Infy Bde relieved 48th Infy Bde in Left Sub-section FONTAINES SECTOR. The Battn relieved 2 Coys. 2nd R Dublin Fus. & 2 Coys 9th R. Dublin Fus. in Left Support. HQ at T22 d. 5.9 near CROISELLES	O/C.
"	4		General improvements work on 'C' Posts, construction of deep dug outs, & generally preparing for bad weather in the winter	O/C.
"	5		As above Lieut B. J. Stuart, 2Lieut V. Mitchell, 2Lieut AB. Kennedy joined Bn	O/C.
"	6/8		As above	O/C.
"	9		Gas alarm 9 pm. To our immediate Right the enemy sent over a smoke cloud & then shelled heavily with gas shells. No gas reached positions occupied by Battn & situation became calm 9.45 pm	O/C.
FRONT LINE	10.		Lieut C J. Coggins, a/adjutant proceeded on leave & Capt. W. G. Groombridge assumed the duties of a/adjt.	
L. SUB SECTOR FONTAINES SECTOR			Battn moved into Front Line about 7.30 pm relieving 7th R. IRISH Rifles in the Left Sub Sect FONTAINE SECTOR. Relief complete 11 pm. Bn HQ in TUNNEL at T.4 d 4.9.	O/C.
"	11		MAJOR G.E.G. Cockburn DSO, MC., R IRISH Fus, joined Bn for duty	O/C.
"	12/15		General drainage & grading of trenches, erecting shelters &c. under R.E. Supervision Artillery activity normal during tour	O/C.

D. D. & L., London, E.C. (A7883) Wt. W703/M1672 350,000 4/17 Sch. 52a Forms/C/2118/14

Instructions regarding War Diaries and Intelligence Summaries are contained in F. S. Regs., Part II, and the Staff Manual respectively. Title pages will be prepared in manuscript.

WAR DIARY
or
INTELLIGENCE SUMMARY.
(*Erase heading not required.*)

Army Form C. 2118.

Place	Date	Hour	Summary of Events and Information	Remarks and references to Appendices
	SEPTEMBER			
FRONT LINE L SUBSECTOR FONTAINES SECTOR	16		48th Infy Bde relieved 49th Infy Bde. In Left Subsection Battn relieved by 2nd R. Dublin Fus. & on completion of relief moved into ARMAGH CAMP arriving 6 pm	CF
ARMAGH CAMP	17		Checking deficiencies, fitting clothing etc.	CF
"	18		Baths. Rifles & LGs inspected by VI Corps Armourer Sgt	CF
"	19/22		Bayonet Fighting & P.T. Ceremonial etc. Work on improvements in Camps	CF
"	23		Lieut C.J. Coggins rejoined off leave & assumed duties of Adjutant. Capt W.G. Greenbridge assumed command of 'A' Coy. Divine Service parades.	CF
"	24		Battalion Sports in afternoon	CF
"	25		G.O.C's inspection of 49th Infy Bde. Battn XI played in final Br. Football Cup v 2 R Irish Rgt. Result 1 goal each	CF
"	26		Battn XI played in final of Brigade Football Cup v 2 R Irish Rgt & lost after a hard game 2 - 0. (replay)	CF
"	27		Gas helmets & box respirators inspected by Div Gas NCOs. Major G. E. G. Cockburn DSO MC assumed command of Bn vice Lieut Col K.C. Weldon DSO to Hospital	CF
LEFT SUPPORT	28		49th Infy Bde relieved 48th Infy Bde in Left Subsection FONTAINE SECTOR. The Battn relieved 2nd R DUBLIN FUS in Left Support. Relief complete by 3.30 pm.	
"	29		General work on positions, erection of dugouts etc. Our own & hostile aircraft very active	
"	30		As for 29th	

D. D. & L., London, E.C. (A7883) Wt. W803/M1672 350,000 4/17 Sch. 52a Forms/C/2118/14

Instructions regarding War Diaries and Intelligence Summaries are contained in F. S. Regs., Part II. and the Staff Manual respectively. Title pages will be prepared in manuscript.

SEPT

WAR DIARY
or
INTELLIGENCE SUMMARY.
(Erase heading not required.)

Army Form C. 2118.

Place	Date	Hour	Summary of Events and Information	Remarks and references to Appendices
			The following awards have been made during the month –	
			Lieut W. Sparks Military Cross	
			2/Lieut. G. J. Forbes "	
			Rev. E. Kelly, C. F. (attd) "	
			No. 8907 C.S.M. Griffin A. D.C.M.	
			The following have been awarded the Military Medal –	
			No. 12764 Sgt. Daley M. No. 4319 Pte Dalton E. No. 16929 Pte Sweeney F.	
			" 18729 Pte Gray F. " 4317 " Dobbins W. " 20194 " Finlay W attd 49 T.M.B.	
			" 20912 " McKee P. " 21495 L.Cpl. Laverty J.	J
			" 24518 " Loughran B. " 19091 Pte Bishop R. " 24049 " Robinson W	
			Bar to Military Medal No. 20165 L/Cpl McCall W.	
			The following Officers, N.C.Os, & men have been awarded Parchment Certificates –	
			Capt. M H. Turnbull, Lieut F. L. Crilly, 2/Lieut J. S. Vorley	
			No. 12764 Sgt. Daley M, No. 16912 Cpl. McMorrow J. No. 6932 Pte Walker M.	
			" 20560 Pte Plunkett J " 20272 Pte Quigley J " 20529 " Garland J	
			" 18431 Cpl. Conlon J. " 21130 " McCaughey P " 15419 " Boyle J	

D. D. & L., London, E.C. (A7883) Wt. W803/M1672 350,000 4/17 Sch. 52a Forms/C/2118/14

Army Form C. 2118.

Instructions regarding War Diaries and Intelligence Summaries are contained in F. S. Regs., Part II. and the Staff Manual respectively. Title pages will be prepared in manuscript.

WAR DIARY
or
INTELLIGENCE SUMMARY.
(Erase heading not required.)

Place	Date	Hour	Summary of Events and Information	Remarks and references to Appendices
SEPTEMBER			Continued List of Awards of Parchment Certificates –	
			No. 18929 Pte Longhurst C, No. 21877 L/Cpl Martin A, No 13438 L/Cpl Morrow W.	C/C.
			" 18787 Sgt. Timmins I.S. " 25133 Pte Austin L. " 15466 Cpl. Nolan C.	
			" 43406 Cpl. Gilliland J. " 25120 " Phillips A. " 23504 Pte Rogers J.C.	
			E. Cockburn Major Commdg. 7/8 Bn. Royal Irish Fusiliers	

2353 Wt. W2544/1454 700,000 5/15 D. D. & L. A.D.S.S./Forms/C. 2118.

13 J.
Lally

W A R D I A R Y

FOR MONTH OF OCTOBER, 1917.

UNIT 1/8th Royal Irish Fuslrs.

VOLUME NUMBER B

7/8 Bn Royal Irish Fusiliers

WAR DIARY
or
~~INTELLIGENCE SUMMARY.~~
(Erase heading not required.)

October, 1917.

Army Form C. 2118.

Instructions regarding War Diaries and Intelligence Summaries are contained in F. S. Regs., Part II. and the Staff Manual respectively. Title pages will be prepared in manuscript.

Ref Sheet. 51 b SW 1/10000

Place	Date	Hour	Summary of Events and Information	Remarks and references to Appendices
Left Support / Left subsection FONTAINE	1917 Oct 1		General work on positions, erection of dugouts etc	G/F
	2		do	G/F
	3		do	G/F
	4		Battalion moved into Front line about 2 P.M relieving 7th Royal Irish Rifles in the left sub section. FONTAINE Sector. Relief complete at 5 P.M.	
	5		Gas shell bombardment on enemy at 7 P.M. Enemy retaliated with many aerial darts on LUMP LANE, and shelled the Right Coys HQRS with heavies.	G/F
	6		Gas shell bombardment on enemy at 6 AM. Enemy retaliation slight.	G/F
	7		Our artillery displayed the usual activity. Enemy was very quiet.	
	8		Hostile T.M's more active. Usual Lewis Gun firing during night.	
	9		Enemy shelled LUMP LANE and HIND SUPPORT – getting some direct hits. Usual activity by our Artillery.	
	10		Shoots were carried out by our Artillery according to plan. During tour in Front line, general drainage, grading and improving trenches etc. was carried on, under R.E supervision	G/F

T2134. Wt. W708–776. 500000. 4/15. Sir J. C. & S.

7/8 Royal Irish Fusiliers

Instructions regarding War Diaries and Intelligence Summaries are contained in F. S. Regs., Part II. and the Staff Manual respectively. Title pages will be prepared in manuscript.

WAR DIARY or ~~INTELLIGENCE~~ SUMMARY.

(Erase heading not required.)

October 1917.

Army Form C. 2118.

Ref. MAP. Sheet 51b SW 1/10000

Place	Date	Hour	Summary of Events and Information	Remarks and references to Appendices
LEFT Sub section FONTAINE	1917 Oct 10		The 48th Inf: Bde (less M G Coy) relieved the 49th Inf Bde (less M. G. Coy) in the left section. The battalion was relieved by 2nd Royal Dublin Fusiliers in the left subsection, and on relief being completed moved to ARMAGH CAMP. (Sheet 51b S. 23. c. 3.3)	G/F
ARMAGH CAMP	11		Checking deficiencies. fitting clothing. cleaning up. Baths etc.	
	12		Company training. Specialist training. etc. Games in afternoon. Improvements in camp	
	13		do	G/F
	14		Church Parade.	G/F
	15		Musketry. Bayonet fighting. specialists training. Wiring (SC.177) Improvements in camp.	G/F
	16/19		do	
	20		do	
	21		Church Parade. Battn sports. Lewis Gun & Bombing &c competitions	WH
Left Sub Section FONTAINE	22		The 49th Inf. Bdge. relieved the 48th Inf Bde in the Left Section. The Battn relieved the 8th R. Dublin Fus in the left sub section. Relief was complete by 4.40 pm. At 5.30 pm 20 shells of 5.9 and 4.2 were put on CLAW TRENCH causing no damage. With the exception of	

T2134. Wt. W708–776. 500000. 4/15. Sir J. C. & S.

1/8th (S) Battn ROYAL IRISH FUSILIERS

WAR DIARY
or
~~INTELLIGENCE SUMMARY.~~
(Erase heading not required.)

OCTOBER 1917

Army Form C. 2118.

Instructions regarding War Diaries and Intelligence Summaries are contained in F. S. Regs., Part II. and the Staff Manual respectively. Title pages will be prepared in manuscript.

Place	Date	Hour	Summary of Events and Information Ref. Sheet 51 b SW 1/10,000	Remarks and references to Appendices
LEFT Sub-sector. FONTAINE			a few whiz-bangs on LUMP LANE in retaliation for our artillery fire on TUNNEL TR. One of our patrols encountered a hostile patrol of about 20 men. They returned & Lewis Gun fire was brought to bear on the hostile patrol. He continued to use green lights for artillery direction, ie to lengthen range.	W.I.
23 · 10 · 17			The day passed unusually quietly owing to bad weather & low visibility. Our Lewis Guns fired 3000 rounds on enemy parapets during the night without drawing retaliation. At 9pm ~~and~~ 1am & 5.30 am the enemy was observed signalling from his front line into No Man's Land.	W.I.
24 10 · 17			With good visibility, our aeroplanes and artillery were active throughout the day. From 12.45pm until 1.30pm a combined M.G, TM & artillery strafe was carried out on our right with good results observed. Enemy retaliation was slight. The night again passed quietly. Enemy machine gun fire was slightly more active. Light signals were used from the front line. At 12 noon a few aerial darts fell in the vicinity of O 7/4.	W.I.
25 · 10 · 17			During the day many small parties of the enemy were observed walking about in rear of their line. We successfully fired on these parties with our Lewis Guns on several	

7/8th (S) Battn R. IRISH FUSILIERS

Instructions regarding War Diaries and Intelligence Summaries are contained in F. S. Regs., Part II. and the Staff Manual respectively. Title pages will be prepared in manuscript.

WAR DIARY
or
INTELLIGENCE SUMMARY.
(Erase heading not required.)

OCTOBER 1917

Army Form C. 2118.

Place	Date	Hour	Ref Sheet 51B. SW 1/10,000 — Summary of Events and Information	Remarks and references to Appendices
LEFT SUB SECTION FONTAINE	25/10/17		occasions. Hostile artillery was inactive. 10 4.2"s fell on front line in 1/2. Owing to the bad weather & change in direction of the wind, we were unable to discharge gas on our immediate right.	W.S.
	26.10.17		Weather conditions during the day were variable but good observation was possible. Our artillery especially the 18-pdrs were more active than usual throughout the day. The enemy retaliation & counter battery was slight. At 10 pm & 3 am we ~~sent over~~ bombarded the enemy front line at TUNNEL TRENCH with gas in shells & mortars. Each bombardment lasted about 10 minutes and in spite of their SOS no retaliating fire was sent over. During the bombardments & at 11.15 pm, he bombed his own wire & our sap at KING'S ~~HEAD~~ POINT. Hostile machine guns were more active during the night, especially during the strafes, traversing LUMP LANE & SHAFT TRENCH. The absence of hostile artillery is very marked.	W.S.
	27.10.17		Day passed very quietly. From 3.15 pm to 3.45 pm, a combined T.M., M.G. and artillery strafe was carried out on our right. The enemy did not retaliate on the front line, sending a few shells well over in the direction of the ~~CHALK~~ QUARRY. Our Lewis Guns fired intermittently throughout the night & assisted during the strafe by enfilading	

T2134. Wt. W708–776. 500000. 4/15. Sir J. C. & S.

7/8th (S) Battn ROYAL IRISH FUSILIERS

WAR DIARY
or
INTELLIGENCE SUMMARY.

(*Erase heading not required.*)

OCTOBER 1917

Army Form C. 2118.

Instructions regarding War Diaries and Intelligence Summaries are contained in F. S. Regs., Part II. and the Staff Manual respectively. Title pages will be prepared in manuscript.

Place	Date	Hour	Summary of Events and Information (Reference Sheet 51b SW 1/10,000)	Remarks and references to Appendices
LEFT SUB-SECTION FONTAINE	27-10-17 (contd)		TUNNEL TRENCH. Night passed very quietly. Our casualties during this tour have been 1 man wounded.	WS
LEFT SUPPORT CROISILLES	28-10-17		The 4th (S.I.H.) Battn ROYAL IRISH Regt relieved the battn in the left sub-section. Relief was complete by 3.30 pm. On relief the battn moved into Brigade support in CROISILLES.	WS
	29-10-17		In support. Supplied daily working parties to RE in forward areas. Continued work on dugouts &c under RE supervision. At 4.45 pm, the 7/8th R. Innis. Fus carried out a successful raid on the right sub-section, taking 3 prisoners, killing and wounding at least 50 of the enemy.	WS
	30-10-17		Remained in support.	WS
	31-10-17		Ditto	

T. O'Donnell Major ~~Lieut.-Col.~~
Comdg. 7/8th (S) Bn. Rl. Irish Fus.

T2131. Wt. W708-776. 500000. 4/15. Sir J. C. & S.

[illegible]

[illegible]

10.3 p.m. [illegible]

[illegible]

10.2 p.m. [illegible]

[illegible]

[illegible] 10.15 p.m. [illegible]

10.10 p.m. [illegible]

[illegible]

10.14 p.m. [illegible]

[illegible]

[illegible]

Saving the [illegible]
[illegible]
the [illegible]
right of [illegible]
[illegible]
[illegible]
[illegible]
[illegible]

[illegible]
[illegible]
[illegible]
[illegible]

27 [illegible]

[illegible]

[illegible]

[illegible]

[illegible]

[illegible]

[illegible]

[illegible]

[illegible]

[illegible]

[illegible]

[illegible]

[illegible]

[illegible]

[illegible] LANE [illegible]

[illegible] PUMP LANE & BURG

SUPPORT [illegible] no damage

AT 3.35 AM [illegible]

[illegible]

[illegible]

[illegible]

27.10.17

W. H. Waters
LIEUT
[illegible]

SECRET. OCTOBER 25th.1917. COPY NO........

7/8th.(S)Battalion The Royal Irish Fusiliers Order No.30.

Reference Map 51.B.,S.W. 4.

1. On the ~~night~~ night 26th/27th.Octoberor the first suitable night after that date,No.3.Special Coy.R.E.will carry out a Gas and Smoke Bombardment with 4" Stokes Mortars of TUNNEL TRENCH from JOVE MEBUS (U.20.b.47.70.) to junction with FRINGE TRENCH (U.7.b.45.40.)

2. The front to be dealt with is divided into four sectors.A.B.C.D. Ten guns will fire on each sector.

3. The Bombardment will be carried out in two shoots as under :-

SHOOT	TIME	SECTOR	MORTARS	ROUNDS PER GUN	TOTAL
(a)	10.0.p.m. Oct.26th.	A.B.C.D.	40.	30.	1200.
(b)	3.0.a.m. Oct.27th.	A.B.C.D. A.	40.	30.	1200.

The 30 rounds per Gun fired on each occasion will be made up as follows:-

15.rounds P.S.
10.rounds C.G.
5.rounds Smoke.

4. Firing will take place in ~~any~~ wind between W and S.S.W.

5.(a) If weather conditions are clearly unfavourable at 1.30.p.m. on October 26th,the code word "CASE"will be sent from Bn.H.Qrs. to all concerned.This will mean"**both** bombardments postponed twenty hours".
four

(b) If the weather conditions appear favourable at 1.0.p.m.October 26th.the code word "JUMP"will be sent out.If subsequently conditions become unfavourable,O.C.Special Coy.R.E.will send the code word "RANDOM"from 49th.Inf.Bde.H.Q.to Div.H.Q.by whom it will be repeated to all concerned.This will only refer to the first bombardment.The second bombardment will take place unless the word "RANDOM"is repeated a second time.
New Code words will be sent out on Oct.27th.and each day following a postponement of both bombardments.

6. O.C."C"Coy.will have the following trenches cleared ten minutes before ZERO in each bombardment.
(a)LUMP LANE (except for sap at U.7.b.10.00.)care will be taken to clear LUMP LANE silently and in small parties only.
Troops will as far as possible be accommodated under cover.
Above positions will be reoccupied 15 minutes after "ALL CLEAR" is given by O.C.Special Coy.R.E. In all cases a careful reconnaissance will be made of all trenches to see that they are clear of "GAS"

7. An Officer No.3.Special Coy.R.E.will be sent to Coy.H.Qrs at junction of LUMP LANE and BURG SUPPORT,and one to Coy.H.Q.in LINCOLN SUPPORT,where Lieut.W.H.WATERS will act as Liason Officer to whom the"all clear" as regards D and C Sectors will be given. Lieut.Waters will report at the first named Coy.H.Qrs.half an hour before ZERO in each bombardment.

SHEET 3.

8. All Dugout Curtains in LINCOLN SUPPORT and N.E. of LINCOLN SUPPORT will be dropped, and extra precautions will be taken to see that all ranks carry their Box Respirators in the "ALERT" position ready to put on at once.

9. The Machine Guns covering the front will enfilade TUNNEL TRENCH, NO MAN's LAND and main communication trenches in rear commencing at each ZERO hour under orders to be issued by D.M.G.O.

10. 16th.D.A. will arrange for bursts of shrapnel on the main Communication trenches and tracks in rear of TUNNEL TRENCH during each discharge from ZERO plus 3. to ZERO plus 15.

11. Signal Time will be sent to all concerned at 5.0.p.m. on the day of the bombardment.

12. ACKNOWLEDGE.

Captain & A/Adjutant.

7/8th.(S)Battalion The Royal Irish Fusiliers.

ISSUED THROUGH SIGNALS AT 3.0.p.m. 25th.inst.

Copy No.1. "A"Coy.
2. "B"Coy.
3. "C"Coy. Map Attached.
4. "D"Coy.
5 & 6. War Diary.

SECRET. OCTOBER 27th.1917 COPY NO...13......

7/8th.(S)Battalion the Royal Irish Fusiliers Order No.51.

---

1. The following relief will be carried out on the [illegible] October 1917.
The 7/8th.Royal Inniskilling Fusiliers will relieve the 2nd.Royal Irish Regiment in the Right Subsection.
The 7th.(S.I.H.)R.Irish Regiment will relieve the 7/8th.Royal Irish Fusiliers in the Left Subsection.
Relief to be complete by [illegible]p.m.

2. On Relief the Battalion will move into Brigade Support as under:-
Battalion H.Qrs. T.[illegible] "A"Coy. T.17.[illegible]
"B"Coy. SHAFT TRENCH. "C"Coy. T.[illegible]
"D"Coy."C.POINT" [illegible] 10. H.Qrs.at [illegible]

3. "B"Coy.S.I.H.will relieve "C"Coy.7/8th.Royal Irish Fusiliers.
"A"Coy.S.I.H. will relieve "A"Coy. 7/8th.Royal Irish Fusiliers
"C"Coy.S.I.H. will relieve "D"Coy.7/8th.Royal Irish Fusiliers.
"D"Coy. S.I.H.will relieve "B"Coy.7/8th.Royal Irish Fusiliers.

4. On Relief "B"Coy.7/8th.Royal Irish Fusiliers will move into the xx position vacated by "B"Coy.S.I.H.

5. <u>GUIDES.</u> Four Guides from "C","D" & "A"Coys' will be at "C"[illegible] at [illegible]p.m.Four Guides from "B"Coy.will be at QUARRY (T.18.b.[illegible]) at [illegible]p.m.Each Guide will be provided with a slip of paper stating the Coy.of the S.I.H. that he is to guide.The Right Coy.must be x clear of JAMES AVENUE by [illegible]p.m.

6. One N.C.O.per Coy.and one from Battalion H.Qrs.will take over from the corresponding Coys.S.I.H.by 12 noon.Trench Returns must be sent in by 12 noon.

7. Twenty four Lewis Gun Drums will be handed over in the line.The ~~Transport Officer will arrange to collect Drums from Transport Lines S.I.H.~~

8. <u>MOVEMENT.</u> Platoons at five minutes interval.The Transport Officer will arrange to send 1/2 limber to "C"Coy.at QUARRY;Maltese Cart and limber to "C"10.for Battalion H.Qrs.and "A"Coy. at [illegible]p.m.

9. <u>HANDING OVER.</u> Great care must be taken in handing over trench stores,defence plans,work in progress and proposed.Trench Store Lists to be sent in by [illegible]p.m. 29th.inst.

10. Rations and Water will be sent up as usual.Cooks and Orderly men will leave for their new positions as soon after dinners as possible. L/Cpl.MILLER will remain behind and hand over

11. Relief complete to be reported to Battalion H.Qrs. in Code.

12. <u>ACKNOWLEDGE.</u>

[signature]

Captain & A/Adjutant.

7/8th.(S)Battalion the Royal Irish Fusiliers

<u>ISSUED THROUGH SIGNALS AT [illegible]p.m.</u>

Copy No.		Copy No.	
1.	"A"Coy.	8.	Signals
2.	"B"Coy.	9.	R.M.O.
3.	"C"Coy.	10.	7.(S.I.H.)R.Irish Regt.
4.	"D"Coy.	11.	H.Q.49.Inf.Bde.
5.	Q.M.	12.	Spare.
6.	T.O.	13.)	War Diary.
7.	M.O.	14.)	

SECRET. OCTOBER 27th.1917 COPY NO.....14.....

7/8th.(S)Battalion The Royal Irish Fusiliers Order No.[illegible]

---

1. The following relief will be carried out on the 28th.October 1917. The 7/8th.Royal Inniskilling Fusiliers will relieve the 2nd.Royal Irish Regiment in the Right Subsection.
The 7th.(S.I.H.)R.Irish Regiment will relieve the 7/8th.Royal Irish Fusiliers in the Left Subsection.
Relief to be complete by [illegible] p.m.

2. On Relief the Battalion will move into Brigade Support as under:-
Battalion H.Qrs. T.[illegible] "A"Coy. T.17.c.[illegible]
"B"Coy. SHAFT TRENCH. "C"Coy. T.[illegible]
"D"Coy."C.POINT" 8.and 10. H.Qrs.at C.9.

3. "B"Coy. S.I.H.will relieve "C"Coy.7/8th.Royal Irish Fusiliers.
"A"Coy.S.I.H. will relieve "A"Coy. 7/8th.Royal Irish Fusiliers
"C"Coy.S.I.H. will relieve "B"Coy.7/8th.Royal Irish Fusiliers.
"D"Coy. S.I.H.will relieve "D"Coy.7/8th.Royal Irish Fusiliers.

4. On Relief "B"Coy.7/8th.Royal Irish Fusiliers will move into the position vacated by "B"Coy.S.I.H.

5. GUIDES. Four Guides from "B","D" & "A"Coys' will be at "C"[illegible] at [illegible] p.m. Four Guides from "C"Coy.will be at QUARRY (T.[illegible]) at [illegible] p.m. Each Guide will be provided with a slip of paper stating the Coy.of the S.I.H.that he is to guide. The Right Coy.must be clear of [illegible] AVENUE by [illegible] p.m.

6. One N.C.O.per Coy.and one from Battalion H.Qrs.will take over from the corresponding Coys.S.I.H.by 12 noon. Grenade Returns must be sent in by 12 noon.

7. Twenty four Lewis Gun Drums will be handed over in the Line. The Transport Officer will arrange to collect Drums from Transport Lines S.I.H.

8. MOVEMENT. Platoons at five minutes interval. The Transport Officer will arrange to send 1/2 limber to "C"Coy.at QUARRY; Maltese Cart and limber to "C"10.for Battalion H.Qrs.and "A"Coy. at [illegible] p.m.

9. HANDING OVER. Great care must be taken in handing over trench stores, defence plans, work in progress and proposed. Trench Store Lists to be sent in by [illegible] p.m. 28th.inst.

10. Rations and Water will be sent up as usual. Cooks and Orderly men will leave for their new positions as soon after dinners as possible. L/Cpl.[illegible] will remain behind and hand over

11. Relief complete to be reported to Battalion H.Qrs. in Code.

12. ACKNOWLEDGE.

[signature]

Captain & A/Adjutant.

7/8th.(S)Battalion The Royal Irish Fusiliers

ISSUED THROUGH SIGNALS AT [illegible] a.m.

Copy No.1.	"A"Coy.	Copy.No. 8.	Signals
2.	"B"Coy.	9.	R.M.O.
3.	"C"Coy.	10.	7.(S.I.H)R.Irish Regt.
4.	"D"Coy.	11.	H.Q. 49.Inf.Bde.
5.	C.O.	12.	Spare.
6.	T.O.	13.}	War Diary.
7.	M.O.	14.}	

SECRET. OCTOBER [illegible]th.1917. Copy No.....14.....

7/8th.S.Bn.ROYAL IRISH FUSILIERS. Order. No. 29.

-:-

Reference Sheet 51 B.S.W.1/10,000.
(less M.G.Coy.)

I. The 49th.Inf.Bde.will relieve the 48th.Inf.Bde.(less M.G.Coy.) in the LEFT SECTION on the 22nd.October.

2. The Battalion will relieve the 8th.R.DUBLIN FUS.in the LEFT SUB-SECTION. Companies will relieve as under :-
"C"Coy.on the right. "A"Coy.on the right centre.
"D"Coy.on the left centre. "B"Coy. on the left.

3. Advance parties consisting of One Officer, One NCO. and One Gas N.C.O., No.Is. of L.G.Teams and Signallers from each Coy., and R.S.M., Gas N.C.O. and necessary Signallers from Headquarters will take over by I p.m.

4. All Officers' kits, etc., to be left behind will be stacked outside H.Q.Mess by 12.30.p.m.
All trench kits, mess kits, etc., will be stacked outside Orderly Room by Coys.at 12.30.p.m.

5. One limber for H.Q., One limber for M.O.and Orderly Room, ½ limber per Coy.for kits will be available. The Transport Officer will arrange to send on the limbers of A,B,and D Coys.to C.IO, and that of C.Coy.to the QUARRY so that limbers can be unpacked before Companies arrive. One servant per Coy.will accompany the limber.

6. Order of March will be :-
"C" and "A"Coys.will march out at 1.0.p.m.
"D"Coy. " " " " 1.20.p.m.
"B"Coy. will " " " 1.35 p.m.
All movement will be by platoons at 5 minutes interval.
Dinners will be at 11.30.a.m.

7. The usual arrangements for rations and water will be made. Rations will be dumped at 5.30.p.m.at
QUARRY......for "C"Coy., STALYBRIDGE....for "A" "D" and "B"Coys.

8. Four guides per Coy.will be sent as under :-
"C"Coys..... ..at QUARRY at 3.0.p.m.
"A" "D" and "B"Coys.at C.IO at 3.0.p.m.

9. Taking over lists will be forwarded to Bn.H.Q.by 9.0.a.m.on the 23rd.Oct. All trench stores, etc., work in progress and proposed will be carefully taken over. Aeroplane photos will not be taken over.

10. Blankets will be rolled in bundles of 10 and handed in to Coy. Stores and clearly labelled. Twenty four Magazines per gun will be taken over from the 8th.R.DUBLIN FUS. A corresponding number will be handed over by the Transport Officer.

II. Completion of relief will be reported to Bn.H.Q.in Code.

12. ACKNOWLEDGE.

[illegible signature]
Capt. & a/Adjutant,
7/8th.S.Bn.R.IRISH FUSILIERS.

[illegible]/8th. R. IRISH FUSILIERS. Copy No. 8.

ACTION IN THE EVENT OF AN ENEMY WITHDRAWAL.

-.-

[illegible]

SECRET.

1. These instructions are issued in order that no time may be lost in following up the Enemy should he withdraw to the QUEANT-DROCOURT Line for the Winter. All previous instructions are cancelled.

2. Very active patrolling by night and careful observation by day is to be maintained in order to prevent the Enemy from abandoning his present line unobserved.
Any indications of a withdrawal are to be reported at once.

3. Process of following up the Enemy should he retire must necessarily be deliberate, but touch with him must be maintained.
If the Battalion is in the Front Line :-
(a) The Right Company will push forward two platoons into the unoccupied portion of [illegible] TRENCH.
(b) Two reconnoitring patrols (one platoon under an officer) from each Company will be pushed forward and establish themselves on the Line,
U.[illegible] - U.[illegible] - U.[illegible]. (Marked on map.)
These patrols will be followed by one platoon from each Coy., who will establish themselves on the INTERMEDIATE OBJECTIVE as a protective detachment.
(c) On completion of above and as soon as the protective detachments have established themselves and got touch with Units on either flank, the two remaining platoons of each Company will advance into the Enemy's trenches and establish themselves as a reserve to their protective detachments.
(d) On communications being established Bn. H.Q. will move to present Left Coy. H.Q.
(e) Right Boundary of the Battalion is the [illegible] LINE (Inclusive.) as far as U.[illegible] 80./ to point U.[illegible].

4. If the Battalion is in Support
(a) Companies will move into positions in our original Front Line.
Two Companies into the Front Line.
Two Companies in Reserve in SHAFT TRENCH.
(b) Bn. H.Q. will move to present Bn. H.Q. in Front Line.

5. If the Battalion is in Divisional Reserve.
The Brigade will be ordered to move up in Support.

[signature]
Capt. & A/Adjutant,
13.10.17. [illegible]/8th. R. IRISH FUSILIERS.

S E C R E T. OCTOBER 3rd.1917 COPY NO..14....

7/8th.(S)Battalion The Royal Irish Fusiliers Order No.37.

Reference SHEET 51,B.,S.W. 1/20,000

1. The Battalion will relieve the 7th.Royal Irish Rifles in the Left Front Subsection on October 5th.1917 Relief to be completed by 5.0.p.m.

2. On Completion of Relief the Battalion will be disposed as follows from Left to Right.
"C"Coy., "B"Coy, "D"Coy., "A"Coy., H.Qrs. at T.6.40.90.

3. "A"Coy.7/8th.R.Irish Fusiliers will relieve "D"Coy.7.R.Irish Rifles.
"B"Coy.7/8th.R.Irish Fusiliers will relieve "A"Coy.7.R.Irish Rifles.
"C"Coy.7/8th.R.Irish Fusiliers will relieve "B"Coy.7.R.Irish Rifles.
"D"Coy.7/8th.R.Irish Fusrs will relieve "C"Coy.7.R.Irish Rifles.

4. GUIDES FOR :-
"A"Coy. 2.0.p.m. at the QUARRY at T.18.b.8.4.NELLY AVENUE and JANET LANE to be cleared by 3.30.p.m.
"C"Coy. 2.30.p.m.at STALYBRIDGE DUMP T.5.b.5.4.
"D"Coy. 2.0.p.m. ditto ditto.
Headquarters and "B"Coy.will make their own arrangements.

5. Advance Parties,composition as usual will report at the various H.Qrs. concerned at 11.0.a.m.The advanced parties of the relieving Unit will report at the same hour

6. Working Hours in the line will be from 9.0. to 12 noon and 2.0.to 4.0pm

7. All work,defence arrangements,trench stores etc.will be carefully handed over.Trench Store Lists will be sent to Bn.H.Qrs.by 9.0.a.m. 5th.inst.

8. All Movement will be by platoons at five minutes interval.Great care must be taken that parties do not come under observation.

9. "A"Coy's rations and water will be drawn from the Quarry,T.18.b.8.4. where a water cart will be kept and cooking done.This cart can be filled by day.H.Qrs.and other Coys.will draw water and rations from STALYBRIDGE DUMP T.5.b.5.4.,where a cookhouse is available.The tank at this dump will be filled by Water Cart daily after dusk.Sufficient Hot Food Containers are available.

10. Completion of relief will be reported to Battalion H.Qrs.by Code.

11. ACKNOWLEDGE.

J. Loggins
Captain & A/Adjutant,
7/8th.(S)Battalion The Royal Irish Fusiliers

ISSUED THROUGH SIGNALS AT 4.0.p.m. 3rd.Oct.1917

Copy No.1. "A"Coy.
2. "B"Coy.
3. "C"Coy.
4. "D"Coy.
5. C.O.
6. M.O.
7. T.O.
8. R.Q.M.Sgt.

COPY NO. 9. R.S.M.
10. Signals.
11. 7.Royal Irish Rifles
12. H.Qrs.49th.Inf.Bde.
13. Spare.
14. File.
15. War Diary.
16. War Diary.

SECRET. OCTOBER 9th, 1917. Copy No...14.......

7/8th.S.Bn.R.IRISH FUSILIERS, Order No.28.

Reference Sheet 51 B.S.W.1/10,000.

I. The 48th.Inf.Bde.(less M.G.Coy.) will relieve the 49th.Inf.Bde.(less M.G.Coy.)in the left section on the 10th.October.

2. The Battalion will be relieved in the LEFT SUB-SECTION by the 2nd. R.DUBLIN FUS.and on completion of relief will move to ARMAGH CAMP. Coy.fronts will be taken over as now held.

3. Two guides from "C" "D" and "B"Coys.and one from H.Q.will be at STANBRIDGE at 2 p.m. "A"Coy.will send two guides to QUARRY at 2 p.m.

4. Advance parties of 2nd.R.DUBLIN FUS.,including Nos.1 of L.G.Teams, Signallers,Snipers and Observers will report atthe various Coy. and Bn.H.Q.to take over. A clean "BILL OF HEALTH" will be obtained by each Coy.Commander.

5. All maps,except aeroplane map,trench stores,details of Defence arrangements,and work in progress will be carefully handed over. Lists will be rendered to Orderly Room by 9 a.m.IIth.Inst.

6. Twelve petrol tins per Coy.and eight for H.Q.will be brought out of the line,and Box Periscopes will be handed over and a separate receipt obtained for them.

7. Lieut.F.L.CRILLY,four C.Q.M.S.,and SGT.Bird will take over ARMAGH Camp reporting there by 12 noon.

8. Half Limber per Coy.and H.Q.,Maltese Cart,and Mess Cart will be at Post C.10 at 3,30 p.m. One limber will be at the QUARRY at 4 p.m. for "A"Coy. Chargers for C.O.,Adjt.,and M.O.will be at Post C.10 at 4.30.p.m.

9. Completion of relief to be reported to Bn.H.Q. by wire,the word " FLEETWOOD" being used.

10. Arrival in Billets to be reported to Orderly Room.

II. ACKNOWLEDGE.

G.J. Coggins
Capt. & a/Adjutant,
7/8th.S.Bn.R.IRISH FUSILIERS.

Issued through Bn.Signals at............ 9.10.17

Copy No.I..........O.C."A"Coy.
Copy No.3...........O.C."C"Coy.
Copy No.5...........C.O.
Copy No.7...........T.O.
Copy No.9...........R.Q.M.S.
Copy No.11.........2nd.Bn.R.DUB.FUS.
Copy No.13 ....Spare.
Copy No.2........O.C."B"Coy.
Copy No.4........O.C."D"Coy.
Copy No.6........M.O.
Copy No.8........R.S.M.
Copy No.10......O.C.Bn.Sigs.
Copy No 12......49th.Inf.Bde.
Copies Nos.14 &15..War Diary.

SECRET OCTOBER 31st.1917. COPY NO.......13.

7/8th.(S)Battalion The Royal Irish Fusiliers Order No.31.

::

REFERENCE SHEET 51.B. 1/40,000.

---

1. The 49th.Infantry Brigade (less M.G.Coy.)will be relieved in the Left Sub-section by the 48th.Infantry Brigade (less M.G.Coy.)on November 1st.1917.

2. The Battalion will be relieved in the Left Support by 8/9th.Royal Dublin Fusiliers.Relief to be completed by 3.0.p.m.

3. On Relief the Battalion will move to A RANCH CAMP.

4. Lieut.C.E.W.MEAT and four C.Q.M.Sgts.will arrange to take over the Camp at 11.0.a.m. on 1st.inst.

5. "A"Coy.8/9.R.Dublin Fusiliers will relieve "B"Coy.7/8.R.Irish Fus.
"B"Coy.8/9.R.Dublin Fusiliers will relieve "D"Coy. ditto.
"C"Coy.8/9.R.Dublin Fusiliers will relieve "C"Coy.7/8.R.Irish Fus.
"D"Coy.8/9.R.Dublin Fusiliers will relieve "A"Coy.7/8.R.Irish Fus.

6. GUIDES Four Guides per Company and one from H.Qrs.will be at the undermentioned places at 1.30.p.m.
"B"Coy.7/8.R.Irish Fusiliers C.10.
"D"Coy. ditto C.6.
H.Q. & "A"Coy. ditto. T.23.d.15.80. (entrance to CROISSELLES)
"C"Coy. ditto. Trench Junction T.21.d.0.3.
Advance parties R.Dublin Fusiliers will arrive about 11.0.a.m.

7. Lewis Gun Drums will not be handed over.

8. All Trench Stores,defence plans,working parties,work in progress and proposed &c.will be carefully handed over.Aeroplane Photos will not be handed ver.Handing over lists to be sent to Battalion H.Qrs.by 7.0.p.m. day of Relief.

9. TRANSPORT Maltese Cart and one limber for H.Qrs.will be in SUNKEN ROAD T.23.d.15.80.at 3.0.p.m.One Limber for LewisGuns and Kit will be at :-
(1) "B"& "D"Coys. C.10. at 1.30.p.m.
(2) "A" &"C"Coys.at Coys.H.Qrs.at 1.30.p.m.
All Transport must be clear by 2.30.p.m.Transport Officer will arrange to send up the necessary boxes for Lewis Guns.Officers' Horses to be sent up,those for Battalion H.Qrs.to T.23.d.15.80.at 3.0.p.m.

10. Grenade Returns will be sent in by 9.0.a.m. 1st.inst.

11. While the Brigade is in Reserve the Transport Officer will arrange to fill the tanks at Bde.H.Qrs.at 9.30.a.m. commencing 2.11.17.

12. Completion of Relief to be reported in CODE.

13. Arrival in Camp to be reported to Orderly Room.

14. ACKNOWLEDGE.

Captain & A/Adjutant.
7/8th.(S)Battalion The Royal Irish Fusiliers.

ISSUED THROUGH SIGNALS AT 5.30.p.m. 31.10.17.

Copy No.1. "A"Coy.
2. "B"Coy.
3. "C"Coy.
4. "D"Coy.
5. Q.M.
6. M.O.
7. T.O.

Copy No.9. R.S.M.
10. Lewis G.Officer.
11. 8/9th.R.Dub.Fus.
12. 49.Inf.Bde.
13. Spare.
14. File.

14 J.

W A R D I A R Y

FOR MONTH OF NOVEMBER, 1917.

VOLUME:- 14

U N I T :- 1/8th R. Irish Fusiliers

Vol 22

7/8th (S) Battn ROYAL IRISH FUSILIERS

Instructions regarding War Diaries and Intelligence Summaries are contained in F. S. Regs., Part II. and the Staff Manual respectively. Title pages will be prepared in manuscript.

WAR DIARY or ~~INTELLIGENCE SUMMARY.~~

(Erase heading not required.)

NOVEMBER 1917

C/130

Army Form C. 2118.

Place	Date	Hour	Summary of Events and Information (Ref. Sheet France 51 B 1/40,000)	Remarks and references to Appendices
ARMAGH CAMP	1/11/17		The 48th Infantry Bde (less M.G. Company) relieved the 49th Inf. Bde (less M.G. Comp) in the Left Sector. The 8/9th R Dublin Fus relieved the Battn in left Support. Relief was complete by 3 pm & Battn moved into reserve at ARMAGH CAMP.	WL
	2/11/17		Day spent in cleaning up checking deficiencies &c.	WL
	3/11/17		Parades. Preliminary orders for the approaching offensive operation against TUNNEL TRENCH and TUNNEL SUPPT Trench.	WL
	4/11/17		Church parades. Recreation.	WL
	5/11/17		Training. Lt Col K.C. Weldon, D.S.O returned from sick leave and took over command of the Battn. A concert was held in the evening.	WL
	6/11/17		Training.	WL
	7/11/17		The 2nd R. Irish Regt and the Battn moved into Left and Right Support respectively, coming under orders of the G.O.C 48th Inf. Bde on relief. The Battn relieved the 1st R. Dublin Fus.	WL
	8/11/17		Remained in support. Provided working parties in the front line. 3 forward dumps of SAA &c.	WL
	9/11/17		" " " " " "	
	10/11/17		" " " " " "	
	11/11/17		"	

2353 Wt. W2544/1454 700,000 5/13 D. D. & L. A.D.S.S./Forms/C. 2118.

7/8th (S) Battn ROYAL IRISH FUSILIERS

Instructions regarding War Diaries and Intelligence Summaries are contained in F. S. Regs., Part II. and the Staff Manual respectively. Title pages will be prepared in manuscript.

WAR DIARY
or
~~INTELLIGENCE SUMMARY~~.
(Erase heading not required.)

NOVEMBER 1914

Army Form C. 2118.

Place	Date	Hour	Summary of Events and Information	Remarks and references to Appendices
			Ref Sheet	
ARMAGH CAMT	12.11.17		The 7/8th R. Innis Fus & 9th (S.I.H) R Irish Regt took over Right & Left Sub-sections. The Battn was relieved in Right support by the 1st R Dublin Fus, 48th Inf Bdge. On relief the Battn moved into Reserve in ARMAGH CAMP.	[illegible]
	13.11.17		Cleaning up, kits inspections &c.	WS.
	14.11.17		Baths. Independent attack practice by all companies in training area	[illegible]
	15.11.17		Practice attack in training area.	
	16.11.17		" " " " "	
	17.11.18		Final attack practice before Corps Commander.	
	18.11.18		~~The~~ D. Company took over the attack front, from KINGS POINT to PEAR LANE relieving a company of the 7/8 R. Inniskilling Fus	

2353 Wt. W2544/1454 700,000 5/15 D. D. & L. A.D.S.S./Forms/C. 2118.

7/8 (S) Battn Royal Irish Fusiliers

WAR DIARY

or

~~INTELLIGENCE SUMMARY.~~

(Erase heading not required.)

NOVEMBER 1917

Army Form C. 2118.

Instructions regarding War Diaries and Intelligence Summaries are contained in F. S. Regs., Part II. and the Staff Manual respectively. Title pages will be prepared in manuscript.

Place	Date	Hour	Summary of Events and Information	Remarks and references to Appendices
			Ref. Sheets 51 B 1/40000 Special Sheet U1 C6 57 C.N.W. 1/20000	
Right Sub Section FONTAINE lez	19.11.17		The Battn relieved the 7/8 R. Innis. Fus in the line. Two Companies being in the Quarry One Company in Sunken Road T 17 A and one Company in the front line	
CROISILLES	20.11.17		The Battn attacked with two Companies "A" and "B" in the line, "C" and "D" in support Special wiring parties having been detailed from "C" Coy. 1st Objective TUNNEL TRENCH. 2nd Objective TUNNEL SUPPORT. At Zero 6.20 a.m. our artillery barrage opened on TUNNEL lasting for 4 minutes, when it was lifted on to TUNNEL SUPPORT The Battn assembled without coming under any hostile shelling. TUNNEL trench was taken by "A" Coy without great opposition. "B" on the left was held up for about 3/4 of an hour by a machine gun post and suffered heavy casualties. The wiring parties were also broken up and wiring was not completed on the new front as arranged until the following night owing to losses ~~by~~ during the attack and by enemy snipers. All opposition was finally overcome by organised bombing parties and the whole of TUNNEL trench taken and consolidated. Strong points were made as previously directed in ① PRINCE trench, ② trench off OLDENBURG leading to PRINCE and ③ in OLDENBURG on left on TUNNEL SUPPORT. "A" Coy meanwhile had pushed on and taken	

2353 Wt. W2544/1454 700,000 5/15 D. D. & L. A.D.S.S./Forms/C. 2118.

Instructions regarding War Diaries and Intelligence Summaries are contained in F. S. Regs., Part II. and the Staff Manual respectively. Title pages will be prepared in manuscript.

7/8th (S) Battn Royal Irish Fusiliers

WAR DIARY
or
~~INTELLIGENCE SUMMARY.~~

(Erase heading not required.)

NOVEMBER 1917

Army Form C. 2118.

Place	Date	Hour	Summary of Events and Information	Remarks and references to Appendices
			page 2 (contd)	
R. Sub Section FONTAINE -les- CROISILLES	20.11.17		Tunnel Support trench. The enemy counter-attacked four times, at 9.30 am 1.30 pm, 2.30 pm and 4.30 pm. but an artillery barrage was put down on each occasion and the attacks dispersed under our rifle and Lewis gun fire. Immediately on reaching Tunnel trench small patrols were sent down to ascertain if there were any enemy present. After a little opposition those present surrendered and the patrols returned. A detachment of the R.E. then proceeded to cut the wires and clear the mines as directed which had been laid throughout the tunnel by the enemy. Information having been received that the enemy would probably attack that night, "C & D" Coys were re-organised and sent up from HdQrs as reinforcements. The Bn stood to during the night 20/21, but no attack was made.	
	21.11.17		The Bn was relieved at 4 pm on the 21st November by the 7/8 R. Inniskilling Fus. and took up its position in Support. Our casualties during the action on the 20th inst were:-	

	K.	W.	D of W	Missing	Total.
Officers	2	2	1	—	5.
O.R	19	79	3	5	106.

4/8th (S) Battn ROYAL IRISH FUSILIERS

WAR DIARY
or
~~INTELLIGENCE SUMMARY.~~
(Erase heading not required.)

NOVEMBER 1917

Army Form C. 2118.

Instructions regarding War Diaries and Intelligence Summaries are contained in F. S. Regs., Part II. and the Staff Manual respectively. Title pages will be prepared in manuscript.

Place	Date	Hour	Summary of Events and Information	Remarks and references to Appendices
Ref Sheet 1.23.c.4.9	22/11/17		The Battn was relieved in Brigade support by the 8/9th R Dublin Fus. On relief the Battn moved to ARMAGH CAMP.	[illegible]
ARMAGH CAMP	23/11/17		Day spent in cleaning up, refitting &c. Burial parties and search parties were sent up to the front line. "C" Company made concertina wire at 154th Coy RE, HAMLINCOURT and completed preparations for putting out another belt of wire in front of the captured trenches.	[illegible]
—do—	24/11/17		A party of 100 men composed of "C" Coy and a ~~mixing~~ ~~for~~ carrying party from "D" Coy, left camp in motor lorries at 4 pm. The party debussed at CROISILLES & carried wire from QUARRY to TUNNEL TR. A complete belt of barbed concertina wire was put out from LUMP LANE to OLDENBURG LANE. The party suffered no casualties.	[illegible]
—do—	25/11/17		At 9 am, orders were received to move up to the front line and relieve the 4th (S.I.H.) Battn R. Irish Regt in the Left Sub Section. The relief was complete by 6 pm; the Battn came under orders of G.O.C. 48th Inf. Bdge on relief. 2 officer reconnoitring patrols were sent out between 4 pm & 9 pm to find out whether the enemy was still in occupation of his present front line system. He was found to be still in occupation.	[illegible]
Left Sub Section FONTAINE lez CROISILLES	26/11/17		Reconnoitring patrols were sent out again between 12 midnight and 3 am. One patrol was fired on. The enemy was inactive during the night except for an occasional sniper. At 12.30 pm, he fired a few gas shells on HORN TR. Hostile aircraft was active at about 1.30 pm over	[illegible]

1/8th (S) Batt R. IRISH FUSILIERS

WAR DIARY
~~or~~
~~INTELLIGENCE SUMMARY.~~
(Erase heading not required.)

NOVEMBER 1917

Army Form C. 2118.

Instructions regarding War Diaries and Intelligence Summaries are contained in F. S. Regs., Part II. and the Staff Manual respectively. Title pages will be prepared in manuscript.

Place	Date	Hour	Summary of Events and Information (Ref Sheet 57 B. 1/40,000 Trench Map. Sheet U.1 to 26.)	Remarks and references to Appendices
LEFT Sub Sector.	26/11/17		FONTAINE. Our artillery displayed their usual activity in firing on trenches, suspected dugouts &c throughout the night harassing fire was maintained on his roads & dumps. Between 7 pm and 10 pm two reconnoitring patrols with the same object went out to ROTTEN ROW and SENSEE TR. Both patrols returned safely after being fired on by M.G's and rifles from these trenches. The night passed quietly on our front. A special order from Major-General W.B. Hickie, CB is attached.	[illegible]
	27/11/17		Our artillery continued their night firing programme on tracks, roads & FONTAINE. Enemy aircraft was more active during the day but his artillery remained inactive throughout the day. Two reconnoitring patrols maintained touch with the enemy in ROTTEN ROW & SENSEE TR. The enemy was found working hard on his front line. The right patrol of 1 off. and an NCO encountered a large hostile patrol & withdrawing to our own lines opened fire with rifles & Lewis Guns.	[illegible]
	28/11/17		The morning passed quietly. The usual movement was observed in FONTAINE. Our artillery was very active during the day & successfully engaged several working parties. About 3pm the enemy registered with 5.9 & 4.2 on our front line in the vicinity of FOP LANE but hostile artillery was inactive. The usual patrols found the enemy wiring his front line at ROTTEN TR & working in SENSEE TR. On the return of these patrols, working parties were engaged with Lewis Gun & artillery fire. At about 11 pm, 'B' & 'C' Coys relieved 'A' & 'D' Coys in the front line	[illegible]

7/8th (S) Battn R. IRISH FUSILIERS

WAR DIARY or ~~INTELLIGENCE SUMMARY.~~

(Erase heading not required.)

NOVEMBER 1917

Army Form C. 2118.

Instructions regarding War Diaries and Intelligence Summaries are contained in F. S. Regs., Part II. and the Staff Manual respectively. Title pages will be prepared in manuscript.

Place	Date	Hour	Summary of Events and Information	Remarks and references to Appendices
			Special sheet 51 B C6 Sheet 51 B S.W. 1/20,000	
LEFT SECTION FONTAINE	29/11/17		Except for slightly increased M.G. fire the night passed quietly. At 5.30 am the enemy put down a heavy barrage of 5.9 and 4.2 on our front line. Gas shells were also used. In response to SOS signals on our right and left, our artillery put down an SOS barrage. Heavy shelling continued for about 3/4 hour when the hostile barrage ceased. No enemy infantry action was attempted against our front. Our heavies continued to retaliate until about 15 minutes after hostile barrage ceased. Our only casualty was 1 O.R. slightly wounded. At about 11 pm, two officer patrols went out & discovered the enemy working on his front line. On being fired on, our patrols withdrew.	W.S. WH
	30/11/17		At 6am to 7am, & from 10am to 12 noon, the enemy heavily shelled our front line, communication trenches and the SENSEE VALLEY with 5.9, 4.2, 77mm & gas shells. His artillery showed greatly increased activity and intensity. The places receiving special attention were FOP FUN & FIT LANES, SHAFT TR & HIND AV. The barrage appeared to be more of a practice or skeleton barrage than destructive. Our casualties were 1 wounded at duty. The 1st R. Dublin Fus relieved the battn in the left sub-section. Relief was complete by 4.30 pm. On relief the battn moved to ARMAGH CAMP, under command of the G.O.C. 48th Inf. Bde.	W.H.

[signature] Lieut. Col.
Comdg. 7/8th (S) Bn. Rl. Irish Fus.

D. D. & L., London, E.C. (A7833) Wt. W803/M1672 350,000 4/17 Sch. 52a Forms/C2118/14

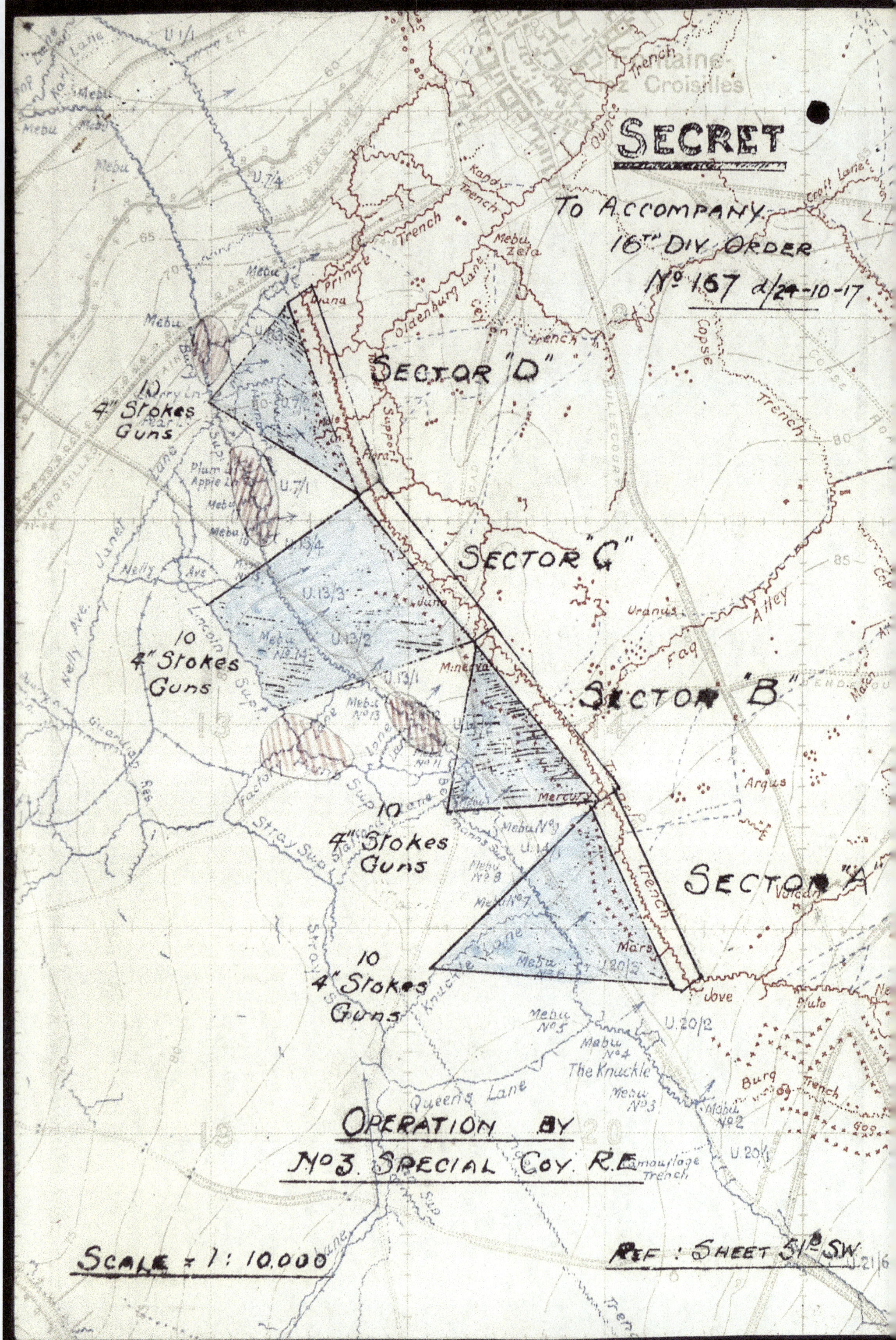
SECRET
TO ACCOMPANY
16TH DIV ORDER
No 167 d/24-10-17
SECTOR "D"
SECTOR "C"
SECTOR "B"
SECTOR "A"
10
4" Stokes
Guns
10
4" Stokes
Guns
10
4" Stokes
Guns
10
4" Stokes
Guns
OPERATION BY
No 3. SPECIAL COY. R.E.
SCALE = 1: 10.000
REF : SHEET 51B SW
Fontaine-lez Croisilles
Kandy Trench
Prince Trench
Oldenburg Lane
Ceylon Trench
Copse Trench
Croft Lane
Fag Alley
Uranus
Minerva
Mercury
Mars
Jove
Argus
Vulcan
Pluto
Burg Trench
The Knuckle
Queens Lane
Knuckle Lane
Lincoln Sup.
Nelly Ave
Stray Sup
Camouflage Trench

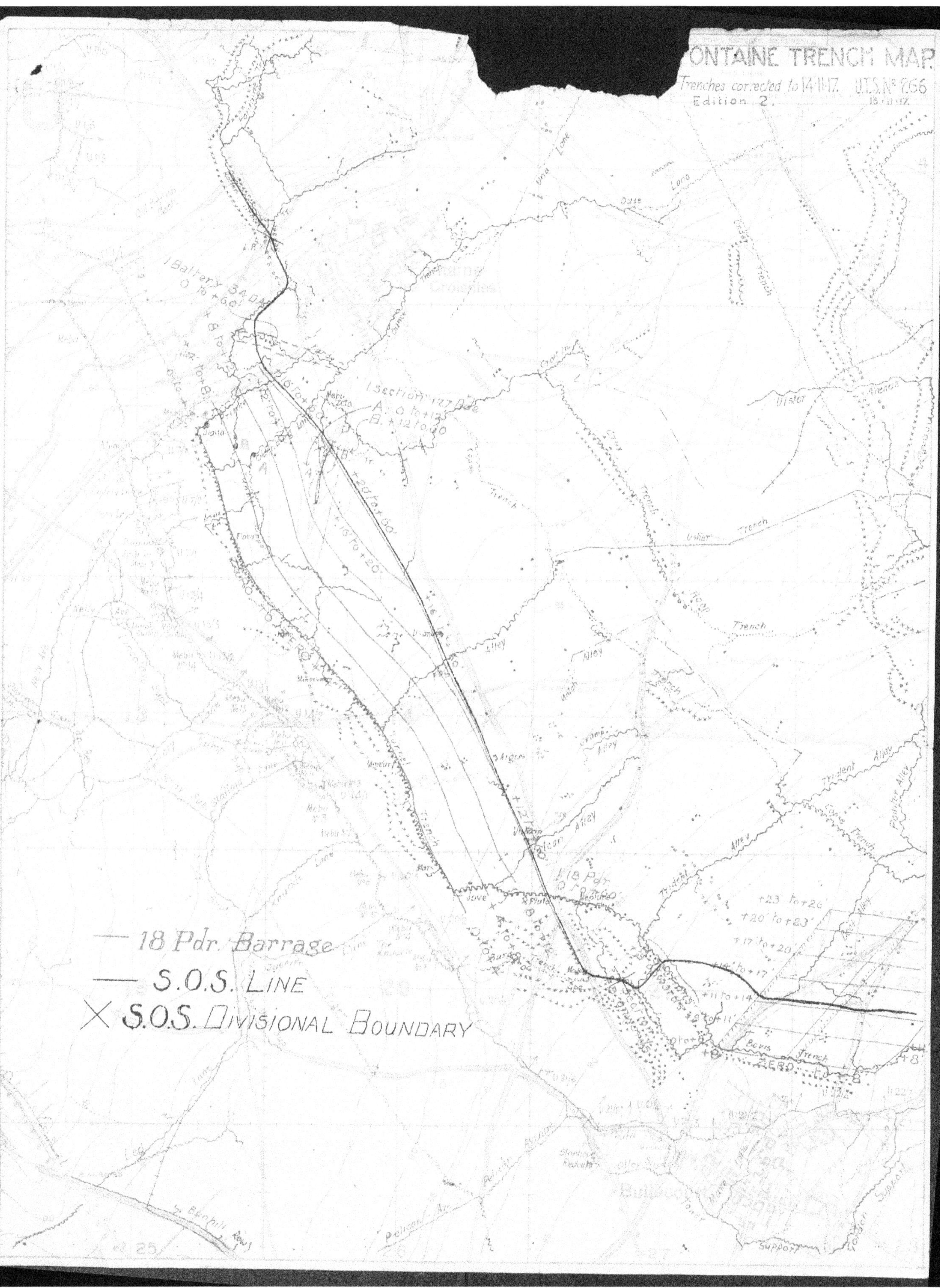

ONTAINE TRENCH MAP
Trenches corrected to 14.11.17.
U.T.S. Nº 266
Edition 2.
18 Pdr. Barrage
S.O.S. Line
S.O.S. Divisional Boundary

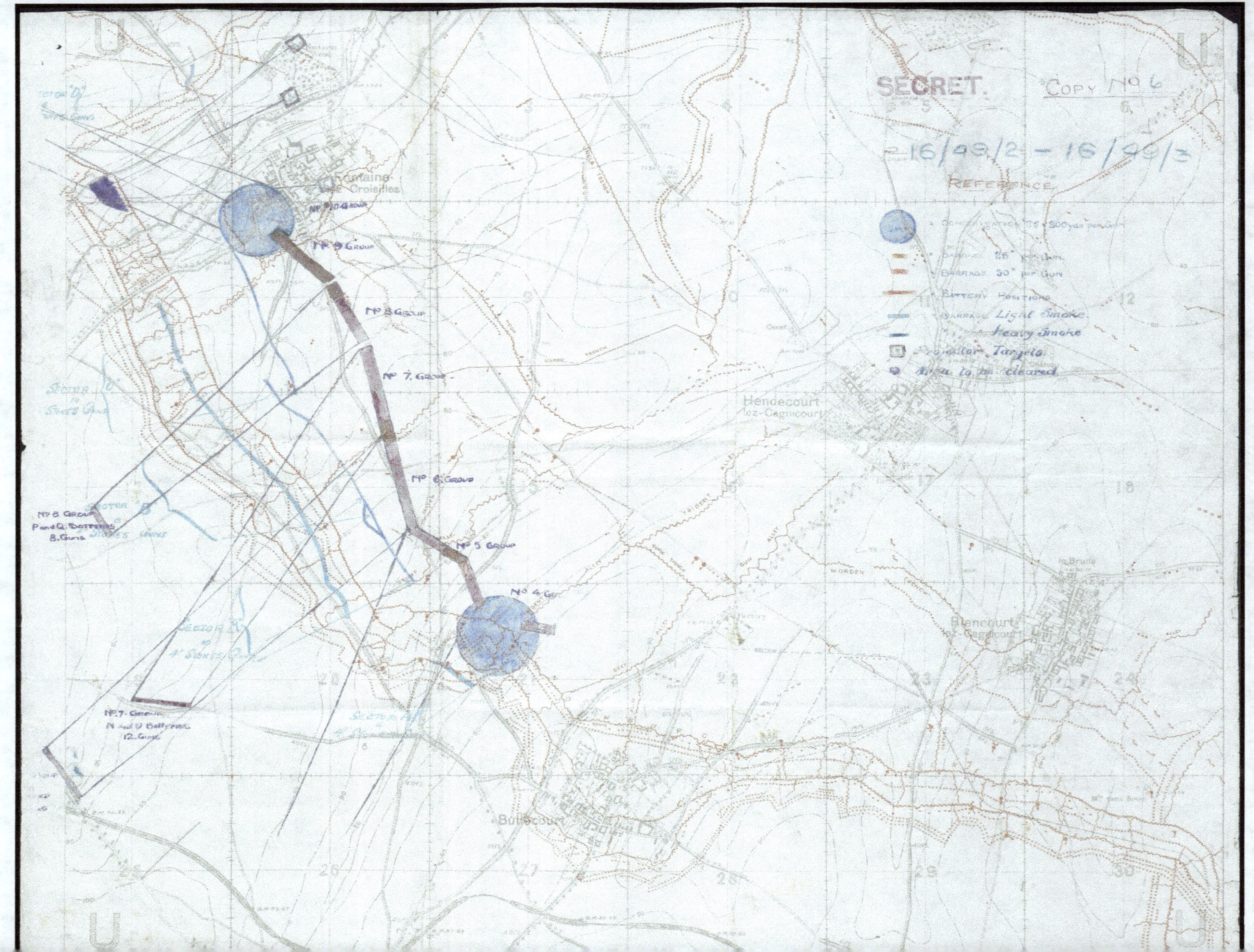

SECRET.
COPY No 6
16/49/2 – 16/49/3
REFERENCE
Light Smoke
Heavy Smoke
Area to be cleared
Hendecourt
lez-Cagnicourt
Riencourt
lez-Cagnicourt
Bullecourt
Fontaine
Croisilles
No 10 Group
No 9 Group
No 8 Group
No 7. Group
No 6. Group
No 5 Group
No 4 Gp
No 8 Group
P and Q. Batteries
8. Guns
No 7. Group
N and O Batteries
12. Guns

SECRET NOVEMBER 6th.1917 COPY NO..13.....

7/8th.(S)Battalion The Royal Irish Fusiliers.Warning Order.

The Battalion will move into Right Support to morrow.Leading Company will move off at about 1.30.p.m.Name of Battalion of the Royal Dublin Fusiliers to be relieved is not yet known.

The usual taking over parties will report to Right Support Battalion Headquarters T.33.d.4.8. for Guides at 11.30.a.m.

DISPOSITIONS ON RELIEF

"A"Company SUNKEN ROAD T.33.c.

"B"Company. SUNKEN ROAD T.33.a.

"C"Company QUARRY T.18.b.8.3.

"D"Company RAILWAY EMBANKMENT T.34.d.6.4.

Officers in charge Advance Parties will arrange for one guide per platoon to meet the Battalion at entrance to CROISSILLES T.23.d.15.80. about 3.0.p.m.

[signature]

Captain & A/Adjutant.

7/8th.(S)Battalion The Royal Irish Fusiliers

ISSUED THROUGH SIGNALS AT 6.30.p.m. 6th.inst.

Copy No.1. "A"Coy.
2. "B"Coy.
3. "C"Coy.
4. "D"Coy.
5. Transport Officer
6. M.Officer

Copy No.7. Quartermaster
8. Signals.
9. Lewis Gun Officer
10. R.S.M.
11. File
12. Spare.

13 & 14 WAR DIARY.

SECRET. NOVEMBER 6th, 1917. COPY NO. 13

7/8th. (S) Battalion The Royal Irish Fusiliers Order No. 54.

Reference Sheet 51.B.1/40,000

1. The 2nd. Royal Irish Regiment and 7/8th. Royal Irish Fusiliers will take over the Left and Right Support Positions of the Left Section to morrow 7th. inst.

2. The Battalion will relieve the 1st. Royal Dublin Fusiliers and on relief will come under orders of G.O.C. 48th. Infantry Brigade

3. Advance parties will proceed as already detailed. One Lewis Gunner per Company will also accompany them

4. Officers taking over will arrange for one guide per platoon at entrance to CROISSILLES (T.33.d.15.80.) at 1.30. p.m. All maps, trench stores, defence plans, working parties and work in progress and proposed will be carefully taken over. Trench Store lists will be sent to Battalion H.Qrs. not later than 7;0. p.m. the day of relief

5. Companies will march out of Camp in the following order.
"C" Coy. 1.30. p.m. "D" Coy. 1.50. p.m. "A" Coy. 2.10. p.m.
"B" Coy. 2.30. p.m. Battalion H.Qrs. 2.50. p.m.

6. Officers Kits etc will be stacked outside the Orderly Room at 12.45. p.m. Kits for the Trenches and those to be left behind must be stacked separately.

7. TRANSPORT One Limber per Coy. and H.Qrs. for Kit and Lewis Guns also Maltese Cart for M.O. will be available and will move in rear of their Companies. Horses ~~will be sent up to~~ for Battalion H.Qrs. at 2.15. p.m.

8. WATER The two filled Water Carts will proceed to T.33.d.15.80. at 3.0. p.m. and await orders. Twelve filled Petrol Tins will be sent up in each Company Limber.
RATIONS. Rations for 8th. inst will be sent up in the Limber.

9. Packs and Blankets will be stacked in Coy. Stores by 12 noon.

10. MEDICAL. R.A.P. is situated in SUNKEN ROAD T.33.c.

11. HANDING OVER
Lieut. C.E.W. NEAT will arrange to hand over the Camp to the 2nd. Royal Dublin Fusiliers at 11.30. a.m.

12. SOCKS. Arrangements about socks will be notified later.

13. Relief complete to be reported to Bn. H.Qrs. in Code.

14. ACKNOWLEDGE.

Captain & A/Adjutant.
7/8th. (S) Battalion The Royal Irish Fusiliers

Issued through Signals at 10.30. p.m.

Copy No. 1. "A" Coy.
2. "B" Coy.
3. "C" Coy.
4. "D" Coy.
5. Q.M.
6. M.O.
7. T.O.
8. Signal Officer

Copy No. 9. R.S.M.
10. Lewis Gun Officer.
11. 1st. R. Dublin Fusiliers
12. 49th. Inf. Bde.
13. Spare.
14. File.
15. & 16. War Diary.

War Diary

SECRET. 12th. November 1917 COPY NO......17....

7/8th.(S)Battalion The Royal Irish Fusiliers Order No.85.

Reference Sheet 51.B.,S.W. 1/10,000.

1. The 7/8th.Battalion The Royal Inniskilling Fusiliers and the 7th. (S.I.H.).R.Irish Regt.will take over the Left and Right Sub-section respectively on the 12th.inst.

2. The 2nd.Royal Irish Regiment and 7/8th.Royal Irish Fusiliers will be relieved in Support on 12th.inst.The Battalion will be relieved by the 1st.Royal Dublin Fusiliers.Relief to be complete by 5.0.p.m.

3. On Relief the Battalion will march to ARMAGH CAMP.

4. "A"Coy.7/8th.R.Irish Fusrs will be relieved by."X"Coy.1.R.Dub.Fusrs.
"B"Coy.R.Irish Fusrs.will be relieved by."W"Coy.1.R.Dub.Fusrs.
"C"Coy.7/8th.R.Irish Fusrs will be relieved by."Z"Coy.1.R.Dub.Fusrs.
"D"Coy.7/8th.R.Irish Fusrs.will be relieved by "Y"Coy.1.R.Dub.Fusrs.

5. GUIDES No Guides will be sent.

6. ADVANCE PARTIESAdvance Parties of 1.R.Dublin Fusiliers will take over four hours before relief commences

7. TRANSPORT
One Limber per Company will be sent upto each Coy.H.Qrs.at.3.0.p.m. One limber for Bn.H.Qrs.will be sent up as far as "A"Coy.,Maltese Cart will be sent to "B"Coy.also H.O's Horse.Horses will be sent up at above hours,and for Battalion H.Qrs. at 4.30.p.m.

8. LEWIS GUN Drums filled will be taken out.

9. HANDING OVER Officers' Commanding Companies will hand over carefully.
(a) All Trench Stores,maps,defence plans &c.
(b) All Work in progress and proposed.
Grenade Returns will be sent in by 12 noon.Reports on work done and work proposed will be sent to Battalion H.Qrs.by 10.0.a.m. 12th.inst. Trench Store Lists will be sent to BATTALION H.QRS. BY. 3.0.p.m.12th. inst.Great care must be taken to check the stores taken over and those handed over

10. TAKING OVER Lieut.F.L.CRILLY will arrange to take over ARMAGH CAMP at 11.0.a.m.

11. The Q.M.will arrange to have a hot meal ready for the Officers.

12. Completion of relief to be reported in "BAB"Code.

13. Arrival in Camp will be reported to Orderly Room.

14. ACKNOWLEDGE.

Captain & A/Adjutant.

7/8th.(S)Battalion The Royal Irish Fusiliers.

ISSUED THROUGH SIGNALS AT 3.0.p.m. 11th.inst.

Copy No.1. "A"Coy.
2. "B"Coy.
3. "C"Coy.
4. "D"Coy.
5. Q.M.
6. T.O.
7. M.O.
8. L.G.O.

Copy No.9. Signals.
10. R.S.M.
12. 1st.R.Dublin Fusrs.
13. 48th.Inf.Bde.
14. 49th.Inf.Bde.
15. File.
16 & 17. War Diary.

S E C R E T.   NOVEMBER 17th 1917   COPY NO.....18.....

7/8th.(S)Battalion The Royal Irish Fusiliers Order No.35.

REFERENCE MAPS:-   SHEETS 51.B., S.W. 1/20,000
                               57.C., N.W. 1/20,000
                        SPECIAL SHEET U.1.to.C.6. 1/10,000.

::

1. The 16th.Division is about to carry out an offensive with the object of occupying and consolidating the TUNNEL TRENCH and TUNNEL SUPPORT from JOVE NEBUS (U.30.b.30,70.) to the Junction of PRINCE and TUNNEL TRENCHES (U.7.b.45.15.) Final Objective marked on attached Map with a green line

2. DISPOSITION OF BRIGADE.

The 49th.Infantry Brigade will attack with the 2nd.Royal Irish Regt. on the RIGHT and the 7/8th.Royal Irish Fusiliers on the LEFT. The 7/8th. Royal Inniskilling Fusiliers will be in Support. The 7th.(S.I.H.) R.Irish Regt. will hold the line North of the CROISSILLES - FONTAINE ROAD.

3. BATTALION BOUNDARIES.

RIGHT.   PEAR LANE inclusive to. U.7.d.63.63. - U.7.d.88.73.
LEFT.   CROISSILLES -- FONTAINE ROAD inclusive.

4. The Battalion will attack with:-
"A"Company on the RIGHT   "B"Company on the LEFT.
"C" and "D"Companies will be in SUPPORT.

5. BOUNDARIES BETWEEN "A" and "B"Companies.
Disused Sap immediately S of LUMP LANE in HUMBER SUPPORT- U.7.d.51.93.
Trench Junction U.7.73;87. (inclusive to "B"Coy.)

6. ASSEMBLY POSITIONS.

"A"Company   HUMBER SUPPORT from PEAR LANE to disused sap immediately S.of LUMP LANE in HUMBER SUPPORT.
Coy.H.Qrs. NEBUS in BURG SUPPORT between PEAR LANE and JANET AVENUE.
"B"Coy. From disused Sap to CROISSILLES - FONTAINE ROAD.
Coy.H.Qrs. in deep dugout in BURG SUPPORT 50 yds.North of CHERRY LANE.
"D"Coy. BURG SUPPORT - PEAR LANE to CHERRY LANE.
Coy.H.Qrs. in deep dug out in BURG SUPPORT 50 yds.North of CHERRY LANE.
At ZERO plus four minutes,each section will move up to its wiring dump,pick up their stores and advance to TUNNEL TRENCH.

7. OBJECTIVES.
GENERAL IDEA.
To take portion of TUNNEL TRENCH and TUNNEL SUPPORT connect TUNNEL SUPPORT with TUNNEL TRENCH;establish Blocking Posts "A","B" and "C" marked on attached map.
"A"Company.
Two platoons take TUNNEL TRENCH from U.7.d.63.63. to U.7.d.51.93.
One Platoon take TUNNEL SUPPORT from U.7.d.88.73. to TRENCH JUNCTION U.7.d.75.88.
One Platoon to dig and man Posts "A" The Lewis Gun Section will cover the remainder of the Platoon. The Officer i/c Left Platoon will take over a flag and plant it at the Trench Junction U.7.d.75.87. as a guide to the Digging party.
"B"Company.
Two Platoons take TUNNEL TRENCH on the Left,and then dig new trench from Trench Junction U.7.d.75.87. to TUNNEL TRENCH at U.7.b.45.15.
On completion of this task these two platoons will man TUNNEL TRENCH to the top of LUMP LANE inclusive.
One Platoon will dig and man Post "B". The Lewis Gun Section will cover the remainder of the Platoon.
One Platoon will dig and man Post "C". The Lewis Gun Section will cover the remainder of the platoon.

SHEET. 3.

7. OBJECTIVES (Contd.)

"C"Company will wire the new position under orders from the C.R.E. On completion of this task they will return to dug out in BURG SUPPORT

"D"Company will remain in Support .When the two platoons 7/8th. Royal Inniskilling Fusiliers move up to BURG SUPPORT, two platoons will be sent to O.C."B"Company on receipt of orders from Bn.H.Qrs. They will assist in digging the new trench.

8. LEWIS GUNS.

"A" and "B"Coys. will establish all four Guns in the GREEN LINE and Blocking Posts."B"Coy.will establish one of the four guns in the top of LUMP LANE

"C"Coy's guns will be attached :- two to "A"Coy. and Two to "B"Coy. These guns will be established in TUNNEL TRENCH and will replace Casualties in the firing line.

"D"Company's Guns will remain with the Company.

9. HEADQUARTERS

Battalion H.Qrs.in Dug out at U.7.d.05.35.

40th.Infantry Brigade in Caves CROISSILLES.

2nd.The Royal Irish Regiment Dug out at U.7.d.15.30.

10. DRESS.

The following dress will be worn by all ranks during the forthcoming operations :-

FIGHTING ORDER.

(a) Clothing,arms and entrenching tool as issued.

(b) Equipment as issued,no haversack,sandbags will be provided for these and surplus kit.Packs will be worn.

(c) ~~Baxrazx~~ Box Respirators and P.H.HELMETS.

(d) Iron Rations,unexpended portion of the day's rations,mess tin and cover.Field dressing.

(e) Water proof sheets.

(f) Riflemen 150 rounds S.A.A.,2.Mills' Bombs.(One Rifle one Hand)

(g) Lewis Gunners 50 rounds S.A.A.,4 Lewis Gun-Drums.

(h) Bombers 100 rounds S.A.A.,Six Mills' Bombs.

(i) Rifle Bombers 100 rounds S.A.A.,Six Rifle Grenades,cartridges to be carried by one man per section in the tin box.

(j) Signallers 50 rounds S.A.A.

(k) Personnel of Company and Platoon H.Qrs.will carry 50 rounds S.A.A. and "P"Bombs.The "P"Bombs will be available at Dumps.

(l) Personnel of Battalion and Company H.Qrs.will carry Very Pistols and Ammunition and Six "S.O.S"Rifle Grenades per H.Qrs.

(m) Every man will carry two sandbags.

(n) Every man will carry a pick or a shovel,in proportion twenty per cent picks to eighty per cent shovels.

All Officers will wear men's equipment and will carry,Map,binoculars, Prismatic compass and watch.

11. No mention of these operations is to be made on any telephone.

12. DUMPS.

Advanced dumps have been formed at :-

"D"DUMP. Head of Sap 4.

"E"DUMP. In Small "T"Head Sap in Sap 4.about U.7.d.20,~~88~~ 66.

"F"DUMP. LUMP LANE U.7.b,23.08.

Each of the above dumps contain :-

S.A.A. ten boxes.,Mills' hand grenades 30 boxes,Mills' Rifle Gdes. 10 ~~X~~ boxes.,Very Lights 1". (White) 3 Boxes.,S.O.S.Rifle Grenades 4 ~~X~~ Boxes (3 in each box.)

An advanced Brigade Dump will be established and maintained in the Vicinity of the Junction of JANET AVENUE and BURG SUPPORT about U.7.d.0.3.This will contain S.A.A. 40 Boxes.,Mills' Hand Grenades 30 ~~X~~ Boxes.,Mills Rifle Grenades 50 Boxes.,Very Lights 1" (White) 4 ~~X~~ Boxes. 1½ Very Lights (White) One Box.,S.O.S.Rifle Grenades 3 ~~X~~ Boxes (Three in each Box.)

S H E E T 3.

12. DUMPS (Contd.)

The Method of establishing Dumps in captured ground is as follows :- O.C."D"Coy.will detail two parties of one N.C.O. and ten men,both under one Officer.As soon after ZERO as possible,these parties will move "D" and "E"Dumps to a site near the Junction of OLDENBURG LANE and TUNNEL TRENCH where two advanced Dumps will be made about ½ thirty yards apart.O.C."D"Company will then arrange to replenish and maintain the "D" and "E"Dumps in SAP 4.from the advanced Brigade Dump.These Dumps should be regarded as specially intended for operations and should not be drawn upon until after ZERO.

13. AEROPLANE.

There will be oneContact Aeroplane flying over the Divisional Frontage

14. MEDICAL.

Regimental Aid Post QUARRY T.18.b.3.4.
Regimental Bearers with a certain number of R.A.M.C.Bearers will clear to R.A.P.Four Drummers will be attached to "A"Coy.and two to "B"Coy.
Walking wounded from Attack Area will be directed by Sign Boards skirting the North and South sides of CROISSILLES to WALKING WOUNDED COLLECTING POST at JUDAS COPSE T.27.d. Central.,thence by Light Railway.Mortuary will be established in disused Sap.

15. PRISONERS OF WAR.

All prisoners will be sent to "D"Company who will then provide escort to the Divisional Cage at T. 33.c.4.7. the escort from "A", "B" or "C"Companies rejoining their Companies.On no account are men from the firing line to take prisoners further than Battalion H.Qrs. A N.C.O.will be detailed from Battalion H.Qrs.to supervise the sending down of prisoners.He will be stationed at the Junction of NELLY AVENUE and BURG SUPPORT.

16. COMMUNICATIONS.

FULLERPHONE. A Pair of lines will be run from Battalion H.Qrs.to the East end of LUMP LANE.When the Objective has been taken this line will be run out to about U.7.d.50.65.in TUNNEL TRENCH where communication will be established with Battalion H.Qrs.by Fullerphone
RUNNERS A Relay Post will be established in the QUARRY.
VISUAL. A Battalion Visual Station will be established in TUNNEL TRENCH T.7.d.60.85.This Station will send to the Brigade Station at T.8.c.30.75.and will be used by both Battalions.
POWER BUZZER. One will be established near Battalion H.Qrs.All messages sent by Power Buzzer must be sent by "B.A.B."Code.or by Field cipher.As any listening apparatus in use by the enemy is unlikely to be affected or disturbed by the proposed operations,it is important that every possible precaution should be taken to prevent the enemy from obtaining useful information in this way both before and after the attack.Code calls have been issued and will take the place of Position Calls from ZERO until further notice.

17. ARTILLERY.

The attack will be made under a creeping barrage.
(a) A Map shewing times of lift will be issued to all concerned.

17. ARTILLERY. (Contd.)

(b) The barrage will be put down at ZERO on the enemy front trench for four minutes. It will then lift on to his Support Line for four minutes and then lift until the protective barrage line is reached.

(c) From the time of reaching the Protective Barrage Line until ZERO plus one hour, 18.pdr.Batteries will fire smoke shells. At ZERO plus one hour fire on the Protective Barrage Line will cease except for "S.O.S."

(d) 18 pdr.Batteries will search Communication Trenches, roads ~~&c~~ etc. ~~At~~ ZERO plus three hours forty minutes.

(e) Area Searches will be carried out on the night following "Z"Day, starting from the "S.O.S"Line to a depth of 1,000 yds. at the following times:-

7.50.p.m.
10.15.p.m.
4.30.a.m.

Each Search will last for ten minutes.

(f) All available heavy batteries will carry out intense neutralization from ZERO to ZERO plus one hour.

18. VETERINARY.
There will be a Veterinary Aid Post at B.3.a.5.8.half a mile West of St LEGER.

19. The primary duty of burying the dead falls on the Unit concerned. and attention is drawn to regulations already issued as regards the disposal of effects. The usual cemeteries will be used. The Mortuary will be established in disused sap.

20. RATIONS.

Rations for "Z"Day will be carried on the man together with his iron rations. Rations for "Z" plus one day will be sent up in the ordinary way. Solidified alcohol has been issued.
WATER Every man carries up a full water bottle. In addition there will be a dump of filled Petrol Tins at Battalion H.Qrs in case of need.

21. TRENCH MORTARS.

Stokes Mortars will fire :-
ZERO to ZERO plus two minutes TUNNEL TRENCH.
ZERO plus 2.minutes to ZERO plus 4 Minutes ON GENERAL LINE OF TUNNEL SUPPORT.

After the enemy's trenches have been captured, four teams will move forward for "S.O.S" Work.

22. GAS AND SMOKE.
Should the weather be favourable the programme of Gas and Smoke Bombardments will be carried out on our own Divisional Front and also that of neighbouring Divisions. Should it not be possible to fire the projectors, the code word "TROUT" will be sent to all concerned.
TASKS OF NO.3. SPECIAL CO.R.E. are :-

(a) A very light smoke screen to simulate a lethal shell bombardment from ZERO plus thirty seconds on front line and Valley N.E. of BULLECOURT. Discharges to take place in any wind.

(b) Heavy Smoke Barrage E.of TUNNEL TRENCH from ZERO plus thirty seconds to ZERO plus fifteen minutes, if wind is between South and N.W.

S H E E T 8.

No.33.(Contd.)

(c) Smoke screen about FONTAINE ROAD Trench until ZERO plus ten minutes.

33. MACHINE GUNS.

VICKERS' GUNS will cover the attack with a barrage, decreasing the rate of fire until ZERO plus one hour and thirty minutes. They will reopen fire on (A) increased hostile shelling
(B) S.O.S.

34. O.C. "A" & "B" Coys will be responsible for seeing that diagonal lines are cut in our wire previous to assault as an exit to attacking troops

35. No papers or orders likely to give information to the enemy are to be carried by Officers or Other Ranks taking part in the attack. All Officers will take the following Maps.
(a) Hectographed sheet issued
(b) BULLECOURT Trench Map 51.B., S.W., 4.Ed.4.a.
(c) GAGNICOURT " " 51.B., S.E.3. Ed.3.a.

36. TUNNEL.

An Officer of the 174th. Tunnelling Coy. R.E. will report at Bn.H.Qrs. and will as soon as TUNNEL TRENCH has been taken, go forward and make a reconnaissance. He will report on completion at Bn.H.Qrs. When TUNNEL TRENCH has been taken, "A" & "B" Coys. will send a party to reconnoitre the TUNNEL. If any opposition is met, the O.C. Coy. should send down to "D", "E" & "F" Dumps for "P" Bombs if required, and attempt to clear TUNNEL with "P" and Mills' Bombs. As few "P" Bombs as possible should be used. O.C. Coys. must notify Battalion H.Qrs. as soon as possible whether opposition is encountered or not. Speciall Tunnelling Parties will make a reconnaissance when informed by the Infantry Commander on the spot that all is clear. The word "SAFE" or DANGER will be marked in chalk at the head of each gallery.

37. A Working Party of 7th. (S.I.H.) R. Irish Regt. will connect the head of LUMP LANE to TUNNEL TRENCH after ZERO.

38 In moving into positions on Y/Z Night, great care must be taken, especially in the case of "A" Coy. that there is no talking, striking of lights or flas hing of torches. The Companies occupying the line will have listening patrols in their wire to see that enemy patrols do not approach our trenches at important places such as heads of Communication trenches &c.

39. General Bearing of the Attack is 59° true.

30. During the operations, flares and S.O.S. Signals as under will be used:-
(a) WHITE FLARES.
(b) The S.O.S. Signal for the VI Corps will be a Rifle Grenade bursting into two red and two green lights.

31. EXTRA RATIONS.
A Chocolate ration will be made on the 18/11/17. This ration is to be regarded as part of the Iron Ration.

33. ACKNOWLEDGE.

Captain & A/Adjutant.

7/8th. (S) Battalion The Royal Irish Fusiliers

SHEET 6.

ISSUED THROUGH SIGNALS AT 8.0.p.m. 17th.inst.

Copy No.1. "A" Coy.
2. "B" Coy.
3. "C" Coy.
4. "D" Coy.
5. Quartermaster.
6. Transport Officer
7. Medical Officer.
8. Lewis Gun Officer.
9. Signals.
10. 49th. Infantry Bde.

Copy. No.11. 2nd. R. Irish Regt.
12. 7/8th. R. Innis. Fusrs.
13. 7th. (S.I.H.). R. Ir. R.
14. C.O.
15. 2nd. in Command.
16. O.C. Echelon "B"
17. War Diary
18. War Diary.
19. Spare.
20. File.

SECRET. NOVEMBER 16th.1917. COPY.NO..........

7/8th.(S)Battalion The Royal Irish Fusiliers Order No.36.

REFERENCE MAP. 51.B., S.W. 1/10,000.

::

1. The Battalion will move into the Line on 18th.November 1917

3. On Relief the Battalion will be disposed as follows :-
"A"Coy. QUARRY. "B"Coy. QUARRY.
"C"Coy. SUNKEN ROAD T.17.a. "D"Company. FRONT LINE & SUPPORT.
Battalion H.Qrs. Dug out at Western End of LUMP LANE.

3. "A"Company will relieve one Company 1st.Royal Dublin Fusiliers
"B"Company will relieve one Company.....
"C"Company will relieve one Company 8/9th.Royal Dublin Fusiliers
"D"Company will relieve one Company 7/8th.Royal Inniskilling Fusrs.

4. Companies will march out at the following times :-
"D"Company 10;0.a.m.
"A"Company 10.20.a.m.
"B"Company at 10.40.a.m.
"C"Company at 11.10.a.m.
Battalion H.Qrs. 11.30.a.m.

5. Taking over parties of one Officer,One N.C.O.,Nos.1.of Lewis Gun Teams per Company,Signal Officer,R.S.M. and Gas N.C.O. for Battalion Headquarters,will report to their various Company H.Qrs.at 9.0.a.m.

6. KITS Fighting Order will be worn.The two sandbags per man to be issued on 17th.November 1917 will be carried.
Packs will only contain:-
(1) Great coat.
(2) Iron Rations plus any extra rations issued.
(3) Mess Tin.
(4) Washing Kit.
All other kit including haversack will be placed in sandbags,issued. They will be stacked in Company Stores by 4.0.p.m. 17/11/17.The Q.M. will arrange to have all these collected by Companies and stored Blankets will be rolled into bundles by half platoons,that is two Bundles to each platoon.Every bundle is to be most clearly marked with the platoon number,Company and Unit.
OFFICERS Kit left behind will be separated into two lots as per instructionsissued.
(a) Valise of 35 lbs.
(b) Surplus Kit. (Clearly marked as such.)
Kits will be sent down and stacked in the Recreation Hut by 9.30.a.m. Trench Kits will be stacked outside Orderly Room by 9.30.a.m.

7. WATER% The Transport Officer will arrange to send up on 18.11.17. to "B"Company in the QUARRY the Hundred Petrol Tins filled.O.C."B"Coy will arrange to have these sent up to Battalion H.Qrs. the same night.This water is not to be used.
Lewis Gun Tin Boxes will also be sent up at the same time,full of magazines to "A"Company and handed over to the Lewis Gun Officer;he will arrange to send up 18 Tin Boxes to each of "D","E" & "F"Dumps. ~~Further instructions will be issued to O.C."B"Company~~."A","B" and "D"Companies will draw water from the QUARRY.A Water Cart will be sent to "C"Company.Twelve filled Petrol Tins per Company and eight for Battalion H.Qrs.will be taken up.

8. TRANSPORT. The following transport will be available:-
Half limber each for "A" and "B"Companies.One Limber each for "C", "D" and Battalion H.Qrs.Rations for the 19th.inst will be sent up and be dumped as follows. "D","A" & "B"& Battalion H.Qrs. QUARRY.
"C"Company at Company Headquarters.

S H E E T...... 3.

9. DINNERS Dinners will be served on arrival. O.C."D"Company will arrange to take up the YUKON PACKS. On the morning of the 19th. inst., he will arrange to have these loaded and packed at "D" & "E"Dumps with a mixed load.

10. BOMBS. With reference to Order No.35, para 10., "DRESS"Bombs, Grenades etc. (except "E"Bombs.) will be drawn. "A" & "B" from Brigade Bomb Store QUARRY on the 19th. inst. "D"Company will complete from Bomb Stores in the Front Line.

11. COMMUNICATION. 49th. Infantry Brigade Advanced H.Qrs. will be established in CROISSILLES CAVES T.24.a.2.8, on 18th. inst. Battalion H.Qrs. Position Call....................

12. LEWIS GUNS. Twenty Four Lewis Gun Magazines per Gun will be carried up by sections in carriers

13. MEDICAL. The Regimental Aid Post will be established at the QUARRY. Maltese Cart will be sent up at a.m.

14. The Second in Command will be respobsible for the general cleanliness and sanitation of the QUARRY.

15. Completion of Relief will be reported to Battalion H.Qrs, by CODE.

16. The above orders to be read in conjunction with BattalionOrder No.5

17. Echelon "B" will not proceed to the Trenches, Quartermaster will make the necessary/arrangements for accommodation and rations etc.

18. ACKNOWLEDGE.

[signature]

Captain.
A/Adjutant.

7/8th. (S)Battalion The Royal Irish Fusiliers.

ISSUED THROUGH SIGNALS AT 10.15.p.m. 18th. inst.

Copy No.1. "A"Coy.
2. "B"Coy.
3. "C"Coy.
4. "D"Coy.
5. Q.M.
6. T.O.
7. M.O.
8. L.G.O.
9. Signals.

Copy. No.10. R.S.M.
11. 49th. Inf. Bde.
12. 1st. R. Dublin Fus.
13. 8/9th. R. Dub. Fus.
14. 7/8th. R. Innis. Fus.
15. ?.
16. FILE.
17. War Diary.
18. War Diary.

No.19 & 20. SPARE.

S E C R E T. November 21st.1917 COPY.NO.........

7/8th.(S)Battalion The Royal Irish Fusiliers Order No.86.

Reference Map 51.B.,S.W. 1/20,000.

---

1. The 7/8th.Royal Inniskilling Fusiliers will relieve the Battalion with this afternoon,with two Companies in the front line,two Platoons in deep mine shaft LAMP LANE,one Coy.Bn.H.Qrs.

2. On Relief the Battalion will be disposed as under:-
H.Qrs. T.22.d.8.9. "B"Coy. QUARRY. "C"Coy.SUNKEN ROAD T.17.c.
"A" and "D"Companies SUNKEN ROAD at T.23.a. "A"Coy.H.Qrs.and one Platoon of "A"Coy.to occupy spare Battalion H.Qrs. at T.22.d.2.9.

3. "A" and "D"Companies will send four guides each with full instructions to Bn.H.Qrs.at 9.0.p.m.

4. Great care must be taken in handing over dumps,methods of defence and any available information regarding the enemy.

5. All Very Pistols [Yukon.] and Lewis Gun Web Carriers will be brought out. All empty Petrol Tins will be brought out.

6. Completion of Relief to be reported to Battalion H.Qrs. by runner.

7. All movement by Platoons at five minutes interval.

8. Efforts are being made to have a hot meal xxxx on arrival in Support.Officers Commanding Companies will be notified of this as soon as arranged.

9. ACKNOWLEDGE.

November 21st.1917 Captain & A/Adjutant.

7/8th.(S)Battalion The Royal Irish Fusiliers.

<u>ISSUED THROUGH SIGNALS AT 1.0.p.m.</u>

Copy No.1. "A"Coy.
2. "B"Coy.
3. "C"Coy.
4. "D"Coy.
5. 7/8th.(S)Bn. The Royal Inniskilling Fusiliers.

S E C R E T   22nd. November 1917   COPY NO...........

7/8th. (S) Battalion The Royal Irish Fusiliers Order No. 37.

Reference Map 51.B., S.W. 1/20,000.

---

1. The Battalion will be relieved to night by the 8/9th. Royal Dublin Fusiliers.

2. Companies on relief will march back to ARMAGH CAMP. Completion of relief to be reported by wire ~~and~~ runner. Code Word "SPLENDID" followed by the ~~returning~~ letter of the relieving Dublin Fusilier Company.

3. Officers Chargers and one limber per Company will be sent up.

4. All Petrol Tins, Yukon Packs and Lewis Gun Tin Boxes will be brought out. O.C. "D" Company will be responsible for seeing that the tin boxes are brought out and if there is not sufficient transport, he must leave surplus stores under a N.C.O.

5. Approximate handing over lists must be made up and sent to this Office.

6. All movement must be by platoons at five minutes interval.

7. Officers chargers will be sent up via the Road.

8. Arrival in billets to be reported to Orderly Room.

9. ACKNOWLEDGE.

10. All ammunition is to be made up before leaving the line.

Captain & A/Adjutant.

7/8th. (S) Battalion The Royal Irish Fusiliers.

ISSUED THROUGH SIGNALS AT 3.45.p.m.

Copies 1.to.4. "A" "B" "C" & "D" Coys.
Copy No.5. L.Gun Officer.
6. Medical Officer.
7. File.
8. Spare.
9 & 10 War diary

S E C R E T. Copy No. 8.

49th Inf. Bde. Order No. 182.

24th Nov. 1917.

1. The 2nd R. Dublin Fus. and 7/8th R. Irish Fus. will relieve the 7/8th R. Innis Fus. and 7th (S.I.H) R. Irish Regt. in the CENTRE and LEFT SUBSECTIONS respectively tomorrow, 25th instant.

2. Details will be arranged between Commanding Officers concerned.

3. 7/8th R. Innis Fus. will attach two platoons complete to the 2nd R. Irish Regt. from tomorrow. O.C. 7/8th R. Innis Fus. will arrange for them to report to 2nd R. Irish Regt. by 12 noon 25th.

4. (a) All trench stores, No. 9 Periscopes, gum boots, ammunition, grenades, etc, will be carefully handed and taken over. A return of above will be rendered to reach this office by 6 p.m. 26th. Particular attention will be paid to No. 9 Periscopes and gum boots.

(b) All work in hand and proposed will be carefully handed over in writing to ensure continuity.

5. Relief of Left Subsection to be complete by 4 p.m. and Centre Subsection by 5 p.m.

6. Advanced parties to include observers, snipers and Nos. 1 of Lewis Gun Teams, will take over 4 hours before their respective reliefs.

7. On completion of relief 7th (S.I.H) R.I.Regt. will march to BELFAST CAMP, and the 7/8th R. Innis Fus. to ENNISKILLEN CAMP. Billeting parties will take over camp by 11 a.m.. 1st R. Dublin Fus. will march to ARMAGH CAMP.

8. All movements will be made by platoons at 5 minutes interval.
Owing to bad state of HOLE LANE it will not be used for purposes of relief during daylight unless completed tonight.

9. Command of LEFT SECTION will pass to G. O. C. 49th Inf. Bde. on completion of relief.
H.Q. 49th Inf. Bde. will then move to HAMELINCOURT.

10. Completion of relief will be notified to 48th and 49th Inf. Bde. H.Q. by Code Word "VICTORY".

11. ACKNOWLEDGE.

✓ W

T. L. MacDonald. Captain,
Brigade Major, 49th Infantry Brigade.

Issued through Signals.

Copy No.		Copy No.	
1	to G. O. C.	11	to 16th Div. (G).
2	Staff Captain.	12	16th Div. (Q).
3	Bde. Signal Officer.	13	16th Div. Artillery.
4	Bde. Int. Officer.	14	180th Bde. R.F.A.
5	2nd R. Irish Regt.	15	47th Inf. Bde.
6	7th (S.I.H)R.I.Regt.	16	48th Inf. Bde.
7	7/8th R. Innis Fus.	17	Left Brigade.
8	7/8th R. Irish Fus.	18	157th Field Coy. R.E.
9	49th M.G.Company.	19	114th Coy. A.S.C.
10	49th T.M.Battery.	20-21	War Diary.
		22	File.

BATTALION ORDERS, No. 39, by Lieut. Colonel K.C. WELDON, D.S.O., Comdg.
7/8th. R. IRISH FUSILIERS. Nov. 29/17.

-:-

COPY No...........

SECRET.

Reference SHEET 51.B.S.W.1/40,000.

1. The 49th. Inf. Bde. will relieve the 48th. Inf. Bde. in the LEFT SECTION on the 30th. November.

2. The 1st. Bn. R. DUBLIN FUS. will relieve the Battalion: relief to be complete by 4.0.p.m.
On relief the Battalion will move to ARMAGH CAMP.

3. GUIDES. 3 guides per Coy. and one from Headquarters will be at C.IO at 2.0.p.m. Lieut. W.H.H. WATERS will be in charge of the guides at C.IO.
Every guide will be in possession of a chit stating what platoon he comes from and the platoon of the R. DUBLIN FUS. he is to relieve.

4. Advance parties will take over four hours before. O.C. "B" "C" and "D" Coys. will send one guide from each Lewis Gun to Bn. H.Q. at 12.15.p.m/The Transport Officer will arrange to send a guide to 1st R. DUB. FUS. at 2.0.p.m. to guide advance parties.

5. The Cook-SERGEANT will arrange to leave sufficient water for teas.

6. I limber per Coy. and H.Q., Maltese Cart will be at C.IO. Bn. H.Q. horses will be sent up at 4.15.p.m. to below C.IO.

7. HANDING OVER. Trench Stores, defence plans, No. 9. Periscopes, work in progress and proposed must be carefully handed over and list sent to Orderly Room on arrival in Camp. Care must be taken to check Grenade Returns handed over. Grenade Returns will reach Orderly Room by 12.0.noon 30th. Inst.

8. MOVEMENT. All movement must be in formed bodies with no straggling. Five minutes interval between platoons.

9. Arrival in Camp to be reported to Orderly Room.
Capt. A.F. CODDINGTON will arrange to take over ARMAGH CAMP by 11.0. a.m. 30th. The Quartermaster will arrange for a hot meal on arrival.

10. ACKNOWLEDGE.

Capt. & a/Adjutant,
7/8th. R. IRISH FUSILIERS...

Issued through Regt. Signals.

Copy No. 1........"A" Coy.
3........"C"
5........M.O.
7........Q.M.
9........L.G.O.
11........49th. Inf. Bde.
13........Sig. Officer.
15........War Diary..
17 ....SPARE.

Copy No. 2..........."B" Coy.
4..........."D"
6. ....Transport Offi er
8...........R.S.M.
10...........48th. Inf. Bde.
12...........1st. R.D.F.
14........Capt. A.F. Coddington
16........File.

Vol 23

WAR DIARY.

FOR MONTH OF DECEMBER, 1917.

VOLUME :- 15.

UNIT :- 7/8th R. Irish Fusiliers

9.P.

15.J.

1/8th (S) Battn R. IRISH FUSILIERS

DECEMBER 1917

C/134

Army Form C. 2118.

WAR DIARY
or
INTELLIGENCE SUMMARY.
(Erase heading not required.)

Instructions regarding War Diaries and Intelligence Summaries are contained in F. S. Regs., Part II. and the Staff Manual respectively. Title pages will be prepared in manuscript.

Place	Date	Hour	Summary of Events and Information (Ref. Sheet. FRANCE. 57.C. Ed. 2)	Remarks and references to Appendices
ARMAGH CAMP HAMLINCOURT	1/12/17		The 48th Inf. Bdge was relieved in Divisional reserve by the 121st Inf. Bdge, 40th Division. On relief by the 10th Middlesex Regt, the Battn marched to HENHAM CAMP NORTH, ACHIET-le-PETIT arriving in camp about 11.30 pm.	WS
ACHIET-le-PETIT	2/12/17		Remained in ACHIET-le-PETIT.	WS
"	3/12/17		The Battn marched to BARASTRE, leaving camp at 8.45 am and arriving in camp at C.10.c at 10.30 am. On arrival the Battn came under orders of G.O.C. 49th I.B.	WS
BARASTRE	4/12/17		Remained at BARASTRE	WS
TINCOURT	5/12/17		The 49th Inf. Bdge group moved to TINCOURT AREA. The Battn was billeted in HAMEL	WS
ST. EMELIE	6/12/17		The 49th Inf. Bdge group moved to ST-EMELIE & remained in divisional reserve.	WS.
"	7/12/17		Battn remained at ST EMELIE and took up "Stand to position" at Cam NW of LEMPIRE	WS
"	8/12/17		"A" & "B" Coys moved up in support to MALASSISSE Fm and MAY CORPS. A working party of 6 off 252 O.R started digging a new support trench in front of OLD COPSE. ST EMELIE was shelled at intervals throughout the night with 4.2 and 4.2.	WS
	9/12/17		As an hostile attack was expected all precautionary measures were taken. The party was provided again & new trench completed.	WS

B. D. & L., London, E.C. (A7853) Wt. W5031/M1672 350,000 1/17 Sch. 52a Forms/C/2118/14

7/8th (S) Battn R. IRISH FUS.

Instructions regarding War Diaries and Intelligence Summaries are contained in F. S. Regs., Part II. and the Staff Manual respectively. Title pages will be prepared in manuscript.

WAR DIARY
or
INTELLIGENCE SUMMARY.
(Erase heading not required.)

DECEMBER 1917

Army Form C. 2118.

Place	Date	Hour	Summary of Events and Information	Remarks and references to Appendices
			EPEHY 62c NE 2 1/10,000 VILLERS-GUISLAIN 1/10,000	
St EMELIE	10/12/17		Hostile artillery was very active in counter battery work & on defensive positions on the EPEHY – LEMPIRE Ridge. Throughout the day hostile aircraft made good use of a clear day. Our anti-aircraft batteries engaged these targets	[initials]
	11/12/17		Remained in St EMILE and provided working parties at night. Hostile artillery was not so active on counter-battery work	[initials]
	12/12/17		The Battn relieved the 9th Leicester Regt, 21st Division in the front line from copse at X 27 c to No 12 copse. Relief was complete by about 8 pm & the night passed very quietly on the front	[initials]
	13/12/17		At 6 pm drum fire commenced about 1 mile N of our line & gradually died down at about 7 pm. The night passed quietly & hostile artillery was not so active owing to bad visibility	[initials]
	14/12/17		During the night the enemy fired salvoes of 77 m in bursts of 20 on F 8 c 0 6. At 5 30 am the rate increased & 5 9 were used. MALASSISSE Fm was engaged during the day with 5 9 & 4 2.	[initials]
	15/12/17		The day passed quietly in the front line. The enemy's batteries were very active on counter-battery work through the day. During the night a new front line was dug by pioneers & large working parties. This trench was wired, with gaps, by the Battn. From 2 30 am to 3-30 am, wiring operations	[initials]

D. D. & L., London, E.C. (A7883) Wt. W5931M1672 350,000 4/17 Sch. 52a Forms C/2118/14

7/8th (S) Battn R. Irish Fusiliers

Army Form C. 2118.

WAR DIARY
or
INTELLIGENCE SUMMARY.
(Erase heading not required.)

December 1917

Instructions regarding War Diaries and Intelligence Summaries are contained in F. S. Regs., Part II, and the Staff Manual respectively. Title pages will be prepared in manuscript.

Place	Date	Hour	Summary of Events and Information	Remarks and references to Appendices
			Ref Sheet Sheet EPEHY VILLERS-GUISLAIN 62c	
	15/12/17	(contd)	interrupted by hostile artillery & MG fire.	[illegible]
EPEHY	16/12/17		The day passed quietly in the forward area. During the night the wire in front of our newly dug front line was completed. All SAA, bomb dumps were formed in the line	[illegible]
	17/12/17		Owing to a fall of snow, artillery activity was nil during the day.	
	18/12/17		49 Inf Bde was relieved by the 48 Inf. Bde in Left Subsection Left Section by the 1st Royal Dublin Fus relief completed by 8-15 PM. On relief Battalion marched to Ste Emilie and entrained for Hamel on light railway. Arrived in billets about 10-15 PM.	
HAMEL	19/12/17		Day was spent in cleaning up generally, fitting clothing etc. Lieut Col K C Weldon D.S.O. assumed command of 49th Inf Bde during the temporary absence of Brig Gen P Leveson Gower D.S.O. Capt & Adjt W. H Stitt MC proceeded to 16th Division to complete Staff Course. Capt. A/Capt. W. Sparks M.C. proceeded on leave & the duties of Adjutant were performed during his absence by Capt. B. J. Start	[illegible]
"	20/12/17		C. O. Inspected each Company on their own parade grounds remainder of the day was spent in checking deficiencies etc	[illegible]

D. D. & L., London, E.C. (A7883) Wt. W807/M1672 350,000 4/17 Sch. 52a Forms C/2118/14

7/8 (S) Batt Royal Irish Fusiliers

WAR DIARY
or
INTELLIGENCE SUMMARY.
(Erase heading not required.)

December 1917

Army Form C. 2118.

Instructions regarding War Diaries and Intelligence Summaries are contained in F. S. Regs., Part II. and the Staff Manual respectively. Title pages will be prepared in manuscript.

Place	Date	Hour	Summary of Events and Information	Remarks and references to Appendices
HAMEL	21/12/17		Day was spent in training	RJS
"	22/12/17		Battalion paraded under Divisional P.T. Instructor for Physical training	
			At 5-30 PM a concert was given by the 16th Divisional Concert Party to the	RJS
"			49th Inf Bde in the CINEMA HALL HAMEL Major J. F. O'Donel M.C proceeded on leave	
St EMELIE	23/12/17		49 Inf Bde relieved the 47th Inf Bde in Right Subsection Batt was in Bde	
"			Reserve & was accommodated in the Huts in the Railway Cutting about	RJS
			E 23. d 5.3. with Batt H.Q. in St Emilie	
"	24/12/17		St Emelie heavily shelled by hostile artillery casualties Nil	RJS
	25/12/17		Xmas day passed very quietly the day was not celebrated in the	RJS
			Battalion	
	26/12/17		Whilst in reserve several large working parties had to be formed making	
"	27/12/17		new hutments for reserve Batt Comfortable the remainder of the Batt	RJS
	28/12/17		was making concertina wire for front line "D" Coy was wiring front line during	
			the nights 27th & 28th one casualty from M.G. fire on latter date	
LEMPIRE	29/12/17		On evening of 29th Battalion relieved 7th (S.I.H.) Royal Irish Reg in the left	RJS
			sub-section relief completed by 8 PM night passed quietly except for	

D. D. & L., London, E.C. (A7883) Wt. W20/M1672 350,000 4/17 Sch. 52a Forms/C/2118/4

7/8 (S) Batt Royal Irish Fusiliers

DECEMBER 1917

Army Form C. 2118.

WAR DIARY
or
INTELLIGENCE SUMMARY.
(*Erase heading not required.*)

Instructions regarding War Diaries and Intelligence Summaries are contained in F. S. Regs., Part II. and the Staff Manual respectively. Title pages will be prepared in manuscript.

Place	Date	Hour	Summary of Events and Information	Remarks and references to Appendices
LEMPIRE	29/12/17		for usual M G fire	
"	30/12/17		About 300yds of wire erected in front line, about mid-night enemy shelled our front line with light trench mortars & 77 m.m guns 4·2 were fired at The Causeway one casualty	[illegible]
"	31/12/17		Day passed quietly but during the evening enemy heavily shelled Batt. H. Q. & EAST LEMPIRE with 77 m.m & 4·2 also again at mid-night two casualties. Lieut Col H. C. Weldon D.S.O. assumed Command of the 49th Inf Bde during the temporary absence of Brig Gen P. Leveson Gower D.S.O. Capt. B. St. J. Galvin M.C. Commanded with Capt. W. W. Neville as 2nd in Command	[illegible]

B St J Galvin Captain
Comdg 7/8 R. Irish Fusrs

D. D. & L., London, E.C. (A7853) Wt. W501/M1672 350,000 4/17 Sch. 52a Forms C/2118/14

S E C R E T. December 2nd.1917. COPY.NO. 11........

7/8th.(S)Battalion The Royal Irish Fusiliers Order No.40.

Reference Sheet LENS 11. Ed.2.a. 1/100,000.

1. The Battalion will move to BARASTRE to morrow the 3rd.inst and on arrival will come under the orders of the/49th.Infantry Brigade. G.O.C.

2. The Battalion will be formed up ready to move off at 4.45.a.m.on the road S.of Camp,head of Column on the road Junction N.of second T. in Achiet-le-Petit.O.C.Coys.will report to head of column when ready to move off.

DRUMS
Battalion H.Qrs.
"B"Coy.
"C"Coy.
"D"Coy.
"A"Coy.
TRANSPORT.

~~XXXXXXXXXXXXXXXXX~~

3. ROUTE ETC.

ACHIET-le-GRAND-- BIHUCOURT--BAPAUME--RIENCOURT--BARASTRE.
DISTANCE..Nine Miles.
Advance Party consisting of 5.C.Q.M.Sgts with bicycles will meet 2/Lieut.H.P.H.MONTGOMERT outside Bn.H.Qrs.Hut at 4.45.a.m.
Officers' Kits will be stacked outside Bn.H.Q.Hut at 4.15.a.m.
Halts. Every hour for ten minutes,before each hour.
Reveille 3.30.a.m., Hot Tea 4.0.a.m. Breakfast on arrival.
Dress.Steel helmets will be worn,one blanket per man to be carried on the man,Water bottles must be filled.

Captain & A/Adjutant.

7/8th.(S)Battalion The Royal Irish Fusiliers

Copy No.1. "A"Coy.
2. "B"Coy.
3. "C"Coy.
4. "D"Coy.
5. Q.M.
6. M.O.

Copy No.7. Transport Officer.
8. L.G.O.
9. R.S.M.
10. File.
11. War Diary
12. War Diary.

S E C R E T. DECEMBER 12th.1917 COPY NO.........

7/8th.(S)Battalion The Royal Irish Fusiliers Order No......
Reference Sheets EPEHY. and VILLERS GUISLAIN.

---

1. The Battalion will relieve the 9th.Leicester Regt.,21st.Division on the night 12/13th.inst.

2. On Relief Companies will be disposed as under:-
"C"Coy. in Posts E.& S.E.of Copse at X.27.c. Coy.H.Q. about X.26.d.30.05
"D"Coy. in Posts in F.2.b.and F.2.d. Coy.H.Qrs.about F. .b.5.9.
"B"Coy. in trenches running South from TETARD WOOD Coy.H.Q. about F.2.a.80.35. Battalion H.Qrs. F.1.d.7.7.

3. "A"Coy. will relieve "A"Coy. 9th.Leicester Regt.
"B"Coy. will relieve "D"Coy. 9th.Leicester Regt.
"C"Coy. will relieve "B"Coy. 9th.Leicester Regt.
"D"Coy. will relieve "C"Coy. 9th.Leicester Regt.

4. No.1's of Lewis Gun Teams from "C"Coy. will report to Battalion H.Qrs. F.1.d.7.7. at 7.0.a.m. 12 th.inst to take over.

5. Guides for Battalion H.Qrs.,"C"&"D"Coy's.will be at Road Junction F.1.c.7.5. at 6.0.p.m. Guides for "B"Coy. at MALASSISSE FARM at 7.0.p.m. Guides for "A"Coy. at Level Crossing F.1.d.7.0. at 7.0.p.m.

6. "A"&"B"Coys. will not move off until relieved by 2nd.R.Irish Regt.

7. Rations for Bn.H.Q.,"A","B" &"D"Coys.will be dumped at Bn.H.Q.where ration parties will be sent as soon after relief as possible."C"Coy's. rations will be dumped in the SUNKEN ROAD about F.3.d.20.25.Twelve filled Petrol Tins will be sent up nightly with rations.All Empty tins must be sent back each night

8. Twenty Four Lewis Gun Drums per Gun to be carried by the teams.The remainder will be sent up:-
"D"Coy.in the Ration Limbers to Bn.H.Qrs.
"C"Coy.in the Ration Limbers,O.C."C"Coy.will send an Officer to intercep the limber on the SUNKEN ROAD nearest his Right Post.

9, As This line is a new one it is important that taking over lists be sent in to Bn.H.Qrs.as soon as possible.Accurate taking over lists together with Grenade and S.A.A. Requirements must be sent at the same time.

10. COOKING. All Cooking will be done at Battalion H.Qrs.Food Containers are available for "C","D"&"A" Coys.
Breakfasts will be sent up at 5.30.a.m.& Dinners after dark.
Hot tea will be sent up during the night if procurable.

11. MOVEMENT. All Ground is under observation by the enemy and there must be no movement by daylight or lighting of fires etc.

12. WATER. There is a Pump at F.1.a.2.3.in case of need.

13 R.E.STORES arrangements will be notified later.No Trench Boards are available.A Limber load of Wire and Pickets will be sent up to O.C."C" Coy.on the night of 11/12th.inst.

14. MOVING OFF. "C"Coy.at 5.30.p.m.,"D"Coy. at 5.40.p.m.,BN.H.Q.550.p.m. Platoons at 200 yards interval.The Transport Officer will arrange for the necessary transport for Bn.H.Q.,"C"&"D"Coys.Trench Kits and Officers' Valises will be stacked separately outside Bn.H.Q. by 4.0.p.m Blankets will be rolled and stacked in Coy.Huts by 8.30.a.m.

15. Completion of Relief to be reported by the Code Word."JANUS"

16. ACKNOWLEDGE.

December 13th.1917 | Captain & A/Adjutant.

7/8th.(S)Battalion The Royal Irish Fusiliers.

Copy. No.1. "A" Coy.
2. "B" Coy
3. "C" Coy.
4. "D" Coy.
5. Quartermaster.
6 Medical Officer.
7. Transport Officer.

Copy No.8. Signals.
9. [illegible]
10. 9th.Leicester Regt.
11. 49th.Inf.Bde.
12. File.
13 War Diary.
14. War Diary.

S E C R E T.   DECEMBER 16th.1917   COPY NO.........

7/8th.(S)Battalion The Royal Irish Fusiliers Order No.43.

Reference Sheet EPEHY & 62.c. 1/40,000.

---

1. The 48th.Infantry Brigade will relieve the 49th.Infantry Brigade on the night of 17/18th.December 1917.

2. The 1st.Royal Dublin Fusiliers will relieve the Battalion in the Left Subsection.

3. An Advance Party consisting of Major T.J.CARRON ROBERT,Sergt.BIRD and four C.Q.M.S.ts.will report to Town Major at TINCOURT at 10.0.a.m. 17th.inst.,who will give them a list of billets to be occupied.

4. On Relief the Battalion will move to HAMEL,Bn.H.Qrs.at K.19.a.2.9. Brigade H.Qrs.at J.18.d.8.1.

5. The 1st.Royal Dublin Fusiliers will take over the same dispositions. GUIDES One per Platoon to be at Battalion H.Qrs.not later than 4.30.p.m.under Lieut.W.H.WATERS.Guides will meet the relieving Battalion at F.1.c.7.5.
X.Coy.1.R.Dublin Fusiliers will relieve "A"Coy.7/8.R.Irish Fusiliers.
Y.Coy.1.R.Dublin Fusiliers will relieve "B"Coy.7/8.R.Irish Fusiliers.
Z.Coy.1.R.Dublin Fusiliers will relieve "D"Coy.7/8.R.Irish Fusiliers.
W.Coy.1.R.Dublin Fusiliers will relieve "C"Coy.7/8.R.Irish Fusiliers.

6. Officers' Kits and Mess Boxes will be stacked outside Battalion H.Qrs. by 5.30.p.m.

7. LEWIS GUNS. One Limber per Company will be on road at F.1.d.2.3. at 6.0.p.m.The Transport Officer will arrange for four empty Lewis Gun wooden boxes per Company to be brought up on limbers.There are ten tin boxes at Battalion H.Qrs.each for "C" & "D"Coys',for extra Lewis Gun Drums in carriers.

8. TRANSPORT.The Transport Officer will arrange for the necessary Transport at the above hours.

9. PETROL TINS. All Petrol Tins must be brought out.The numbers brought out by Companies will be checked by the Q.M.and on going into the Line again the same number as brought out will be issued to Companies.

10. HANDING OVER. All Trench Stores,Ammunition,Grenades,Defence Schemes, work in progress and proposed will be carefully handed over.Handing Over Lists to be sent to Battalion H.Qrs.by 10.0.a.m. 18th.inst. Accurate Grenade Returns to be sent to Battalion H.Qrs early on the 17th.inst.

11. The Battalion will entrain at Ste.EMILIE.Further details as to entraining etc will be issued later.

12 Completion of Relief to be reported to Bn.H.Qrs.in Code.

13. ACKNOWLEDGE.

Captain & A/Adjutant.
7/8th.(S)Battalion The Royal Irish Fusiliers.

Issued through Signals.at 10.30.p.m. 16th.inst.

Copy No.1. "A"Coy.
2. "B"Coy.
3. "C"Coy.
4. "D"Coy.
5. Q.M.
6. M.O.
7. T.O.

Copy.No.8. L.G.O.
9. Signals.
10. R.S.M.
11. 49th.Inf.Bde.
12. 1.R.Dublin Fusiliers.
13. File.
14. War Diary.

S E C R E T.   DECEMBER 17th.1917   COPY NO..........

7/8th.(S)Battalion The Royal Irish Fusiliers Order to be read in conjunction with Order No.43 dated 16.12.17.

::

1. There are three trains "A","B" & "C" allotted for moving 2nd.The Royal Irish Regiment,7/8th.R.Innis.Fusrs & 7/8.R.Irish Fusrs. to Ste.EMILIE

2. Capacity of each train ~~800~~ 600 all ranks.Entraining Point,siding in F.13.c. Detraining Point-Siding at K.13.c.
Departure of Trains :- "A" 9.0.p.m.
"B" 9.30.p.m.
"C" 10.0.p.m.

3. Each Coy.will entrain as a complete and separate Unit under the direction of/Staff Captain,in order of arrival at the entraining point,irrespective of the Battalion to which they belong.O's.C.Coys.will therefore ensure that their platoons are collected before entraining.

4. One N.C.O.per Company and Battalion H.Qrs.will report to the Adjutant at 6.0.p.m.This party under Lieut.W.H.WATERS will report to the Staff Captain at F.13.c.1.5. at 8.30.p.m.Each N.C.O.will know the strength of all ranks in his Company.

5. In order to avoid confusion,equipment will be worn.

6. During entraining there is not to be any talking or shouting except by those on duty;the lighting of candles,striking of matches or unnecessary shining of Electric Lights is forbidden.

7. Advance Parties will meet their Companies at the Detraining Point K.13.c.

Captain & A/Adjutant.

7/8th.(S)Battalion The Royal Irish Fusiliers.

ISSUED THROUGH SIGNALS AT 10.30.a.m. 17/12/17.

Copy No.1. "A"Coy.
2. "B"Coy.
3. "C"Coy.
4. "D"Coy.
5. Q.M.
Copy No.6. T.O.
7. L.G.O.
8. Lieut.W.H.WATERS
9. R.S.M.
10. FILE
11 & 12 War Diary.

SECRET. December 28th. 1917. War Diary Copy No. 16

1st Bn. The Royal Irish Fusiliers Order No. 110.

1. The Battalion will relieve the 7th. (S. I. H.) R. Irish Regiment in the Left Subsection Right Section on 29th. December 1917.
The Bn. will relieve as follows, "moving" off at hours shewn against each Coy's name.

3.30 p.m. "D" Coy. 1st R. Ir. Fusrs. will relieve "B" Coy S. I. H. in Posts.
4.0 p.m. "C" " 1/F " " " " "A" Coy. S. I. H. in SART FARM
4.30 p.m. "B" " 1/F " " " " "C" Coy S. I. H. as Left Front Coy.
6.0 p.m. "A" " 1/F " " " " "B" Coy S. I. H. as Right Front Coy.
6.30 p.m. Bn. H. Qrs.

2. Advance Parties:-
Advance parties composed as under will report to H. Qrs. S. I. H. as under:
At 2.0 p.m. 1 Officer & 1 N.C.O. per Coy, Coy. Gas N.C.O. Nos. 1. of each Lewis Gun and one N.C.O. for H. Qrs.

4. Guides:-
Guides will be provided for this Battalion as under:
For Advance Party two for each Coy. & one for Bn. H.Q at [illegible] to RONSSOY VILLAGE. (F. 21. a. 3. 9) at 2.0 p.m.
For Main Body one per platoon and one per Bn. H.Q. [illegible] F. 22. c. 3. 9 at 4.0 p.m.

5. Lewis Guns:-
One Lewis Gun and personnel from both "A" & "C" Coys. will be attached to "B" Coy during the tour in the Front Line. Coys will arrange to ration accordingly.
Lewis Guns and 8 filled drums per Gun will be carried by Lewis Gunners. The remaining drums in tin boxes will be brought up as follows together with empty boxes from which drums have been taken.
"A" & "B" Coys. to LONDON ROAD.
"C" & "D" Coys. to Bn. H. Qrs (F. 16. a. 8. 9)
They will be carried from here under Coy arrangements.

6. Movement:
All movement will be by Platoons at 200 yds. interval.

7. Rations etc.:-
Rations will be dumped as follows:
"A" & "B" at LONDON ROAD. Cooking for these Coys. will be done at LONDON ROAD.
"C" & "D" Coys & Bn. H. Q. will be dumped at Bn. H. Q. where cooking for these Coys will also be done.
The Transport Officer will arrange to send two water carts to Bn. H. Q. nightly to fill tanks there. Twelve filled petrol tins of water will be sent up nightly with each Coy's rations.
As only 8 food containers are available in the Line 4 have been allotted to "A" & 4 to "B" Coys. Cooking for all Coys. will be done in Camp heaters.

Transport:-
All Officer's Kits will be stacked as under, Transport Officer making necessary arrangements for their removal.
For trenches:- Outside Bn. H. Q. by 3.30 p.m.
For Q.M. Stores by Railway Cutting at 4.30 p.m.

9. Taking Over:-
All Trench Stores, defence arrangements, [illegible] Work in Progress will be carefully taken over & Trench Store lists sent to Bn. H. Q. by 9.0 a.m. 30th. inst.

10. Completion of Relief to be reported by word "Peace".

11. Acknowledge.

J. J. Hart
Capt. a/Adjutant
7/8th. Roy. Irish Fusrs.

Issued through Signals at 7.30 p.m.

Distribution.

Copy No 1. "A" Coy.	Copy No. 2. "B" Coy.
" " 3. "C" "	" " 4. "D" "
" " 5. Q. M.	" " 6. I. O.
" " 7. M. O.	" " 8 Signals.
" " 9. R. S. M.	" " 10 49 Inf. Bde.
" " 11. 7th (S.I.H.) R. Ir. Regt.	" " 12 2nd 7th R. Irish Regt.
" " 13 Spare	" " 14 File.

15 & 16 War Diary.

S E C R E T. File D E C E M B E R 31st.1917 COPY NO...12...

7/8th.(S)Battalion The Royal Irish Fusiliers Order No.46.

---

1. There will be an Inter-Company Relief to morrow 1st.Prox.as under:- "C"Company will relieve "A"Coy.as Right Front Coy,moving off at 8.0.p.m. from present position.
"D"Company will relieve "B"Company as Left Front Coy.moving off at 5.0.p.m. from present position.

2. ADVANCE PARTIES
Advance Parties of "C" & "D"Coys.consisting of One Officer and one N.C.O.per Company also Gas N.C.O's and ~~men~~ Nos.1.of Lewis Guns will proceed to take over,reporting to "A" & "B"Coys' H.Qrs.at 2.0.p.m. Advance Parties of "A" & "B"Coys. each consisting of one Officer per Company and one N.C.O.per Platoon will commence taking over at 2.0.p.m.The One N.C.O.per Platoon will act as Guide for the relieving platoon of that Coy,thereafter guiding their own platoons to the new position..

3. LEWIS GUNS.
Lewis Gun Drums will be handed over in their boxes complete.
"B"Coy.will hand over to "D"Coy.one complete Lewis Gun and personnel.
"C"Coy.will do likewise to "A"Coy.
The Lewis Gunners now attached to "C"Coy. under instruction will come under "A"Coy. and remain at SART FARM,the rations being adjusted by Company Commanders.Sergt.CUNNINGHAM will take up the duties of Instructor from Sergt.COLLINS,the latter explaining how far the class has progressed

4. TAKING OVER
A sketch of positions showing the wire erected by Coys.vacating the position will be handed over to the relieving Coys.and a copy sent to Bn.H.Qrs.with Trench Store Lists by 9.0.a.m. 2nd.prox.

5. RATIONS etc.
Q.M. will make the necessary arrangements for reversing the conditions for dumping rations as to that order stated in B.O.45.para 7.dated 28.12.17.

6. Completion of Relief to be reported by Code Words "BLACK LIGHTS". A Second Code Word will be used by the Coys that are relieved from the front line when they are in position in their respective places Code Word "WHISKEY"

7. ACKNOWLEDGE BY WIRE.

Captain & A/Adjutant.
7/8th.(S)Battalion The Royal Irish Fusiliers.

ISSUED THROUGH SIGNALS AT P.M.31.12.17.

Copy No.1. "A"Coy.	Copy No.7. 49th.Infantry Bde.
2. "B"Coy.	8. R.S.M.
3. "C"Coy.	9. Sig.Officer
4. "D"Coy.	10. Intelligence Officer.
5. Q.M.	11 File
6. M.O.	12 War Diary

Cancelled

S E C R E T.

Copy No 6

19th Inf. Bde. Order No. 188.

3rd December 1917.

Ref. Map Sheet 57.C.
1/40,000.

1\. (a). The 16th Division (less Artillery) will concentrate tomorrow (4th December) in the area METZ-EN-COUTURE - BERTINCOURT - LECHELLE. The above area is at present occupied by 36th Division and is to be cleared by that Division by 3 p.m. 4th December.

(b). The 19th INF. BDE. GROUP will move to the BERTINCOURT - RUYAULCOURT area according to the attached March Table.

2\. The regulation halts i.e. from 50 minutes to the clock hour - will be observed

3\. Distances as follows will be observed :-

200 yards between Companies.
200 yards between battalions.
200 yards between each battalion and its own transport.
200 yards between all other units.

4\. Billeting parties as follows will report to Staff Captain at Town Major's Office, BERTINCOURT at 11 a.m.

Battalions (each) 1 Officer & 5 O.R. on horses or cycles.
M.G.Company. 1 Officer, 2 O.R. on horses or cycles.
T.M.Battery. 1 N.C.O on cycle.
Brigade H.Q. Sgt Johnston on cycle.

113th Field Amb. 1 Staff Sgt. on cycle or horse.
144th Coy, A.S.C. 1 Warrant Officer on cycle or horse.
Interpreters - M. LAGUERRE and M. ROISEL (to be warned by 7/8th R. Irish Fus. and 2nd R. Irish Regt. respectively).

Maps as above must be taken and billeting strengths known.

5\. Supply Wagons of units will march with 144 Coy, A.S.C.

6\. Motor Lorries for blankets have been asked for, but information regarding these will be issued separately.

7\. Camps must be left scrupulously clean, but no rear parties will be left for handing over.

8\. Brigade H.Q. will close at BARASTRE at 2.30 p.m. and will open on arrival in the new area. Location will be notified to all concerned.

9\. ACKNOWLEDGE.

Captain,
A/Brigade Major, 49th Infantry Brigade.

Issued through Signals at 11.30 PM.

Copy No.		Copy No.	
1 to	G. O. C.	12 to	48th Inf. Bde.
2	Staff Captain.	13	16th Division (G).
3	2nd R.Irish Regt.	14	16th Division (Q).
4	7th (S.I.H)R.I.Rgt.	15	144th Coy, A.S.C.
5	7/8th R. Innis Fus.	16	113th Field Ambulance.
6	7/8th R.Irish Fus.	17	Area Comdt. BARASTRE.
7	49th M.G.Company.	18	A.D.M.S. 16th Div.
8	49th T.M.Battery.	19	16th Div. Train.
9	Bde. Transport Officer.	20-21	War Diary.
10	Bde. Signal Officer.	22	File.
11	47th Inf. Bde.		

MARCH TABLE TO ACCOMPANY 49th I.F.BDE. ORDER No. 188.

Unit.	Starting Point.	Time.	Route.	Destination.		Remarks.
Brigade H.Q.	O.16.a.0.3.	2.30 pm.	O.18.b.95.00 - P.7.a.9.7 P.7.a.9.5 - P.1.d.95.00 P.8.a.5.8 - P.3.d.1.4. I.2.d.5.1.	-	Billeting parties will meet units on line of march.	
7/8th R.Innis Fus.		2.35 pm.		RUYAULCOURT		
7/8th R.Irish Fus.		2.40 pm.		RUYAULCOURT.		
7th (S.I.H.) R.I.Rgt.		3.05 pm.		BERTINCOURT.		
2nd R.Irish Rgt.		3.30 pm.		do.		
49th M.G.Company.		3.35 pm.		-		
49th T.M.Battery.		3.40 pm.		-		
113th Field Amb.		3.45 pm.		-		
1[illegible]th Coy.A.S.C.		3.50 pm.		-		

S E C R E T.   Copy No ...6.

49th Inf. Bde. Order No. 189.

Ref. Map Sheets 57.C)   4th December 1917.
and 62.C)1/40,000.

1. The 49th Inf. Bde. Group will march tomorrow, 5th December 1917, to TINCOURT AREA according to attached table.

2.(a) Regulation halts - i.e. from every 50 minutes to the clock hour - will be observed.

(b) Distances as follows will be kept :-

200 yards between units.

(c) First line transport will march with units.

3. Billeting Parties (as laid down in Bde. Order No. 188) will report to Staff Captain at Town Major's Office, TINCOURT at 11 a.m.

Maps as above must be taken.

4. Dinners will be cooked enroute and served out on arrival in camp.

5. Supply Wagons will march with 144th Coy, A.S.C.

6. Motor lorries for blankets have been asked for. Guides from units will report at Brigade H.Q. at 7 a.m. tomorrow to conduct same to units' camps. When filled these lorries should go to TINCOURT and report to Staff Captain at Town Major's Office.

7. Camps must be left scrupulously clean, but no rear parties will be left for handing over.

8. Brigade H.Q. will close at BARASTRE at 8.45 a.m. Reports to head of column while on march. Brigade H.Q. will open in TINCOURT area on arrival.

9. The 155th Field Coy, R.E. will join rear of column as it passes through [illegible] about 10.30 a.m. and will continue on the march under orders of G.O.C. 49th Inf. Bde. A billeting party of 2 N.C.O's on cycles will report to Staff Captain as detailed in para. 3.

10. ACKNOWLEDGE.

[illegible signature]

Captain,

a/Brigade Major, 49th Infantry Brigade.

Issued throught signals at 10.30 p.m.

Copy No.		Copy No.	
1 to	G. O. C.	14 to	Bde. Sig. Officer.
2	Staff Captain.	15	Bde. Int. Officer.
3	2nd R.Irish Rgt.	16	16th Div. (G).
4	7th(S.I.H)R.I.Rgt.	17	16th Div. (Q).
5	7/8th R. Innis Fus.	18	47th Inf. Bde.
6	7/8th R.Irish Fus.	19	48th Inf. Bde.
7	49th M.G.Company.	20	A.D.M.S. 16th Div.
8	49th T.M.Battery.	21	16th Div. Train.
9	155th Field Coy,R.E.	22-23	War Diary.
10	157th Field Coy,R.E.	24	File.
11	144th Coy, A.S.C.		
12	113th Field Amb.		
13	Bde. Transport Off.		

MARCH TABLE TO ACCOMPANY BRIGADE ORDER NO. 189

UNIT.	STARTING POINT.	TIME.	ROUTE.	REMARKS.
Bde. H.Q.	Q.15.d.5.8.	9 a.m.	O.21.c.3.1. - U.27.a.7.7. - MOCQUIGNY -- LE MESNIL-EN-ARROUAISE -- U.4.c.1.6. -- U.11.b.6.2 -- LANANCOURT -- LOISLAINE -- TEMPLEUX-LA-FOSSE -- J.4.d.5.5. -- J.16.c.5.2.	Billeting Guides will meet Units on Route.
7/R. Irish Regt.,		9.5 a.m.		
2/R. Irish Regt.,		9.15 a.m.		
7/8 R. Irish Fus.,		9.25 a.m.		
7/8 R. Innis. Fus.		9.35 a.m.		
157 Fd. Coy. R.E.		9.45 a.m.		
49th M.G. Coy.		9.50 a.m.		
49th T.M.B.,		10.5 a.m.		
113 Fd. Amb.		10.10 a.m.		
144 Coy. A.S.C.		10.15 a.m.		

SECRET.

Copy No. 6

49th Inf. Bde. Order No. 190.

5th December 1917.

Ref. Map Sheet 62.C Scale 1/40,000.

1\. (a) The 16th Division (less Artillery) is to relieve 55th Division (less artillery) in the line from F.[illegible].a.0.0 to the MALASSISE ROAD inclusive. Relief to be complete by 10 a.m. December 7th, when command of the front will pass to G.O.C. 16th Division with Headquarters at VILLERS FAUCON.

(b) The 49th Inf. Bde. will move tomorrow, 6.12.17, as detailed in Table attached, to STE. EMELIE and front line area.

2\. Distances as follows to be observed:-

200 yards between Companies and similar units.
200 yards between units transport.

3\. One blanket will be carried on the man. Instructions re second blanket will be issued later.

4\. Billeting parties will report to Staff Captain at the present Brigade H.Q. in STE.EMELIE at 9 a.m.

5\. Supply Wagons filled will report to units at 9.30 a.m. and will march with each units' transport to destination where rations will be immediately offloaded and wagons sent back to 144th Coy, A.S.C.

6\. R.E. and Medical Reliefs will be carried out under arrangements to be made by C.R.E. and A.D.M.S. respectively.

7\. All working parties, guards, anti-aircraft defences, maps, defence schemes, ammunition including S.O.S. Signals and reserve rations will be taken over. A list of all ammunition, showing locations of dumps, will be sent at once to Staff Captain, Brigade Headquarters.

8\. Brigade H.Q. close at TINCOURT at 10.30 a.m. and reopen on arrival at STE. EMELIE.

9\. ACKNOWLEDGE (stating time of receipt).

Captain,

A/Brigade Major, 49th Infantry Brigade.

Issued through Signals at 1 a.m.

Copy No.	1 to	G.O.C.	14 to	C.R.E.
"	2	Staff Captain.	15	A.D.M.S.
"	3	2nd R.Irish Regt.	16	113th Field Ambulance.
"	4	7th (S.I.H) R.I.Rgt.	17	155th Field Coy, R.E.
"	5	7/8th R. Innis Fus.	18	55th Division.
"	6	7/8th R.Irish Fus.	19	47th Inf. Bde.
"	7	49th M.G.Company.	20	48th Inf. Bde.
"	8	49th T.M.Battery.	21	164th Inf. Bde.
"	9	157th Field Coy, R.E.	22	Bde. Transport Officer.
"	10	144th Coy, A.S.C.	23	Bde. Signal Officer.
"	11	113th Field Amb.	24	Bde. Int. Officer.
"	12	16th Div. (G).	25-26	War Diary.
"	13	16th Div. (Q).	27	File.

VII Corps Q

TABLE TO ACCOMPANY 49th Inf. Bde. Order No. 190.

Unit.	Starting Point.	Time.	Route.	Remarks.
Brigade H.Q. (less T'port) 49th M.G.Company. (less T'port) 2nd R.Irish Regt. (less T'port)	J.18.d.8.3. do. do.	10.30 a.m. 10.35 a.m. 10.40 a.m.	By lorries via ROISEL - STE.EMELIE to E.23.c.5.0. where units will debus on North side of road facing lorries.	Units to be detailed before marching off from unit parade grounds into lorry loads of 25 each.
7/8th R.Irish Fus. (less T'port) 7th (S.I.H) R.I.Regt. (less T'port) 49th T.M.Battery.	J.18.d.8.3. do. do.	11.15 a.m. 11.25 a.m. 11.35 a.m.	By march route via MARQUAIX - ROISEL - K.16.b.3.3 - VILLERS-FAUCON to E.22.d.9.4. where billeting guides will meet units.	
49th M.G.Coy. T'port 2nd R.Irish Regt. T'port. Brigade H.Q. T'port. 7/8th R.Irish Fus. T'port. 7th (S.I.H) R.I.Regt. T'port. 7/8th R.Innis Fus. T'port.	J.18.d.8.3. do. do. do. do. do.	11.40 a.m. 11.50 a.m. 12.10 p.m. 12.15 p.m. 12.25 p.m. 12.35 p.m.	Via MARQUAIX - ROISEL - K.16.b.3.3 to VILLERS FAUCON.	Under command of Bde. Transport Officer.
7/8th R.Innis Fus. (less T'port)	J.18.d.8.3.	2.40 p.m.	By lorries via ROISEL - STE.EMELIE to E.23.c.5.0 where unit will debus on North side of road facing lorries.	Units to be detailed before marching off from unit parade ground to lorry loads of 25 each.

SECRET.

Copy No........6

49th Infantry Brigade Order No. 191.

6th December, 1917.

Disposition. The 49th Inf.Bde. will be in support to 48th Inf.Bde. who is holding the line F.24.a.0.0. to MALASSISE FARM inclusive.

2nd Royal Irish Regt. MALASSISE FARM and ground to West as far as F.9.c.5.0.

7th Royal Irish Regt.)
7/8th Royal Innis. Fus.) Billets in ST.EMILIE.
7/8th Royal Irish Fus.)

Disposition 48th Inf. Bde. 3 Battalions in line.
1 Battalion holding posts in and about LEMPIRE & RONSSOY.

The 21st Division is on our ~~Right~~. LEFT
The 24th Division is on our ~~left~~. RIGT

Appreciation of Tactical Situation.

The enemy are occupying the line A.19.b.5.0. to about X.28.central, the northern part of which above F.5.c.2.8. they have recently captured from us.

The ridge EPEHY - MALASSISE FARM - RONSSOY is of great importance. It covers our communications and gives us good observation. If the enemy captured this ridge it would give him a very good flank to proceed with his attack west, but the ridge must be held at all costs.

Action of Support Brigade.

2nd R.Irish Regt. Hold their position MALASSISE FARM extending S.E.

7/8th R.Irish Fus. Will move out of billets and will be in position at 6 a.m./6.12.7. just south of road from about F.8.d.5.5. to F.15.a.8.5.

7th R.Irish R.(S.I.H.) will occupy the posts running N. from ST.EMILIE towards EPEHY. To be in position 6 a.m. 7.12.17.

7/8th Innis. Fus. will stand to in ST.EMILIE.

Battalions will report to Brigades when in position. X

7/8th Innis. Fusiliers will reconnoitre generally ground S.W. of EPEHY - RONSSOY RIDGE, today.

In case of attack the 7/8th R.Irish Fus. will strengthen line on ridge and hold 2 companies for counter attack to keep Ridge in their possession.

7/8th Innis. Fus. will be kept in reserve to counter attack on any portion of Divisional front.

Brigade H.Q., will be at ST.EMILIE with 48th Bde. H.Qs., to which place all reports will be sent.

ACKNOWLEDGE (stating time of receipt).

H. J. Bowen

Captain,
A/Brigade Major, 49th Infantry Brigade.

Issued to Signals at ..3.45. p.m.

Copy No. 1 - G.O.C.
2 - Staff Captain.
3 - 2nd R.Irish Regt.
4 - 7th (S.I.H) R.I.Regt.
5 - 7/8th R.Innis. Fus.
6 - 7/8th R.Irish Fus.
7 - 49th M.G.Coy.
8 - 49th T.M.Battery.
9 - 157th Field Co.R.E.
10 - 144th Coy.A.S.C.
11 - 113th Field Ambce.
12.- 16th Div. 'G'.
13 - 16th Div. 'Q'.
14 - C.R.E.
15 - A.D.M.S.
16 - 55th Div. 'G'.
17 - 55th Div. 'Q'.
18 - 47th Inf.Bde.
19 - 48th Inf.Bde.
20.- Bde.Transport Offr.
21 - Bde. Signal Offr.
22 - Bde. Int.Officer.
23 - War Diary.
24 - -do-.
25 - File.
26 - VII Corps 'Q'.

S E C R E T.

Copy No 7

49th Inf. Bde. Order No. 192.

7th December 1917.

Ref. Maps Sheets
57.c.S.E.
62.c.N.E.
1/20,000.

1. The 7th (S.I.H) R. Irish Regt. will relieve the 1st R. Dublin Fus. in the Left Subsection of the SECTOR held by the 48th Inf. Bde. tonight (7th/8th December 1917).

Arrangements will be made between C.O's concerned.

2. The head of the 7th (S.I.H) R. Irish Regt. is to be at the road junction F.10.c.35.60 (Sheet 62.c.N.E) by 8 p.m., where guides from 1st R. Dublin Fus. will meet them.

3. All trench stores, periscopes, gum boots, ammuntion and grenades will be carefully taken over, and list of same will be forwarded to Brigade H.Q. by 6 p.m. 8th December 1917.

4. Completion of relief to be reported to 49th Inf. Bde. H.Q. by the code word "POINTER".

5. On completion of relief the command of the portion held by the 7th (S.I.H) R.Irish Regt. will pass to G. O. C. 49th Inf. Bde.

6. ACKNOWLEDGE.

Captain,

A/Brigade Major, 49th Infantry Brigade.

Issued through Signals at 6.15 p.m.

Copy No. 1 to G. O. C.
.. 2 48th Inf. Bde.
.. 3 7th (S.I.H) R.Irish Regt.
.. 4 Staff Captain.
.. 5 2nd R. Irish Regt.
.. 6 7/8th R. Innis Fus.
.. 7 7/8th R. Irish Fus.
.. 8 49th M.G.Company.
.. 9 49th T.M.Battery.
.. 10 Bde. Transport Officer.
.. 11 Bde. Signal Officer.
.. 12 Bde. Int. Officer.
.. 13 113th Coy, A.S.C.
.. 14 157th Field Coy, R.E.
... 15 113th Field Ambulance.
.. 16 16th Division (G).
.. 17 16th Division (Q).
.. 18 16th Div. Artillery.
.. 19 C. R. E.
.. 20 A.D.M.S.
.. 21 21st Division.
.. 22 110th Inf. Bde.
.. 23 D. M. G. O.
.. 24 D. T. M. O.
.. 25-26 War Diary.
.. 27 File.

S E C R E T. Copy No 2....

49th Inf. Bde. Order No. 193.

8th December 1917.

1.(a)The 2nd R. Irish Regt. will relieve the 8/9th R. Dublin Fus. in the line from F.11.a.8.6 inclusive to the right of the 7th (S.I.H) R.Irish Regt. about F.4.d.8.9, and in ZEBRA and YAK POSTS today, and during the night of 7th/8th December 1917.

(b). The 7/8th R. Irish Fus. will relieve the 2nd R.Irish Regt. in MALASSISE FARM and ground to the S.E. today and during the night of 7th/8th December 1917.
Arrangements will be made between C.O's concerned.

2. All trench stores, maps, defence plans, etc, to be taken over carefully and list of same sent to Brigade H.Q. by 6 p.m. 8th December.

3. Completion of (a) & (b) reliefs respectively will be wired to Brigade H.Q. by 2nd R. Irish Regt. by the Code Word "SUPPORTS", and by the 7/8th R.Irish Fus. by the Code Word "PIQUETS".

4. On completion of relief the command of the Right Subsection of the 49th Inf. Bde. Front from F.11.a.8.9 inclusive to the right of the 7th (S.I.H) R.I.Regt. about F.4.d.8.9, and of ZEBRA and YAK POSTS will pass to the O.C. 2nd R. Irish Regt.

5. ACKNOWLEDGE.

[signature]

Capta[in]

A/Brigade Major, 49th Infantry Brigade.

Issued [th]rough Signals at 2.10 p.m.

Copy No. 1 to 2nd R.Irish Regt.
" 2 7/8th R.Irish Fus.
" 3 48th Inf. Bde.
" 4 8/9th R.Dublin Fus.(On Ins[tructions] from G.O.C. 48th Inf. Bde.)

SECRET. Copy No 6

49th Inf. Bde. Order No. 198

15th December 1917.

WARNING ORDER.

Ref: Maps 57.c.S.E.
62.c.N.E.
1/20,000.

1. The 48th Inf. Bde. (less M.G.Company) will relieve the 49th Inf. Bde. (less M.G.Company) in the Left Section of the Div. Front from F.11.a.8.6 to X.26.d.50.45 on night 17th/18th December as follows :-

2nd R. Dublin Fus. will relieve 7/8th R. Innis Fus.
1st R. Dublin Fus. will relieve 7/8th R. Irish Fus.
10th R. Dublin Fus. will relieve 2nd R. Irish Regt.
8/9th R. Dublin Fus. will relieve 7th (S.I.H) R.I.Regt.
48th T.M.Battery will relieve 49th T.M.Battery.

Arrangements as to guides etc will be made between C.O's concerned.

2. On relief 49th Inf. Bde. will move as follows :-

Brigade Headquarters to HAMEL at J.18.d.8.1.
H.Q. 2nd R. Irish Regt. to TINCOURT at J.23.b.8.4.
H.Q. 7th (S.I.H) R.I.Regt. to BUIRE J.27.d.8.8.
H.Q. 7/8th R. Innis Fus. to J.18.d.9.0.
H.Q. 7/8th R. Irish Fus. to K.19.a.2.9.
H.Q. 49th T.M.Battery to J.24.b.3.8.

3. M.4. Advance Parties will report to Town Major, TINCOURT, at 11 a.m. 17th instant, who will give them a list of billets to be occupied.

4. ✓ ACKNOWLEDGE.

[signature] Captain,
A/Brigade Major, 49th Infantry Brigade.

Issued through Signals.

Copy No. 1 to G. O. C.
" 2 Staff Captain.
" 3 2nd R. Irish Regt.
" 4 7th (S.I.H) R.I.Regt.
" 5 7/8th R. Innis Fus.
" 6 7/8th R. Irish Fus.
" 7 49th M.G.Company.
" 8 49th T.M.Battery.
" 9 157th Field Coy, R.E.
" 10 113th Coy, A.S.C.
" 11 113th Field Ambulance.
" 12 Bde. Transport Officer.
" 13 Bde. Sig. Officer.
" 14 Bde. Int. Officer.
" 15-16 War Diary.
" 17 File.

SECRET

Copy No. 7

49TH INFANTRY BRIGADE.

ADMINISTRATIVE INSTRUCTION NO. 39. 16-12-17.

Reference 49th Infantry Brigade Order 198.

---

1. BAGGAGE WAGONS.
Baggage Wagons have been instructed to report to Transport Lines of Units at 9 a.m. 17th inst.

2. BLANKETS.
7/R.Irish Regt., will hand over at its present Camp, to the Battalion relieving it, 1000 blankets, rolled in bundles of 10.
The remaining three Battalions will hand over at their present Q.M. Stores, to advance parties of Units relieving them, 1000 blankets, rolled in bundles of 10.
The 49th T.M.B. will carry their blankets in the motor lorry which will bring the 48th Brigade to relieve them. They will also take their guns, kits, etc in this lorry.
Brigade H.Q, will hand over at the QUARRY, 168 blankets.
Any Unit having more than 1000 blankets in possession must arrange to carry these additional blankets either on the man or on their Regimental Transport.
Each Advance Party from Battalions will take over at the Billet they are proceeding to, 1000 blankets.

3. Information as to entraining for the 2/R.Irish Regt., 7/8 R.Innis,Fus., 7/8 R.Irish Fus., and 49th T.M.B., will be issued later.

4. Advance parties from Battalions and T.M.B, should report to Town Major, TINCOURT at 10 a.m. 17th inst., and not at 11 a.m. as previously stated. One Officer must be sent with each Advance Party.

W. [illegible] Statt.
Captain,
for Staff Captain.
49th Infantry Brigade.

Issued through signals at 3.55 P.M.

Issued to:-
1. G.O.C,
2. Brigade Major.
3. Staff Captain.
4. 2/R.Irish Regt.
5. 7/R.Irish Regt.
6. 7/8 R.Innis.Fus,
7. 7/8 R.Irish Fus.
8. 49th T.M.B.,
9. Q.M. 2/R.Irish Regt.,
10. Q.M. 7/R.Irish Regt.,
11. Q.M. 7/8 R.Innis,Fus.,
12. Q.M. 7/8 R.Irish Fus.,

SECRET. COPY NO. 7

49TH INFANTRY BRIGADE.

ADMINISTRATIVE INSTRUCTION NO. 30. 16.12.17.

Reference 49th Infantry Brigade Order No. 198 and Administrative Instruction No. 29 both dated 16.12.17.

---

1. TRAINS.
The following are the Train arrangements for movement of 2/R.Irish Regt., 7/8 R.Innis.Fus., 7/8 R.Irish Fus., and 49th T.M.B., on night 17/18th Dec. 1917, from ST. EMILIE to Divisional Reserve in TINCOURT Area.
There will be 3 trains, to be known as "A" Train, "B" Train and "C" Train.

Capacity of each train,	600 all ranks.
Entraining Point,	Siding in F.13.c.
Detraining Point,	Siding in K.13.c.
Departure of trains	"A" Train, 9.0 p.m.
	"B" " 9.30 p.m.
	"C" " 10.0 p.m.

Each Company and T.M.B., will entrain as a complete Unit. Companies will entrain under direction of Staff Captain in order of arrival at entraining point, irrespective of the Battalion to which they belong.

3. One N.C.O. per Company and T.M.B., and 1 Officer per Battalion will report to Staff Captain at F.13.c.1.5 at 8.30 p.m. Each N.C.O. must know the strength in all ranks, of his Company. (F.13.c.1.5 at 8.30)

4. In order to avoid confusion, equipment will be worn.

5. During entraining there is to be no talking or shouting except by those on duty; and the lighting of candles, striking of matches or unnecessary shining of electric lamps is forbidden.

6. Advance Parties should arrange to meet their Companies at detraining Point, K.13.c.

Issued at 7.15 p.m. [illegible] Captain,
s/ Staff Captain,
49th Infantry Brigade.

Issued to:-

1. G.O.C.
2. Brigade Major.
3. Staff Captain.
4. 2/R.Irish Regt.,
5. 7/R.Irish Regt.,
6. 7/8 R.Innis.Fus.,
7. 7/8 R.Irish Fus.
8. 49th T.M.B.,
9. 16th Div., "Q".
10. Capt. [illegible].J.Forbes, M.C.

S E C R E T. Copy No ..10

49th INF. BDE ORDER No. 199.

16th December 1917.

Ref. Maps 57.c.S.E.
62.c.N.E.
1/20,000.

1. (a) 48th Inf. Bde. (less M.G.Company) will relieve 49th Inf. Bde. (less M.G.Company) in the Left Section of Div. Front from F.11.a.8.6 to X.26.d.50.45 on the night 17th/18th December.
(b) In accordance with above, reliefs, as per table below, will take place, unit commanders concerned being responsible for arranging guides and other details of reliefs.

RELIEF TABLE.

Unit.	Relieved by	Location.
7/8th R.Innis Fus.	2nd R. Dublin Fus.	Right Subsection from F.11.a.8.6 to MALASSISE Fm. Rd.)inclusive).
7/8th R. Irish Fus.	1st R.Dublin Fus.	Left Subsection from MALASSISE Fm. Rd (exclusive) to X.26.d.50.45.
2nd R.Irish Regt.	10th R.Dub. Fus.	In support in MALASSISE FM Area., and in ZEBRA & YAK POSTS.
7th (S.I.H)R.I.Rgt.	8/9th R.Dub.Fus.	In Bde. Reserve in STE. EMILIE.
49th T.M.Battery.	48th T.M.Battery.	

2. All (a) Trench Stores, (b) Ammunition, (c) Written Defence Schemes, (d) Written schemes of work in progress and proposed, and all other documents connected with the line will be carefully handed over to relieving units, and receipts taken for same.
Copies of (c) and (d) to reach Bde. H.Q. by noon 17th, and of (a) and (b) (with receipts) by 6 p.m. 18th.

3. (a) Completion of relief will be wired by code as under to Brigade Headquarters in the form of a message in reply to one numbered "B.M.C. 535".

2nd R. Irish Regt.	"NIL RETURN".
7th (S.I.H)R.I.Regt.	"NONE TO RECOMMEND".
7/8th R. Innis Fus.	"VACANCIES ALLOTTED".
7/8th R.Irish Fus.	"1483 Sgt G. BAKER".
49th T.M.Battery.	"2466 Cpl T. WILSON".

(b) Brigade H.Q. REPORT CENTRE will close at STE. EMILIE on completion of relief and will reopen at same hour at HAMEL (J.18.d.8.1).

4. On relief the 49th Inf. Bde. will move back into DIV. RESERVE in HAMEL-TINCOURT Area, according to attached Move Table.

5. ACKNOWLEDGE.

Captain,

Brigade Major, 49th Infantry Brigade.

Issued through Signals.

Copy No. 1 to G. O. C.
.. 2 Staff Captain.
.. 3 Asst. Staff Captain.
.. 4 Bde. Int. Officer.
.. 5 Bde. Signal Officer.
.. 6 Bde. Transport Officer.
.. 7 2nd R. Irish Regt.
.. 8 7th (S.I.H) R.I.Regt.
.. 9 7/8th R. Innis Fus.
.. 10 7/8th R. Irish Fus.
.. 11 49th M.G.Company.
.. 12 49th T.M.Battery.
.. 13 157th Field Coy, R.E.
.. 14 144th Coy, A.S.C.
.. 15 113th Field Ambulance.
.. 16 16th Div. (G).
.. 17 16th Div. (Q).
.. 18 16th Div. Artillery.
.. 19 D.M.G.O.
.. 20 C.R.E.
.. 21 A.D.M.S.
.. 22 47th Inf. Bde.
.. 23 48th Inf. Bde.
.. 24 21st Division.
.. 25 110th Inf. Bde.
.. 26 Left Group R.F.A.
.. 27-28 War Diary.
.. 29 File.

MOVE TABLE TO ACCOMPANY 49TH INF. BDE. ORDER No. 199.

UNIT.	From.	To.	Remarks.
Brigade Headquarters	STE.EMILIE.	HAMEL J.18:d.8.1.	By March.
7th (S.I/H) R.Irish Regt.	STE. EMILIE.	BUIRE.	By March. Dinners to be cooked enroute and had on arrival at destination. 200 yards distance between Companies and between rear Coy. and Transport.
2nd R. Irish Regt.	Support.	TINCOURT.	By train. Instructions re entraining and detraining points, times, etc, issued later by Staff Captain.
7/8th R. Innis Fus.	Right Subsection.	do.	do.
7/8th R. Irish Fus.	Left Subsection.	do.	do.
49th T.M.Battery.	Line.	do.	do.

S E C R E T.   Copy No ..9.

49th INF. BDE. ORDER No. 200.

20th December 1917.

1. The 49th Inf. Bde. will relieve the 47th Inf. Bde. in the Right Section on the 23rd December in accordance with attached table.
   All details will be arranged between Officers Commanding units concerned.

2. The following will be carefully taken over by relieving units:-
   (a) Trench Stores.
   (b) Ammunition and Grenades.
   (c) Written Defence Schemes.
   (d) Written schemes of work in progress & proposed.
   (e) All maps and other documents connected with the line.

   Copies of (a) and (b) will be forwarded to Brigade H.Q. by 6 p.m. 24th December.

3. Advance parties, to include snipers, observers and Nos. 1 of Lewis Gun Teams will take over during daylight and will proceed by march route.

4. A map showing dispositions of battalions will be forwarded to Brigade Headquarters by 6 p.m. 24th December.

5. 49th Inf. Bde. H.Q. will close at HAMEL and reopen at STE. EMILIE on completion of relief.

6. Completion of reliefs will be reported by wire by the code word "SALVAGE".

7. ACKNOWLEDGE.

I. L. MacDonald. Captain,
Brigade Major, 49th Infantry Brigade.

Issued through Signals.

Copy No.			
1 to	G.O.C.	15 to	16th Division (G).
.. 2	Staff Captain.	16	16th Division (Q).
.. 3	Bde. Int. Officer.	17	16th Div. Artillery.
.. 4	Bde. Sig. Officer.	18	D.M.G.O.
.. 5	Bde. T'port Officer.	19	C. R. E.
.. 6	2nd R. Irish Regt.	20	A.D.M.S.
.. 7	7th (SIH) R.Irish Rgt.	21	47th Inf. Bde.
.. 8	7/8th R. Innis Fus.	22	48th Inf. Bde.
.. 9	7/8th R. Irish Fus.	23	24th Division.
.. 10	49th M.G.Company.	24	Left Bde.24th Div.
.. 11	49th T.M.Battery.	25	Right Group R.F.A.
.. 12	157th Field Coy,R.E.	26-27	War Diary.
.. 13	144th Coy, A.S.C.	28	File.
.. 14	113th Field Amb.		

RELIEF TABLE TO ACCOMPANY 49th INF. BDE. ORDER No. 200.

Relieving Unit.	Unit to be relieved.	Location.	Remarks.
2nd R. Irish Regt.	6th R. Irish Regt.	Right Subsection.	Relieving unit not to be East of LEMPIRE before 5.30 p.m. Proceed by train leaving TINCOURT siding at 3 p.m. (K.13.c).
7th (SIH) R.Irish Rgt.	6th Connaught Rangers.	Left Subsection.	By march route. Relieving unit not to be East of LEMPIRE before 5 p.m.
7/8th R. Innis Fus.	1st R. Munster Fus.	Support. LEMPIRE.	By train leaving TINCOURT siding at 5.30 p.m. Relieving unit not to enter LEMPIRE before 6 p.m. One Company to proceed by train leaving 3 p.m.
7/8th R.Irish Fus.	7th Leinster Regt.	Reserve. STE.EMILIE.	By march route. Relief to be complete by 1 p.m.
49th T.M.Battery.	47th T.M.Battery.	Right Section.	By march route under arrangements to be made by O.C. 49th T.M.Battery.
49th Inf. Bde.H.Q.	47th Inf. Bde. H.Q.	STE.EMILIE.	Move to be arranged by Staff Captain.

NOTE.- All movement East of STE. EMILIE will be by platoons at 5 minutes interval.
Units will report at the train 15 minutes before time of starting.

3.30pm

SECRET.

Copy No. 8.

49th INF. BDE. ORDER No. 201.

28th December 1917.

1. The 7/8th R. Innis Fus. will relieve the 2nd R. Irish Regt. and the 7/8th R. Irish Fus. will relieve the 7th (SIH) R. Irish Regt. in the Right and Left Subsections of the Right Section respectively on the night December 29th/30th.

2. On completion of relief the 2nd R. Irish Regt. will proceed to Brigade Reserve in STE. EMILIE and the 7th (SIH) R. Irish Regt. to Brigade Support in LEMPIRE and RONSSOY.

3. Advance parties, to include snipers, observers and Nos. 1 of Lewis Gun Teams will proceed by daylight to take over. Taking over parties from units being relieved will report at Support and Reserve Battalion H.Q. by 2 p.m. 29th instant.

4. Order of relief will be as follows :-

7/8th R. Irish Fus. will not be East of LEMPIRE before 4.30 p.m. Their leading two Companies will relieve the two rear Companies of the 7th (SIH) R. Irish Regt. who will at once relieve two Companies of the 7/8th R. Innis Fus. in the LEMPIRE DEFENCES. As soon as latter relief is complete, the 7/8th R. Innis Fus. will commence to relieve the 2nd R. Irish Regt. Officers Commanding Battalions will maintain touch with their Companies during the relief. All movement will be by platoons at 500 yards interval.

5. All other details will be arranged between Commanding Officers concerned.

6. The following will be carefully handed and taken over:-

(a) Trench Stores.
(b) Defence arrangements.
(c) Work in progress and proposed.
(d) Working Parties.

Copies of (a) and (c) to reach Brigade H.Q. by 4 p.m. 30th instant.

7. Completion of relief in front line will be notified to Brigade H.Q. by code word "MARGARINE".
7th (SIH) R. Irish Regt. and 2nd R. Irish Regt. will notify Brigade H.Q. when they arrive in Support and Reserve respectively by code word "BUTTER".

8. The 48th Inf. Bde. is being relieved by 47th Inf. Bde. on the night December 29th/30th.

9. ACKNOWLEDGE.

[illegible] Captain,
Brigade Major, 49th Infantry Brigade.

Issued through Signals.

Copy No. 1 to G.O.C.
" 2 Staff Captain.
" 3 Bde. Sig. Officer.
" 4 Bde. Int. Officer.
" 5 2nd R. Irish Rgt.
" 6 7th (SIH) R. Irish Rgt.
" 7 7/8th R. Innis Fus.
" 8 7/8th R. Irish Fus.
" 9 49th M.G. Company.
" 10 49th T.M. Battery.
" 11 155th Field Coy. R.E.
12 to 11?th Coy. A.S.C.
13 113th Field Amb.
14 16th Division (G).
15 16th Division (Q).
16 16th Div. Artillery.
17 D.M.G.O.
18 LEFT ~~Right~~ Bde. 24th Div.
19 47th Inf. Bde.
20 48th Inf. Bde.
21 Right Group.
22-23 War Diary.
24 File.

7/8 R. Irish Fus.

To all Coys.

S P E C I A L   O R D E R.

The Division completes today its second year of War.

During that year it has added to its history the glorious deeds of WYTSCHAETE, FREZENBERG and CROISILLES HEIGHTS.

The Divisional Commander congratulates all ranks on the manner in which they have upheld the spirit of our motto. We enter our third year with pride in the records of the Past, with confidence in the present, and with determination to act up in the future to the traditions of the Irish Division,

"EVERYWHERE AND ALWAYS FAITHFUL".

W. B. Hickie,

Major-General,

Dec. 17th. 1917.   Commanding 16th.(Irish)Division.

Copy to each Coy

16. J.
G.D.

Vol 24

WAR DIARY,

FOR MONTH OF JANUARY, 1918.

VOLUME :- 16.

UNIT :- 7/8th R. Irish Fusilrs.

7/8th (S) Battn Royal Irish Fusiliers

Instructions regarding War Diaries and Intelligence Summaries are contained in F. S. Regs., Part II. and the Staff Manual respectively. Title pages will be prepared in manuscript.

WAR DIARY
or
INTELLIGENCE SUMMARY.
(Erase heading not required.)

JANUARY 1918

Army Form C. 2118.

Place	Date	Hour	Summary of Events and Information	Remarks and references to Appendices
			Ref Map 62 c. N	
Left sub Sect Right Sect	1/1/18		'A' + 'B' Coys relieved 'C' + 'D' Coys in the front line day very quite	
H. Q. LEMPIRE			enemy shelled back area	
	2/1/18		Hostile artillery shelled Batt H. Q. two of the being wounded	
	3/1/18		Very quite, no operations took place during the day, at night	
			there very heavy shelling on the Batt front on our left	
Left Sub Section Right	4/1/18		The 49th Inf Bde was relieved by the 48th Inf Bde. The Battn was relieved by the 2nd R Dub.	
			Fus and on relief moved into Divisional Reserve at HAMEL	
HAMEL	5/1/18		Day spent in cleaning up, checking deficiencies &c	
	6/1/18		Remained in divisional reserve. The men were given their Xmas dinner as the Battn was in	
			the line on the 25th Dec. The whole Battn sat down together in the village theatre	
	7/1/18		Remained in divisional Reserve	
	8/1/18		and provided a working party of 6 officers and 200	
			O.R. at RONSOY.	
	9/1/18		Remained in reserve. Several officers reconnoitred the support line	
	10/1/18		The 49th Inf. Bde relieved the 47th Inf Bde in the left section. The Battn	
			moved up on light railway & relieved the 7th Leinster Regt in support.	

7/8th (S) Battn Royal Irish Fusiliers

WAR DIARY
or
INTELLIGENCE SUMMARY.
(Erase heading not required.)

JANUARY 1918

Army Form C. 2118.

Instructions regarding War Diaries and Intelligence Summaries are contained in F. S. Regs., Part II. and the Staff Manual respectively. Title pages will be prepared in manuscript.

Special Sheet. LEMPIRE 1/10,000

Place	Date	Hour	Summary of Events and Information	Remarks and references to Appendices
LEFT SUPPORT LEMPIRE	11/1/18		The day passed quietly. Hostile artillery intermittently fire over scattered areas. Owing to the thaw setting in all trenches were in a flooded state and bad condition.	[illegible]
	12/1/18		The day passed quietly with low visibility & slight artillery activity. Bn. H.Q., MALASSISSE Fm were lightly shelled during the day. The night passed quietly except for a lively bombardment on our left at 2.15 am	[illegible]
	13/1/18		More snow fell during the morning and with excellent visibility our own and enemy aircraft very active. One of our planes brought down an EA out of control at 10.5 am and another in flames at 10.15 am	[illegible]
	14/1/18		In support. The day passed quietly except for occasional shelling of MALASSISSE Fm	[illegible]
	15/1/18		" " . Every available man was at work under the RE. Hostile artillery was more active than usual shelling MALASSISSE Fm & the ground west of it with 4.2 & 5.9".	[illegible]
	16/1/18		The Battn relieved the 2nd R Irish Regt in the left sub-section. Relief was complete by 8 pm. From 9 pm to 10.30 pm hostile artillery traversed the ground from MALASSISSE Fm to Sunken Rd 4.2	[illegible]
	17/1/18		At 3.55 am the enemy put down a heavy barrage on our right and sent over a raiding party against the Battn on our right. The barrage ceased at 4.15 am	

D. D. & L., London, E.C. (A7853) Wt. W20j/M1672 350,000 5/17 Sch. 52a Forms/C/2118/14

7/8th (S) Battn ROYAL IRISH FUSILIER

Instructions regarding War Diaries and Intelligence Summaries are contained in F. S. Regs., Part II, and the Staff Manual respectively. Title pages will be prepared in manuscript.

WAR DIARY
or
INTELLIGENCE SUMMARY.
(*Erase heading not required.*)

JANUARY 1918

Army Form C. 2118.

Place	Date	Hour	Special Sheet LEMPIRE 1/10,000 Summary of Events and Information	Remarks and references to Appendices
Left Sub-Sector EPEHY	17/1/18		Our artillery was active throughout the day firing concentration shoots on the ridge in F 29. From 7pm to 11 pm a patrol reconnoitred the MALASSISE Rd. A large enemy party was encountered. Our patrol lay in wait, but the enemy move off in a southerly direction towards PRIEL Fm. The night passed quietly.	Wg
	18/1/18		The day pass fairly quietly. The night was exceptionally quiet except for slightly increased enemy M.G. fire. A fighting patrol could find no trace of the enemy in No Man's Land	Wg
	19/1/18		At 5.45 am our artillery opened up a slow rate of fire chiefly opposite VILLERS-GUISLAIN as an enemy raid was anticipated. Artillery activity increased and our artillery carried out Divisional concentrations four times during the day. Hostile artillery did not retaliate. Our usual fighting patrol was out	Wg
	20/1/18		At 4 am, divisional artillery carried out a 'dummy' raid on HOLTS BANK without drawing retaliation. At about 6.20 am, the division on the right carried out a raid, support by the artillery of this division. The situation did not become normal until 7.30 am. An escaped German prisoner was recaptured by one of our men in No Man's Land early in the morning. Hostile artillery was	

D. D. & L., London, E.C. (A7833) Wt. W593/M1672 350,000 4/17 Sch. 52a Forms/C/2118/14

1/8th (S) Battn ROYAL IRISH FUSILIERS

WAR DIARY
or
INTELLIGENCE SUMMARY.
(*Erase heading not required.*)

JANUARY 1918

Army Form C. 2118.

Instructions regarding War Diaries and Intelligence Summaries are contained in F. S. Regs., Part II. and the Staff Manual respectively. Title pages will be prepared in manuscript.

Place	Date	Hour	Special LEMPIRE SHEET — Summary of Events and Information	Remarks and references to Appendices
			chiefly on back areas and counter battery work. The night passed unusually quietly.	[illegible]
EPEHY	22/1/18		The day passed very quietly, our own & hostile artillery was inactive. Aerial activity from 10 am to 12 noon. The Battn was relieved in the Left Sub-Section by the 2nd R. Irish Regt and on relief moved into Brigade reserve in St EMELIE. Total casualties during this tour amounted to 1 O.R. killed, [illegible] wounded, 1 O.R. wounded at duty.	[illegible]
St EMELIE	23/1/18		Remained in reserve, supplied working parties of 72 O.R's	[illegible]
	24/1/18		" " " "	[illegible]
	25/1/18			[illegible]
	26/1/18 27/1/18			[illegible]
	28/1/18		The Battn relieved the 2nd R Irish Regt in the Left Sub-Section. The night passed quietly. Owing to bright moonlight, our own & enemy aircraft carried out night flights.	[illegible]
	29/1/18		A fighting patrol of an Officer's party, supported by a Lewis Gun, reconnoitred the vicinity of CATELET COPSE without encountering an enemy. Aerial activity was very marked on both sides owing to excellent visibility. Hostile artillery was active on	

D. D. & L., London, E.C. (A7883) Wt. W1o/M1672 350,000 4/17 Sch. 52a Forms/C/2118/14

7/8th (S) Battn R. IRISH FUSILIERS

JANUARY 1918

Army Form C. 2118.

WAR DIARY
or
INTELLIGENCE SUMMARY.
(Erase heading not required.)

Instructions regarding War Diaries and Intelligence Summaries are contained in F. S. Regs., Part II, and the Staff Manual respectively. Title pages will be prepared in manuscript.

Place	Date	Hour	Special LEMPIRE Sheet — Summary of Events and Information	Remarks and references to Appendices
29/1/18	(Contd)		counter battery & back areas, but the forward zone remained untouched	[illegible]
30/1/18			Our artillery was active during the day, firing 3 concentration shoots. Hostile artillery intermittently shelled EPEHY & battery zone with 15 cm, 10.5 cm & 77 mm. Otherwise the day passed quietly. A fighting patrol reconnoitred CATELET COPSE and found no sign of the enemy.	[illegible]
31/1/18			A thick fog lasted throughout the day & prevented operations of any kind. Our usual patrol was out during the night	[illegible]
1/1/18			Owing to continued misty weather, no operations were possible. Hostile MG's were active during the day firing through the mist. A large patrol found CATELET COPSE unoccupied	[illegible]

[illegible] Lieut. Col.
Comdg. 7/8th (S) Bn. Rl. Irish Fus.

D. D. & L., London, E.C. (A7883) Wt. W803/M1672 350,000 2/17 Sch. 52a Forms/C/2118/14

SECRET. JANUARY 3rd.1918 COPY NO....

7/8th.(S)Battalion The Royal Irish Fusiliers Order No.47.

---

1. The 48th.Infantry Brigade (less M.G.Coy) will relieve the 49th. Infantry Brigade(Less M.G.Coy.) in the Right Section on the night of 4/5th.January 1918.

2. The Battalion will be relieved by the 2nd.Royal Dublin Fusiliers in the Left Sub-section as under:-
"A"Coy.2.R.Dublins will relieve "D"Coy.7/8th.R.Irish Fusiliers
"B"Coy.2.Dublins will relieve "A"Coy.7/8th.R.Irish Fusiliers.
"C"Coy.2nd.R.Dublins will relieve "C"Coy.7/8th.R.Irish Fusrs.
"D"Coy.xxxxxxxxxxxxx 2nd.DUBLINS will relieve "B"Coy.7/8.R.Irish Fus.

3. GUIDES.
Guides as under will report to the Adjutant at Bn.H.Qrs.
FOR ADVANCE PARTY
One N.C.O.per Company and one from H.Qrs.will be at Bn.H.Qrs.at 1.30.p.m.and be sent to F.21.c.3.9. by 2.0.p.m.
MAIN BODY
One Guide per Platoon i.e . four per Company together with 2/Lieut. O'CONNELL will report at Bn.H.Qrs.at 4.0.p.m. and be sent to F.21.c.3.9. by 4.30.p.m.

4. HANDING OVER The following will be carefully handed over:-
(a) Trench Stores etc.
(b) Defence Schemes etc.
(c) Ammunition,Grenades &c.
(d) All Work in progress and proposed.
Copies of (c) will reach Battalion H.Qrs.by 9.0.a.m. 4th.inst.and copies of (a) by 9.0.a.m. 5th.inst.Great care must bev taken so that (c) agrees with those handed over in (a).

5. TRANSPORT.
Owing to the fact that Transport has to be reduced to a minimum on the Ste.EMELIE - RONSSOY ROAD the following are the arrangements.
(a) All Officers' Mess Boxes only will be stacked outside Bn.H.Qrs. between dusk and xxxxx 5.0.p.m.These will be cleared by one limber at that hour.Any boxes not there by 5.0.p.m.will not be available for use until the following morning.
(b) The remaining Trench Kits.,L.G.Drums etc.will be dumped at each Coy's Ration Dump and H.Q.at H.Q.Dump.One limber each will be sent so as to clear these dumps by 9.30.p.m.A N.C.O.is to be left i/c of each Dump.
All Petrol Tins and Periscopes not taken over in the line as Trench Stores, are to be brought out by the Company on whose charge they xxx are at present.The petrol Tins will be handed over to and checked by the Q.M.

6. On Completion of relief the Brigade will be in Divisional Reserve,the Battalion being billetted in HAMEL,the necessary arrangements for xxxx taking over these billets will be made by Major T.J.C.ROBERTS in conjunction with the Q.M.

7. MOVE TO HAMEL. The Battalion will move to Ste.EMILIE and entrain there for HAMEL.All movement East Of Ste.EMILIE will be by Platoons at five minutes interval..Trains will leave Ste.EMILIE at 6.30.p.m. and 7.30.p.m Lieut.W.H.WATERS will entrain the Battalion and report to a represent-ative of 49th.Inf.Bde.before dusk.Each Train accommodates 600.No Coys. will entrain in less numbers than a Platoon and each Company Comdr.will be responsible that every man of his Coy.is on the train.
Trains will move off when full irrespective of Units on board.

8. Completion of Relief to be reported in Code Word."JUGGLER"
9. ACKNOWLEDGE

Captain & A/Adjutant.
7/8th.(S)Battalion The Royal Irish Fusiliers

ISSUED THROUGH SIGNALS AT P.M. 3/1/18.

Copy No. 1.	"A" Coy.	Copy No. 8.	Sigs.
2.	"B" Coy.	9.	R.S.M.
3.	"C" Coy.	10.	49th. Inf. Bde.
4.	"D" Coy.	11.	2nd. Dublins.
5.	Q.M.	12.	Lieut. WATERS
6.	T.O. (Maj. T.J.C. ROBERTS)	13	Spare.
7.	M.O.	14.	File.

15 & 16 War Diary.

SECRET. JANUARY 9th. 1918 COPY NO..........

7/8th. (S) Battalion The Royal Irish Fusiliers Order No. 46.

---

1. The 48th. Infantry Brigade will relieve the 47th. Infantry Brigade in the Left Section on the night 10th/11th. January 1918.

2. The Battalion will relieve the 7th. LEINSTERS in Support and on relief will be disposed as under :-

		Coy. H. Q.
Battalion H. Qrs.	LEMPIRE F.16.a.9.3.	
"A" Company	LEMPIRE - UPTON WOOD-MAY COPSE.	LEMPIRE.
"B" Company	MALASSISE FARM	In Farm.
"C" Company.	Railway Cutting in F.9.c.	In Cutting
"D" Company.	Posts North of MALASSISE FARM	ditto.

3. Advance Parties consisting of one Officer, No's 1. of L.Gun Teams, Gas N.C.O., one N.C.O. from Battalion H.Qrs. will reportat their respective H.Qrs. at 2.0.p.m.

4. One Guide per Platoon and Battalion H.Qrs. will be at [meet the Bn.] CROSS ROADS F.8.c.15.70. Each Guide will be provided with a slip of paper stating the Company that he comes from.

5. "A" Company 7/8th. R. Irish Fusrs. will relieve "D" Coy. 7th. LEINSTERS.
"B" Company 7/8th. R. Irish Fusrs. will relieve "C" Coy. 7th. LEINSTERS.
"C" Company 7/8th. R. Irish Fusrs. will relieve "B" Coy. 7th. LEINSTERS
"D" Company 7/8th. R. Irish Fusrs. will relieve "A" Coy. 7th. LEINSTERS.

6. One Blanket per man will be stacked by Companies at Q.M. Stores, rolled in bundles of ten by 9.30.a.m.

7. Officers Valises as to be left behind will be stacked outside Bn.H.Q. at 2.0.p.m. The Transport Officer will arrange for 1 Limber per Coy. and two limbers for Battalion H.Qrs. to be at Bn.H.Qrs. by 3.0.p.m. for 20 L.Gun Magazines per Gun, Officers Trench Kits and Mess Boxes.

8. Lewis Guns and 24 L.Gun Magazines per Gun will be carried by the teams.

9. Rations will be sent up and dumped at their various H.Qrs.
WATER 12 Tins per Company, 8 for Bn.H.Qrs. will be sent up. O.C. "B", "C" & "D" Coys. will arrange to send back their empty tins each night. "A" Coy. & Battalion H.Qrs. will refill from POINT in LEMPIRE. A Water Cart will be sent up nightly to fill tanks at "C" Coy. and MALASSISE FARM.

10 The Platoon of "A" Coy. in MAY COPSE will be attached to "B" Coy. for Rations and Tactical Purposes. Rations [& water] for this Platoon will be sent to "B" Coy.

11. The Four Lewis Gunners per Company under instruction will be temporarily attached to "A" Coy. under the L.G.O. and will entrain with "A" Coy.

12. ENTRAINING -- ORDER OF . DEPART AT ENTRAINING SIDING AT.

"A" Company	3.45.p.m.
"B" Coy.	3.45.p.m.
"C" Company	4.15.p.m.
"D" Company.	4.15.p.m.
Battalion H.Qrs.	4.15.p.m.

All movement EAST of Ste EMILIE by Platoons at 5 minutes interval.

13. The following will be carefully taken over:-
(a) Defence Schemes and documents excep t Aeroplane Photos.
(b) All work in progress and proposed (in writing.)
(c) Trench Stores.
(d) S.A.A. and Grenades.
Copies of (b) and (c) together with a rough sketch showing disposition and positions of Lewis Guns to reach Bn.H.Q. by 10.0.a.m. 11th. inst.

14. SOCKS A clean pair of Socks per man will be issued on the morning of the 10th.inst. Starting on the night of the 11th.inst. one clean pair per man will be sent up. O.C.Coys. must ensure that the equivalent number of dirty socks are sent down in empty limbers.

15. Completion of relief to be reported by Code Word "CECIL"

16. ACKNOWLEDGE.

Captain
A/Adjutant.
9/8th.(S)Battalion The Royal Irish Fusiliers.

ISSUED THROUGH SIGNALS AT 8:30 p.m. 9/1/17.

Copy No. 1. "A" Coy. ✓
2. "B" Coy. ✓
3. "C" Coy. ✓
4. "D" Coy. ✓
5. Q.M.
6. T.O.
7. M.O.

Copy No. 8. R.S.M.
9. 49th. Infantry Brigade.
10. 7th. LEINSTER REGT.
11. File.
12. War Diary.
13. War Diary.
14. Lewis Gun Officer.

15. Signals. ✓

~~SECRET.~~ JANUARY 16th.1918 COPY NO. 16

7/8th.(S)Battalion The Royal Irish Fusiliers Order No.40.
REFERENCE Special Sheet LEMPIRE.

1. The Battalion will relieve the 2nd.Bn.The Royal Irish Regt. in the Left Sub-Section on the night of the 16th/17th.January 1918.

2. "A" Coy.7/8th.R.Irish Fusrs. will relieve "C" Coy. 2.R.Ir.Regt. Left. Front.
"B" Coy.7/8th.R.Irish Fusrs. will relieve "D" Coy. 2.R.Ir.Regt. Right Front.
"D" Coy.7/8th.R.Irish Fusrs. will relieve "B" Coy. 2.R.Ir.Regt. in Support.
"C" Coy.7/8th.R.Irish Fusrs. will relieve "A" Coy. 2.R.Ir.Regt. in Reserve.

3. GUIDES.	COMPANY.	Place	Time
	"B" Company	MALASSISE FARM	4.30.p.m.
	"C" Company "D" Company "A" Company	"C" Coy.H.Qrs. in CUTTING about F.[illegible]	4.0.p.m.

Each Platoon 7/8th.Royal Irish Fusiliers will detail a reliable guide to take ~~back~~ the relieved Platoon of 2nd.R.Irish Regt. to the position vacated.

4. Rations for "A", "C" & "D" Coys. /& Battalion H.Qrs. will be sent to the Cutting in F.[illegible]
Rations for "B" Coy. will be sent to No.12.COPSE.
Hours of Meals :-
BREAKFASTS 8.0.a.m. DINNERS 5.0.p.m.
~~WATER~~ Filled Petrol Tins will be sent ~~nightly~~ to Cookhouses. Water Carts will report nightly; one at Battalion H.Qrs. one at cookhouses (to make two journeys)

5. ADVANCE PARTIES Advance parties of One Officer, One N.C.O. and Nos.1. of Lewis Gun Teams will report at Battalion H.Qrs. of 2nd.R.Irish Regt. at F.1.d.7.8. at 10.0.a.m.

6. HANDING OVER. The following will be carefully handed over; copies of (a) & (c) to be sent to this Office by 10.0.a.m. 17th.inst.
(a) Trench Stores
(b) Defence Schemes.
(c) Work in progress and proposed.
(d) ~~Working Parties~~. Grenade Returns

Grenade Returns for the 16th.inst. will be sent to this Office by 12.noon that date, also (c)

7. A Limber will report to Battalion H.Qrs. as soon after dark as possible to take Mess Kit and O.Room Boxes to the new Battalion H.Qrs. The ~~XXXXXXXXXXXX~~ Maltese Cart will also be sent to convey the M.O.'s.kit &c. to new Aid Post.

8. All Working Parties will be found in the morning, but will not work after 12 noon.

9. ACKNOWLEDGE.

Captain.
A/Adjutant.
7/8th.(S)Battalion The Royal Irish Fusiliers

ISSUED THROUGH SIGNALS AT P.M. 16.1.18.

Copy No.1. "A" Coy. ✓
2. "B" Coy.
3. "C" Coy.
4. "D" Coy.
5. Q.M.
6. T.O.
7. M.O.
8. L.G.O. ✓

Copy No.9. R.S.M.
10. Cook Sergt.
11 Signals. ✓
12. 49th.Inf.Bde.
13. 2nd.The R.Irish Regt
14. Spare.
15. File.
16. War Diary.

COPY NO..........15..... JANUARY 21st.1918. SECRET..

7/8th.(S)Battalion The Royal Irish Fusiliers Order No.30.

---

1. The 2nd.Battalion The Royal Irish Regiment will relieve the Battalion in the Left Sub-Section on the night of the 22nd/23rd.inst. On relief the Battalion will move into Brigade Reserve in Ste.EMILIE.

2. "C"Coy.2nd.R.Irish Regt.will relieve "B"Coy.7/8.R.Ir.Fus.Right Front.
"D"Coy.2nd.R.Irish Regt.will relieve "A"Coy.7/8.R.Ir.Fus.Left Front.
"B"Coy.2nd.R.Irish Regt.will relieve "C"Coy.7/8.R.Ir.Fus.in RESERVE
"A"Coy.2nd.R.Irish Regt.will relieve "D"Coy.7/8.R.Ir.Fus.in SUPPORT.

3. Three guides per Company for "D","A"&"B"Coys.2nd.R.Irish Regt.will be at the AID POST in CUTTING (F.2.c.1.8.) at 5.30.p.m.,and guides for "C"Company 2nd.R.Irish Regt.will be at MALASSISE FARM at 5.30.p.m.

4. Advance Parties will report at the various Coy.H.Qrs.at 2.0.p.m. except in the case of the Right Company.

5. TRANSPORT &c..

(a) Two Limbers at Battalion H.Qrs.as soon after dark as possible.
One Limber at SUNKEN ROAD for "C"Company.
One Limber at "D"Company's Headquarters at 6.0.p.m.
One Limber at "A"Company's Headquarters at 6.0.p.m. (X.30.d.35.20.)
One Limber for "B"Company at WILLOW TREES F.3.c.5.9.
This Transport is for Officer's Kits.,Mess Boxes and Lewis Guns.
The Transport Officer will arrange to send up the necessary tin boxes and wooden boxes.

(b) Dinners will be served before coming out.The Q.M.will arrange for a hot meal on arrival in Ste.EMILIE.

(c) TAKING OVER. The Quartermaster with a party will report at Bn.H.Q. 7th.(SIH)R.Irish Regt.at 4.0.p.m.to take over.

HANDING OVER.

(a) TRENCH STORES.
(b) Defence Arrangements.
(c) Work in progress and proposed (in writing)
(d) Grenade Returns.

Copies of (c) & (d) to reach Battalion H.Qrs.by first runner on 22nd.inst.Copies by 12 noon 23rd.inst duly countersigned.
Gum Boots must be handed over.

(d) The Q.M.will arrange to send up Officers' Valises,Blankets &c.

6. BATHS..

Baths at VILLERS FAUCON(100 men per hour)are allotted as under for the 23rd.inst.
8.0.a.m. to 9.15.a.m. "C"Company. 9.30.a.m. to 10.30.a.m. "B"Coy. 11.30.a.m. to 1.0.p.m. "A"Company. 2.45.p.m. to 3.30.p.m. and 4.0.p.m. to 4.30.p.m. "D"Company..
The R.S.M.will be responsible that Battalion H.Qrs.parade with their Companies.

7. Completion of relief will be reported in Code Word "T/30.noted"

8. Companies will report their arrival in billets to Orderly Room.

9. ACKNOWLEDGE.

Captain.
A/Adjutant.
7/8th.(S)Battalion The Royal Irish Fusiliers

ISSUED THROUGH SIGNALS AT 8.0.P.M. 21.1.18.

Copy No.1. "A"Coy.
2. "B"Coy.
3. "C"Coy.
4. "D"Coy.
5. Q.M.
6. T.O.
7. M.O.
8. Signals.

Copy No.9. R.S.M.
10. Lewis Gun Officer.
11. 49th.Infantry Bde.
12. 7th.(SIH)R.Irish Regt.
13. Spare.
14 2nd.The R.Irish Regt.
15. War Diary.
16. File.

SECRET. JANUARY 27th.1916. COPY NO. 15

7/8th.(S)Battalion The Royal Irish Fusiliers Order No.. 31.

1. The Battalion will relieve the 2nd.Royal Irish Regiment in the Left Sector on the night 28th/29th.January 1916.

2. "A" Coy.7/8th.R.Irish Fusrs.will relieve "C" Coy.2nd.R.Irish Regt.Right FRONT.
"B" Coy.7/8th.R.Irish Fusrs.will relieve "D" Coy.2nd.R.Irish Regt Left FRONT.also 2.Platoons 2nd.R.Irish Regt.in [illegible].
"C" Coy.7/8th.R.Irish Fusrs.will relieve "A" Coy.2.R.Ir.Regt.in SUPPORT.
"D" Coy.7/8th.R.Irish Fusrs.will relieve "B" Coy.2.R.Ir.Regt.in RESERVE.

3. O.C."C" Coy.will take over the posts with one Platoon and an extra [illegible] No.4.& 6 Posts.He will arrange patrols in relief [illegible] etc.Two Platoons of "C" Coy.will take up position in [illegible].
O.C."D" Coy.will occupy the trenches and Posts in [illegible] occupied by the SUPPORT COY.during the last tour.O.C."B" & "C" Coys.will arrange details of GUIDES &c.with the Company Commanders concerned.

4. GUIDES.
1.per Platoon for "B" Coy. by [illegible] at 4.30.p.m.
1.per Platoon for other Coys. at [illegible] at 5.15.p.m.

5. Companies will pass the Starting Point at [illegible]
"C" Company 5.0.p.m. "D" Company 5.15.p.m. "A" Coy. 5.30.p.m.
"B" Company 5.45.p.m. Bn.H.Qrs. 6.0.p.m. Five minutes interval between Platoons.

6. TRANSPORT &c.
(1) BLANKETS. To be rolled in bundles of 10 and stacked by Companies by [illegible] Quartermaster will arrange to collect.
RATIONS) ~~[illegible]~~ "B" Coys.Rations will be sent
COOKING) to [illegible]. Other Coys. rations for tomorrow will be dumped at their respective cookhouses at 7.30pm.
[illegible]
(2) [illegible] to be stacked outside [illegible] by [illegible] p.m. [illegible] for the trenches to be stacked separately by Coys.together with the [illegible] Gun Drums,per Coy. "B" and "C" Coys.will stack their [illegible] etc.at their [illegible].
(3) TRANSPORT. Two Limbers for Battalion H.Qrs.,One per Company for [illegible] L.Gun Drums etc.

7. ADVANCE PARTIES.
Advance Parties to report to Battalion H.Qrs.2nd.Royal Irish Regt.at [illegible] "C" & "B" Coys.will warn their parties specially.

8. The Quartermaster will arrange to hand over the present Billets.

9. [illegible]
Twenty four [illegible] to be carried by the [illegible] Officer will arrange for [illegible] for 24 magazines to be sent up in Coy.Limbers.

10. Every man is to rub his feet with Whale Oil before moving off.

11. TRENCH STORES.
The following are to be carefully taken over.Copies of (a) to be sent to Bn.H.Qrs.by first runner after [illegible] Numbers in (d) must agree with those shown in (a)
(a) Trench Store Lists.
(b) Defence Schemes and Information
(c) Work in Progress and proposed.
(d) Grenade Return.

12. Completion of Relief to be reported by Code word "[illegible]"

13. ACKNOWLEDGE.

[signature]
CAPTAIN
A/Adjutant.
7/8th.(S)Battalion The Royal Irish Fusiliers.

[illegible] 30 P.M. [illegible]

Copy Nos. 1. "A" Coy. — 9. [illegible]
2. "B" Coy. — 10. [illegible]
3. "C" Coy. — 11. [illegible]
4. "D" Coy. — 12. [illegible]
5. [illegible] — 13. [illegible]
6. [illegible] — 14. [illegible]
7. [illegible] — 15. [illegible]
8. [illegible] — 16. [illegible]

17. J.
Lalbury

Vol 25

W A R D I A R Y .

FOR MONTH OF FEBRUARY, 1918.

VOLUME:- 14

UNIT:- 1/8th R. Irish Fusrs.

7/8th (S) Battn ROYAL IRISH FUSILIERS

FEBRUARY 1918

C/153

Army Form C. 2118.

WAR DIARY
or
~~INTELLIGENCE SUMMARY.~~
(Erase heading not required.)

Instructions regarding War Diaries and Intelligence Summaries are contained in F. S. Regs., Part II. and the Staff Manual respectively. Title pages will be prepared in manuscript.

Place	Date	Hour	Summary of Events and Information	Remarks and references to Appendices
			Special Sheet LEMPIRE Sheet FRANCE 62 C. ~~1/40,000~~	
Left Sub Section EPEHY	1/2/18		Owing to the thick mist continuing no operations were possible. Hostile M.G. were active throughout the day firing through the mist. A large patrol found CATELET COPSE unoccupied	[initials]
	2/2/18		The following places were lightly shelled during the morning, 12 COPSE & MALASSISE Fm. Our Lewis guns dispersed two working [parties] during the day in STONE TR. Increased hostile MG fire. Otherwise the day passed quietly	[initials]
	3/2/18		The enemy registered on RELIEF COPSE, FOUR TREES [illegible] & 12 copse during the morning & showed increased activity in artillery fire on the forward zone. The Battn was relieved in the left sub-section by the 10th R Innis. Fus. & on relief moved into Divisional Reserve in VILLERS-FAUCON.	App 1 [initials]
VILLERS FAUCON	4/2/18		Remained in Divisional Reserve. Getting clothes cleaning up &c	[initials]
	5/2/18		Provided working parties. Intimation was received that the Battn was to be broken up under a new system in which each brigade was composed of only 3 Inf Battns	[initials]
	6/2/18		Remained in Reserve & provided working parties	
	7/2/18		During the afternoon the Battn was relieved by the 7/8th R. Innis. Fus. and on relief moved to HAMEL.	[initials] App 2

D. D. & L., London, E.C. (A7883) Wt. W693/M1672 350,000 4/17 Sch. 52a Forms/C2118/14

7/8th (S) Battn ROYAL IRISH FUSILIERS

WAR DIARY
or
INTELLIGENCE SUMMARY.
(*Erase heading not required.*)

FEBRUARY 1918

Army Form C. 2118.

Instructions regarding War Diaries and Intelligence Summaries are contained in F. S. Regs., Part II. and the Staff Manual respectively. Title pages will be prepared in manuscript.

Place	Date	Hour	Summary of Events and Information (Sheet FRANCE 62 c 1/40,000)	Remarks and references to Appendices
HAMEL	8/2/18		The day was spent in preparing drafts for the 1st & 9th Battns R. IRISH Fus., making up deficiencies, change of clothing, making out nominal rolls &c.	[illegible]
"	9/2/18		A draft of 9 officers & 240 O.R (approx) & 9 Off. & 220. O.R were sent to the 1st & 9th Battns R. Ir. Fus respectively. The party left in motor lorries	[illegible]
"	10/2/18		Drafts of 32 O.R was sent to the 6th Connaught Rangers, & O.R to the 1st R. Munster Fus. The only men then remaining with the Battn were those on the War Establishment of Bn HQ (Transport, S.B's &c)	[illegible]
"	11/2/18		The following numbers show the approximate postings of officers & men of the Battn on disbandment	
			1st R. Irish Fus — 12 officers — 240. O.R	
			9th R. " " — 11 " — 220 "	
			6th Connaught Rangers — 2 " — 34 "	
			7/8th R. Innis Fus — 1 " — 34 "	
			1st R. Munster Fus — 1 " — 44 "	
			R. I. L. I — – " — 18 "	[illegible]

P. Jolliffe Capt.

7/8 (S) BN. R. IRISH FUSILIERS.

D. D. & L., London, E.C. (A7883) Wt. W803/M1672 350,000 4/17 Sch. 52a Forms/C/2118/14

SECRET. [illegible] FEBRUARY 2nd.1918. COPY NO.........

7/8th.(S)Battalion The Royal Irish Fusiliers Order No. 82.

REFERENCE SHEET 62.C..1/40,000.

1. The Battalion will be relieved in the Left Sub-section by the 10th. Royal Dublin Fusiliers on the night of the 3rd/4th.February 1918.

2. "A"Company Royal Dublin Fusrs.will relieve "A"Coy.7/8.R.Irish Fusrs.
"B"Company Royal Dublin Fusiliers will relieve "D"Coy.R.Irish Fusrs.
"C"Company Royal Dublin Fusrs.will relieve "C"Company R.Irish Fusrs.
"D"Coy.R.Dublin Fusiliers will relieve "B"Coy.7/8.R.Irish Fusrs.

3. Advance Parties of 10th.Royal Dublin Fusiliers will report at Bn.H.Q. during the afternoon of the 3rd.inst.

4. GUIDES.
"A"Company will send Guides to HALA SNIPE FARM at 5.45.p.m.
"B","C","D"Coys.& Bn.H.Qrs.Guides will report to Captain [illegible].NEVILLE at Battalion H.Qrs.at 5.30.p.m.Three guides per Company to be sent and each guide ~~[illegible]~~ to have a slip of paper stating the Coy. 10th.R.Dublin Fusiliers he is to guide.

5. TRANSPORT.
The Transport Officer will arrange the following transport.:-
2.Limbers for Battalion H.Qrs.at 6.0.p.m.
1.Limber "A"Coy.at No.12.COPSE at 6.15.p.m.
1.Limber "D"Coy.at [illegible] F.R.O. at 6.15.p.m.
1.Limber each for "B" & "C"Coys.at [illegible] F.R.L.G.7[illegible]
These limbers are for Lewis Guns,L.Gun Drums and Officers Kits.

6. TAKING OVER. The Quartermaster with Billeting Party will report to [illegible] VILLERS FAUCON at 10.0.a.m. 3rd.February.the Q.M.will arrange to meet Companies as they march in at the Railway Crossing at [illegible].
The Quartermaster will arrange for a hot meal on arrival.

7. HANDING OVER &
(a) Trench Stores.
(b) Work in Progress and proposal in writing.
(c) Grenade Return to be countersigned by the relieving Coy.
Copies ~~[illegible]~~ of (a) to be sent to Battalion H.Qrs.by [illegible] 4th.inst.
Copies of (b) to be sent to Battalion H.Qrs.by first D.R.on the 3rd.inst.O.C."A"&"D"Coys.will hand over the reserve rations in No.12. COPSE and [illegible] WOOD.

8. Baths at VILLERS FAUCON are allotted as under:-
FEBRUARY 4th 3.0.p.m. to 4.0.p.m. "A"Company.
4.0.p.m. to 5.0.p.m. "B"Company.
6.0.p.m. to 7.0.p.m. "D"Company.
Battalion H.Qrs.will not bathe with their Companies.The remainder of the Battalion will bathe on the 5th.inst.

9. The Transport Officer will arrange to send [illegible] limber to Battalion H.Qrs.at 9.0.a.m.on the 3rd.inst.to convey a L.Gun Team of "D"Coy.to 1[illegible]th.R.F.A. Wagon lines,at [illegible].
O.C."D"Company will arrange for a complete team with equipment to be at Battalion H.Qrs.at that hour.

10. "A"& "D"Coys.will each arrange to have a patrol of one Officer and one N.C.O.and six O.Ranks out to cover the relief.these patrols will be withdrawn when relieved by the 10th.Royal Dublin Fusiliers.

11. Code Word for relief."[illegible] "A".NIL."

12. Arrival in Billets to be reported to Orderly Room.

13. ACKNOWLEDGE BY WIRE.

CAPTAIN & A/ADJUTANT

7/8th.(S)Battalion The Royal Irish Fusiliers

ISSUED THROUGH SIGNALS at 4.0.p.m.2/2/18.

Copy No.1. "A"Coy.	Copy No.2. "B"Coy.	Copy No.3. "C"Coy.
4. "D"Coy.	5. Q.M.	6. T.O.
7. M.O.	8. Signals.	9. R.S.M.
10. L.G.O.	11. 49.Inf.Bde.	12. 10.R.Dub.F
13. Spare.	14 File	15.&.16. War Diary

App. 2

SECRET.

FEBRUARY 6th.1918.... COPY NO.........

7/8th.(S)Battalion The Royal Irish Fusiliers Order No.33.

---

1. The Battalion will relieve the 7/8th.Royal Inniskilling Fusiliers to morrow 7th.inst.& will move to HAMEL by march route .

2. Advance Parties consisting of 2/Lieut.H.P.H.MONTGOMERY & four C.Q.M.Sgts.& 1 N.C.O.for Bn.H.Qrs. will rendezvous at Town Major's Office HAMEL at 10.0.a.m.

3. WORKING PARTIES
The party detailed in Bn.R.O.44 of to day will parade at 8.30.a.m. instead of at 9.0.a.m. O.C.Coys.must ensure that their men are carrying haversack rations.This party will stack their kits before parading.each Coy.leaving an N.C.O.to look after them.The party on completion of their task will march back to Camp,the Q.M.will arrange to leave their cookers so that the party can have dinners before marching to HAMEL.
The party of 4.N.C.O.'s & 48 men detached to TUNNELLING COY.will be relieved by 9.0.a.m. on 8th.inst.The Transport Officer will arrange to send transport to SAULCOURT at 8.30.a.m. 8th.inst.to pick up blankets etc.

4. TRANSPORT
Blankets will be rolled and stacked by Companies by 9.0.a.m. Officers' Valises and Mess kit will be packed ready by 2.0.p.m. O.C.Coys.will notify the T.Officer at what time they need their horses.
The T.Officer will arrange the necessary transport at above hours.

5. MARCH DISCIPLINE.
Companies will march independently to HAMEL,and the strictest attention is to be paid to march discipline."B"Coy.& Bn.H.Qrs.will march off as soon as relieved with the Drums."A","C" & "D"Coys. on return from work.Intervals of 500 yards between Coys.

6. Quartermaster will arrange to hand over the Camp.

7. O.C.Coys.will arrange to bring on the kit of the men who are receiving medal ribbons.

8. Acknowledge

[signature]
CAPTAIN
A/ADJUTANT.

7/8th.(S)Battalion The Royal Irish Fusiliers.

ISSUED THROUGH SIGNALS AT 9.35.P.M.

Copy No.1. "A"Coy.
2. "B"Coy.
3. "C"Coy.
4. "D"Coy.
5. Q.M.
6. T.O.
7. L.G.O.

Copy No.8. L.G.O.
9. M.O.
10. R.S.M.
11. Signals.
12. 49th.Inf.Bde.
13 & 14 War Diary
15 File.

SECRET   February 8th.1918   COPY NO.........

7/8th.(S)Battalion The Royal Irish Fusiliers Order No. 54.
REFERENCE SHEET 62 c.

::

1. The Drafts proceeding to the 1st.Royal Irish Fusiliers and 9th.Royal Irish Fusiliers will embus at 10.0.a.m. on 9th.inst at J.18.d.6.3.

2. The convoy will be in two sections.
   Section "A"   12 Lorries   } Each Lorry holds 22 men.
   Section "B"   11 Lorries.. }
   One bus is reserved for 25 Officers.

3. Section "A" will be for O.Ranks posted to the 1st.Royal Irish Fusiliers and will consist of 11 Lorries for the men, and one lorry for the Blankets, Officers' Kits and rations for the 10th.inst .
   Section "B" will be for O.Ranks posted to the 9th.Royal Irish Fusiliers and will consist of 10 Lorries for the men and one lorry for Blankets, Officers' Kits and rations for the 10th.inst.

4. The whole personnel proceeding will be formed up on the SOUTH SIDE of the road at 9.45.a.m.

5. The drafts for the 1st.& 9th.Battalions will form up separately. Draft for 1st.Royal Irish Fusiliers under Captain B.StJ.GALVIN M.C. about 300 yards WEST of CROSS ROADS at J.18.d.7.4.
   Draft for 9th.Battalion Royal Irish Fusiliers under 2/Lieut.W.F. REID will be formed up 200 yards WEST of these CROSS ROADS at J.18.d.7.4. The order from WEST to EAST is.
   Officers for 1st.Royal Irish Fusiliers.
   O.Ranks for 1st.Royal Irish Fusiliers.
   Officers for 9th.Royal Irish Fusiliers.
   O.Ranks for 9th.Royal Irish Fusiliers.
   Men will be detailed in parties of 22 for embussing purposes.
   O.C.each section will detail an Officer to report to the Staff Captain at 10.0.a.m.

6. The Quartermaster will arrange to Section "A" & "B" Rations in separate Limbers to Battalion H.Qrs. at 8.0.a.m. Drivers will report to the Adjutant before off loading. Lorries will pick up loads at Bn.H.Qrs.

7. O.C.Coys.will arrange to send two blankets per man, Officers' Valises to Battalion H.Qrs.at 8.0.a.m. where two separate dumps will be made under the supervision of the Quartermaster.

8. Section "A" will parade by Companies on road opposite CINEMA HALL at 8.30.a.m. in full marching order.
   Section "B" will parade by Companies on road opposite CINEMA HALL at 8.30.a.m.
   Officers i/c Sections are responsible for checking the rolls of their Sections and will report to the Adjutant at once any absentees. All O.Ranks who remain in Billets after the departure of these drafts, will parade outside Orderly Room at 11.0.a.m..

9. O.C."Coys.are responsible that all the men proceeding on the draft are in possession of their days' rations, iron rations and complete kits. They are also responsible that all men belonging to their Coys. detailed for either draft are warned for the parade.

[illegible] Captain & A/Adjutant.
7/8th.(S)Battalion The Royal Irish Fusiliers.

Copy No.1.. "A" Coy.
2. "B" Coy.
3. "C" Coy.
4. "D" Coy.
5. Q.M.
6. T.O.
Copy No.7. Captain B.St.J.GALVI[illegible]
8. Lieut.W.F.REID.
9. R.S.M.
10. War Diary.
11. War Diary.
12 Spare.
13 & 14 File.

11th Bn Roy Ir. Fus.

48th Bde 16th DIV.

France (Formed June 1918)
France July 1918.
Absorbed by 5th Bn. Aug 1918.

Aug 18

1918 JULY – 1918 AUG

ABSORBED by 5 BN

4 5th [illegible]

Abroad [illegible] 27/4/18

Instructions regarding War Diaries and Intelligence Summaries are contained in F. S. Regs., Part II. and the Staff Manual respectively. Title pages will be prepared in manuscript.

WAR DIARY
or
~~INTELLIGENCE SUMMARY.~~

(Erase heading not required.)

11th Bn Royal Irish Fus

48 Bde / 16

Army Form C. 2118.

Vol 1

Place	Date	Hour	Summary of Events and Information	Remarks and references to Appendices
COURSET	Aug 1		Strength 30 officers 262 O.R. The Battalion raised at GREATHAM under BOURLEY CAMP ALDERSHOT, commenced its active service yesterday, when we landed at BOULOGNE and marched to OSTROHOVE Rest Camp. At 10.40 am this morning, the battalion left BOULOGNE and entrained for SAMER, marching thence to the village of COURSET, where billets were in readiness for us	RWS
—	Aug 2		A and B Coys moved out to village of SACRIQUIER there being cookhouses, latrines etc., already constructed there. In anticipation of drafts arriving we are now in a position to accommodate them. Today was spent in settling in our new Billets. The weather was as bad as possible it raining almost the whole time	
—	Aug 3		Signallers taken in buzzer work by Sig Officer — L.G. Officer took L.G. Instructions. Remainder of Bn had a route march of some six miles. One man unable to complete. First mail arrives since leaving [illegible]	RWS
—	Aug 4		Training areas for the Bn were decided upon today and pointed out to Company commanders. The Bn attended Baths. Orders issued to Bn abolishing Left Hand Salute.	RWS

D. D. & L., London, E.C.
(A10266) Wt W5300/P713 750,000 2/18 Sch. 52 Forms/C2118/16.

Instructions regarding War Diaries and Intelligence Summaries are contained in F. S. Regs., Part II. and the Staff Manual respectively. Title pages will be prepared in manuscript.

WAR DIARY
or
~~INTELLIGENCE~~ SUMMARY.

(Erase heading not required.)

Army Form C. 2118.

11th Bn. Royal Irish Fus

Place	Date	Hour	Summary of Events and Information	Remarks and references to Appendices
COURSET	Aug 5		We supplied a working party 2 officers 50 ORs to work on assault course COURSET. Officers issued with Field Advance Pay Books	RWS
— " —	Aug 6		Working party supplied as for 5th inst. Major G.C. Carpenter joined today and assumed duties of Second in Command vice Capt. P.S. Maclean. Rev. W. GREENHALGH ceased to be attached to the Bn	RWS
— " —	Aug 7		Imprest a/c opened, companies received first issue of pay in France. Brigade route march of six miles. Dress Fighting Order, marching good. Time taken 2½ hours	RWS
— " —	8		All officers except Specialists met CO at SACRIQVIER at 10 AM and discussed an OUTPOST SCHEME — Scheme Order No 6	RWS
— " —	9		Name of 2/LIEUT. G COLEMAN submitted for Infantry course	RWS
— " —	10		FGCM assembled at BN HQRS COURSET to try Privates DUKE, RICHARDSON, McCREADY and DOUGAN. This is the first CM since the Bn formed. Battalion spent the day firing Musketry Practice.	RWS
— " —	11		A draft of ten WO's and NCOs arrived today, including instructors in Lewis Gun, Gas and Musketry. This is our first draft since leaving ENGLAND.	RWS
— " —	12		Battalion employed on Tactical Exercises	

D. D. & L., London, E.C.
(A10266) Wt W5300/P713 750,000 2/18 Sch. 52 Forms/C2118/16.

Instructions regarding War Diaries and Intelligence Summaries are contained in F. S. Regs., Part II. and the Staff Manual respectively. Title pages will be prepared in manuscript.

WAR DIARY ~~or~~ INTELLIGENCE ~~SUMMARY.~~

(Erase heading not required.)

Army Form C. 2118.

11th Bn. R. Irish Fusiliers

Place	Date	Hour	Summary of Events and Information	Remarks and references to Appendices
COURSET	Aug 13		Transport Draft 6 ORs from 1st DUBLINS attached to us, to assist in Training Transport. Censor stamp for Bn arrived.	R.S.
— —	" 14		C.O. attended Lecture and Demonstration by the Inspector General of Training at CHATEAU DE LA HAIE.	R.S.
— —	" 15		Major REV E.D. DELANY CF RC joined for duty today	R.S.
— —	" 16		Officers and NCOs attended Lecture and Demonstration on Bayonet Fighting by COL CAMPBELL at DESURES. — Warning Order 48 I.B. No 15 Copy No 7 issued to us, transfer from 22nd CORPS to 1st CORPS on 19th AUG.	R.S.
— —	" 17		6 ORs Transport Personel of 22 NORTHUMBERLAND FUS. attached for Transport Duties	R.S.
— —	" 18		Copy No 7 of 48 I.B. ORDER No 16 received, giving further instructions of the move to 1st CORPS area.	
— —	" 19		Our SECRET Order No 7 issued referring to move from DESURES area to BARLIN area.	R.S.
— —	20		Instructions issued to be read with SECRET ORDER No 7 of 19/8/18. C.O. and four COY COMMANDERS proceeded to new area in advance.	R.S.

D. D. & L., London, E.C.
(A10266) Wt W5300/P713 750,000 2/18 Sch. 52 Forms/C2118/16.

Instructions regarding War Diaries and Intelligence Summaries are contained in F. S. Regs., Part II. and the Staff Manual respectively. Title pages will be prepared in manuscript.

WAR DIARY
~~or~~
~~INTELLIGENCE SUMMARY.~~
(Erase heading not required.)

11th Bn. R. Irish Fus

Army Form C. 2118.

Place	Date	Hour	Summary of Events and Information	Remarks and references to Appendices
COURSET.	Aug 21		Regimental Transport left COURSET for BARLIN area at 5 PM.	R.S.
— " —	22		We Embussed on the COURSET – LACOURTEAU road at 8·30 am today. EMBUSSING STRENGTH, less Transport 21 Officers 184 ORS. We passed through THEROUANNE, and NOEUX-LES-MINES, a journey of about 60 KILOS, debussing at our BIVOUACS at 3 PM — Here we relieved the 49th BRIGADE, and are in CORPS reserve. The camp consists of a number of scattered BIVOUACS	R.S.
BARLIN	23		Our Transport arrived at NOEUX-LES-MINES. Notification received from Brigade that our Bn is to be disbanded on amalgamation with 5th R. IRISH FUS	R.S.
— " —	24		Transport of 5th R IRISH FUS arrived and quartered with our own Transport	R.S.
— " —	25		Col JOHNSTON, CO of 5th BN arrived in camp from DIVISIONAL RECEPTION CAMP, and arrangements were entered into as to the number of NCOS & MEN to be transferred from 11th BN to 5th BN	R.S.

D. D. & L., London, E.C.
(20348) Wt W3300/P713 750,000 3/18 E 2688 Forms C/2118/14.

Instructions regarding War Diaries and Intelligence Summaries are contained in F. S. Regs., Part II. and the Staff Manual respectively. Title pages will be prepared in manuscript.

WAR DIARY
or
~~INTELLIGENCE SUMMARY.~~
(Erase heading not required.)

Army Form C. 2118.

11th Bn. Royal Irish Fus.

Place	Date	Hour	Summary of Events and Information	Remarks and references to Appendices
BARLIN	Aug 26		Five officers: — Capt MACLEAN Capt CROSS Lieut LYONS Lieut BELL and Lieut LAIRD transferred to 9th BN. R IRISH FUS — Three officers Lieut SANDILANDS Lieut REYNELL and Lieut LEWIS transferred to 5th R. IRISH FUS	RS
— " —	" 27		One hundred and fifty one men were transferred to 5th BN to complete their establishment, and the remainder proceeded to 16th DIV RECEPTION CAMP for transfer to other units. Part of our Stores Equipment, HORSES etc handed to 5th BN, remainder going back to ORDNANCE. The COL ADJT and QUARTERMASTER remained to hand over, and all other OFFICERS proceeded to 16 DIVISIONAL RECEPTION CAMP at BOIS DE OLHAIN for reposting.	RS

R [illegible] Lt Col [illegible]
R I F

D. D. & L., London, E.C.
(10340) Wt W5300/P713 750,000 3/18 E 2688 Forms C/2118/16.

7 RDF

Vol 2

June

D.A.G.
3rd Echelon
G.H.Q.

Ref your minute of 3/9/18 the 7th R. Dub. Fus (less Training Staff) was absorbed by 2nd R. Dub. Fus on 7/6/18. The Training Staff was transferred to the 11th R. Irish Fusiliers in England on 20/6/18, & no copy of a War Diary for the Training Staff for the period 7-20/6/18 is now available. Please see 2 R. Dub Fus minute of 20/9/18 beneath.

W Dickson
Capt & Adjt
5 R. I. Fus
for O.C. 11 R. I. Fus

PA

D.A.G. ~~3rd Echelon GHQ~~ ~~B.E.F.~~

O/c 11 R. Dr. Gus.

ORDERLY ROOM
20 SEP 1918
No. 887
2ND BATT'N. ROYAL DUBLIN FUSRS.

Ref. reverse.

Will you please reply direct in so far as the period 7/6/18 till date on which 7th R.D.F. training personnel was absorbed into 11 R. Dr. Gus. is affected. The 7th Bn. War Diary Book has been forwarded to Home Records, this covering period Oct. '17 – 7/6/18

[signature] Capt. for Lieut Colonel
Comdg. 2nd Battn. Royal Dublin Fusrs.

Headquarters,
Division.

The War Diaries of the undermentioned Units have not been received for the months stated against them.

It is requested that they may be forwarded as soon as possible, and the attention of the Officers Commanding be called to Field Service Regulations para 140, and G.R.O. 1598.

UNIT.	PERIOD.
7th Battn Royal Dublin Fus.	June & ~~July~~.

G.H.Qrs,
3rd Echelon,
3/9/18.

Major,
D.A.A.G. for
D.A.G.

www.ingramcontent.com/pod-product-compliance
Lightning Source LLC
Chambersburg PA
CBHW080813010526
44111CB00015B/2552

* 9 7 8 1 4 7 4 5 1 0 1 7 2 *